2005
Guidebook to
GEORGIA
TAXES

**State and Local Tax Group
Alston & Bird LLP
Contributing Editors**

CCH INCORPORATED
Chicago

A WoltersKluwer Company

Editorial Staff

Editor .... Fred Conklin

Production Coordinator .... Linda Barnich

Production .... Emily Atwood, Joyce Maranzani

This publication is designed to provide accurate and authoritative information in regard to the subject matter covered. It is sold with the understanding that the publisher is not engaged in rendering legal, accounting, or other professional service and that the authors are not offering such advice in this publication. If legal advice or other expert assistance is required, the services of a competent professional person should be sought.

ISBN 0-8080-1157-X

©2004, CCH INCORPORATED

4025 W. Peterson Ave.
Chicago, IL 60646-6085
1 800 248 3248
http://tax.cchgroup.com

No claim is made to original government works; however, within this Product or Publication, the following are subject to CCH's copyright: (1) the gathering, compilation, and arrangement of such government materials; (2) the magnetic translation and digital conversion of data, if applicable; (3) the historical, statutory, and other notes and references; and (4) the commentary and other materials.

All Rights Reserved
Printed in the United States of America

PREFACE

This *Guidebook* gives a general picture of the taxes imposed by the state of Georgia and the general property tax levied by the local governments. All 2004 legislative amendments received as of press time are reflected, and references to Georgia and federal laws are to the laws as of the date of publication of this book.

The emphasis is on the law applicable to the filing of income tax returns in 2005 for the 2004 tax year. However, if legislation has made changes effective after 2004, we have tried to note this also, with an indication of the effective date to avoid confusion.

The taxes of major interest—income and sales and use—are discussed in detail. Other Georgia taxes, including estate taxes, are summarized, with particular emphasis on application, exemptions, returns, and payment.

Throughout the *Guidebook,* tax tips are highlighted to help practitioners avoid pitfalls and use the tax laws to their best advantage.

The *Guidebook* is a quick-reference work that describes the general provisions of the various tax laws, regulations, and administrative practices. It is useful to tax practitioners, businesspersons, and others who prepare or file Georgia returns or who are required to deal with Georgia taxes.

The *Guidebook* is not designed to eliminate the necessity of referring to the law and regulations for answers to complicated problems, nor is it intended to take the place of detailed reference works such as the CCH GEORGIA TAX REPORTS. With this in mind, specific references to the publisher's Georgia and federal tax products are inserted in most paragraphs. By assuming some knowledge of federal taxes, the *Guidebook* is able to provide a concise, readable treatment of Georgia taxes that will supply a complete answer to most questions and will serve as a time-saving aid where it does not provide the complete answer.

SCOPE OF THE BOOK

This *Guidebook* is designed to do three things:

1. Give a general picture of the impact and pattern of all taxes levied by the state of Georgia and the general property tax levied by local governmental units.

2. Provide a readable quick-reference work for the personal income tax and the tax on corporate income. As such, it explains briefly what the Georgia law provides and indicates whether the Georgia provision is the same as federal law.

3. Analyze and explain the differences, in most cases, between Georgia and federal law.

HIGHLIGHTS OF 2004 GEORGIA TAX CHANGES

The most important 2004 Georgia tax changes received by press time are noted in the "Highlights of 2004 Georgia Tax Changes" section of the *Guide-*

book, beginning on page 11. This useful reference gives the practitioner up-to-the-minute information on changes in tax legislation.

FINDERS

The practitioner may find the information wanted by consulting the general Table of Contents at the beginning of the *Guidebook,* the Table of Contents at the beginning of each chapter, the Topical Index, or the Law and Regulation Locator.

The Topical Index is a useful tool. Specific taxes and information on rates, allocation, credits, exemptions, returns, payments, collection, penalties, and remedies are thoroughly indexed and cross-referenced to paragraph numbers in the *Guidebook.*

The Law and Regulation Locator is an equally useful finders tool. Beginning on page 365, this finding list shows where sections of Georgia statutory law and administrative regulations referred to in the *Guidebook* are discussed.

October 2004

About the Editors

Mary T. Benton

Mary T. Benton is a partner in Alston & Bird LLP's State and Local Tax Practice Group, concentrating her practice on controversy and litigation matters involving property, sales & use and income taxation. She also maintains a multistate transactional practice involving all tax types, emphasizing property and sales & use taxation.

Ms. Benton has represented clients in property tax disputes in many jurisdictions, appearing before Boards of Equalization and litigating matters in both bench and jury trials and practicing before the appellate courts. She has represented clients in sales/use and income tax disputes before state revenue agencies, in administrative hearings, trial and appellate courts, and has managed multistate controversy and litigation matters.

Ms. Benton received her J.D. degree, with honors, from the University of Texas School of Law. She received her B.A. degree, cum laude and with honors, from Southern Methodist University, where she was a member of Phi Beta Kappa. Ms. Benton serves as chair of the Taxation Section of the State Bar of Georgia and is a member of the Atlanta Bar Association (Taxation Section) and the Institute for Professionals in Taxation.

John L. Coalson, Jr.

John Coalson is a partner in Alston & Bird LLP's State and Local Tax Group. His practice focuses on counseling/planning as well as dispute and litigation work in the state and local tax area. He has extensive experience in most areas of state and local taxation, ranging from the more common areas of income, sales and use, and property taxes to less common areas, including business license taxes, gross receipts and gross premiums taxes, real estate transfer and recording taxes, intangible property taxes, and other tax disciplines.

Mr. Coalson is a past chair of the Taxation Section of the State Bar of Georgia, and has served as the Tax Section's Liaison with the Georgia Department of Revenue since 1996. Mr. Coalson also serves as a Trustee and member of the Paul Hartman Memorial Institute on State and Local Taxation, Editorial Board of the *Journal of Multistate Taxation*, and is a past chair and continuing member of the Executive Committee of the National Association of State Bar Tax Sections.

Mr. Coalson has authored or co-authored more than a dozen law review articles. He is listed in *The Best Lawyers in America* and is also a frequent speaker at state and local tax seminars.

Mr. Coalson received his B.B.A. degree, with highest distinction, in accounting at Emory University, and his J.D. degree, summa cum laude, from the University of Georgia School of Law, where he was the First Honor Graduate and served as Executive Editor of the Georgia Law Review and was a member of the Order of the Coif.

Timothy J. Peaden

Tim Peaden is a partner in Alston & Bird LLP's State and Local Tax and Federal Income Tax Groups. He concentrates his practice on federal, state and local tax litigation. Mr. Peaden has handled numerous state and local tax cases involving a variety of issues. He has been involved in over 30 bench and jury trials in the income, sales and use, and property tax areas. The issues have included nexus, apportionment of income, the manufacturing exemption from sales tax, various property tax exemptions, and the valuation of real and personal property for property tax purposes.

In the federal tax area, Mr. Peaden also has been involved in numerous disputes with over a dozen trials in the United States Tax Court, Court of Federal Claims, and local district courts, as well as a number of subsequent appeals to several different Circuit Courts of Appeals. He was part of the team that tried one of the seminal cases involving intangible assets, *Citizens and Southern Corp. v. Commissioner*, and worked on a number of subsequent cases involving the valuation of intangible assets.

Mr. Peaden is a frequent author and speaker on tax litigation topics. He has spoken to numerous professional organizations, including the American Bar Association, the Committee on State Taxation, the Institute for Professionals in Taxation, the American Society of Appraisers, the Interstate Tax Report Conference, the Georgia Institute for Continuing Legal Education, the Georgia Society of Certified Public Accountants, and the American Accounting Association.

Mr. Peaden received his J.D. degree from Vanderbilt University and his undergraduate and graduate degrees in accounting from Wichita State University. He is a Certified Public Accountant. He is a member of the tax sections of the American and Georgia Bar Association, and has served on numerous committees in those sections. Mr. Peaden is a past chairman of the Georgia State Bar Taxation Section, and is also a member of the Georgia Society of Certified Public Accountants, the Institute for Professionals in Taxation, and the Atlanta Tax Forum.

Michael T. Petrik

Mike Petrik is a partner and serves as chair of the Alston & Bird LLP's State and Local Tax Group. Mr. Petrik concentrates his practice on multistate tax planning for businesses, including income tax, franchise tax, sales/use tax, and other state and local taxes.

Mr. Petrik has extensive experience in developing and implementing new corporate structures designed to achieve multistate tax efficiency. He also maintains an active administrative tax dispute and negotiation practice, including audit appeals, the negotiation of special filing or apportionment methods, and anonymous "amnesty" applications.

Mr. Petrik is a frequent author and speaker on state tax topics, including constitutional questions involving the due process and commerce clauses. He is a frequent lecturer before professional groups, including the Council on State Taxation, Tax Executives Institute, and the National Tax Association. He is listed in *The Best Lawyers in America* for his tax expertise. Mr. Petrik is a

About the Editors

member of CCH's State Income Tax Alert Advisory Board, and his writings on state and local tax issues are extensive.

Mr. Petrik received his J.D. from Duke University School of Law and his B.A. degree from Eastern Illinois University. He is a member of the Tax Sections of the State Bar of Georgia, Atlanta Bar Association, and American Bar Association.

R. Mark Williamson

Mark Williamson is a partner in Alston & Bird LLP's Wealth Planning Group and his practice encompasses estate planning, exempt organizations and general tax matters.

Before joining Alston & Bird, he practiced with the Milwaukee law firm of Foley & Lardner and was an adjunct professor of law at the University of Wisconsin in Madison. Mr. Williamson was on the faculties of the 1997 and 1999 Annual Estate Planning Institutes in Athens, Georgia, and the 1997 and 2000 Fiduciary Law Institutes in St. Simons, Georgia, and he received the Estates and Trusts Magazine 1997 Best Young Author Award for a series of articles he co-authored with Professor Jeffrey Pennell of Emory University.

He received his J.D., with highest honors, from the Florida State University College of Law, where he was a member of the Order of the Coif and served as executive editor of the Law Review. Previously, he received his B.M., cum laude, in music from Louisiana State University and his M.M. in music from North Texas State University, and he also studied at the doctorate level at Louisiana State University and the Catholic University of America.

Jeffrey C. Glickman

Jeff Glickman is an associate in Alston & Bird LLP's State and Local Tax Practice Group. His practice focuses on mergers and acquisitions and multi-state tax planning for businesses, including income tax, franchise tax, sales/use tax, real estate transfer tax, telecommunications tax, and other state and local taxes.

Mr. Glickman is a frequent author and speaker on state tax topics, including constitutional issues relating to income and sales and use taxation, taxation of passive investment companies, residency issues, and the state tax aspects of mergers and acquisitions. He has authored or contributed to articles appearing in State Income Tax Alert, Mergers and Acquisitions, and the Journal of Multistate Taxation, and is a member of the editorial staff of *The State and Local Tax Lawyer*, an American Bar Association publication. Mr. Glickman also serves as an adjunct professor at Emory Law School, where he teaches a class in multistate taxation.

Mr. Glickman received his LL.M. in Taxation (1999) and his J.D. (1998) from New York University School of Law, where he was a member of the Moot Court Board. Mr. Glickman received his B.S., with distinction, from Cornell University in 1995, where he majored in Consumer Economics and Housing. He is a member of the Tax Sections of the State Bar of Georgia, Atlanta Bar Association, and American Bar Association.

Alice M. Nolen

As Counsel in Alston & Bird LLP's State and Local Tax Group, Ms. Nolen concentrates her practice on state tax incentives and unclaimed property matters, as well as the general areas of income, sales and use, and property taxes.

Prior to joining Alston & Bird, Alice was a Manager in the state tax consultancy practice at Ernst & Young LLP. She assisted corporate clients in securing millions of dollars in state tax credits and other state incentives. Ms. Nolen frequently lectures before professional groups on incentives and other multistate tax issues.

Ms. Nolen received her J.D. degree from the University of Alabama in 1990 and M.B.A. degree from Tulane University, where she was a Morton A. Aldrich Scholar, in 1993. Alice received her B.A. degree from the University of Alabama in 1987. She is a Certified Public Accountant and a member of the Tax Sections of the State Bar of Georgia and the Atlanta Bar Association.

CONTENTS

Chapter	Page
Highlights of 2004 Georgia Tax Changes	11
Tax Calendar	17

PART I—TABLES

Tax Rates: Personal Income Tax, Corporate Income Tax, Corporate Net Worth (Franchise) Tax, Sales and Use Taxes, Estate Tax	21
Federal/State Comparisons of Key Features	23
Business Incentives and Credits	32

PART II—PERSONAL INCOME TAX

1.	Imposition of Tax, Rates, Exemptions, Credits	37
2.	Computation of Tax	59
3.	Subtractions from Federal Adjusted Gross Income	67
4.	Additions to Taxable Income	73
5.	Allocation and Apportionment of Nonresident Income	75
6.	Returns, Estimates, Payment of Tax, Withholding	79
7.	Fiduciaries, Partnerships, Limited Liability Companies	95
8.	Administration, Deficiencies, Penalties, Refunds, Appeals	99

PART III—CORPORATE INCOME TAX

9.	Imposition of Tax, Rates, Exemptions, Credits	103
10.	Computation of Taxable Net Income	129
11.	Additions to Federal Base	137
12.	Subtractions from Federal Base	139
13.	Allocation and Apportionment	143
14.	Returns, Estimates, Payment of Tax	155
15.	Administration, Deficiencies, Penalties, Refunds, Appeals	163

PART IV—CORPORATE NET WORTH (FRANCHISE) TAX

16.	Imposition of Tax, Rates, Exemptions	169
17.	Basis of Tax	173
18.	Returns and Payment of Tax; Administration	175

PART V—BANKS AND FINANCIAL INSTITUTIONS TAX

19.	Tax on Depository Financial Institutions	179

PART VI—SALES AND USE TAXES

20.	Persons and Transactions Subject to Tax	183
21.	Basis and Rate of Tax	209

Chapter	Page
22. Exemptions and Credits	227
23. Returns, Payments, and Records	249
24. Collection of Tax, Refunds	257

PART VII—ESTATE TAX

25. Imposition of Tax and Rates	263

PART VIII—PROPERTY TAXES

26. Property Taxes	267

PART IX—MISCELLANEOUS TAXES

27. Unemployment Insurance	297
28. Other State Taxes	309
Alcoholic Beverages Taxes	309
Cigarettes and Tobacco Taxes	311
Insurance Taxes	313
Motor Fuel Taxes	317
Motor Vehicles	321
Rental Vehicles	325
Motor Carriers	325
Environmental Taxes	327
Realty Transfer and Recording Taxes	327
Utilities	330
Lodgings Taxes	331

PART X—ADMINISTRATION AND PROCEDURE

29. Georgia Administration and Procedure	335
30. Audits, Assessment, and Collection of Tax	341
31. Taxpayer Remedies	353
32. Georgia Resources	359

PART XI—DOING BUSINESS IN GEORGIA

33. Fees and Taxes	361
Law and Regulation Locator	365
Topical Index	371

HIGHLIGHTS OF 2004 GEORGIA TAX CHANGES

The most important tax changes and new developments in 2004 are noted below:

Multiple Taxes

● *Jobs credit expanded*

Georgia has increased and expanded the jobs credit, available against Georgia corporate and personal income taxes, for businesses in less developed areas, effective for tax years beginning after 2003. The maximum jobs credit amount that may be claimed by a taxpayer in a single taxable year is increased to 100% (previously, 50%) of the taxpayer's corporate or personal income tax liability that is attributable to income derived from operations in Georgia during that taxable year.

The Georgia Commissioner of Community Affairs is authorized to designate the following additional areas as less developed: (1) any area comprised of one or more census tracts adjacent to a federal military installation where pervasive poverty is evidenced by a poverty rate of at least 15% as reflected in the most recent federal decennial census, and (2) any area comprised of two or more contiguous census block groups with a poverty rate of at least 20% as determined from data in the most recent federal decennial census, if the area is also located within a state enterprise zone; a redevelopment plan has been adopted; and in the Commissioner's opinion the area displays pervasive poverty, underdevelopment, general distress, and blight. In areas determined to be suffering from pervasive poverty, credits may be claimed by any lawful business and are not limited to business enterprises. Also, for credit eligibility purposes, new jobs created by a taxpayer are not required to be held by residents of less developed areas. Previously, 30% of new jobs created by the taxpayer had to be held by residents of less developed areas. (H.B. 984), Laws 2004.) (¶ 913)

● *Federal tie-in updated*

For taxable years beginning after 2003, Georgia conforms with the Internal Revenue Code as amended as of January 1, 2004. However, for Georgia corporate and personal income tax purposes, Georgia has not adopted the increased limits applicable to the expensing of assets under IRC Sec. 179 that were enacted by the federal Jobs and Growth Tax Relief Reconciliation Act (JGTRRA) (P.L. 108-27). (H.B. 1437, Laws 2004.) (¶ 101, 204, 901, 1002, 1007)

● *Penalty threshold for dishonored checks increased*

For purposes of all Georgia taxes, after June 30, 2004, the 2% penalty for a dishonored check or money order to the Commissioner applies to checks or money orders in the amount of at least $1,250 (previously, $750). If a check or money order is less than $1,250, the penalty is $25 (previously, $15 or the amount of the check or money order). Also, the penalty for filing a frivolous corporate or personal income tax return is increased to $1,000 (previously, $500). (H.B. 1437, Laws 2004.) (¶ 3003)

● *Joint development authority jobs credit limited*

For purposes of the jobs credit allowed against corporate and personal income taxes, the additional credit allowed to a business enterprise located in a county that belongs to more than one joint development authority is limited to $500 for each new full-time position created. (Act 664 (S.B. 444), Laws 2004.) (¶ 913)

Personal Income Tax

● *Organ donation expenses deductible beginning in 2005*

Applicable to all taxable years beginning on or after January 1, 2005, organ donation expenses incurred in accordance with the federal National Organ Procurement Act (P.L. 98-507) may be subtracted from a taxpayer's federal adjusted gross income in figuring Georgia net taxable income for Georgia personal income tax purposes. The exclusion may be taken in the taxable year in which the donation is made; may be claimed only for unreimbursed travel expenses, lodging expenses, and lost wages incurred as a direct result of the organ donation; and may not exceed $10,000. (H.B. 1410, Laws 2004.) (¶ 311)

● *Joint liability amended; credit eligibility limited*

Provisions on spousal liability and eligibility for the low income credit have been amended, effective May 13, 2004, as follows (H.B. 1437, Laws 2004.)

Joint liability: A taxpayer is relieved of joint liability for an understatement on a Georgia joint personal income tax return if the taxpayer has made the proper election under IRC Sec. 6015. Previously, a taxpayer that made the proper federal election also had to meet certain other statutory requirements to be relieved of Georgia liability. (¶ 109)

Low income credit: Any individual incarcerated or confined in any city, county, municipal, state, or federal penal or correctional institution for any part of a taxable year is not eligible to claim the low income credit against personal income tax. (¶ 117)

Sales and Use Taxes

● *Georgia may enter into Streamlined Agreement*

Legislation authorizing Georgia to enter into the Streamlined Sales and Use Tax Agreement has been enacted. The legislation does not make the substantive changes to Georgia law necessary for the state to come into actual compliance with the Agreement. Subsequent legislation will be necessary to achieve that compliance.

The Agreement was approved by the Streamlined Sales Tax Implementing States on November 12, 2002. The Implementing States consist of those states that have passed some version of the authorizing legislation. With

Highlights of Tax Changes

enactment of this legislation, Georgia becomes a member of the Implementing States. (H.B. 1437, Laws 2004.) (¶ 2003)

● *Exemption added for corporate tourist attractions*

Until December 31, 2007, sales of tangible personal property to, or used in or for the new construction of, an eligible corporate attraction are exempt from Georgia sales and use taxes. "Corporate attraction" means any tourist facility constructed on or after May 17, 2004, dedicated to the history and products of a corporation that (1) has costs that exceed $50 million; (2) has greater than 60,000 square feet of space; and (3) has associated facilities, including parking decks and landscaping owned by the same owner as the corporate attraction. For purposes of this exemption, a seller must collect tax unless the purchaser furnishes the seller with an exemption determination letter certifying that the purchase is exempt. (Act 794 (H.B. 1528), Laws 2004.) (¶ 2201)

● *Certain child care nonprofits exempted*

Sales of tangible personal property and services to or by a child-caring institution, a child-placing agency, or a maternity home are exempt from Georgia sales and use taxes, beginning May 17, 2004, if the entity is engaged primarily in providing child services and is a nonprofit exempt organization under IRC Sec. 501(c)(3). The entity must obtain an exemption determination letter from the Commissioner. (Act 727 (H.B. 1744), Laws 2004.) (¶ 2201)

● *Bidders for state contracts must be registered to collect taxes*

Any nongovernmental vendor, or its affiliates, bidding on a state agency contract that exceeds $100,000 per year is required to register with the state and to collect and remit Georgia sales and use tax on all retail sales occurring in Georgia, effective May 13, 2004 (Act 499 (H.B. 1457), Laws 2004.) (¶ 2304)

● *Exemption for U.S. government contractors extended*

The Georgia sales and use tax exemption for sales to government contractors of overhead materials used in performance of contracts with the U.S. Department of Defense or the National Aeronautics and Space Administration will remain in effect until January 1, 2007. The exemption was previously scheduled to be repealed January 1, 2005. (H.B. 1238), Laws 2004, effective July 1, 2004.) (¶ 2201)

● *Collection allowance for timely payment reduced*

A vendor may deduct 0.5% of the total amount of prepaid Georgia sales and use taxes if payment of the tax is timely, effective July 1, 2004. Previously, the deduction was an amount equal to 3% of the first $3,000, and 0.5% of the excess. (Act 500 (H.B. 1459), Laws 2004) (¶ 2302)

Property Taxes

● *Deadlines changed for exemptions and special assessments*

The homestead exemption application deadline and the deadlines for certain military personnel to file a special assessment application and a notice of appeal have been extended, as follows (Act 515 (S.B. 393), Laws 2004):

Homestead exemption: Effective June 1, 2005, an applicant seeking a homestead exemption may file a written application and schedule at any time during the calendar year subsequent to the property becoming the applicant's primary residence, up to and including March 1 of the following year.

Military personnel: Effective May 13, 2004, a member of the U.S. armed forces serving outside the continental United States may file the member's initial or renewal application for special property tax assessment at any time within six months following the member's return to the continental United States.

If an individual is absent from his or her residence because of duty in the armed forces, the deadline for filing a property tax notice of appeal or notice of arbitration is tolled for 90 days. During that period, a family member or friend of the individual may notify the taxing authority of the individual's absence due to military service and submit written notice of representation for the limited purpose of the appeal. Upon receipt of this notice, the taxing authority will initiate the appeal. (¶ 2604, 2609)

● *Conservation use property expanded*

Effective July 1, 2004, the term "bona fide conservation use property" includes land used for the production of fish or wildlife by maintaining no less than 10 acres of wildlife habitat either in its natural state or under management. Effective January 1, 2005, and applicable to taxable years beginning on or after that date, the term also includes land within buffer zones adjacent to rivers or perennial streams within which land-disturbing activity is prohibited by state or local law. (Act 476 (H.B. 1107), Laws 2004; Act 477 (H.B. 1416), Laws 2004.) (¶ 2605)

● *Veterans' organizations' vehicles exempted*

Effective January 1, 2005, a motor vehicle owned by or leased to a veterans organization is exempt from all state and local property taxes. (Act 497 (H.B. 1446), Laws 2004.) (¶ 2604)

Motor Fuel Taxes

● *Collection allowance expanded; nonhighway use refund allowed*

A motor fuel distributor may deduct a 1% allowance to cover the losses and expenses incurred in reporting motor fuels tax, effective July 1, 2004. Previously, this allowance was 1% of the first 5.5¢ per gallon of the motor fuels tax.

Every purchaser of fuel oil (other than dyed fuel oils) who buys 25 gallons or more for use in operating equipment for nonhighway purposes may claim a

Highlights of Tax Changes

refund (without interest) of the motor fuels tax paid on the fuel oils, effective July 1, 2004. Refund applications must be filed within 18 months from the date the fuel oil was purchased. (Act 500 (H.B. 1459), Laws 2004.) (¶ 2805)

Insurance Taxes

● *Credits for capital contributions repealed*

Effective May 13, 2004, provisions that would have allowed a credit against Georgia insurance premium tax for an insurance company that contributed certified capital to a certified capital company were repealed. (H.B. 1507, Laws 2004.) (¶ 2804)

Administration and Procedure

● *Confidential information may be disclosed with taxpayer's permission*

Confidential Georgia taxpayer information or records may be disclosed to or discussed with another party if the taxpayer has granted express written authorization to the Georgia Department of Revenue, effective May 13, 2004. (Act 501 (H.B. 1461), Laws 2004.) (¶ 2903)

● *Penalty enacted for false independent contractor claims*

Effective July 1, 2004, it is unlawful for any person to knowingly coerce, induce, or threaten an individual to falsely declare himself or herself an independent contractor, or to falsely claim that an individual employed by that person is an independent contractor, in order to avoid or evade the withholding or payment of any Georgia tax. Penalties range from the total amount of tax owed, for a first offense, to four times the tax owed, for multiple offenses. (Act 525 (S.B. 491), Laws 2004.) (¶ 607, 3003)

TAX CALENDAR

The following table lists significant dates of interest to Georgia taxpayers and tax practitioners.

January

1st—Annual reports of corporations due between January 1 and April 1

    Assessment date for property subject to taxation

    Property tax rolls open

    Distilled spirits license renewals due

15th—Final declaration and payment of estimated tax due for calendar-year corporations and individuals

    Declaration of estimated tax (for preceding year) by farmers and fishermen due

20th—Public Service Commission fees due

31st—Income tax withholding returns for semi-weekly, monthly, quarterly, and annual payers

    Employer's withholding statement furnished to employees

    Final return and balance of tax due (in lieu of final declaration) for individuals

February

28th—Employer's annual withholding return due

March

1st—Complete returns and full amount of tax due (in lieu of declaration) from farmers and fishermen

    Airline companies, special franchises and public utilities must file returns by this date

    All domestic, foreign or alien insurance companies must file annual return and payment by this date

    Declaration and first quarterly payment of estimated tax due for calendar-year corporations and individuals

15th—Corporate income and net worth returns due

31st—Fire insurance companies' additional premium tax due

April

1st—Annual reports of corporations due between January 1 and April 1

 Applications for homestead exemption due

 Property tax rolls close

15th—Franchise taxes and returns of calendar-year corporations due

 Personal income tax returns and payments due

30th—Income tax withholding returns for semi-weekly, monthly, and quarterly payers

June

15th—Declaration (if not met by April 1) and installment payment of estimated tax due for calendar-year corporations and individuals

30th—Cigarette distributors' licenses expire

 Licensed tobacco distributor to pay any liability due for purchase of tobacco tax stamps

July

1st—Franchise tax for corporations receiving charter or commencing business on or after this date is one-half the annual fee

 Rural telephone companies' fees due

 All domestic, foreign or alien insurance companies must pay license fee by this date

31st—Income tax withholding returns for semi-weekly, monthly, and quarterly payers

August

15th—First installment of property taxes due

September

15th—Declaration (if not met by June 1) and installment payment of estimated tax due for calendar-year corporations and individuals

October

31st—Income tax withholding returns for semi-weekly, monthly, and quarterly payers

November

1st—Brewers, brokers, importers, wholesalers and retailers of malt beverages must renew applications for occupational licenses

 Renewal applications for wine licenses must be made

 Renewal applications for alcoholic liquor licenses must be made

15th—Second installment of property taxes due

Tax Calendar

December

1st—Public service corporations and utilities receive notice of the fees due

20th—Annual property tax payments due to state or county

QUARTERLY RECURRING DATES

15th April, June, Sept., Jan.—Declarations and payment of estimated tax for calendar-year corporations and individuals

15th Jan., April, July, Oct.—Surplus line brokers' affidavits and tax payments due

20th Jan., April, July, Oct.—Sales and use tax returns due for certain dealers with minimum tax liability

20th March, June, Sept., Dec.—Installment prepayments of annual premium taxes due

Last day of April, July, Oct., Jan.—Income tax withholding returns and payments due for quarterly payers

    Motor carriers' motor fuel report and tax payment due

MONTHLY RECURRING DATES

10th—Cigarette distributors' reports due

    Cigarette users' reports and tax due

    Report and payment of tax due on all cigars and little cigars sold, used or disposed of during previous month if not paid with sales price

15th—Income tax withholding return and payment due the next month for monthly payers

    Reports and tax payments of wine wholesalers, importers and brokers due by this date next following the month of purchase

20th—Gasoline distributors' reports and taxes due

    Reports by transporters of motor fuel due

    Gasoline reports by persons other than distributors due

    Licensed tobacco distributors required to pay in full for tobacco tax stamps purchased during previous month

    Sales and use taxes and returns due for preceding month

    Dealer's payment of estimated sales tax liability due

    Reports and tax payments of licensed malt beverage wholesalers due

PART I

TABLES

Tax Rates
¶ 1   Personal Income Tax
¶ 5   Corporate Income Tax
¶ 10 Corporate Net Worth (Franchise) Tax
¶ 15 Sales and Use Taxes
¶ 20 Estate Tax

Federal/State Comparison of Key Features
¶ 40 Personal Income Tax Comparison
¶ 45 Corporate Income Tax Comparison

Business Incentives and Credits
¶ 50 Introduction
¶ 55 Personal Income Tax
¶ 60 Corporate Income Tax
¶ 65 Sales and Use Taxes
¶ 70 Property Tax
¶ 75 Insurance Gross Premiums Tax

TAX RATES

¶ 1 Personal Income Tax

Georgia personal income tax is computed using the following tax rate schedule (¶ 105):

Single Person

If Georgia taxable net income is:	The tax is:
Not over $750	1%
Over $750 but not over $2250	$7.50 plus 2% of amount over $750
Over $2250 but not over $3750	$37.50 plus 3% of amount over $2250
Over $3750 but not over $5250	$82.50 plus 4% of amount over $3750
Over $5250 but not over $7000	$142.50 plus 5% of amount over $5250
Over $7000	$230.00 plus 6% of amount over $7000

Married Person Filing a Separate Return

If Georgia taxable net income is:	The tax is:
Not over $500	1%
Over $500 but not over $1500	$5.00 plus 2% of amount over $500
Over $1500 but not over $2500	$25.00 plus 3% of amount over $1500
Over $2500 but not over $3500	$55.00 plus 4% of amount over $2500
Over $3500 but not over $5000	$95.00 plus 5% of amount over $3500
Over $5000	$170.00 plus 6% of amount over $5000

Head of Household and Married Persons Filing a Joint Return

If Georgia taxable net income is:	The tax is:
Not over $1000	1%

¶ 1

Over $1000 but not over $3000	$10.00 plus 2% of amount over $1000
Over $3000 but not over $5000	$50.00 plus 3% of amount over $3000
Over $5000 but not over $7000	$110.00 plus 4% of amount over $5000
Over $7000 but not over $10,000	$190.00 plus 5% of amount over $7000
Over $10,000	$340.00 plus 6% of amount over $10,000

● *Personal and dependent exemptions*

A personal exemption of $2,700 is allowed for the taxpayer and a $5,400 exemption is allowed for the taxpayer and spouse if a joint return is filed (¶ 301).

An estate is allowed a deduction of $2,700 in lieu of a personal exemption deduction. A trust is allowed a deduction of $1,350 in lieu of a personal exemption deduction.

For 2004, the dependent exemption is $3,000 (¶ 301). The amount of a dependent's unearned income that is included in the federal adjusted gross income of a parent's return must be subtracted from federal adjusted gross income.

¶ 5 Corporate Income Tax

Georgia corporate income tax is imposed at a rate of 6% on the corporation's taxable income from property owned and business done in Georgia (¶ 905).

¶ 10 Corporate Net Worth (Franchise) Tax

Georgia corporate net worth (franchise) tax is imposed at the following graduated rates on the full corporate net worth of domestic and domesticated corporations, and on the apportioned net worth of foreign corporations (¶ 1605):

Corporations with Net Worth Including Issued Capital Stock, Paid-in Surplus and Earned Surplus		Amount of Tax
Over	But Not Over	
.....	$ 10,000	$ 10
$10,000	25,000	20
25,000	40,000	40
40,000	60,000	60
60,000	80,000	75
80,000	100,000	100
100,000	150,000	125
150,000	200,000	150
200,000	300,000	200
300,000	500,000	250
500,000	750,000	300
750,000	1,000,000	500
1,000,000	2,000,000	750
2,000,000	4,000,000	1,000
4,000,000	6,000,000	1,250
6,000,000	8,000,000	1,500
8,000,000	10,000,000	1,750
10,000,000	12,000,000	2,000
12,000,000	14,000,000	2,500
14,000,000	16,000,000	3,000
16,000,000	18,000,000	3,500

Part I—Tables											23

18,000,000	20,000,000	4,000
20,000,000	22,000,000	4,500
22,000,000		5,000

¶ 15 Sales and Use Taxes

Georgia sales and use tax is imposed at the rate of 4% (¶ 2102).

The joint county and municipal sales and use tax, homestead option sales and use tax, special county sales and use tax, educational local option sales and use tax, and Metropolitan Atlanta Rapid Transit Authority tax may be imposed at the rate of 1%.

¶ 20 Estate Tax

Georgia estate tax is equal to the maximum credit allowable under the federal estate tax.

FEDERAL/STATE COMPARISON OF KEY FEATURES

¶ 40 Personal Income Tax Comparison

The following compares federal and state treatment of major personal income items, deductions, and credits.

The comparisons below do not reflect the differences that may arise as a result of the enactment of the Working Families Tax Relief Act of 2004 (P.L. 108-311) or the American Jobs Creation Act of 2004. For highlights of the amendments made by these Acts and the adjustments that may be required on the Georgia return, see ¶ 101, 201.

Adoption expenses (IRC Sec. 23 and Sec. 137).—The same as IRC Sec. 137 because the starting point for Georgia taxable income is federal adjusted gross income. Georgia has no credit similar to the federal adoption expense credit (IRC Sec. 23).

Alimony (IRC Sec. 71 and Sec. 215).—The same as federal because the starting point for Georgia taxable income is federal adjusted gross income.

Alternative minimum tax (IRC Sec. 55—Sec. 59).—Georgia does not impose an alternative minimum tax on tax preference items.

Asset expense election (IRC Sec. 179).—Generally, the same as federal because the starting point for Georgia taxable income is federal adjusted gross income. However, Georgia does not allow the $100,000 expense deduction enacted by the federal Jobs and Growth Tax Relief Reconciliation Act of 2003 (JGTRRA) (P.L. 108-27).

Bad debts (IRC Sec. 166).—The same as federal because federal deductions are adopted by reference (¶ 201).

Business deductions (IRC Sec. 162).—The same as federal because the starting point for Georgia taxable income is federal adjusted gross income.

Capital gains and capital losses (IRC Sec. 1(h) and Sec. 1211).—The same as federal because the starting point for Georgia taxable income is federal adjusted gross income.

¶ 40

Charitable contributions (IRC Sec. 170).—The same as federal because the starting point for Georgia taxable income is federal adjusted gross income.

Child care credit (IRC Sec. 45F).—A Georgia credit similar to the federal child care credit is available to employers for costs associated with providing or sponsoring an on-site day-care center for their employees (see ¶ 911). Georgia also allows a credit for the cost of all property acquired for use exclusively in the construction, expansion, improvement, or operation of a licensed day-care facility. Taxpayers claiming the credit for qualified child care property must increase Georgia taxable income by the amount of any depreciation deductions used in determining federal taxable income.

Child tax credit (IRC Sec. 24).—Georgia does not offer a child tax credit corresponding to IRC Sec. 24.

Depreciation (IRC Sec. 167 and Sec. 168).—The same as the federal treatment of depreciation, except that Georgia has not adopted the federal bonus depreciation provisions of IRC Sec. 168(k). Federal depreciation must be added back to federal adjusted gross income and depreciation must be computed separately for Georgia purposes (¶ 204). For most assets, there is no adjustment required for depreciation. However, certain types of property of child care facilities (¶ 404) and certain property placed in service before March 11, 1987, (¶ 204) may be entitled to special depreciation treatment under Georgia law, in which case a modification adjustment may be required for Georgia purposes.

Earned income credit (IRC Sec. 32(b)).—Georgia has no equivalent to the federal earned income credit.

Education assistance benefits (IRC Sec. 127) and educationIRAs (IRC Sec. 530).—The same as federal because federal adjusted gross income is the starting point for determining Georgia taxable income (¶ 201).

Education credits (IRC Sec. 25A).—Georgia has no equivalent to the federal education credit.

Exclusion of gain on sale of residence (IRC Sec. 121).—The same as federal because the starting point for Georgia taxable income is federal adjusted gross income.

Extraterritorial income (IRC Sec. 114).—The same as federal because the starting point for Georgia taxable income is federal adjusted gross income.

Filing status (IRC Sec. 1).—Georgia requires taxpayers to use the same filing status on the Georgia return as is used on the federal return.

Health insurance premiums for self-employed taxpayers (IRC Sec. 162(l)).—Generally, the same as federal because the starting point for Georgia taxable income is federal adjusted gross income. However, a self-employed taxpayer may subtract the portion of the self-employed health insurance that is not allowed as a deduction on the federal return and that the taxpayer does not claim as an itemized deduction (¶ 309).

Interest on federal obligations (IRC Sec. 61).—Interest and dividends on U.S. government obligations, net of related expenses, are exempt

Part I—Tables   **25**

from Georgia income tax and are subtracted from the taxable base in computing Georgia adjusted gross income (¶ 303).

Interest on indebtedness (IRC Sec. 163 and Sec. 221).—The same as federal because the starting point for Georgia taxable income is federal adjusted gross income.

IRAs, SEPs, and Keoghs (IRC Sec. 401—Sec. 404, Sec. 408, Sec. 408A, and Sec. 530).—Georgia generally conforms to federal provisions regarding IRAs, SEPs, and Keoghs because the starting point for Georgia taxable income is federal adjusted gross income. Georgia provides a retirement income exclusion if the taxpayer is 62 years of age or older, or the taxpayer is totally and permanently disabled. Georgia has no credit comparable to the credit allowed for IRA contributions (IRC Sec. 25B).

Itemized deductions (IRC Sec. 63(d)).—Generally, the same as federal because the starting point for Georgia taxable income is federal adjusted gross income. However, federal itemized deductions have to be reduced by taxes that are paid to states other than Georgia (¶ 403) and for investment interest expenses related to the production of income exempt from Georgia income tax.

Kiddie tax (IRS Sec. 1(g)).—Unlike federal law, Georgia does not have a "kiddie tax" on unearned or investment income of children under age 14.

Losses not otherwise compensated (IRC Sec. 165).—The same as federal because federal adjusted gross income is the starting point for determining Georgia adjusted gross income.

Lump-sum distributions (IRC Sec. 402(d)).—The deduction allowed under federal law, relating to the ordinary income portion of a lump-sum distribution is not allowed in Georgia; the amount deducted on the federal return must be added to Georgia taxable income (¶ 402).

Medical savings account (IRC Sec. 138 and Sec. 220).—The same as federal because the starting point for Georgia taxable income is federal adjusted gross income.

Practitioner Comment: Health Savings Accounts

Georgia also conforms to the treatment of health savings accounts ("HSAs"—IRC Section 223).

Michael T. Petrik, Esq., Alston & Bird

Military combat zone compensation (IRC Sec. 112).—The same treatment as the federal because federal adjusted gross income in the starting point for determining Georgia adjusted gross income. In addition, Georgia allows an exemption for military combat pay received by a member of the National Guard and any reserve component of the armed services (¶ 108). Unlike IRC Sec. 112, Georgia does not limit the exemption for commissioned officers to the "maximum enlisted amount."

¶ 40

Moving expenses (IRC Sec. 62 and Sec. 217).—The same as federal because federal adjusted gross income is the starting point for determining Georgia adjusted gross income.

Net operating loss (IRC Sec. 172).—The amount of any federal net operating loss deducted on the federal return must be added back to federal adjusted gross income in computing Georgia taxable income (208). However, Georgia allows taxpayers to carry over and carry back net operating losses after adjustments to federal adjusted gross income and to the extent the loss is attributable to operations in the state. Georgia follows IRC Sec. 172 with respect to the net operating loss carryback and carryover periods.

Personal exemptions (IRC Sec. 151).—Generally, Georgia follows the same treatment of personal and dependency exemptions as federal law (¶ 104). However, under federal law a dependency exemption is not allowed if the dependent files his or her own return and claims a personal exemption; Georgia allows a dependency exemption for such a dependent.

Retirement benefits (IRC Sec. 61, Sec. 86, and Sec. 401—Sec. 403).—Social security and railroad retirement benefits may be subtracted from federal adjusted gross income to the extent that the benefits are included in federal adjusted gross income. In addition, Georgia provides an exclusion for retirement income otherwise included in Georgia taxable income if the taxpayer is 62 years of age or older, or the taxpayer is totally and permanently disabled (¶ 304).

Student loan interest (IRC Sec. 221).—The same as federal because federal adjusted gross income is the starting point for determining Georgia adjusted gross income.

Taxes paid (IRC Sec. 164).—Income taxes paid to jurisdictions other than Georgia must be added to Georgia taxable income to the extent that such taxes were deducted in determining federal adjusted gross income (¶ 403). A Georgia resident is allowed a credit against Georgia personal income tax liability for any income taxes paid to another state (¶ 120).

Tuition expenses and programs (IRC Secs. 222 and 529).—The same as IRC Sec. 222, because the starting point for Georgia taxable income is federal adjusted gross income. Georgia allows a deduction from federal adjusted gross income for contributions to, and the earnings portion of qualified withdrawals from, the Georgia Higher Education Savings Plan established pursuant to IRC Sec. 529 (¶ 310). Earnings attributable to nonqualified withdrawals from the plan must be added to federal adjusted gross income.

Victims of terrorism or disaster (IRC Secs. 139 and 692).—The same as federal because federal adjusted gross income is the starting point for determining Georgia adjusted gross income.

¶ 45 Corporate Income Tax Comparison

The following is a comparison of key features of the Georgia corporate income tax law and the federal income tax law. Georgia generally adopts the provisions of the Internal Revenue Code (see ¶ 1002). State modifications to taxable income required by law differences are discussed beginning at in Chapters 11 and 12.

¶ 45

Part I—Tables

The comparisons below do not reflect the differences that may arise as a result of the enactment of the Working Families Tax Relief Act of 2004 (P.L. 108-311) or the American Jobs Creation Act of 2004. For highlights of the amendments made by these Acts and the adjustments that may be required on the Georgia return, see ¶ 1002.

IRC Sec. 27 foreign tax credit.—Georgia has no equivalent to the federal foreign tax credit and does not allow a deduction for foreign income, franchise, or capital stock taxes measured by net income, regardless of whether the federal foreign tax credit was taken. However, Georgia allows a subtraction from federal taxable income for any foreign dividend gross-up included in federal taxable income under IRC Sec. 78 (see ¶ 1203).

IRC Sec. 29 fuel from nonconventional source credit.—Georgia has no equivalent to the fuel from nonconventional source credit.

IRC Sec. 30 qualified electric vehicles credit.—Georgia has no equivalent to the qualified electric vehicles credit. However, Georgia allows a credit for purchases or leases of new low-emission vehicles or conversions of conventional vehicles to low-emission vehicles (¶ 915). Georgia also allows a credit for the purchase of electric vehicle chargers.

IRC Sec. 40 alcohol fuel credit.—Georgia has no equivalent to the alcohol fuel credit.

IRC Sec. 41 incremental research expenditures credit.—Georgia businesses that are allowed a federal income tax credit for qualified research expenses are also allowed such a credit against their Georgia income taxes.

IRC Sec. 42 low-income housing credit.—Georgia allows a tax credit for each Georgia housing project that qualifies as a low-income building under IRC Sec. 42 and that is placed in service after January 1, 2001. The amount of the credit is equal to the federal low-income housing tax credit allowed with respect to the qualified project (¶ 922).

IRC Sec. 43 enhanced oil recovery credit.—Georgia has no equivalent to the enhanced oil recovery credit.

IRC Sec. 44 disabled access credit.—Georgia has no equivalent to the disabled access credit.

IRC Sec. 45 renewable electricity production credit.—Georgia has no equivalent to the renewable electricity production credit.

IRC Sec. 45A Indian employment credit.—Georgia has no equivalent to the Indian employment credit. However, Georgia allows a deduction from federal taxable income for salary and wage deductions that are reduced in computing federal taxable income because the corporation has taken the federal Indian employment credit (¶ 1204).

IRC Sec. 45B employer social security credit.—Employers electing to take the federal employer social security credit are allowed an income tax deduction equal to the credit for purposes of calculating Georgia net income taxes (¶ 1206).

IRC Sec. 45C orphan drug credit.—Georgia has no equivalent to the orphan drug credit.

¶ 45

IRC Sec. 45D new markets credit.—Georgia has no equivalent to the new markets credit.

IRC Sec. 45E small business pension startup costs credit.—Georgia has no equivalent to the federal small business pension startup costs credit.

IRC Sec. 45F employer-provided child care credit.—Georgia does not conform to the federal employer-provided child care credit. However, Georgia allows similar child day care credits to employers for costs associated with providing or sponsoring an on-site day care center for their employees (¶ 911). Georgia also allows a credit for the cost of all property acquired for use exclusively in the construction, expansion, improvement, or operation of a licensed day-care facility (¶ 911). Taxpayers claiming the credit for qualified child care property must increase Georgia taxable income by the amount of any depreciation deductions used in determining federal taxable income.

IRC Sec. 46—Sec. 49 investment credit (former law).—Georgia has no equivalent to the former federal investment credit or to the current investment credits. However, Georgia does provide a manufacturer's and telecommunications investment credit (¶ 916). An alternative manufacturer's and telecommunications investment credit is available for most businesses that increase their port traffic at in-state facilities (¶ 924). Georgia also provides credits to taxpayers that establish or relocate corporate headquarters in the state (¶ 920) and to manufacturers that construct new facilities (¶ 926, 927).

IRC Sec. 51—Sec. 52 work opportunity credit.—Georgia has no equivalent to the federal work opportunity or welfare-to-work credits. However, Georgia allows a deduction from federal taxable income for salary and wage deductions that are reduced in computing federal taxable income because the corporation has taken the federal work opportunity and welfare-to-work credits (see ¶ 911). Also, Georgia provides job tax credits to businesses that increase employment by creating new full-time jobs (¶ 913).

IRC Sec. 55—Sec. 59 tax preferences.—There is no Georgia equivalent to the federal alternative minimum tax on tax preference items.

IRC Sec. 78 deemed dividends.—Georgia allows a subtraction from federal taxable income for any foreign dividend gross-up included in federal taxable income under IRC Sec. 78 (¶ 1203).

Interest on federal obligations.—Interest or dividends on obligations of any authority, commission, instrumentality, territory, or possession of the United States that are exempt from federal income tax but not from state income taxes must be added to federal taxable income (¶ 1102). Interest and dividends on obligations of the United States, its territories and possessions or of any authority, commission, or instrumentality of the United States are subtracted from federal taxable income to the extent they were included in gross income for federal income tax purposes but are exempt from state income taxes (¶ 1202).

IRC Sec. 103 interest on state obligations.—Interest income derived from obligations of any state or political subdivision, except Georgia and political subdivisions of Georgia, is added to federal taxable income to the

¶ 45

Part I—Tables

extent that the interest income is not included in gross income for federal income tax purposes (¶ 1102).

IRC Sec. 114 extraterritorial income.—The same as federal because the IRC is incorporated by reference (¶ 1002).

IRC Sec. 163 interest on indebtedness.—Same as federal because the IRC is incorporated by reference (¶ 1002). For the subtraction of interest related to federally tax-exempt income, see ¶ 1202.

IRC Sec. 164 income and franchise tax deductions.—Any taxes imposed by any taxing jurisdiction, except the State of Georgia, on, or measured by, net income or net profits that were deducted from federal taxable income are added back for Georgia purposes (¶ 1103).

IRC Sec. 165 losses.—The same as federal, except that losses incurred in any year in which the taxpayer was not subject to taxation in Georgia must be added back to federal taxable income (¶ 1004). Also, previously reported income, losses and deductions may never be used again in computing Georgia taxable income.

IRC Sec. 166 bad debts.—The same as federal because the IRC is incorporated by reference (¶ 1002).

IRC Sec. 167 and Sec. 168 depreciation.—The same as federal because the IRC is incorporated by reference (¶ 1002) with the exception of bonus depreciation under IRC Sec. 168(k). Employers who claim the tax credit available with respect to qualified child care property (¶ 911) must add to their taxable income the amount of any depreciation deductions attributable to such property to the extent that these deductions are used in determining federal taxable income (¶ 1104).

IRC Sec. 168(f) safe harbor leasing (pre-1984 leases).—Georgia does not recognize federal safe harbor leases.

IRC Sec. 169 pollution control facilities amortization.—The same as federal because the IRC is incorporated by reference (¶ 1002). Georgia also provides a tax credit to manufacturers and telecommunications providers for investments in pollution control equipment and facilities (¶ 916)

IRC Sec. 170 charitable contributions.—The same as federal because the IRC is incorporated by reference (¶ 1002).

IRC Sec. 171 amortizable bond premium.—The same as federal because the IRC is incorporated by reference (¶ 1002).

IRC Sec. 172 net operating loss.—The same as federal because the IRC is incorporated by reference (¶ 1002). However, Georgia allows a separate deduction for carryovers and carrybacks of net operating losses after adjustments to federal taxable income and to the extent the loss is attributable to operations in the state (¶ 1002). Georgia follows IRC Sec. 172 with respect to the net operating loss carryback and carryover periods.

IRC Sec. 173 circulation expenditures.—The same as federal because the IRC is incorporated by reference (¶ 1002).

IRC Sec. 174 research and experimental expenditures.—The same as federal because the IRC is incorporated by reference (¶ 1002).

¶ 45

IRC Sec. 175 soil and water conservation expenditures.—The same as federal because the IRC is incorporated by reference (¶ 1002). Georgia also provides credits for water conservation (¶ 918).

IRC Sec. 179 asset expense election.—Generally, the same as federal because the starting point for Georgia taxable income is federal taxable income. However, Georgia does not allow the expense deduction enacted by the federal Jobs and Growth Tax Relief Reconciliation Act of 2003 (JGTRRA) (P.L. 108-27), which raised the limit for expensing of assets from $25,000 to $100,000 and the phase-out threshold from $200,000 to $400,000 (¶ 1007).

IRC Sec. 179A clean-fuel vehicles.—The same as federal because the IRC is incorporated by reference (¶ 1002). Georgia also allows a credit for purchases or leases of new low-emission vehicles or conversions of conventional vehicles to low-emission vehicles and a credit for the installation of diesel particulate emission reduction technology equipment at a truck stop, depot, or other facility (¶ 915).

IRC Sec. 180 deduction for fertilizer.—The same as federal because the IRC is incorporated by reference (¶ 1002).

IRC Sec. 190 deduction for barriers removal.—The same as federal because the IRC is incorporated by reference (¶ 1002).

IRC Sec. 193 deduction for tertiary injectants.—The same as federal because the IRC is incorporated by reference (¶ 1002).

IRC Sec. 194 reforestation amortization.—The same as federal because the IRC is incorporated by reference (¶ 1002).

IRC Sec. 195 start-up expenditures.—The same as federal because the IRC is incorporated by reference (¶ 1002).

IRC Sec. 197 amortization of intangibles.—The same as federal because the IRC is incorporated by reference (¶ 1002).

IRC Sec. 198 environmental remediation costs.—The same as federal because the IRC is incorporated by reference (¶ 1002).

IRC Sec. 243—Sec. 245 dividends received deduction.—The same as federal because the IRC is incorporated by reference (¶ 1002). In addition, dividends to the extent included in net income that were received from affiliated corporations within the United States by a corporation engaged in business in Georgia and subject to Georgia income tax may be subtracted if first reduced by any expenses directly attributable to the dividend income (¶ 1203).

IRC Sec. 301—Sec. 385 corporate distributions and adjustments.—The same as federal because the IRC is incorporated by reference (¶ 1002).

IRC Sec. 401—Sec. 424 deferred compensation plans.—The same as federal because the IRC is incorporated by reference (¶ 1002).

IRC Sec. 441—Sec. 483 accounting periods and methods.—Although Georgia incorporates the IRC by reference, Georgia law contains specific provisions concerning the taxpayer's authorized tax year and the accounting methods used in the computation of Georgia taxable net income (¶ 907). The annual accounting period and the accounting method regularly employed in

¶ 45

Part I—Tables 31

keeping the taxpayer's books are used in the computation of the taxpayer's net income. A fiscal accounting period may be used with the Commissioner's approval. The Commissioner has authority to require use of a method clearly reflecting income in a case where either no accounting method is employed or the method used does not clearly reflect income.

IRC Sec. 501—530 exempt organization.—The same as federal (¶ 903). Unrelated business income is subject to Georgia corporate income tax.

IRC Sec. 531—565 corporations used to avoid shareholder taxation.—Georgia has no provisions regarding corporations used to avoid shareholder taxation. Georgia does not impose a tax on accumulated earnings or on personal holding companies.

IRC Sec. 581—Sec. 597 banking institutions.—The same as federal because the IRC is incorporated by reference (¶ 1002). Banks and financial institutions are also subject to a gross receipts tax (Chapter 19). However, Georgia allows a credit to depository financial institutions in an amount equal to the gross receipts and occupation taxes paid by the institution (¶ 919).

IRC Sec. 611—Sec. 638 natural resources.—The same as federal because the IRC is incorporated by reference (¶ 1002).

IRC Sec. 801—Sec. 848 insurance companies.—There is no Georgia equivalent to the federal provisions relating to insurance companies. Insurance companies that pay the gross premiums tax are exempt from corporate income tax (¶ 903).

IRC Sec. 851—Sec. 860L RICs, REITs, REMICs, and FASITs.—The same as federal because the IRC is incorporated by reference (¶ 1002).

IRC Sec. 901—Sec. 912 foreign source income.—Georgia allows a subtraction from federal taxable income for dividends received from sources outside the United States and included in federal taxable income, including foreign gross-up dividends, Subpart F income, qualified electing fund income, and income attributable to an increase in United States property by a controlled foreign corporation (¶ 1203).

IRC Sec. 921—Sec. 927 foreign sales corporations (former law).—Georgia has no special provisions on FSCs.

IRC Sec. 991—Sec. 997 domestic international sales corporations.—Georgia has no special provisions on DISCs.

IRC Sec. 1001—Sec. 1092 gain or loss on disposition of property.—The same as federal except that when the gain or loss on the sale or exchange of real or tangible personal property located in Georgia is not recognized because the taxpayer has received or purchased similar property (IRC Sec. 1031 like-kind exchange), the nonrecognition will be allowed for Georgia tax purposes only if the replacement property is also located in Georgia (¶ 1004). Georgia also requires a gain or loss adjustment measured by the difference between the Georgia basis and the federal basis, but limited to the amount of such difference included in federal taxable income.

IRC Sec. 1201 alternative capital gains tax.—Georgia does not impose a different rate of tax on capital gains.

¶ 45

IRC Sec. 1211 and Sec. 1212 capital losses.—The same as federal except that Georgia does not allow a deduction for losses that occurred in a year in which the taxpayer was not subject to tax in Georgia or for losses that were previously reported (¶ 1004).

IRC Sec. 1221—1260 determining capital gains and losses.—The same as federal because the IRC is incorporated by reference (¶ 1002).

IRC Sec. 1301 averaging farm income.—The same as federal because the IRC is incorporated by reference (¶ 1002).

IRC Sec. 1361—Sec. 1379 S corporations.—The same as federal because the IRC is incorporated by reference (¶ 1002). However, for a federal S corporation election to apply for Georgia income tax purposes, all stockholders must either be subject to tax in Georgia or be nonresident stockholders who pay Georgia income tax on their portion of the corporation's income (¶ 1006).

IRC Sec. 1391—1400J empowerment zones and renewal communities.—Georgia has no provisions equivalent to the federal provisions relating to empowerment zones and renewal communities. However, Georgia allows a deduction from federal taxable income for salary and wage deductions that are reduced in computing federal taxable income because the corporation has taken the federal empowerment zone employment credit under IRC Sec. 1396 (¶ 911). Georgia also provides various tax credits to businesses that create jobs and make investments in distressed areas (¶ 908).

IRC Sec. 1501—Sec. 1504 consolidated returns.—Corporations that file their federal income tax return on a consolidated basis must also file consolidated returns for Georgia income tax purposes if all of their income is from sources within Georgia. Unless the Department of Revenue either requires or gives prior approval to the filing of a consolidated return for Georgia income tax purposes, corporations that file a consolidated federal income tax return, but derive income from sources outside Georgia, must file separate returns for Georgia income tax purposes (¶ 1403).

BUSINESS INCENTIVES AND CREDITS

¶ 50 Introduction

Georgia has created a number of tax incentives designed to attract business to the state, stimulate expansion, and/or encourage certain economic activity. These incentives are listed below, by tax, with a brief description and a cross-reference to the paragraph at which they are discussed in greater detail. Exemptions and deductions, which are too numerous to be included below, are discussed under the taxes to which they apply (see the Table of Contents or the Topical Index).

¶ 55 Personal Income Tax

● *Employment-related incentives*

Credits against personal income tax are available to employers who:

—increase their full time employment (¶ 125, 129);

—provide or sponsor an approved retraining program (¶ 112);

Part I—Tables   **33**

   —provide a basic skills education program (¶ 113);

   —provide or sponsor child care (¶ 114);

   —provide transportation (¶ 126) or qualified transportation fringe benefits (¶ 115).

● *Credit for zero-emission or low-emission vehicles and equipment*

Georgia allows a credit for business enterprises that purchase or lease new zero-emission or low-emission vehicles or convert conventional vehicles (¶ 116). Credits are also available for the purchase or lease of electric vehicle chargers and for installation of diesel particulate emission reduction technology.

● *Rural physicians' credit*

A physician who practices in a rural county and resides in a rural county or an adjacent county, primarily admits patients to a rural hospital, and practices in a family practice, obstetrics and gynecology, pediatrics, internal medicine, or general surgery may receive a credit against personal income tax (¶ 118).

● *Deduction for payments to minority subcontractors*

A state contractor may subtract from federal adjusted gross income for Georgia personal income tax purposes a portion of the amount paid to a minority subcontractor for goods, property, or services delivered to the state under the contract (¶ 305).

● *Low income housing credit*

Georgia allows a credit equal to the federal credit under IRC Sec. 41 for low income housing placed in service after 2000 (¶ 124).

● *Credit for rehabilitation of historic property*

Beginning after 2003, a credit is available for taxpayers that substantially rehabilitate historic property (¶ 127).

● *Deduction for organ donation expenses*

Beginning in 2005, organ donation expenses incurred in accordance with the federal National Organ Procurement Act may be subtracted from a taxpayer's federal adjusted gross income in figuring Georgia net taxable income for Georgia personal income tax purposes (¶ 311).

¶ 60   Corporate Income Tax

● *Job tax credits*

Georgia allows a credit for certain business taxpayers that increase their full time employment by specified numbers of jobs, depending upon their location in the state (¶ 913).

Related additional jobs credits are available for taxpayers who also increase their traffic at Georgia port facilities (¶ 924).

¶ 60

A jobs credit is available to employers who create at least 100 new full time jobs by establishing their corporate headquarters in Georgia or relocating from out of state (¶ 920).

A manufacturer who creates at least 1,800 jobs in a new manufacturing facility may claim a credit for up to 3,300 new jobs (¶ 926).

● *Other employment-related incentives*

In addition to the credits for increasing employment, credits are available to employers who:

—provide or sponsor an approved retraining program (¶ 909);

—provide a basic skills education program (¶ 910);

—provide or sponsor child care (¶ 911);

—provide transportation (¶ 923) or qualified transportation fringe benefits (¶ 914);

—construct new manufacturing facilities in Georgia (¶ 926, 927).

● *Deduction for payments to minority subcontractors*

A state contractor may subtract from federal taxable income for Georgia corporate income tax purposes a portion of the amount paid to a minority subcontractor for goods, property, or services delivered to the state under the contract (¶ 1205).

● *Investment tax credit*

Georgia allows an investment tax credit for taxpayers that have operated a manufacturing or telecommunication facility in Georgia for the immediately preceding three years and that purchase or acquire real or personal property used to construct or expand a manufacturing facility in Georgia (¶ 916).

Related additional investment credits are available for taxpayers who also increase their traffic at Georgia port facilities (¶ 924), or who construct new manufacturing facilities (¶ 927).

● *Business growth credit*

Georgia allows a credit for Georgia business enterprises with current net taxable income that exceeds the prior year's net taxable income by 20% or more, and whose net taxable income for the previous two years exceeded their prior years' net taxable income by 20% or more (¶ 912).

● *Credit for zero-emission or low-emission vehicles and equipment*

Georgia allows a credit for business enterprises that purchase or lease new zero-emission or low-emission vehicles or convert conventional vehicles (¶ 915). Credits are also available for the purchase or lease of electric vehicle chargers and for installation of diesel particulate emission reduction technology.

¶ 60

Part I—Tables

● *Qualified research credit*

Georgia business enterprises that are allowed a federal income tax credit for qualified research expenses under IRC Sec. 41 are also allowed a qualified research credit for Georgia tax purposes (¶ 917).

● *Water conservation credit*

A credit is available for business enterprises that purchase water from a qualified water conservation facility and reduce groundwater consumption by at least 10% per year (¶ 918).

● *Credit for increasing cigarette exports*

Cigarette manufacturing businesses that increase their exports of cigarettes to foreign countries by 50% or more may receive a credit against Georgia corporate income tax (¶ 921).

● *Low income housing credit*

Georgia allows a credit equal to the federal credit under IRC Sec. 41 for low income housing placed in service after 2000 (¶ 922).

● *Credit for rehabilitation of historic property*

Beginning after 2003, a credit is available for taxpayers that substantially rehabilitate historic property (¶ 925).

¶ 65 Sales and Use Taxes

Sales of property used in the production of tangible personal property are exempt from sales and use tax in certain circumstances (¶ 2201). Specific incentives, in the form of exemptions, apply to:

—agricultural materials, fuel, and irrigation equipment;

—computer equipment sold or leased to high technology companies;

— corporate tourist attractions;

—manufacturing machinery;

—medical supplies;

—pollution reduction equipment;

—telecommunications, broadcasting, and film production.

¶ 70 Property Tax

Incentive exemptions for business apply to the following (¶ 2604):

—specified agricultural products;

Enterprise Zone property;

—inventory (Freeport exemption);

—pollution control equipment;

¶ 70

● *Specially valued property*

The following property is valued at its current use, rather than at its highest and best use, for property tax purposes (¶ 2605):

—agricultural land;

—conservation use or residential transitional property.

● *Historic property*

The fair market value of rehabilitated historic property and landmark historic property is computed by a special formula for the first nine years it is specially classified.

¶ 75 Insurance Gross Premiums Tax

● *Low income housing credit*

Georgia allows a credit equal to the federal credit under IRC Sec. 41 for low income housing placed in service after 2000 (¶ 2804).

PART II

PERSONAL INCOME TAX

CHAPTER 1

IMPOSITION OF TAX, RATES, EXEMPTIONS, CREDITS

¶ 101   Overview
¶ 102   Residency
¶ 103   Tax Base
¶ 104   Personal and Dependent Exemptions
¶ 105   Tax Rates
¶ 106   Accounting Periods and Methods
¶ 107   Accounting Method on Decedent's Return
¶ 108   Military Personnel
¶ 109   Innocent Spouse Relief
¶ 110   Credits Against Tax—In General
¶ 111   Aged and Disabled Caregiving Expenses Credit
¶ 112   Approved Retraining Programs Credit
¶ 113   Basic Skills Education Programs Credit
¶ 114   Credit for Child Care Provided by Employers
¶ 115   Federal Qualified Transportation Fringe Benefits Credit
¶ 116   Low Emission Vehicles and Equipment Credit
¶ 117   Credit for Low Income Residents and Working Poor Persons
¶ 118   Rural Physicians Credit
¶ 119   Credit for Taxes Paid on Returned Income Amounts
¶ 120   Credit for Taxes Paid to Another State
¶ 121   Credit for Taxes Withheld and Estimated Tax
¶ 122   Credit for Disaster Assistance Recipients
¶ 123   Driver's Education Expenses Credit
¶ 124   Low-Income Housing Credit
¶ 125   Business Expansion Credit
¶ 126   Credit for Employer-Provided Transportation
¶ 127   Credit for Rehabilitation of Historic Property
¶ 128   Credit for Accessible Residence
¶ 129   Job Tax Credit

¶ 101 Overview

Law: Secs. 14-11-1104, 48-1-2(14), 48-7-20, 48-7-22, 48-7-23, Code (CCH GEORGIA TAX REPORTS ¶ 15-001, 15-101, 15-105, 15-120, 15-130, 15-135, 15-201, 16-101).

The Georgia personal income tax is based on the federal income tax (¶ 103). Various adjustments to the federal base are made for Georgia tax purposes (see Chapters 3 and 4).

Current law is set forth in Title 48 of the Code of Georgia of 1981 as amended. Title 48 may be cited as the "Georgia Public Revenue Code."

The tax is imposed on resident individuals, estates, and trusts and on nonresident individuals, estates, and trusts that derive income from sources within Georgia. For part year residents, the tax is prorated on the basis of the time spent within Georgia. Fiduciaries that receive income from business done in Georgia, have charge of funds or property located in Georgia, or have charge of funds or property for the benefit of a Georgia resident are also subject to tax.

Partnerships and limited liability companies (LLCs) classified as partnerships are not subject to tax, but the partners and members are subject to tax on their distributive shares of the partnership's or LLC's income.

The tax is imposed on net taxable income in accordance with the Georgia tax rate schedule appropriate for the taxpayer's filing status. The rates in the schedule range from 1% to 6% (¶ 105). Several credits are available to taxpayers who qualify (¶ 110).

This chapter discusses the imposition of tax, rates, exemptions, and credits. Chapter 2 covers computation of tax. Chapter 3 deals with subtractions from federal adjusted gross income. Additions to taxable income are discussed in Chapter 4. Allocation and apportionment of nonresident income are covered in Chapter 5. Chapter 6 deals with returns, estimates, payment of tax, and withholding. Fiduciaries, partnerships, and limited liability companies are discussed in Chapter 7, and Chapter 8 deals with administrative provisions specific to personal income taxes; however, general administrative provisions are covered in Part IX, "Administration and Procedure," beginning at Chapter 29. Corporate income tax is discussed beginning with Chapter 9.

● *Internal Revenue Code references*

For taxable years beginning after 2003, Georgia conforms with the Internal Revenue Code as amended as of January 1, 2004. However, Georgia has not adopted the increased limits applicable to the expensing of assets under IRC Sec. 179 that were enacted by the federal Jobs and Growth Tax Relief Reconciliation Act (JGTRRA) (P.L. 108-27). Further, because Georgia does not incorporate the IRC as amended to date, amendments made by the Working Families Tax Relief Act (WFTRA) of 2004 or the American Jobs Creation Act (AJCA) of 2004 have not yet been adopted.

Part II—Personal Income Tax

Practitioner Comment: IRC Reference Updates

Since 1986, Georgia has updated its reference to the Internal Revenue Code annually.

Michael T. Petrik, Esq., Alston & Bird LLP

Federal bonus depreciation: Georgia does not adopt the bonus depreciation provisions of IRC Sec. 168(k), nor the New York Liberty Zone provisions of IRC Sec. 1400L.

Classroom supplies: A federal provision (IRC Sec. 62(a)(2)(D) for teachers and other educators allowing a deduction of up to $250 for out-of-pocket expenses incurred in providing classroom supplies is allowed for tax years beginning on or after January 1, 2003.

This federal deduction, which would have expired after 2003, was extended by the federal Working Families Tax Relief Act of 2004. However, because Georgia does not incorporate the Internal Revenue Code as amended to date, the extension of this provision will not be effective for Georgia personal income tax purposes without further state legislation.

Economic Growth and Tax Relief Reconciliation Act (EGTRRA): The EGTRRA (P.L. 107-16), which Georgia has adopted, provides a broad range of federal income tax benefits, many of which are time-delayed with varying effective dates spanning up to 10 years.

The EGTRRA provides a number of retirement savings incentives, including an increase in the contribution limits for individual retirement accounts (IRAs), 401(k)s, and other defined contribution plans, among other pension and retirement savings benefits.

The EGTRRA also implements cuts in the various federal income tax rates and gradually eliminates the marriage penalty tax starting in 2005. Additionally, the federal child tax credit, adoption credit, dependent care credit, and employer-provided child care facilities credit will be increased.

Education benefits are provided in the form of a temporary college tuition deduction, increased education IRA limits, and enhanced student loan deductions.

Working Families Tax Relief Act of 2004: Because Georgia does not incorporate the Internal Revenue Code as amended to date, Georgia does not incorporate the federal amendments made by the Working Families Tax Relief Act of 2004. See ¶ 201.

¶ 102 Residency

Law. Sec. 48-7-1(5), (10), and (11), 48-7-20, Code (CCH Georgia Tax Reports ¶ 15-101, 15-105, 15-110).

The term "resident" is defined as:

—an individual who is a legal resident of Georgia on income tax day,

—an individual who, though not necessarily a legal resident of Georgia, nevertheless resides within Georgia on a more or less regular or permanent basis, and not on the temporary or transitory basis of a visitor or sojourner, including on income tax day, *i.e.*, December 31 of each calendar year or the last day of the taxpayer's fiscal year, and

—an individual who on income tax day has been residing within Georgia for at least 183 days or part days during the immediately preceding 365 day period.

Resident status continues until an individual establishes legal residency or domicile in another state and the individual no longer resides in Georgia for at least 183 days or part days during the preceding year.

● *Taxable nonresidents*

Nonresidents are taxable with respect to their Georgia taxable net income, not otherwise exempt, that is received from services performed, property owned, or from business carried on in Georgia, or lottery prizes of $5,000 or more awarded by the Georgia Lottery Corporation.

A "taxable nonresident" is an individual who is not a resident but who:

—regularly (and not casually or intermittently) engages within Georgia in employment, trade, business, professional or other activity for financial gain or profit (either himself, or by means of employees, agents, or partners). This includes, but is not limited to the rental of real or personal property located within Georgia or for use within Georgia;

—sells, exchanges, or otherwise disposes of tangible property that has a taxable situs within Georgia;

—sells, exchanges or otherwise disposes of intangible personal property that has acquired a business or commercial situs within Georgia;

—receives the proceeds of any lottery prize of $5,000 or more awarded by the Georgia Lottery Corporation; or

—is an individual who makes an unqualified withdrawal from a savings trust account used solely for qualified higher education expenses (¶ 207).

There is an exception to the taxable nonresident definition for a legal resident of another state whose only activity for financial gain or profit in Georgia consists of performing services for an employer in Georgia, when the remuneration for the services does not exceed 5% of the income received by the individual for performing services in all places during any taxable year.

The allocation and apportionment of nonresident income is discussed in Chapter 5.

¶ 103 Tax Base

Law: Sec. 48-7-27(a), Code (CCH GEORGIA TAX REPORTS ¶ 15-310).

Comparable Federal: Sec. 63 (U.S. MASTER TAX GUIDE ¶ 1005—1010).

Form: Form 500 (Individual Income Tax Return).

Georgia taxable net income is computed by using the taxpayer's federal adjusted gross income as a starting point.

Part II—Personal Income Tax 41

¶ 104 Personal and Dependent Exemptions

Law: Secs. 48-7-26(a), (b), and (d), 48-7-27(a)(2), Code (CCH GEORGIA TAX REPORTS ¶ 15-410, 15-420).

Comparable Federal: Secs. 151, 213 (U.S. MASTER TAX GUIDE ¶ 133—149).

Form: Form 500 (Individual Income Tax Return).

An individual's federal adjusted gross income may be reduced by the amounts of personal and dependent exemptions that are allowable in computing Georgia taxable net income. For current amounts, see ¶ 301.

Personal exemptions are also allowed for estates and trusts (¶ 301).

¶ 105 Tax Rates

Law: Sec. 48-7-20(a) and (b), Code (CCH GEORGIA TAX REPORTS ¶ 15-201).

Comparable Federal: Sec. 1 (U.S. MASTER TAX GUIDE ¶ 25, 1401—1480).

Form: Form IT-511 (Individual Income Tax Booklet).

Tax is imposed on every Georgia resident with respect to the taxpayer's Georgia taxable net income and on every taxable nonresident (¶ 102) with respect to the taxpayer's Georgia taxable net income that the taxpayer receives for services performed in Georgia, property owned in Georgia, business carried on in Georgia, or lottery prizes of $5,000 or more awarded by the Georgia Lottery Corporation.

The tax on Georgia taxable net income is computed using the following tax rate schedule:

Single Person

If Georgia taxable net income is:	The tax is:
Not over $750	1%
Over $750 but not over $2250	$7.50 plus 2% of amount over $750
Over $2250 but not over $3750	$37.50 plus 3% of amount over $2250
Over $3750 but not over $5250	$82.50 plus 4% of amount over $3750
Over $5250 but not over $7000	$142.50 plus 5% of amount over $5250
Over $7000	$230.00 plus 6% of amount over $7000

Married Person Filing a Separate Return

If Georgia taxable net income is:	The tax is:
Not over $500	1%
Over $500 but not over $1500	$5.00 plus 2% of amount over $500
Over $1500 but not over $2500	$25.00 plus 3% of amount over $1500
Over $2500 but not over $3500	$55.00 plus 4% of amount over $2500
Over $3500 but not over $5000	$95.00 plus 5% of amount over $3500
Over $5000	$170.00 plus 6% of amount over $5000

Head of Household and Married Persons Filing a Joint Return

If Georgia taxable net income is:	The tax is:
Not over $1000	1%
Over $1000 but not over $3000	$10.00 plus 2% of amount over $1000
Over $3000 but not over $5000	$50.00 plus 3% of amount over $3000
Over $5000 but not over $7000	$110.00 plus 4% of amount over $5000
Over $7000 but not over $10,000	$190.00 plus 5% of amount over $7000
Over $10,000	$340.00 plus 6% of amount over $10,000

¶ 106 Accounting Periods and Methods

Law: Sec. 48-7-33(a), Code (CCH GEORGIA TAX REPORTS ¶ 15-620).

Comparable Federal: Secs. 441, 446, 481 (U.S. MASTER TAX GUIDE ¶ 1501—1577).

The annual accounting period and the accounting method regularly employed in keeping the taxpayer's books are used in the computation of the taxpayer's net income. However, the State Revenue Commissioner may require the use of a method clearly reflecting income if no accounting method is employed or the method used does not clearly reflect income.

● *Calendar or fiscal year*

Ordinarily, net income is computed on the basis of the calendar year. Further, if the taxpayer has no annual accounting period or does not keep books, the net income must be computed on the basis of the calendar year. However, the Commissioner may approve the computation of net income on the basis of a fiscal year.

¶ 107 Accounting Method on Decedent's Return

Law: Sec. 48-7-33(f), Code (CCH GEORGIA TAX REPORTS ¶ 15-620).

If a return is filed on behalf of a decedent within three years after the decedent's death occurred, the method of accounting to be used on the return must be the same method, cash or accrual, used on the decedent's last income tax return. If no return was filed on behalf of the decedent within the three year period, the cash method must be used unless the State Revenue Commissioner certifies that the cash method is not reasonable to either the state or the interest of heirs, devisees or legatees. If the Commissioner certifies that the cash method is unreasonable, the Commissioner may require the use of the accrual method.

¶ 108 Military Personnel

Law: Secs. 48-7-27, 48-7-36, 48-7-56, Code (CCH GEORGIA TAX REPORTS ¶ 17-520).

Comparable Federal: Sec. 112 (U.S. MASTER TAX GUIDE ¶ 889—896, 1078, 2609, 2533).

Georgia's taxation of pay and benefits received by members of the U.S. Armed Forces is generally the same as federal because the starting point for Georgia taxable income is federal adjusted gross income (¶ 201). Military provisions apply to all regular and reserve components of the uniformed services subject to the jurisdiction of the Secretaries of Defense, Army, Navy, or Air Force, including members of the Marines and Coast Guard. Members of the National Oceanic and Atmospheric Administration also are included, but not members of the Merchant Marine.

The following income of military personnel is subject to both federal and Georgia income taxes:

—active duty and reserve training pay;

—enlistment and reenlistment bonuses;

—incentive pay;

—lump-sum payments for accrued leave;

Part II—Personal Income Tax

—severance, separation, or release pay;

—readjustment pay;

—travel and per diem allowances;

—payments received from a former employer, even if paid directly to dependents;

—personal allowances for high-ranking officers;

—military retirement pay based on age or length of service;

—scholarships and student loan repayments.

● *Residency and domicile*

Under the provisions of the Soldiers' and Sailors' Civil Relief Act of 1940, a member of the Armed Forces retains, while in service, the same domicile as when entering military service. Military personnel (usually career personnel) may change their domicile from Georgia to another state just as any other individual. Conclusive evidence must be submitted showing that their Georgia domicile has been abandoned and a new residence or domicile established in another state.

Residents: Military personnel whose home of record is in Georgia or who otherwise are residents of Georgia are subject to Georgia personal income tax upon all income regardless of source or where earned, unless specifically exempt by Georgia law. The time for filing tax returns and payment of tax by members of the U.S. armed services returning from service outside the continental United States is extended without application to six months after the military person returns to the continental United States. No penalties or interest accrue during this period.

Nonresidents: Nonresident military personnel whose home of record is not in Georgia and who are not otherwise Georgia residents are not required to file a Georgia personal income tax return unless they have earned income from Georgia sources other than military pay. If they have earned income in Georgia from sources other than military pay, they are required to file a return and Schedule 3. A married nonresident with income earned in Georgia whose spouse is a nonresident with no Georgia source income may file either a separate return claiming only himself or herself or a joint return claiming total personal exemption and credit for dependents, prorated per Schedule 3. Schedule 3 must be completed for computation of Georgia taxable income.

● *Combat pay exclusion*

Members of the Armed Forces may exclude combat pay and hostile fire pay for any month for which such pay is received. However, the exclusion for a commissioned officer is limited to the highest rate of enlisted pay for each month.

National Guard and reservists: For tax years beginning after 2002, an exemption from Georgia personal income tax is allowed for military income received by a member of the National Guard or any reserve component of the armed services of the U.S. military for the time the person is stationed in a combat zone as a result of military orders.

¶ 108

CCH Tip: Officers' Pay

Unlike the federal exclusion for combat pay, the Georgia exclusion for combat pay received by National Guard members and reservists is not limited to the highest rate of enlisted pay.

Hospitalization: The monthly exclusion also applies if the service member is hospitalized anywhere as the result of wounds, disease, or injury sustained while serving in a combat zone, but is limited to two years after the termination of combatant activities in the combat zone. Payments for leave accrued during service in a combat zone are also excluded.

● *Tax forgiveness for decedents*

Income tax is forgiven for members of the Armed Forces who die as the result of wounds, disease, or injury incurred in a combat zone or as a result of wounds or injuries sustained in terroristic or military action. Forgiveness includes the entire taxable year in which the death occurs, not just the shortened tax year, and extends to any earlier year ending on or after the first day of service in a combat zone. Taxes for those years are abated, credited, or refunded. However, refunds are subject to the statute of limitations.

CCH Tip: Spouse of Deceased Member

The tax forgiveness applies only to the deceased person, not to the spouse.

The forgiveness provisions also include astronauts who die in the line of duty.

● *Combat zones and hazardous duty areas*

There are three designated combat zones, which include the airspace above, as follows:

—**Arabian Peninsula.** Beginning January 17, 1991: Bahrain, Iraq, Kuwait, Oman, Qatar, Saudi Arabia, the United Arab Emirates, Gulf of Aden, Gulf of Oman, Persian Gulf, Red Sea, and part of the Arabian Sea. Beginning January 1, 2003: Israel and Turkey. Beginning April 11, 2003: part of the Mediterranean Sea.

—**Kosovo.** Beginning March 24, 1999: Yugoslavia (Serbia and Montenegro), Albania, the Adriatic Sea, and the northern Ionian Sea. Additional areas have been designated in support of Operation Enduring Freedom, including Pakistan, Tajikistan, and Jordan (beginning September 19, 2001); Incirlik Air Base, Turkey (beginning September 21, 2001); Kyrgyzstan and Uzbekistan (beginning October 1, 2001); Phillipines (beginning January 9, 2002); Yemen (beginning April 10, 2002); and Djibouti (beginning July 1, 2002).

—**Afghanistan.** Beginning September 19, 2001.

¶ 108

Part II—Personal Income Tax   **45**

A "qualified hazardous duty area" is treated as if it were a combat zone. Bosnia, Herzegovina, Croatia, and Macedonia have been designated as hazardous duty areas.

● *Other nontaxable items*

Miscellaneous items of income received by service members are nontaxable, as follows:

—living allowances, including Basic Allowance for Quarters (BAQ), Basic Allowance for Subsistence (BAS), Variable housing Allowance (VHA), and housing and cost-of-living allowances abroad.

—family allowances, including those for emergencies, evacuation, separation, and certain educational expenses for dependents.

—death allowances, including those for burial services, travel of dependents, and the death gratuity payment to eligible survivors.

CCH Tip: *Military Death Benefit Increased*

The Military Family Tax Relief Act of 2003 (P.L. 108-121) doubled the death benefit from $6,000 to $12,000 for deaths occurring after September 10, 2001. The act also made the death benefit fully tax free (previously, only 50% of the benefit had been excludable).

—moving allowances for dislocation, moving household and personal items, moving trailers or mobile homes, storage, and temporary lodging.

—other benefits, including dependent care, disability, medical benefits, group-term life insurance, professional education, defense counseling, ROTC allowances, survivor and retirement protection plan premiums, uniform allowances for offices, and uniforms furnished to enlisted personnel.

● *Sale of residence*

Two important benefits are available to members of the military who sell their homes.

Homeowner's Assistance Program (HAP): The HAP reimburses military homeowners for losses incurred on the private sale of their homes after a base closure or reduction in operations. The HAP payment is the difference between 95% of the home's fair market value before the closure or reduction announcement and the greater of the home's fair market value at the time of sale or the actual sale price.

HAP payments made after November 11, 2003, are excludable from gross income. Payments made before that date are taxable as compensation.

Capital gains: All homeowners may exclude up to $250,000 ($500,000 on a joint return) of gain on the sale of a home if they have owned and used the home as their personal residence for two of the five years preceding the date of sale. Because members of the military, Public Health Service officers, and Foreign Service officers may be required to move frequently, the Military

¶ 108

Family Tax Relief Act of 2003 provided for these personnel by suspending the five-year testing period for up to 10 years. The suspension applies whenever the person is on qualified official extended duty for more than 90 days and is stationed at least 50 miles from the person's residence or is under orders to reside in government quarters.

● *Moving expenses*

Armed forces members, their spouses and dependents may deduct moving expenses without regard to the distance and time requirements that otherwise would apply. The move must be pursuant to a military order that results in a permanent change of station.

● *Filing requirements*

Members of the military are generally subject to the same filing requirements as other taxpayers (¶ 601), but for service members stationed outside the U.S. or Puerto Rico, the federal due date is automatically extended to June 15th. However, interest accrues on any unpaid tax liability from April 15th, regardless of any extensions.

Georgia allows armed forces members serving outside the continental United States an automatic filing extension, without penalty or interest, until six months after the member's return to the continental U.S.

Members in combat zones: For service members in designated combat zones, hazardous duty areas, hospitalized outside the U.S. due to a combat injury, or deployed in contingency operations, the due date is postponed without interest or penalties until 180 days after the member's return to the U.S. The extended due date also applies to filing amended returns.

● *Veterans*

Payments to veterans for benefits administered by the Veterans Administration are tax-free. Such items include education, training, or subsistence allowances; veterans' pensions, insurance proceeds, and dividends paid to veterans or their families or beneficiaries; grants to disabled veterans for motor vehicles or homes with disability accommodations; and disability compensation.

¶ 109 Innocent Spouse Relief

Law: Sec. 48-7-86(g), Code (CCH GEORGIA TAX REPORTS ¶ 17-840).

Comparable Federal: Sec. 6015 (U.S. MASTER TAX GUIDE ¶ 162).

A taxpayer is relieved of joint liability for an understatement on a joint personal income tax return if the taxpayer has made the proper election under IRC Sec. 6015.

¶ 110 Credits Against Tax—In General

(CCH GEORGIA TAX REPORTS ¶ 16-101).

Georgia personal income tax credits are authorized for aged and disabled caregiving expenses (¶ 111); approved retraining programs (¶ 112); basic skills education programs (¶ 113); child care provided by employers (¶ 114); federal

Part II—Personal Income Tax 47

qualified transportation fringe benefits (¶ 115); low emission vehicles (¶ 116); low income residents and working poor persons (¶ 117); rural physicians (¶ 118); taxes paid on returned income amounts (¶ 119); taxes paid to another state (¶ 120); taxes withheld and estimated tax (¶ 121); disaster assistance recipients (¶ 122); driver's education expenses (¶ 123); low-income housing (¶ 124); business expansion (¶ 125), employer-provided transportation (¶ 126), rehabilitation of historic property (¶ 127), and housing accessibility (¶ 128). A jobs tax credit, discussed at ¶ 913, is also available to certain businesses.

Some credits may not exceed 50% of the taxpayer's tax liability in a year. Excess credits may, in most cases, be carried over to one or more subsequent years. However, some credits are good only for the year in which they arise.

¶ 111 Aged and Disabled Caregiving Expenses Credit

Law: Sec. 48-7-29.2, Code; Reg. Secs. 560-7-8-.43, 560-7-8-.44 (CCH GEORGIA TAX REPORTS ¶ 16-125).

Taxpayers may receive a credit against personal income tax for a portion of certain caregiving expenses incurred on behalf of qualifying aged or disabled family members.

Credit amount: The credit amount may be up to 10% of the total amount expended on such care, but may not exceed the taxpayer's total tax liability or $150, whichever is less.

Qualified expenses: Qualified caregiving expenses include payments made for home health services, personal care services, personal care attendant services, homemaker services, adult day care, respite care, or health care equipment and supplies that a physician has determined to be medically necessary. Expenses that the taxpayer has deducted in calculating Georgia taxable net income and expenses excluded from net income do not qualify for the credit.

Qualifying family members: Qualifying family members include the taxpayer or a person related to the taxpayer by blood, marriage, or adoption who is at least 62 years of age or is disabled. The family member does not have to be a Georgia resident and does not have to be a dependent of the taxpayer.

Limitations and carryforwards: Unused credit may not be carried forward or applied against tax liability from prior years.

CCH Tip: Double Benefit Prohibited

A taxpayer may not receive a double benefit by taking the credit for medical expenses that have been deducted on the individual's federal income tax return. If a taxpayer has enough medical itemized deductions to exceed the federal percentage limitation, then, to determine the portion of expenses that are not allowed for purposes of the disabled care credit, the ratio of the medical itemized deductions that are allowed after the federal percentage limitation to the total medical itemized deductions before the federal percentage limitation must be applied to the qualified caregiving expenses

¶ 111

included in the medical itemized deductions before the federal percentage limitation (Reg. Sec. 560-7-8-.43).

¶ 112 Approved Retraining Programs Credit

Law: Sec. 48-7-40.5, Code (CCH GEORGIA TAX REPORTS ¶ 16-180).

Employers that provide or sponsor an approved retraining program may receive a credit against personal income tax.

Credit amount: The credit amount is equal to one-half of the costs of retraining per full time employee, or $500 per full time employee, whichever is less, for each employee who has successfully completed an approved retraining program. However, the credit amount may not exceed 50% of the amount of the taxpayer's income tax liability for the taxable year as computed without regard to this credit.

Limitations and carryforwards: An employer will not receive the credit if the employees are required to reimburse or pay the employer for the cost of retraining.

An approved retraining program credit claimed may be carried forward 10 years from the close of the taxable year when the credit was granted.

Filing requirements: The employer must certify the name of the employee, the course work successfully completed by the employee, the name of the provider of the approved retraining, and other information that may be required to ensure that the credit is granted only to employers that provide or sponsor approved retraining and only with respect to employees who successfully complete approved retraining.

¶ 113 Basic Skills Education Programs Credit

Law: Sec. 48-7-41, Code (CCH GEORGIA TAX REPORTS ¶ 16-170).

Employers that provide approved basic skills education programs for their employees may receive a credit against personal income tax.

An approved basic skills education is employer-provided or employer-sponsored education that enhances reading, writing, or mathematical skills to the twelfth grade level. Education costs include direct instructional costs, instructor salaries, materials, supplies, and textbooks. The credit does not apply to costs associated with renting or securing space.

Credit amount: The credit amount for each employee successfully completing an approved basic skills education program is one-third of the cost per full time equivalent student or $150 per full time equivalent student, whichever is less.

Limitations: The credit may not exceed the amount of the tax liability for the tax year. An employer may not receive a credit if the employee is required to reimburse or pay the employer for the education costs.

Filing requirements: The employer must certify the name of the employee, the course work successfully completed by the employee, the name of the approved basic skills education provider, and other information required

Part II—Personal Income Tax 49

¶ 114 Credit for Child Care Provided by Employers

Law: Sec. 48-7-40.6, Code (CCH GEORGIA TAX REPORTS ¶ 16-190).

Employers that provide or sponsor child care for their employees may receive a credit against personal income tax.

Credit amount: The credit amount is equal to 75% of the cost of operation to the employer, minus any amounts paid by the employees during a taxable year.

Limitations and carryforwards: The credit may not exceed 50% of the amount of the taxpayer's income tax liability for the taxable year as computed without regard to any other credits.

Credit amounts claimed but not used may be carried forward for five years from the close of the taxable year when the cost was incurred.

Practitioner Comment: Partnerships

Businesses operating as a partnership are permitted to pass through this credit to resident and non-resident partners.

Michael T. Petrik, Esq., Alston & Bird

● *Credit for placing qualified child care property into service*

An additional credit is available to employers who place qualified child care property into service on or after July 1, 1999.

Credit amount: The credit equals 100% of the cost of the qualified property, to be claimed at 10% per year over 10 years, but may not equal more than 50% of the tax liability for a given year. An employer's Georgia taxable income must be increased by any depreciation deductions attributable to qualified child care property that are taken in determining the employer's federal taxable income.

Qualified child care property: Qualified child care property includes tangible personal property and real property acquired or purchased on or after July 1, 1999. This property must be used solely for improving, expanding, constructing, or operating a child care facility operated by an employer with the following limitations: (1) the facility must be commissioned or licensed by the Department of Human Resources; (2) at least 95% of children using the facility must be the children of the taxpayer's employees, children of employees of joint and several owners of the facility, or children of employees of a corporation in the taxpayer's affiliated group; and (3) the taxpayer must not have claimed credit for operating costs of such a facility before taxable years beginning on or after January 1, 2000. Qualified child care property also includes funds spent on acquiring land, fixtures, improvements, buildings, equipment, building improvements and furniture.

¶ 114

Carryforward of credit: Any credit claimed but not used in a given tax year may be carried forward three years.

Recapture of credit: The credit is subject to recapture under certain circumstances.

CCH Tip: Filing Requirements

The taxpayer must attach a schedule to the return showing the following: (1) a description of the facility; (2) amounts of qualified property acquired during the tax year and their cost; (3) the amount of the credit claimed for the tax years; (4) amounts and costs of qualified property acquired in previous tax years; (5) any tax credits claimed in previous tax years; (6) amounts of tax credit carried forward from previous years; (7) amounts of tax credits currently used; (8) the amount of tax credit being carried forward to subsequent years; and (9) a description of any recapture event that has occurred during the tax year, a calculation of the reduction in allowable tax credits in the recapture and future tax years, and a calculation of the tax increase for the recapture year.

¶115 Federal Qualified Transportation Fringe Benefits Credit

Law: Sec. 48-7-29.3, Code (CCH GEORGIA TAX REPORTS ¶ 16-145).

Comparable Federal: Sec. 132 (U.S. MASTER TAX GUIDE ¶ 863).

Taxpayers that provide federal qualified transportation fringe benefits to their employees may receive a credit against personal income tax.

Credit amount: The credit amount is equal to $25 per employee receiving the benefit.

Limitations and carryforwards: The credit amount may not exceed the annual benefit expenditure or the taxpayer's total income tax liability.

Any unused credit may be carried forward for three successive years but may not be used against liability from prior years.

¶116 Low Emission Vehicles and Equipment Credit

Law: Secs. 48-7-40.16, 48-7-40.19, Code; Reg. Sec. 391-3-25-.01 (CCH GEORGIA TAX REPORTS ¶ 11-242, 16-165, 16-167).

A taxpayer that purchases or leases a new low emission vehicle or converts a conventional vehicle to a low emission vehicle may receive a credit against personal income tax if the vehicle is registered within a particular geographic area.

Credit amount: The credit amount for each new vehicle is $2,500, except that the credit for zero emission vehicles is $5,000. For converted vehicles, the credit amount equals the cost of conversion, but no more than $2,500 for each converted vehicle.

Part II—Personal Income Tax   51

Qualifying vehicles: In order to qualify for the credit, the vehicle must be registered in an area that has not attained or maintained the ozone level set in the federal Clean Air Act or in any county adjacent to such an area. A low emission vehicle operates on alternative fuel and meets the emission standards set by the Board of Natural Resources. A zero emission vehicle has no tailpipe or evaporative emissions.

Low-speed vehicles designed to transport 10 passengers or less may qualify for the credit, but only if the low-speed vehicle was placed in service during the taxable year ending December 31, 2001.

Carryforward of credit: The credit may be carried forward five years (three years, prior to 2001).

● *Electric vehicle chargers*

A business that purchases or leases an electric vehicle charger located in a particular geographic area may receive a credit against personal income tax.

Credit amount: The credit amount is equal to $2,500 per charger.

Limitations and carryforwards: This credit may be claimed only by an ultimate purchaser or lessee of a new electric vehicle charger at retail. This credit may be carried forward five years.

● *Equipment to reduce diesel particulate emissions*

Taxpayers may receive a credit against personal income tax for installing diesel particulate emission reduction technology equipment at a truck stop, depot, or other facility.

Credit amount: The credit amount is 10% of the cost of the equipment and installation.

Limitations and carryforwards: The credit is allowed for the tax year when the taxpayer first places the equipment in use. This credit may not be carried forward.

¶ 117   Credit for Low Income Residents and Working Poor Persons

Law: Secs. 48-7A-1—48-7A-3, Code (CCH GEORGIA TAX REPORTS ¶ 16-140).

Low income Georgia residents and working poor persons may receive a credit against personal income tax. Each resident taxpayer who files an individual income tax return for a taxable year, and who is not claimed or eligible to be claimed as a dependent by another taxpayer for federal or state income tax purposes, may claim a credit for each dependent that the taxpayer is entitled to claim for the taxable year. For purposes of the credit, "dependent" means the taxpayer, the spouse of the taxpayer, and a natural or legally adopted child of the taxpayer.

A resident who has no income, or no taxable income, and who is not considered a dependent for purposes of the credit, may claim the tax credit. However, a husband and wife filing jointly are each deemed a dependent for purposes of the joint return, and spouses filing separately for a taxable year

¶ 117

when a joint return could have been filed must claim only the credit amount that they would have been entitled to if they filed a joint return been filed.

● *Credit amount*

The credit amount depends on the taxpayer's adjusted gross income and is determined as follows:

Adjusted Gross Income	Tax Credit
Under $6,000	$26
$6,000 but not more than $7,999	20
$8,000 but not more than $9,999	14
$10,000 but not more than $14,999	8
$15,000 but not more than $19,999	5

CCH Tip: Seniors Receive Double Credit

Taxpayers who are age 65 or older may receive double the amount of the tax credit shown above.

● *Limitations*

Individuals receiving food stamp allotments for all or any part of the taxable year are not entitled to claim the credit.

An individual incarcerated or confined in any city, county, municipal, state, or federal penal or correctional institution for any part of a taxable year is not eligible to claim the credit.

● *Refund of excess credit*

If the tax credit exceeds the amount of income tax due from a taxpayer, the excess amount will be refunded. A tax credit properly claimed by a resident individual who has no income tax liability will be paid to that individual. However, no refunds or payment on account of the tax credit will be made for amounts less than $1.

● *Filing requirements*

All claims for the credit, including amended claims, must be filed by the end of the 12th month following the close of the taxable year for which the credit is claimed. Failure to do so constitutes a waiver of the right to claim the credit.

¶ 118   Rural Physicians Credit

Law: Sec. 48-7-29, Code; Reg. Sec. 560-7-8-.20 (CCH GEORGIA TAX REPORTS ¶ 16-195).

A physician who (1) practices in a rural county and resides in a rural county or, beginning in 2003, resides in a county contiguous to a rural county, (2) primarily admits patients to a rural hospital, and (3) practices in a family

Part II—Personal Income Tax

practice, obstetrics and gynecology, pediatrics, internal medicine, or general surgery may receive a credit against personal income tax.

A rural county is a county with no more than 65 people per square mile. A rural hospital is an acute care hospital located in a rural county and containing fewer than 100 beds (80 beds, prior to 2003).

Credit amount: The credit amount is up to $5,000, and the credit may be claimed for no more than five years. No carryforward or carryback of unused amounts is permitted.

Limitations and carryforwards: Physicians practicing in rural counties as of July 1, 1995, are not eligible for the credit. Furthermore, physicians who had previously practiced in a rural county are not eligible for the credit unless they return after July 1, 1995, to a rural county practice after having practiced in a nonrural county for at least three years.

Unused credit may not be carried forward to apply to a taxpayer's tax liability for succeeding years. Furthermore, no credit is allowed against a taxpayer's tax liability for prior years.

¶ 119 Credit for Taxes Paid on Returned Income Amounts

Law: Sec. 48-7-28.1, Code (CCH GEORGIA TAX REPORTS ¶ 16-115).

Comparable Federal: Sec. 1341 (U.S. MASTER TAX GUIDE ¶ 1543).

Taxpayers may receive a refundable tax credit against personal income tax if they have paid taxes on a prior year's income and, in a subsequent tax year, repay a portion of that income to the payor. The credit is applicable only in the year of the repayment and only if a similar tax benefit is allowed under IRC Sec. 1341.

Credit amount: The credit amount equals the tax on the current year's income as reduced by the repayment amount, or the reduced tax on the prior year's income as recalculated excluding the repaid income.

Limitations: The credit will be allowed only if Georgia income tax was actually paid in the prior year. If the taxpayer was not subject to Georgia income tax, the credit is not allowed.

¶ 120 Credit for Taxes Paid to Another State

Law: Sec. 48-7-28, Code (CCH GEORGIA TAX REPORTS ¶ 16-110).

Qualifications for credit and amount: A resident individual who has an established business in another state, has investment in property having a taxable situs in another state, or engages in employment in another state may deduct from the tax due upon the entire net income the tax paid upon the net income of the business, investment, or employment in the other state.

Limitations: The credit is available only if the business, investment, or employment is in a state that levies a tax upon net income. The credit may not exceed the tax that would be payable to Georgia upon a like amount of taxable income.

¶ 121 Credit for Taxes Withheld and Estimated Tax

Law: Sec. 48-7-20(c), Code (CCH GEORGIA TAX REPORTS ¶ 16-130).

Comparable Federal: Secs. 31, 6315 (U.S. MASTER TAX GUIDE ¶ 105, 1372).

An employee is allowed as a credit against personal income tax the amount deducted and withheld by the employer from the employee's wages. Amounts paid by an individual as estimated tax constitute payments on account of the tax. The amount withheld or paid during any calendar year may be taken as a credit or payment for the taxable year beginning in the calendar year when the amount is withheld or paid.

¶ 122 Credit for Disaster Assistance Recipients

Law: Sec. 48-7-29.4, Code (CCH GEORGIA TAX REPORTS ¶ 16-147).

A taxpayer who receives disaster assistance during the tax year from the Georgia Emergency Management Agency or the Federal Emergency Management Agency may receive a credit against Georgia personal income tax.

Credit amount: The credit equals $500 or the actual amount of the disaster assistance, whichever is less. The credit may not exceed the taxpayer's income tax liability for a given tax year.

Limitations and carryforwards: To claim the credit, the approval letter from the federal or state agency granting assistance must be submitted with the return.

Any unused credit may be carried forward to future tax years but may not be used against liability from prior years.

¶ 123 Driver's Education Expenses Credit

Law: Sec. 48-7-29.5, Code (CCH GEORGIA TAX REPORTS ¶ 16-146).

Taxpayers may claim a credit for the amount spent to provide their minor dependent children with a driver's education course at a licensed private driver's training school.

Credit amount: The credit amount for each dependent child equals the actual amount spent for the course or $150, whichever is less.

Filing requirements: To receive the credit, a taxpayer must submit a claim and written proof of the successful completion of the course by the child and the amount spent on the course.

Limitations: The credit may be taken only once for each child. The credit is not allowed with respect to driver's education expenses that have been deducted or subtracted in arriving at net taxable income or with respect to any driver's education expenses for which amounts were excluded from net taxable income. This credit may not exceed the taxpayer's income tax liability.

Part II—Personal Income Tax

¶124 Low-Income Housing Credit

Law: Sec. 48-7-29.6, Code (CCH GEORGIA TAX REPORTS ¶16-131).

Comparable Federal: Sec. 42 (U.S. MASTER TAX GUIDE ¶1334).

Taxpayers may claim a credit for each Georgia housing project that qualifies as a low-income building under IRC Sec. 42 and that is placed in service after January 1, 2001.

Credit amount: The credit amount is equal to the federal low-income housing tax credit allowed with respect to the qualified project.

Limitations and carryforwards: Credits claimed by a taxpayer may not exceed the taxpayer's income tax liability, but unused portions of the credit may be carried forward for a period of three years. Unused credits may not be carried back.

Allocation of credit: The credit may be allocated among some or all of the partners, members, or shareholders of the entity owning the project, regardless of whether such persons are allocated or allowed any portion of the federal housing tax credit with respect to the project.

Recapture of credit: If any portion of the federal housing tax credit is recaptured, the state tax credit must be recaptured proportionally.

¶125 Business Expansion Credit

Law: Sec. 48-7-40.21, Code (CCH GEORGIA TAX REPORTS ¶16-175).

A credit against monthly or quarterly personal income withholding taxes that must be remitted by an employer is available for an expansion of an existing business, not including a retail business, that creates 500 new jobs and has a beneficial effect on the region for which it is planned. For details, see ¶913.

Each employee whose employer receives this credit will also receive a credit against his or her Georgia personal income tax liability for the corresponding tax year for the full amount of the credit that the employer received for the employer's withholding taxes.

¶126 Credit for Employer-Provided Transportation

Law: Sec. 48-7-40.22, Code (CCH GEORGIA TAX REPORTS ¶16-144).

A personal income tax credit is available to any business located in a tier 1 or tier 2 county that purchases or leases a new motor vehicle that is used exclusively for providing transportation for its employees.

Credit amount: A business located in a tier 1 county receives a $3,000 credit for each vehicle purchased or leased, and a business located in a tier 2 county receives a $2,000 credit for each qualified vehicle.

Planning considerations: The business must certify that each vehicle for which a credit is claimed has an average daily ridership of at least four employees. This credit may not exceed the business' income tax liability and may be carried forward for one year.

¶126

¶ 127 Credit for Rehabilitation of Historic Property

Law: Sec. 48-7-29.8, Code (CCH GEORGIA TAX REPORTS ¶ 16-148).

For taxable years beginning after 2003, a credit is available for taxpayers that substantially rehabilitate historic property.

A substantial rehabilitation is a rehabilitation of a certified structure for which the qualified rehabilitation expenditures exceed (1) for a historic home, the lesser of $25,000 or 50% of the adjusted basis of the property, or, in the case of a historic home located in a target area, $5,000, or (2) for any other certified structure, the greater of $5,000 or the adjusted basis of the property. At least 5% of the rehabilitation expenditures must be allocable to the exterior during a 24-month period (a 60-month period may be substituted under certain circumstances) selected by the taxpayer ending with or within the taxable year.

Credit amount: For a historic home, the credit is equal to 10% of the qualified rehabilitation expenditures, and if the home is located within a target area, an additional 5% of qualified expenditures. For any other certified historic structure, the credit is equal to 20% of the qualified rehabilitation expenditures. The credit may not exceed $5,000 in any 120-month period.

Planning considerations: To be eligible to receive the credit, the taxpayer must attach to the taxpayer's state tax return a copy of the Department of Natural Resources certification verifying that the improvements to the certified structure are consistent with the Department standards for rehabilitation.

The credit may be carried forward for 10 years, and may not be carried back. Furthermore, the credit may be transferred to subsequent purchasers of the property. However, if the property owner, other than a nonprofit corporation, sells the property within three years of receiving the credit, then the seller must recapture the credit and remit the applicable amount to the Department of Revenue.

The credit may be allocated among partners, members, or shareholders of flow-through entities.

¶ 128 Credit for Accessible Residence

Law: Sec. 48-7-29.1, Code; Reg. Sec. 560-7-8-.44 (CCH GEORGIA TAX REPORTS ¶ 16-124).

Disabled persons who purchase a new single family home with features accessible to disabled persons or who retrofit an existing home with accessible features are entitled to a credit for a portion of the cost. To be considered new, the home must be brand new, and not just new to the owner, and contain all of the following accessibility features:

—one no-step entrance allowing access into the residence;

—an interior passage door providing at least a 32-inch wide clear opening;

—reinforcements in bathroom walls allowing later installation of grab bars around the toilet, tub, and shower; and

—light switches and outlets placed in accessible locations.

Part II—Personal Income Tax

In the case of retrofitting an existing home, the entire home does not have to be retrofitted with the particular accessibility feature. Part of the home could be retrofitted with one feature and the next year the other part of the home could be retrofitted with the same feature. In this case, a credit would be allowed for each year.

A taxpayer who rents his or her home is entitled to the credit if he or she pays for an accessibility feature.

To be eligible for the credit, a taxpayer must be a permanently disabled person who has been issued either a permanent parking permit or a special permanent parking permit by the Department of Public Safety. The taxpayer's spouse is eligible for credit if a joint return is filed. The taxpayer's dependent does not qualify for the credit.

Credit amount: The credit is $500 credit for the purchase of a new single family home with accessibility features or $125 for each accessibility feature installed in an existing home up to a maximum of $500. The credit may not exceed the tax liability of the taxpayer. If the taxpayer lives in more than one home, then the credit is allowed for each home in which the taxpayer resides.

Planning considerations: The credit may be carried forward for three years but may not be carried back.

¶ 129 Job Tax Credits

Law: Secs. 36-62-5.1, 48-7-40—48-7-40.4, 48-7-40.21, 48-7-40.22, Code; Reg. Sec. 560-7-8-.36 (CCH GEORGIA TAX REPORTS ¶ 12-070, 12-070a, 16-182).

Certain businesses that increase their number of employees may receive job tax credits against personal or corporate income tax. Minimum qualifying increases depend on the county and year in which the jobs are created. The counties are ranked into tiers on the bases of their unemployment rate, per capita income level, percentage of residents below poverty level, and average weekly manufacturing wage, with the least developed counties designated as tier 1 counties and the most developed counties designated as tier 3 or 4 counties.

For details, see ¶ 913.

PERSONAL INCOME TAX

CHAPTER 2

COMPUTATION OF TAX

¶ 201 Taxable Net Income
¶ 202 Prior Year Income, Deductions, and Losses
¶ 203 Sale or Exchange of Property
¶ 204 Depreciation of Property
¶ 205 S Corporations
¶ 206 Teachers Retirement System Contributions
¶ 207 Higher Education Savings Withdrawals
¶ 208 Net Operating Loss

¶ 201 Taxable Net Income

Law: Sec. 48-7-27(a) and (e), Code (CCH GEORGIA TAX REPORTS ¶ 15-320).

Comparable Federal: Sec. 61 (U.S. MASTER TAX GUIDE ¶ 1005—1010).

Form: Form 500 (Individual Income Tax Return).

Georgia taxable net income is computed by using the taxpayer's federal adjusted gross income as a starting point.

● *Subtractions from federal adjusted gross income*

Individual taxpayers may subtract from the federal base:

—personal and dependent exemptions,

—itemized nonbusiness deductions used in computing federal taxable income or a standard deduction,

—income from federal obligations,

—certain retirement income,

—qualified payments to minority subcontractors,

—certain employer expenses,

—certain mortgage interest,

—self-employment health care costs,

—contributions to higher education trust accounts, and

—organ donation expenses.

For discussion of these deductions, see Chapter 3.

¶ 201

● *Additions to federal adjusted gross income*

Taxpayers must add to the federal base:

—any income from obligations of governments outside Georgia, to the extent that the income was excluded for federal tax purposes but taxed by Georgia,

—all non-Georgia income taxes deducted for federal purposes,

—any depreciation deductions attributable to qualified child care property, to the extent that these deductions are used in determining federal taxable income, and

—income from lump sum distributions.

For detailed discussion of these additions, see Chapter 4.

CCH Tip: Impact of 2004 Federal Legislation

Because Georgia does not incorporate the Internal Revenue Code as amended to date, Georgia does not yet incorporate the federal amendments enacted by the Working Families Tax Relief Act (WFTRA) of 2004 (P.L. No. 108-311), or the American Jobs Creation Act (AJCA) of 2004.

Working Families Tax Relief Act (WFTRA) of 2004: In addition to extending the federal research credit (IRC Sec. 41) and numerous other federal credits through 2005, WFTRA extends the availability of the following deductions through the 2005 tax year. However, absent legislative action, Georgia does not allow these extended deductions and, therefore, addition modifications will be required on Georgia's returns for taxpayers that claim these deductions on their 2004 federal tax returns:

—the $250 above-the-line deduction for teachers' expenses (IRC Sec. 62(a)(2)(d));

—the enhanced charitable deduction for computer technology donated to schools and public libraries (IRC Sec. 170(e)(6)(g));

—the election to deduct environmental research expenses (IRC Sec. 198(h));

—the increased depreciation deduction resulting from the shortened MACRS recovery periods for Indian reservation property (IRC Sec. 168(j)(8)); and

—the increased depletion deduction resulting from the suspension of the taxable income limit on the percentage depletion allowance for oil and gas produced from marginal wells (IRC Sec. 613(A)(c)(6)(H)).

The WFTRA also eliminates the phase-out limitation for qualified clean-fuel vehicles placed in service in 2004 and 2005. As a result of this change, a taxpayer who purchases a qualified vehicle in 2004 and 2005 may claim 100 percent of the otherwise allowable deduction on their federal, but not their Georgia return (IRC Sec. 179A).

¶ 201

Part II—Personal Income Tax

Taxpayers claiming this deduction on their Georgia return must reduce the deduction by 25% during the 2004 tax year.

In addition, the WFTRA modifies the definition of a "qualifying child" for purposes of the qualifying criterial head of household filing status, personal exemptions, and various credits. Taxpayers should consult the Instructions to the Georgia's individual income tax return to see what, if any, impact this has on taxpayer's filing a Georgia return.

Finally, under the WFTRA a state that is approved by the Secretary of the Treasury may participate in a combined federal and state employment tax reporting program through December 31, 2005 (IRC Sec. 6103(d)(5)).

American Jobs Creation Act (AJCA) of 2004: The American Jobs Creation Act of 2004 makes extensive changes to the IRC—adding and amending over 300 IRC code provisions. The biggest changes that may affect the preparation of a taxpayer's Georgia 2004 tax returns are:

—Allowing individual taxpayers to elect to claim an itemized deduction for sales taxes rather than income taxes;

—Indexing the IRC Sec. 179 asset expense election allowing taxpayers to deduct up to $102,000 for property valued up to $410,000 during the 2004 tax year;

—Allowing a 15-year recover period for depreciation purposes for qualified leasehold improvements and restaurant property and extending the first year bonus depreciation deduction to restaurant property;

—Limiting the depreciation deduction for SUV vehicles;

—Tightening the eligibility rules for charitable contribution deductions for donations of vehicles and intellectual property.

CCH Tip: Capital Gains Election

With respect to capital gains, a taxpayer may elect to adjust Georgia taxable net income in an amount equal to any full or partial deduction from federal adjusted gross income for federal income tax purposes.

¶ 202   Prior Year Income, Deductions, and Losses

Law: Sec. 48-7-27(b)(4) and (5), Code (CCH Georgia Tax Reports ¶ 15-330).

No portion of any deductions or losses, including net operating losses, that occurred in a year when the taxpayer was not subject to Georgia personal income tax may be deducted in any tax year. If federal adjusted gross income includes deductions or losses that are not allowed because of this provision, the taxpayer must make an adjustment deleting them.

¶ 202

Income, losses, and deductions previously used in computing Georgia taxable income must not be used again in computing Georgia taxable income.

¶ 203 Sale or Exchange of Property

Law: Sec. 48-7-27(b)(6), Code (CCH GEORGIA TAX REPORTS ¶ 15-330).

Comparable Federal: Sec. 121, Sec. 1031 (U.S. MASTER TAX GUIDE ¶ 1719—1734).

If gain or loss on the sale or exchange of property is not recognized for federal income tax purposes because the taxpayer purchases similar property, the nonrecognition treatment generally is allowed for Georgia income tax purposes only if the replacement property is located in Georgia. However, in the case of the sale of a personal residence located in Georgia, if no gain or loss is recognized because a taxpayer receives or purchases similar property, the nonrecognition will apply if the taxpayer purchases another personal residence anywhere in the United States within the time period allowed by the Internal Revenue Code of 1986.

Practitioner Comment: Replacement Property

The requirement that replacement property be Georgia property in order for nonrecognition to apply is of questionable constitutionality.

Michael T. Petrik, Esq., Alston & Bird LLP

¶ 204 Depreciation of Property

Law: Sec. 48-7-39, Code (CCH GEORGIA TAX REPORTS ¶ 15-335).

Comparable Federal: Sec. 167 (U.S. MASTER TAX GUIDE ¶ 1201—1284).

Georgia adopts the federal treatment of depreciation with the exception of bonus depreciation under the Job Creation and Worker Assistance Act of 2002 (26 U.S.C. § 167; 26 U.S.C. § 168) and the Jobs and Growth Tax Relief Reconciliation Act of 2003 (JGTRRA) (P.L. 108-27). Generally, federal law allows a deduction for depreciation of property used in a trade or business. The current system, Modified Accelerated Cost Recovery System (MACRS), uses statutory recovery periods and conventions, and either straight-line, 200%-declining, or 150%-declining methods. For most assets, there is no adjustment required for depreciation. However, depreciation on child care facilities must be added back under certain circumstances (¶ 404).

Bonus depreciation: Georgia disallows the 30% and 50% bonus depreciation allowed under IRC Sec. 168(k).

IRC Sec. 179 expensing: Georgia has not adopted the increased limits applicable to the expensing of assets under IRC Sec. 179 that were enacted by the federal Jobs and Growth Tax Relief Reconciliation Act (JGTRRA) (P.L. 108- 27).

¶ 203

Part II—Personal Income Tax

● *Pre-1987 property*

For certain property placed in service in taxable years ending before March 11, 1987, a taxpayer could elect to (1) continue to depreciate or otherwise recover the cost of the property according to the same method used for Georgia income tax purposes for the taxable year the property was placed in service and make such adjustments to federal taxable income as required to reflect the effect of this election, or (2) depreciate or otherwise recover the cost of the property according to the method used for federal income tax purposes for the taxable year the property was placed in service.

The election had to be made for a taxpayer's first taxable year ending on or after January 1, 1987. This election applies to all subsequent taxable years, to the determination of deductions for depreciation or cost recovery of affected property, and to the determination of gain or loss on the sale or other disposition of the property.

¶ 205   S Corporations

Law: Sec. 48-7-27(d)(1) and (2), Code (CCH GEORGIA TAX REPORTS ¶ 15-350).

Comparable Federal: Secs. 1361, 1362.

Georgia resident shareholders of S corporations may make an adjustment to federal adjusted gross income for S corporation income where another state does not recognize an S corporation.

Practitioner Comment: No Comparable Adjustment

Georgia law does not provide for a comparable adjustment for LLC income attributable to states that subject LLCs to entity-level income tax.

Michael T. Petrik, Esq., Alston & Bird LLP

Nonresident shareholders of a Georgia S corporation must execute a consent agreement to pay Georgia income tax on their portion of the corporate income in order for the S corporation to be recognized for Georgia purposes. This consent agreement must be filed by the corporation with its corporate tax return.

Practitioner Comment: Consent Agreements

The failure of a single shareholder to execute the consent agreement will result in subchapter C status. This can be an opportunity as well as a pitfall.

Michael T. Petrik, Esq., Alston & Bird

Shareholders of a federal S corporation that is not recognized for Georgia purposes may make an adjustment to federal adjusted gross income in order to avoid double taxation on this type of income. Adjustments will not be allowed unless tax was actually paid by the corporation.

¶ 205

Practitioner Comment: Undistributed Pass-Through Income
The purpose of this provision is to allow shareholders of federal S corporations that are treated as C corporations for Georgia tax purposes to exclude the undistributed pass-through income that is otherwise included in federal AGI from Georgia tax, since such income has been subject to Georgia tax at the corporate level. It is the position of the Department of Revenue that this exclusion is limited to the amount of undistributed pass-through income that has actually been subject to Georgia tax.

Michael T. Petrik, Esq., Alston & Bird LLP

¶ 206 Teachers Retirement System Contributions

Law: Sec. 48-7-27(a)(9), Code (CCH GEORGIA TAX REPORTS ¶ 15-465).

Comparable Federal: Sec. 403.

Contributions to the Teachers Retirement System of Georgia, made between July 1, 1987, and December 31, 1989, that were not subject to federal income tax but were subject to state tax are excluded when computing Georgia taxable net income. The purpose of the exclusion is to allow a recovery adjustment for the amount of contributions made after the retirement system begins distributions, and to establish the same basis for federal and state income tax purposes.

¶ 207 Higher Education Savings Withdrawals

Law: Secs. 20-3-630 *et seq.*, 48-7-27(b)(10), Code (CCH GEORGIA TAX REPORTS ¶ 15-490).

Comparable Federal: Sec. 529.

Qualified withdrawals from the Georgia Higher Education Savings Plan used solely for qualified higher education expenses are not subject to Georgia income tax. A "qualified withdrawal" is a withdrawal by an account contributor or beneficiary for qualified higher education expenses, or as otherwise permitted under IRC Sec. 529 without a penalty. Nonqualified withdrawals must be included in the taxable income of the account owner.

The deduction for contributions to higher education savings trust accounts is discussed at ¶ 310.

¶ 208 Net Operating Loss

Law: Reg. Sec. 560-7-4-.01 (CCH GEORGIA TAX REPORTS ¶ 15-330).

Comparable Federal: Sec. 172 (U.S. MASTER TAX GUIDE ¶ 1173—1188).

The number of years an individual net operating loss may be carried back or forward is the same as provided in I.R.C. Sec. 172, except that Georgia did not adopt the provisions of the federal Job Creation and Worker Assistance Act (JCWAA) (P.L. 107-147), which extended the carryback period for net operating losses to five years for 2001 and 2002.

Part II—Personal Income Tax 65

● *Waiver of carryback*

Under I.R.C. Sec. 172(b)(3), the deadline for waiver of the carryback period is the due date (including extensions) for filing the taxpayer's tax return for the taxable year of the net operating loss. A taxpayer who makes a timely federal election to waive the carryback is bound by that election for Georgia income tax purposes and would have to waive the carryback period.

If there is a Georgia net operating loss and no federal net operating loss, the taxpayer may make an election by the due date (including extensions) of the Georgia return to waive the carryback period. An affirmative statement must be attached to the return indicating that the election was made (*Policy Statement IT-2000-07-15-1,* Georgia Department of Revenue, Income Tax Division, July 15, 2000; CCH GEORGIA TAX REPORTS ¶ 200-407).

● *Refund of net operating loss*

A claim for a refund of a net operating loss must be filed by no later than 40 months and 15 days following the close of the taxable year in which the loss was incurred. If the taxpayer fails to file a claim for a refund by that time, the taxpayer is statutorily barred from receiving a refund for those carryback years. However, if the loss is not fully absorbed in the carryback years, amended returns can be filed to determine the amount of the loss that is available to be carried forward to years that are not barred by the statute. (*Policy Statement IT-2000-07-15-1,* Georgia Department of Revenue, Income Tax Division, July 15, 2000; CCH GEORGIA TAX REPORTS ¶ 200-407)

CCH Example: Refund of NOL

In November 2003, Tom Taxpayer realizes that he has a Georgia net operating loss for 1998 that he did not carry back and did not elect to waive the carryback period when he filed his 1998 return. Accordingly, the loss would have to be carried back to 1995, 1996, and 1997 and then carried forward to 1999. Since a claim for refund would have to have been filed by April 15, 2002, no refunds would be issued for 1995, 1996, and 1997. Additionally, since the statutory period has also expired for 1999, Tom cannot claim a refund for 1999. However, any excess loss that was not applied to 1995, 1996, 1997, and 1999 would be available to be carried forward to 2000.

¶ 208

Part II—Personal Income Tax 67

PERSONAL INCOME TAX

CHAPTER 3

SUBTRACTIONS FROM FEDERAL ADJUSTED GROSS INCOME

¶ 301	Personal and Dependent Exemptions
¶ 302	Itemized Nonbusiness Deductions or Standard Deduction
¶ 303	Income from Federal Obligations
¶ 304	Retirement Income
¶ 305	Payments to Minority Subcontractors
¶ 306	Salary and Wage Expenses Eliminated for Federal Jobs Credit Purposes
¶ 307	Employer Social Security Deduction
¶ 308	Mortgage Interest
¶ 309	Self Employed Individuals' Health Insurance Costs
¶ 310	Contributions to Higher Education Savings
¶ 311	Organ Donation Expenses

¶ 301 Personal and Dependent Exemptions

Law: Secs. 48-7-26(a), (b), and (d), 48-7-27(a), Code (CCH GEORGIA TAX REPORTS ¶ 15-410, 15-420).

Comparable Federal: Secs. 151, 213 (U.S. MASTER TAX GUIDE ¶ 133—149, 860, 1020).

An individual's federal adjusted gross income is reduced by the amount of personal exemptions allowable in computing Georgia taxable net income. An exemption of $2,700 is allowed for the taxpayer and a $5,400 exemption is allowed for the taxpayer and spouse if a joint return is filed.

● *Dependent exemption*

An individual's federal adjusted gross income is reduced by the amount of dependent exemptions allowable in computing Georgia taxable net income.

For tax years beginning on or after January 1, 2003, the dependent exemption is $3,000.

The amount of a dependent's unearned income that is included in the federal adjusted gross income of a parent's return must be subtracted from federal adjusted gross income.

¶ 301

● *Estates and trusts*

An estate is allowed a deduction of $2,700 in lieu of a personal exemption deduction. A trust is allowed a deduction of $1,350 in lieu of a personal exemption deduction.

¶ 302 Itemized Nonbusiness Deductions or Standard Deduction

Law: Sec. 48-7-27(a), Code (CCH GEORGIA TAX REPORTS ¶ 15-440).

Comparable Federal: Sec. 63 (U.S. MASTER TAX GUIDE ¶ 126).

An individual's federal adjusted gross income may be reduced by either the itemized nonbusiness deductions used in computing federal taxable income or a standard deduction.

Practitioner Comment: Itemized Non-business Deductions

The Georgia Department of Revenue interprets "itemized non-business deductions in computing federal taxable income" to mean the amount after the reduction under IRC Sec. 68 is taken into account.

Michael T. Petrik, Esq., Alston & Bird LLP

The standard deduction amounts are: $2,300 for a single taxpayer or a head of household; $1,500 for a married taxpayer filing a separate return; and $3,000 for a married couple filing a joint return.

● *Age deduction*

A taxpayer who has attained the age of 65 before the close of the taxable year is allowed an additional $1,300 deduction. An additional $1,300 deduction for a taxpayer's spouse is allowed if a joint return is filed and if the spouse has attained the age of 65 before the close of the taxable year.

● *Blindness deduction*

A taxpayer who is blind at the close of the taxable year is allowed an additional $1,300 deduction. An additional deduction of $1,300 is allowed for a taxpayer's spouse if a joint return is filed and if the spouse is blind at the close of the taxable year. If either the taxpayer or the spouse dies during the taxable year, qualification for the blindness deduction is determined at the time of death.

¶ 303 Income from Federal Obligations

Law: Sec. 48-7-27(b)(2), Code (CCH GEORGIA TAX REPORTS ¶ 15-450).

Comparable Federal: Sec. 3124(a) (U.S. MASTER TAX GUIDE ¶ 731).

Interest and dividends on obligations of the United States and its territories and possessions or of any authority, commission, or U.S. instrumentality are subtracted from taxable income to the extent they are includable in gross

¶ 302

Part II—Personal Income Tax 69

income for federal income tax purposes but exempt from state income taxes under federal law. In subtracting exempt interest or dividends that were includable in federal gross income, the amount to be subtracted is first reduced by any expenses directly attributable to the production of the interest or dividends.

¶ 304 Retirement Income

Law: Secs. 48-2-100, 48-2-110, 48-7-27(a), Code; Reg. Sec. 560-7-4.02 (CCH GEORGIA TAX REPORTS ¶ 15-460).

Comparable Federal: Sec. 401 (U.S. MASTER TAX GUIDE ¶ 2101—2199).

Eligible taxpayers may exclude a specified amount of income received from public pension and retirement funds, programs, or systems if the income is included in the taxpayer's federal adjusted gross income.

● *Eligibility*

To qualify for the exclusion, a taxpayer must be at least 62 years old during any part of the taxable year, or must be permanently and totally disabled and incapable of gainful employment.

● *Taxpayers who are not retired*

A taxpayer is considered retired if he or she does not have earned income of more than $1,200 during the taxable year. A taxpayer who is not retired during the tax year may apply the exclusion only to retirement income, *i.e.*, income based on years of service, age, or contributions to qualified pension plans.

● *Maximum retirement income exclusion*

A taxpayer's retirement income exclusion may not exceed $15,000 for taxable years after 2002 and before 2006. These limits are doubled for an eligible married couple filing jointly.

The amount of retirement income excluded from Georgia personal income tax will be increased to $25,000 for the 2006 tax year, to $30,000 for the 2007 tax year, and to $35,000 for tax years beginning after 2007.

● *Sources of income*

Retirement income consists of both earned and unearned income. Of that amount, the earned income portion is limited to $4,000.

Unearned retirement income includes income from interest, dividends, rental property, capital gains, royalties, pensions, and annuities.

For both the earned and unearned income portions of the exclusion, losses must be offset against income. If, after each portion is separately computed, either portion is less than zero, then the portion that is less than zero cannot be offset against the other portion.

¶ 304

● *Computation*

Part-year residents and nonresidents must prorate the retirement exclusion using the ratio of the Georgia source income before the retirement income exclusion to the Georgia adjusted gross income before the retirement income exclusion, computed as if the taxpayer were a resident of Georgia for the entire year.

The exclusion is in addition to other adjustments to Georgia taxable income. Therefore, the other income and loss adjustments to Georgia taxable income must be computed first to arrive at Georgia taxable income before computing the retirement income exclusion.

● *Social Security and railroad retirement benefits*

Social Security benefits and tier 1 railroad retirement benefits may be subtracted from federal taxable income, to the extent they are included.

¶ 305   Payments to Minority Subcontractors

Law: Secs. 48-7-27(a)(6), 48-7-38(a), (b), and (c), Code (CCH GEORGIA TAX REPORTS ¶ 15-470).

For Georgia personal income tax purposes, a taxpayer's federal adjusted gross income may be reduced by 10% of the qualified payments made to minority subcontractors during the taxable year. The maximum reduction is $100,000 per year.

The payments must be made to a subcontractor who is certified as a minority contractor. Furthermore, the payments must be made in return for goods, personal property, or services that are furnished by the minority subcontractor to the taxpayer and delivered by the taxpayer to the state pursuant to a state contract.

A minority is an individual who is a member of one of the following groups: African-American, Hispanic, Asian-Pacific American, Native American, or Asian-Indian American.

¶ 306   Salary and Wage Expenses Eliminated for Federal Jobs Credit Purposes

Law: Sec. 48-7-27(a)(3)(A), Code; Reg. Sec. 560-7-7-.05 (CCH GEORGIA TAX REPORTS ¶ 15-475).

Comparable Federal: Secs. 38, 51.

An individual's federal adjusted gross income may be reduced by the amount of salary and wage expenses eliminated in computing the individual's federal adjusted gross income if the individual claimed a federal jobs tax credit requiring the elimination of related salary and wage expenses.

Part II—Personal Income Tax 71

¶ 307 Employer Social Security Deduction

Law: Sec. 48-7-28.2, Code (CCH GEORGIA TAX REPORTS ¶ 15-476).

Comparable Federal: Sec. 45B(a).

Employers claiming the federal employer social security credit for portions of employer social security taxes paid with respect to employee cash tips under IRC Sec. 45B(a) are allowed a deduction in an amount equal to their federal employer social security credit.

¶ 308 Mortgage Interest

Law: Sec. 48-7-27(a)(3)(B), Code (CCH GEORGIA TAX REPORTS ¶ 15-480).

Comparable Federal: Secs. 25, 163 (U.S. MASTER TAX GUIDE ¶ 1308).

An individual's federal adjusted gross income may be reduced by the amount of mortgage interest eliminated from federal itemized deductions for the purpose of computing the mortgage interest credit on the federal return.

¶ 309 Self Employed Individuals' Health Insurance Costs

Law: Sec. 48-7-27(a)(10), Code (CCH GEORGIA TAX REPORTS ¶ 15-485).

Comparable Federal: Sec. 162(*l*) (U.S. MASTER TAX GUIDE ¶ 908).

An individual taxpayer who is self employed and treated as an employee under IRC Sec. 401(c)(1) may deduct from federal adjusted gross income the amount paid during the taxable year for health insurance for the individual and the individual's spouse and dependents if the amount is not deductible for federal income tax purposes because the applicable percentage under IRC Sec. 162(*l*) is less than 100%.

¶ 310 Contributions to Higher Education Savings

Law: Secs. 20-3-630 *et seq.*, 48-7-27(a)(11), Code (CCH GEORGIA TAX REPORTS ¶ 15-490).

Comparable Federal: Sec. 529.

For tax years beginning after 2001, amounts contributed by parents or guardians to a Georgia Higher Education Savings Plan for their dependents may be deducted from federal adjusted gross income for purposes of computing Georgia personal income tax. Contributions can be made until the total balance for all accounts for a beneficiary reaches $235,000. The parents or guardians must be the account owners of the designated beneficiary's account.

The maximum annual deduction is $2,000 per beneficiary. If the parents or guardians are married and file separately, the sum of these educational deductions on their returns cannot exceed $2,000. To claim the full deduction, the parents or guardians must (a) itemize deductions on their federal return, and (b) have federal adjusted gross income of less than $100,000 per year for joint filers and $50,000 per year for single filers. The maximum deduction is decreased by $400 for each $1,000 of income over $100,000 for a joint return or $50,000 for a separate or single return.

The exclusion for qualified withdrawals from a Higher Education Savings Plan is discussed at ¶ 207.

¶ 310

¶ 311 Organ Donation Expenses

Law: Sec. 48-7-27(13), Code (CCH Georgia Tax Reports ¶ 15-491).

Effective January 1, 2005, and applicable to all taxable years beginning on or after that date, organ donation expenses incurred in accordance with the federal National Organ Procurement Act (P.L. 98-507) may be subtracted from a taxpayer's federal adjusted gross income in figuring Georgia net taxable income for Georgia personal income tax purposes.

The subtraction may be taken in the taxable year in which the donation is made. It may include only unreimbursed travel expenses, lodging expenses, and lost wages incurred as a direct result of the organ donation. The amount of the subtraction is limited to $10,000.

PERSONAL INCOME TAX

CHAPTER 4

ADDITIONS TO TAXABLE INCOME

¶ 401	Income from State or Local Obligations
¶ 402	Lump Sum Distributions
¶ 403	Income Taxes Deducted on Federal Return
¶ 404	Depreciation Deductions on Child Care Property

¶ 401 Income from State or Local Obligations

Law: Sec. 48-7-27(b)(1)(A), Code (CCH Georgia Tax Reports ¶ 15-510).

Dividend and interest income on obligations of any state or political subdivision, except Georgia and its political subdivisions, must be added to Georgia taxable income to the extent the dividend or interest income is not included in the gross income for federal income tax purposes.

¶ 402 Lump Sum Distributions

Law: Sec. 48-7-27(b)(1)(C), Code (CCH Georgia Tax Reports ¶ 15-515).

Comparable Federal: Sec. 402(d) (U.S. Master Tax Guide ¶ 2153).

Income consisting of lump sum distributions from an annuity, pension plan, or similar source must be added to Georgia taxable income if it is removed from federal adjusted gross income for the purpose of special federal tax computations or treatment.

¶ 403 Income Taxes Deducted on Federal Return

Law: Sec. 48-7-27(b)(3), Code (CCH Georgia Tax Reports ¶ 15-520).

Comparable Federal: Sec. 164(a) (U.S. Master Tax Guide ¶ 1021).

Any income taxes imposed by any taxing jurisdiction except the state of Georgia must be added to Georgia taxable income to the extent that such taxes were deducted in determining federal taxable income.

> *Practitioner Comment: Acceleration of Deductions*
>
> A self-employed individual should consider making the fourth quarterly payment of Georgia estimated taxes in December rather than January in order to accelerate the taxpayer's federal and Georgia deductions.
>
> *Michael T. Petrik, Esq., Alston & Bird LLP*

¶ 404 Depreciation Deductions on Child Care Property

Law: Sec. 48-7-27(b), Code (CCH GEORGIA TAX REPORTS ¶ 15-525, 16-190).

Employers who claim the tax credit available with respect to qualified child care property first placed into service on or after July 1, 1999, must add to their taxable income the amount of any depreciation deductions attributable to such property, to the extent that these deductions are used in determining federal taxable income.

Part II—Personal Income Tax

PERSONAL INCOME TAX

CHAPTER 5

ALLOCATION AND APPORTIONMENT OF NONRESIDENT INCOME

¶ 501 Nonresident Income
¶ 502 Formula Apportionment
¶ 503 Deduction of Expenses
¶ 504 Part Year Residents
¶ 505 Returns Based on Books of Account

¶ 501 Nonresident Income

Law: Secs. 48-7-20(a), 48-7-30(a), (b), and (c), Code (CCH GEORGIA TAX REPORTS ¶ 15-710, 15-720, 15-730).

Nonresident individuals are subject to Georgia personal income tax on taxable activities carried on within Georgia. The tax is imposed only on net income, not otherwise exempted, that is received by the taxpayer from services performed, property owned, or business carried on in Georgia and from lottery prizes of $5,000 or more awarded by the Georgia Lottery Corporation. For the definition of a "taxable nonresident," see ¶ 102.

Separate accounting: A nonresident may use separate accounting if the separate accounting correctly reflects the income fairly attributable to Georgia. The use of separate accounting must be approved by the State Revenue Commissioner. Otherwise, the amount of taxable income is determined in the same manner income is allocated and apportioned by corporations engaged in multistate business (¶ 502).

Computation of tax: Nonresidents are subject to the same computation provisions as residents.

A taxpayer may apply for permission to base a return on his or her books of account (¶ 505).

Practitioner Comment: Pension Income

Pension income received by a Georgia resident is attributable to Georgia even if the income is received from another state; however, pension income received by a non-resident from Georgia is not attributable to Georgia.

Michael T. Petrik, Esq., Alston & Bird

¶ 501

¶ 502 Formula Apportionment

Law: Sec. 48-7-30(b), (c), and (e), Code (CCH GEORGIA TAX REPORTS ¶ 15-710, 15-730, 15-770).

If a separate accounting method is not used, the amount of taxable income is determined in the same manner income is allocated and apportioned by corporations engaged in business within and without the state.

Nonresidents whose income is derived from activities carried on within Georgia must compute net taxable income as if they were Georgia residents. That net taxable income must be apportioned using the apportionment formula that corporations use if they carry on a business within and outside Georgia. Formula apportionment for corporations is discussed in Chapter 13.

Special rules for part year residents: Persons who change from resident to nonresident status or from nonresident to resident status may allocate and apportion their income under special rules (¶ 504).

¶ 503 Deduction of Expenses

Law: Sec. 48-7-30(d)(1) and (2), Code (CCH GEORGIA TAX REPORTS ¶ 15-740, 15-750).

Nonresidents may deduct allowable expenses, interest, taxes, losses, bad debts, depreciation, and similar business expenses if their income is derived from employment, a trade, a business, a profession, or other activity performed or carried on entirely within Georgia. For income that is derived both within and outside Georgia, a nonresident may deduct such items only if the State Revenue Commissioner allows the taxpayer to use separate accounting. Direct allocation of expenses is allowed if the income is derived from the rental of real or personal property located within Georgia or for use within Georgia and from the sale of tangible or intangible property having a situs in Georgia.

Expenses may be deducted only to the extent that the expenses are attributable to the production of income that is allocable to and taxable by Georgia.

CCH Tip: Deductions that Are Personal in Nature

Allowable deductions that are personal in nature may be deducted only in the ratio that gross income allocated to Georgia bears to the total gross income of the nonresident, computed as if the nonresident were a resident of Georgia. The Commissioner may accept total federal gross income as the equivalent of total Georgia gross income for purposes of this allocation. Personal expenses that are subject to this ratio include contributions to charitable organizations, alimony, medical expenses, the optional standard deduction, personal exemptions, and credits for dependents.

Part II—Personal Income Tax

¶ 504 Part Year Residents

Law: Secs. 48-7-1(5), (10)(D), and (E), 48-7-85, Code (CCH GEORGIA TAX REPORTS ¶ 15-110).

Taxpayers who move into or out of Georgia during a taxable year, and thus are not liable for Georgia personal income tax for the entire year, may be allowed to prorate their Georgia tax and exemptions on the basis of time spent within Georgia. For information on residency status, see ¶ 102.

¶ 505 Returns Based on Books of Account

Law: Sec. 48-7-34, Code (CCH GEORGIA TAX REPORTS ¶ 15-760).

Nonresident taxpayers may apply to the State Revenue Commissioner for permission to base their personal income tax return on their books of account. In the books of account, the taxpayer must employ a detailed allocation of receipts and expenditures that clearly reflects the income attributable to the taxpayer's trade or business within Georgia. The application must be filed at least 60 days before the return due date and must be accompanied by a full and complete explanation of the method employed.

Part II—Personal Income Tax

PERSONAL INCOME TAX

CHAPTER 6

RETURNS, ESTIMATES, PAYMENT OF TAX, WITHHOLDING

¶ 601 Returns—Time and Place for Filing
¶ 602 Persons Required to File
¶ 603 Extensions of Time
¶ 604 Estimated Tax
¶ 605 Payment of Tax
¶ 606 Forms
¶ 607 Withholding—In General
¶ 608 Withholding—Amounts Subject to Withholding
¶ 609 Withholding—Nonwage Income
¶ 610 Withholding—Returns and Payments

¶ 601 Returns—Time and Place for Filing

Law: Secs. 48-2-39, 48-7-56(a), 48-7-82(e)(1) and (2), Code (CCH GEORGIA TAX REPORTS ¶ 17-520, 17-540).

Comparable Federal: Secs. 6072, 6081, 6091 (U.S. MASTER TAX GUIDE ¶ 3, 118—122, 1501, 2525—2545).

Forms: Form 500, Form 500-EZ, Form 525-TV (telefiling voucher), Form 8453 (declaration for electronic filing).

Annual returns of calendar year taxpayers must be filed on or before April 15 of each year. Fiscal year taxpayers must file their returns by the 15th day of the fourth month after the close of the fiscal year.

Due date on weekend or holiday: If a filing or payment due date falls on a Saturday, Sunday, or legal holiday, the filing of the return and the payment of the tax may be postponed until the next day that is not a Saturday, Sunday, or legal holiday.

● *Federal change or correction*

A taxpayer who is notified by the federal taxing authorities that a final determination changes or corrects federal net income for any year must file an amended Georgia return reporting the change or correction in income within 180 days after the date of the federal determination.

● *Extensions of time*

Extensions of time are discussed at ¶ 603.

¶ 601

● *Electronic filing*

Individual income tax returns with a zero balance or a refund amount may be filed with the Department of Revenue by residents, nonresidents, and part-year residents filing a Form 500 or 500EZ via the Federal/State Electronic Filing Program. A signature document, GA8453/8453OL, is required. If a credit is taken for taxes paid to another state, taxpayers must attach a copy of the other state's tax return to the back of the signature document.

If the IRS approves a taxpayer for filing federal electronic returns with the IRS Memphis Service Center, the Georgia Department will recognize this approval for purposes of the Federal/State Electronic Filing Program. A separate application form is not required to file electronically in Georgia. The Department conducts suitability checks on IRS-approved applicants and will notify only those applicants who are ineligible to participate in the Georgia program. Notification is not sent to those who are approved for electronic filing.

Payment: Taxpayers who file their return electronically or by telefiling must complete the payment voucher (Form 525-TV) and mail the voucher, together with a check or money order for any tax due, to the Department of Revenue. Taxpayers who file electronically must file Form 8453 or Form 8453OL (declaration for electronic filing).

Exclusions from electronic filing: In addition to the returns excluded from federal electronic filing listed in IRS Publication 1345, the following Georgia returns are also excluded:

—balance due returns;

—amended returns;

—prior year returns; and

—decedent returns, including joint returns filed by the decedent's spouse (*Georgia Electronic Filing Handbook,* Georgia Department of Revenue, 1999).

¶ 602 Persons Required to File

Law: Secs. 48-7-50, 48-7-53, Code; Reg. Sec. 560-7-8-.01 (CCH GEORGIA TAX REPORTS ¶ 15-220, 15-230, 17-510, 17-515).

Comparable Federal: Secs. 6012, 6013, 6014, 6017 (U.S. MASTER TAX GUIDE ¶ 109—124).

Forms: Form 500, Form 500-EZ, Form 700 (Partnership Income Tax Return), Form IT-CR (Composite Return for Nonresident Partners and Shareholders).

An income tax return must be filed by (1) every resident who is required to file a federal income tax return for the taxable year, (2) every nonresident who has federal gross income from sources within Georgia, (3) every resident estate or trust that is required to file a federal income tax return, (4) every nonresident estate or trust that has federal gross income from sources within Georgia, and (5) every resident or nonresident who has taxable income subject to Georgia income tax for the taxable year who does not have taxable income subject to federal income tax for the same taxable year.

¶ 602

Part II—Personal Income Tax   **81**

● *Partnership returns*

Every partnership whose members are subject to Georgia income tax must file a return (Form 700) for each taxable year. The return should state specifically the items of the partnership's gross income and the deduction allowed against the income. The return should also include the names and addresses of the individuals who would be entitled to share in the net income of the partnership if the net income were distributed and should specify the amount of the distributive share of each individual. The return must be sworn to by one of the partners.

Partnerships with nonresident partners are required to withhold on distributions made to the nonresidents. For details, see ¶ 609.

● *Returns filed by husband and wife*

A husband and wife must use the same marital status on their Georgia personal income tax return that they use on their federal income tax return (Georgia Personal Income Tax Return Instructions, Form IT-511).

● *Head of household*

A person filing a federal return as head of household must also file as head of household on the Georgia return (Georgia Individual Income Tax Return Instructions, Form IT-511).

¶ 603   Extensions of Time

> *Law:* Secs. 48-2-36, 48-7-36, 48-7-56(a) and (b), Code (CCH GEORGIA TAX REPORTS ¶ 17-520).
>
> *Comparable Federal:* Sec. 6081 (U.S. MASTER TAX GUIDE ¶ 120, 2509).
>
> *Form:* IT-303.

An extension of time to file a return may be granted in cases of sickness, disability, or other good cause. A taxpayer granted an extension may be required to file a tentative return stating the estimated amount of tax believed to be due.

Generally, the maximum total period for extensions of time equals six months. An extension of time for filing a return does not delay the required payment of the tax unless a satisfactory bond is posted.

CCH Tip: Federal Extension

The state of Georgia recognizes the federal automatic four-month extension of time to file. For Georgia purposes, a copy of the federal extension must be attached to the Georgia return when filed. An extension of time to file does not extend the time to pay. Prepayment of tax should be made with the filing of Form IT-560 before April 15 (Instructions to Georgia Form 500).

¶ 603

● *Military personnel*

Members of the U.S. Armed Forces serving outside the continental United States may file their return for a taxable year ending during such service at any time within a period of six months following their return to the continental United States. During the period of extension, no interest accrues and no penalties are imposed.

In the case of an individual serving in the U.S. Armed Forces, or in support of the U.S. Armed Forces, in an area designated as a combat zone at any time during the period of combatant activities in such zone, the period of service in the combat zone and the next 180 days thereafter is disregarded for the purpose of determining whether a return has been filed on time. Further, in the case of an individual hospitalized as a result of injury received while serving in a combat zone during the period of combat activities and in the case of an individual confined as a prisoner of the forces opposing the United States in a combat zone, the period of continuous hospitalization attributable to the injury plus any period of confinement, and the next 180 days thereafter, are disregarded for the purpose of determining whether a return has been filed on time.

¶ 604 Estimated Tax

Law: Secs. 48-2-32(f)(2), 48-7-114(b), (c), (d), and (e), 48-7-115(a), (b), and (c), 48-7-116(a), (b), and (d), 48-7-120(b) and (e), Code (CCH GEORGIA TAX REPORTS ¶ 17-601, 17-610, 17-620, 17-630, 17-640).

Comparable Federal: Sec. 6654 (U.S. MASTER TAX GUIDE ¶ 101—107, 2679—2697).

Forms: Form 500-ES, Form 500-UET.

Resident and nonresident individuals and fiduciaries who can reasonably be expected to file a Georgia personal income tax return for the current taxable year must pay estimated tax if their gross income can reasonably be expected to include more than $1,000 from nonwage sources and to exceed $1,500, for single persons and married persons living separately who expect to claim only $1,500 of the marital exemption, or $3,000, for married persons living together and expecting to claim the full marital exemption.

Taxpayers are not required to pay estimated tax if (1) the sum of the allowable credits shown on their income tax return for the tax year exceeds the precredit tax liability shown on the return and (2) they reasonably expected that the conditions in (1) above would be satisfied for the tax year.

● *Electronic funds transfer*

Any person or business owing more than $10,000 of estimated tax must pay by electronic funds transfer. Details concerning electronic funds transfers are discussed in Chapter 29, "Georgia Administration and Procedure."

● *Filing dates*

Generally, estimated tax must be paid by April 15 of the taxable year.

However, taxpayers who meet the filing requirements for estimated tax after March 31 of the taxable year may file the declarations later. If the filing

Part II—Personal Income Tax 83

requirements are first met on or after April 1 and before June 1 of the taxable year, estimated tax must be filed on or before June 15 of the taxable year. If the filing requirements are first met on or after June 1 and before September 1 of the taxable year, estimated tax must be filed on or before September 15 of the taxable year. Finally, if the filing requirements are first met on or after September 1 of the taxable year, estimated tax must be filed on or before January 15 of the succeeding taxable year.

Farmers and fishermen: Individuals whose estimated gross income from farming or fishing for the taxable year is at least two-thirds of the total estimated gross income from all sources for the taxable year may file the declaration of estimated tax at any time on or before January 15 of the succeeding taxable year.

Fiscal years: For a taxable year beginning on any date other than January 1, the corresponding months must be substituted for those specified above.

● *Installment payments of estimated tax*

Estimate filed by April 15: If the estimate is filed on or before April 15 of the taxable year, the estimated tax must be paid in four equal installments, with the first one paid at the time of filing the declaration, the second one paid by June 15 of the taxable year, the third one paid by September 15 of the taxable year, and the fourth one paid by January 15 of the succeeding year. Three equal installment payments are required if the taxpayer files an estimate during the period from April 16 through June 16 of the taxable year. Two equal installment payments are required if the taxpayer files an estimate during the period from June 16 through September 15 of the taxable year. Taxpayers filing an estimate after September 15 of the taxable year must pay the estimated tax in full at the time of filing the estimate.

Payment upon late filing of estimate: If the estimate is filed after the time prescribed, all installments that would have been payable on or before such time must be paid at the time of filing, even if an extension of time for filing has been granted. For the remaining installments, the due dates and amounts are the same as if the estimate were timely filed.

Farmers and fishermen: If an individual whose estimated gross income from farming or fishing for the taxable year is at least two-thirds of the total estimated gross income from all sources for the taxable year files estimated tax after September 15 of the taxable year and on or before January 15 of the succeeding year, the estimated tax must be paid in full at the time of the filing of the declaration.

Installments paid in advance: At the election of the individual, any installment of the estimated tax may be paid prior to the date prescribed for its payment.

● *Return of estimated tax*

If a taxpayer files a return on or before January 31 of the succeeding taxable year (or March 1 of the succeeding taxable year for a farmer or fisherman) for a taxable year requiring a declaration and pays in full the amount computed on the return as payable, the return is considered as the

¶ 604

declaration if the declaration is not required to be filed during the taxable year but is required to be filed on or before January 15.

● *Underpayment of estimated tax*

If an underpayment is made, an addition to tax equal to 9% of the underpayment per year, for the period of underpayment, may be added. For additional information, see ¶ 3003.

¶ 605 Payment of Tax

Law: Secs. 48-2-33, 48-7-80, Code (CCH GEORGIA TAX REPORTS ¶ 17-710).

Comparable Federal: Sec. 6151 (U.S. MASTER TAX GUIDE ¶ 5, 2529).

The total amount of tax must be paid by April 15 following the close of the calendar year. For a fiscal year return, the tax must be paid on or before the 15th day of the fourth month following the close of the fiscal year.

Checks should be made payable to the Georgia Income Tax Division (Instructions to Georgia Individual Income Tax Return, Form IT-511).

Taxpayers may request a receipt for payment of taxes.

See ¶ 2902 for the penalty for tendering a check that is not payable upon presentation.

¶ 606 Forms

Law: Sec. 48-1-3, Code (CCH GEORGIA TAX REPORTS ¶ 17-570).

The following forms are in current use:
Form IT-511—Individual Income Tax Booklet
Form 500—Individual Income Tax Return
Form 500-EZ—Short Individual Income Tax Return
Form 501—Fiduciary Income Tax Return
Form 500-X—Amended Individual Income Tax Return
Form IND-CR—Individual Income Tax Credit
Form IT-303—Application for Extension of Time for Filing State Income Tax Returns
Form IT-550—Claim for Refund of Georgia Income Tax Erroneously or Illegally Collected
Form IT-553—Application for Tentative Carry-Back Adjustment—Taxpayers other than Corporations
Form IT-560—Tax Prepayment
Form 500-ES—Individual Estimated Tax Return
Form 500-UET—Underpayment of Estimated Tax by Individuals/Fiduciary
Form RD-1061—Power of Attorney
Form GA-8453—Individual Income Tax Declaration for Electronic Filing—To be Retained by Practitioners
Form GA-8453OL—Individual Income Tax Declaration for Electronic Filing
Form 700—Partnership Income Tax Return
Form IT-CR—Composite Return for Non-Resident Partners and Shareholders
Form 303—Application for Extension of Time for Filing State Income Tax Returns
Form RD-1061—Power of Attorney

¶ 605

Part II—Personal Income Tax

Form IT-553—Application for Tentative Carry-back Adjustment (other than corporations)

Tax forms may be obtained at the Georgia Department of Revenue website, http://www2.State.Ga.us/departments/dor/inctax/individual_income_tax_forms.shtml.

For address information, see Chapter 32, "Georgia Resources."

¶ 607 Withholding—In General

Law: Secs. 48-7-100, 48-7-101, 48-7-108, 48-7-109, 48-7-126, Code (CCH GEORGIA TAX REPORTS ¶ 17-101, 17-130, 17-301).

Comparable Federal: Secs. 3401, 3402 (U.S. MASTER TAX GUIDE ¶ 2601—2663).

Employers must withhold income tax from wage payments made to employees. Ordinarily, employers must file returns and pay the tax on a quarterly basis. The amount of an employee's wages subject to withholding is reduced by the employee's withholding exemption allowance and standard deduction allowance.

The employer is subject to penalties and interest for any failure to adhere to the withholding tax provisions.

● *Wages*

In general, payment as remuneration constitutes wages even if the remuneration is not paid in cash. However, wages do not include remuneration paid for the following: (1) agricultural labor; (2) domestic services in private homes, fraternities, or sororities; (3) services performed by a minister; (4) services performed for a foreign government or an international organization; (5) services not in the course of the employer's trade or business, unless performed by a regular employee and the remuneration is $50 or more; (6) services not in the course of the employer's trade or business to the extent that the remuneration is not paid in cash; (7) newspaper or shopping news delivery by an individual under age 18 and newspaper sales by an individual whose compensation is based on retaining an excess of the price charged; (8) services performed by a Georgia resident or domiciliary in another state, if the employer is required to withhold tax for the other state; (9) services performed by a seaman who is a crew member on a vessel engaged in trade, to the extent withholding is prohibited by federal law; and (10) services performed by a nonresident who has been employed in Georgia for no more than 23 days during the calendar quarter. Furthermore, wages do not include remuneration paid (1) as fees to a public official for services employed by an employee for his employer or (2) to or on behalf of an employee (a) from or to a trust that forms part of an exempt employee stock ownership, pension, or profit sharing plan described in IRC Sec. 401(a), unless the payment is made to the trust's employee as remuneration for services and not as a beneficiary of the trust or (b) under an annuity plan that satisfies the vesting and antidiscrimination requirements of IRC Sec. 401(a)(3), (4), and (5).

¶ 607

> ***CCH Tip: Payments Constituting Wages***
>
> If payments made by an employer to an employee for services performed during one-half or more of any payroll period up to 31 consecutive days constitute wages, all the payments made by the employer to the employee for the period are deemed to be wages. Conversely, if payments by an employer to an employee for services performed during more than one-half of any payroll period up to 31 consecutive days do not constitute wages, then none of the payments made by the employer to the employee for the period are deemed to be wages.

● *Employer liability for tax*

An employer is liable for the payment of tax that the employer is required to deduct and withhold, regardless of whether the employer has deducted or withheld the taxes as required.

● *Employee payment of tax*

If an employer fails to deduct and withhold the required personal income tax from an employee and the employee later pays the tax, the tax required to be withheld and deducted will not be collected from the employer. However, the employer may nevertheless be liable for penalties or additions to tax imposed for failure to withhold the tax as required.

● *False independent contractor claims*

It is unlawful for any person to knowingly coerce, induce, or threaten an individual to falsely declare himself or herself an independent contractor, or to falsely claim that an individual employed by that person is an independent contractor, in order to avoid or evade the withholding or payment of any Georgia tax. For penalties, see ¶ 3003.

● *Penalties and interest assessable as tax*

Penalties and interest (¶ 3003) are assessed and collected in the same manner as income taxes are assessed and collected.

¶ 608 Withholding—Amounts Subject to Withholding

Law: Secs. 48-7-27(a)(1), 48-7-101(a), (b), and (g), 48-7-102(c), 48-7-105(a) and (b), Code; Reg. Sec. 560-7-8-.33 (CCH GEORGIA TAX REPORTS ¶ 15-440, 17-150, 17-160, 17-210, 17-230).

Comparable Federal: Sec. 3402 (U.S. MASTER TAX GUIDE ¶ 2601—2663).

Form: Form G-4, Employee's Withholding Certificate.

The amount of wages subject to withholding is equal to the amount of each wage payment minus the total withholding exemption and standard deduction allowances applicable to the wage payment. The standard deduc-

¶ 608

Part II—Personal Income Tax

tion allowances, determined according to the payroll period and marital status of the employee, are as follows:

Payroll Period	Married Filing Jointly	Single	Married Filing Separately
Weekly	$ 57.50	$ 44.25	$ 28.75
Biweekly	115.00	88.50	57.50
Semimonthly	125.00	95.75	62.50
Monthly	250.00	191.50	125.00
Quarterly	750.00	575.00	375.00
Semiannual	1,500.00	1,150.00	750.00
Annual	3,000.00	2,300.00	1,500.00
Daily or Miscellaneous	8.20	6.30	4.10

● *Withholding exemption allowance*

The total withholding exemption allowance applicable to each wage payment is deducted from the wages paid, in addition to the standard deduction allowance, to determine the amount of wages subject to withholding. The employee withholding exemption allowance is the sum of the employee's exemption, either as a single person or married person, plus the exemption for dependents. The number of dependent exemptions the taxpayer claims is multiplied by the allowance for each dependent exemption to compute the total dependent exemption for withholding purposes. The exemption allowances for the various payroll periods are shown in the chart below.

Payroll Period	Col. 1 Single Exemption	Col. 2 Marital Exemption	Col. 3 Each Dependent Exemption
Weekly	$ 51.92	$ 103.85	$ 51.92
Biweekly	103.85	207.69	103.85
Semimonthly	112.50	225.00	112.50
Monthly	225.00	450.00	225.00
Quarterly	675.00	1350.00	675.00
Semiannual	1,350.00	2,700.00	1,350.00
Annual	2,700.00	5,400.00	2,700.00
Daily or Miscellaneous	7.40	14.79	7.40

Nonstandard payroll period: If wages are paid for a miscellaneous payroll period or with respect to a period that is not a payroll period, the withholding exemption allowance with respect to each payment of the wages is the exemption allowed for a daily payroll period multiplied by the number of days in the period in which the wages are paid. Saturdays and Sundays are included within this computation.

Employee exemption certificate: Employees must give their employer a signed withholding exemption certificate before beginning to work for the employer. If an employee fails to provide a completed certificate or gives false information, the employer withholds the tax as if the exemption status were single and zero until a complete and correct withholding certificate is received. If an employee has provided a federal exemption certificate, the employer may withhold tax according to the exemption status and exemptions claimed on the federal exemption certificate if the certificate contains sufficient information to allow the withholding exemptions claimed.

¶ 608

An exemption certificate is effective as of the beginning of the first payroll period that ends on or after the date when the certificate is furnished and remains effective until the employee furnishes the employer with another certificate.

CCH Tip: No Income Tax Liability for Employee

An exemption certificate may indicate that the employee incurred no income tax liability for the preceding taxable year and anticipates no income tax liability for the current taxable year, and if such a certificate is filed the employer is not required to deduct and withhold tax.

If an employee's exemption status or number of dependency exemptions changes, the employee should file a new exemption certificate indicating the change within 10 days of the change or before December 21 for the next calendar year.

- *Statement to employees*

Employers required to withhold taxes must furnish their employees with a statement of wages paid and taxes withheld by January 31 of each year.

¶ 609 Withholding—Nonwage Income

Law: Secs. 48-7-101(h), 48-7-106, 48-7-128, 48-7-129, Code; Reg. Secs. 560-7-8-.34 and 560-7-8-.35, 560-7-8-.39 (CCH GEORGIA TAX REPORTS ¶ 17-185, 17-190, 17-195, 17-197, 17-235).

Comparable Federal: Sec. 3402 (U.S. MASTER TAX GUIDE ¶ 2601—2663).

Forms: Form G2-A (Withholding on Distributions to Nonresident Members/Shareholders), Form G-4P (Withholding Certificate for Pension or Annuity Payments), Form G-2RP (Withholding on Sales or Transfers of Real Property and Associated Tangible Personal Property by Nonresidents).

Withholding of income tax is required for payments from pensions, annuities, and other periodic payments; distributions to nonresident members of partnerships, S corporations, and limited liability companies (LLCs); property transfers by nonresidents; and other nonwage income.

- *Pensions, annuities, and other periodic payments*

The payor of any periodic payment such as a pension or annuity must withhold from the payment the amount that would be required to be withheld if the payment were wages, unless the payee elects not to have the tax withheld. Such an election remains in effect until it is revoked by the payee.

- *Distributions to nonresident members of pass-through entities*

Distributions to nonresident members of a partnership, S corporation, or LLC are subject to personal income tax withholding at the rate of 4%.

Exclusions: Withholding requirements do not apply if (1) a composite return is filed on behalf of nonresident members, (2) the aggregate annual

Part II—Personal Income Tax 89

distributions made to a member are less than $1,000, (3) a federal S corporation is subject to corporate income tax because it failed to properly elect S corporation status, (4) compliance with withholding tax requirements will cause undue hardship, or (5) the partnership is a publicly traded partnership treated as a corporation under IRC Sec. 7704. Also, if distributions paid or credited to nonresident members of partnerships, S corporations, or LLCs are subject to withholding under other Georgia law provisions, or represent a return of a member's investment or capital, the distributions are exempt from these withholding provisions. Finally, distributions are exempt from withholding if the partnership, S corporation, or LLC earns its income exclusively from transactions in and ownership of securities that it manages on its own behalf.

Apportionment of withholding: If the entity making the distribution owns property or does business within and outside Georgia, withholding is required only on that portion of the income that is reasonably attributable to the property owned or business done in Georgia.

Computing the tax for composite returns: For each member, an entity may choose one of the following three computation options that may be changed annually:

(1) The entity may compute the tax by multiplying the member's income from the entity's business done in Georgia by the tax rate applicable to the member.

(2) The entity may compute the tax by determining its Georgia taxable income and calculating the tax due on the member's share of the Georgia income. Under this option, the member may take a standard deduction and a personal exemption and credit for dependents to the extent that they apply to Georgia income. This option does not allow for adjustments to income on the basis of self employment, self employed health insurance, Keogh, or other adjustments normally allowed in computing adjusted gross income.

(3) The entity may compute the tax for the member making adjustments to income that are based on allowable itemized deductions and personal exemptions and the credit for dependents. The member's income and adjustments should be calculated on the basis of the ratio of the member's Georgia income to the member's total income.

CCH Tip: Options on the Composite Return (Form IT-CR)

Although option 1 is the simplest and least burdensome method for computing income tax liability, it also generates the greatest tax liability. Although option 3 allows an adjustment for itemized deductions and option 2 only allows an adjustment for the standard deduction, option 2 may generate greater tax savings than option 3. Even though the adjusted itemized deductions (adjustment to eliminate deductions not allowable under Georgia law if the taxpayer itemizes) may be a larger deduction for the individual members than the standard deduction, because option 2 uses the nonresident member's share of total partnership or S corporation income as the starting point for computing taxable income and option 3 uses the nonresident member's federal income after Geor-

¶ 609

gia adjustments as the starting point, option 2 may generate greater tax savings. A nonresident member's share of total partnership or S corporation income is not necessarily the same as the member's federal income after Georgia adjustments. The computations for options 2 and 3 should be calculated separately for each individual member. Each individual member can then choose which option to elect based on their personal tax liability. Trusts and estates must elect option 1 or 2. If the trust chooses to elect option 2, the standard deduction is not allowed. Instead of the standard deduction, trusts and estates claim an exemption.

• *Property transfers by nonresidents*

Withholding is required for certain transfers of real property and related personal property located in Georgia that is sold by a nonresident if the purchase price is $20,000 or more. The tax is equal to 3% of the purchase price or consideration paid for the property sold or transferred. The tax is withheld by the purchaser or transferee, who is personally liable for the tax if the tax is not withheld.

Returns and payment: The initial required return and payment are due by the last day of the month after the sale or transfer occurred. The initial payment is calculated by taking 3% of the purchase price less the installment note, or 3% of the gain that would be recognized as a result of the proceeds received at the time of closing. Each subsequent return and payment must be filed by the last day of the month after the month in which the cumulative amount withheld for the year, less any payments already made for the year, exceeds $300. If $300 threshold is not reached, the buyer must file the return and payment by the last day of the month following year in which the tax was withheld. The withholding on subsequent payments is calculated by taking 3% of the principal amount included in each payment, or 3% of the amount of each principal payment that represents gain.

Practitioner Comment: Avoidance of Withholding

Georgia regulations permit the avoidance of withholding in cases of transfers that are exempt from income tax or that do not recognize gain. In additions, a seller may limit withholding to 3% of the recognized gain by providing the purchaser with an appropriate form affidavit.

Michael T. Petrik, Esq., Alston & Bird LLP

• *Lottery proceeds*

All lottery proceeds exceeding $5,000 are subject to income tax withholding in an amount equal to 6% of the proceeds. The Georgia Lottery Corporation issues a form to the prize winner showing the amount of the lottery prize proceeds and the amount of income tax withheld.

¶ 609

Part II—Personal Income Tax 91

● *Employer's sale of business*

If an employer sells out its business or stock of goods or quits the business, any of the employer's successors or assigns must withhold a sufficient amount of the purchase money to cover the amount of the withholding, interest, and penalties due and unpaid until the former owner provides a receipt from the Revenue Commissioner showing that the taxes, interest, and penalties have been paid or a certificate from the Commissioner stating that no withholding taxes, interest, or penalties are due.

Failure of purchaser to withhold: If the purchaser of a business or stock of goods fails to withhold tax from the purchase money as required, the purchaser is personally liable for the payment of the withholding tax, interest, and penalties accruing and unpaid by any former owner or assignor. The personal liability of the purchaser in such a case does not exceed the amount of the total purchase money. The property being transferred, in all cases, is subject to the full amount of the tax lien arising from the delinquencies of the former owner.

Practitioner Comment: Tax Clearance Letters

This requirement presents a potential trap for purchasers of a business in an asset aquisition. In order to avoid successor liability for withholding taxes, a purchaser should require his seller to provide a certificate from the Department of Revenue stating that the seller has no outstanding withholding tax liabilities. These certificates, commonly called "tax clearance letters," can usually be obtained within two or three weeks, assuming the seller has filed all returns that are due and has paid all taxes shown due on such returns. Requests for tax clearance letters usually do not cause an audit.

Michael T. Petrik, Esq., Alston & Bird LLP

¶ 610 Withholding—Returns and Payments

Law: Secs. 48-2-32(f)(2), 48-7-103, 48-7-106, 48-7-107(a), 48-7-128(f), 48-7-129(b) and (d), Code; Reg. Secs. 560-7-8-.33, 560-7-8-.34 (CCH GEORGIA TAX REPORTS ¶ 17-195, 17-197, 17-220, 17-225, 17-235, 17-240).

Comparable Federal: Secs. 3402, 3403, 3501, 6011 (U.S. MASTER TAX GUIDE ¶ 2650).

Forms: GA-7 (Withholding Return), Form G-1003 (Income Statement Transmittal Form).

Employers required to withhold income taxes equal to $800 or less per year must file a return and pay the tax by the last day of January following the end of that year. Employers required to withhold income taxes equal to $200 or less per month must file a return and pay the tax by the last day of the month following the end of the quarter. Employers required to withhold taxes of $50,000 or less in the aggregate for the lookback period (July 1—June 30) must file and pay the tax by the 15th day of the following month, unless the Commissioner permits the taxpayer to file on a quarterly basis. Filing returns and paying the tax on an annual basis may also be permitted. The

¶ 610

Commissioner of Revenue has the authority to permit employers to make estimated payments of taxes withheld.

● *Electronic funds transfers*

Any person or business owing more than $10,000 in personal income tax withholding must pay by electronic funds transfer (EFT). Details concerning electronic funds transfers are discussed at ¶ 2902.

Every employer whose employee withholding taxes exceed $50,000 in the aggregate for the lookback period (July 1-June 30) must pay the taxes by EFT as follows:

—for paydays occurring on Wednesday, Thursday, or Friday, the taxes must be remitted on or before the following Wednesday, or, in the case of a holiday, the next banking day thereafter;

—for paydays occurring on Saturday, Sunday, Monday, or Tuesday, the taxes must be remitted on or before the following Friday, or, in the case of a holiday, the next banking day thereafter.

Employers whose employee withholding taxes exceed $100,000 must remit these taxes by electronic funds transfer by the next banking day. A 10% penalty may be assessed against any employer that is required to file and remit withholding taxes electronically, but fails to do so.

● *Annual and final returns*

Employers must file an annual return on or before February 28 of each year for the preceding calendar year. An employer who has ceased to pay wages must file the return by the 30th day after the date when the final payment of wages is made. Copies of employee statements of wages paid and taxes withheld generally must be attached to an employer's annual or final return.

Employer's sale of business: Employers who are liable for withholding, interest, or penalty, who sell out their business or stock of goods or equipment or quit the business, must file a final return.

● *Return for transfers of property owned by nonresident*

Purchasers required to deduct and withhold tax on transfers of nonresident-owned Georgia property must file a return and remit payment to the Georgia Department of Revenue by the last day of the calendar month following the month when the sale occurred.

● *Return for distributions to nonresident members of pass-through entities*

For distributions to nonresident members of partnerships, S corporations, and limited liability companies (LLCs), personal income tax withholding returns must be filed and tax payments must be made by the last day of the calendar month following the month when the distribution was paid or credited. In the alternative, an entity may file a composite return and pay the applicable income tax due on behalf of its nonresident members (¶ 609).

¶ 610

Distributions of less than $1,000: Partnerships, S corporations, and limited liability companies need not withhold tax for a nonresident member if the aggregate annual distribution to that member is less than $1,000.

Practioner Comment: Unclear Definition of "Credited"

The term "credited" in this context is the subject of some continuing uncertainly in Georgia. Whether the term includes a "credit" posted to a partner, shareholder, or member's capital account is unclear. Many Georgia practitioners believe that such an interpretation is not compatible with the principle that withholding apply only to "distributions," since it would effectively require withholding on the entirety of a nonresident's subchapter K income whether or not actually distributed.

Michael T. Petrik, Esq., Alston & Bird LLP

Part II—Personal Income Tax

PERSONAL INCOME TAX

CHAPTER 7

FIDUCIARIES, PARTNERSHIPS, LIMITED LIABILITY COMPANIES

¶ 701 Fiduciaries
¶ 702 Partners and Partnerships
¶ 703 Limited Liability Companies

¶ 701 Fiduciaries

Law: Secs. 48-1-2(9), 48-7-20(d), 48-7-22, Code (CCH GEORGIA TAX REPORTS ¶ 15-120).

Comparable Federal: Sec. 7701 (U.S. MASTER TAX GUIDE ¶ 64, 501—585).

Form: Form 501, Fiduciary Income Tax Return.

Fiduciaries who receive income from business done in Georgia, have charge of funds or property located in Georgia, or have charge of funds or property for the benefit of a Georgia resident are required to pay Georgia personal income tax. A fiduciary may be a resident or a nonresident. The net income and tax rate are computed the same way as for an individual.

● *"Fiduciary" defined*

"Fiduciary" means a guardian, trustee, executor, administrator, receiver, conservator, or any person, whether individual or corporate, acting in any fiduciary capacity for any person.

● *Taxable income of fiduciary*

A fiduciary is taxed annually upon the following income:

—the part of the net income of an estate or trust that has not become distributable during the taxable year;

—the taxable net income received during the taxable year by a deceased individual who at the time of death was a taxpayer and who died during the taxable year or subsequent to the taxable year without having made a return; and

—the entire net income of an insolvent or incompetent person, regardless of whether any portion of the taxable net income is held for future use of the beneficiaries, when the fiduciary has complete charge of the net income.

¶ 701

● *Nontaxable income of fiduciary*

Income received by a resident fiduciary is not taxable if the income is accumulated for, is distributed, or becomes distributable during the taxable year to a nonresident of Georgia and if the income was received from business done outside Georgia; property held outside Georgia; or intangible property (other than from the licensing for use of the property) held by a fiduciary such as gains from the sale or exchange of the property.

● *Taxable year*

If the taxable year of a beneficiary and that of the estate or trust differ, the beneficiary includes in net income an amount that is based on the income of the estate or trust for any taxable year of the estate or trust ending with or within the beneficiary's taxable year.

● *Charge against the estate or trust*

The tax imposed upon a fiduciary constitutes a charge against the estate or trust.

¶702   Partners and Partnerships

Law: Secs. 48-7-23, 48-7-24, 48-7-53, Code; Reg. Sec. 560-7-3-.08 (CCH GEORGIA TAX REPORTS ¶ 15-130).

Comparable Federal: Secs. 701—761, 1361, 7701 (U.S. MASTER TAX GUIDE ¶ 63, 401—481).

Form: Form 700, Partnership Income Tax Return.

Partnerships, as such, are not subject to taxation, but are required to make returns. Members are taxable upon their distributive shares of the net income of the partnership, regardless of whether the shares are distributed, and are required to include the distributive shares in their returns. If the result of partnership operation is a net loss, the loss is divisible by the partners in the same proportion as net income would have been divisible (unless the partnership states otherwise) and may be taken by the partners in their return of income.

● *"Partnership" defined*

The term partnership includes (but is not limited to) a member in a syndicate, group, pool, joint venture, or other unincorporated organization through or by means of which a business, financial operation, or venture is carried on. The term does not include a trust, estate, or corporation.

● *Computation of net income*

Partnerships compute net income in the same manner and on the same basis as an individual computes net income. However, the deduction for charitable contributions or gifts is not permitted, as these are allowable (subject to limitations) to the respective partners on their individual returns. Payments made to a partner for services rendered and for interest on capital contributions are also not deductible in computing the net income of the partnership because such payments represent a division of profits.

Part II—Personal Income Tax

● *Taxation of the partners*

Individuals carrying on business in a partnership are liable for income tax only in their individual capacity and each partner must include on the individual return the partner's distributive shares (whether distributed or not) of the net income of the partnership for the taxable year. If the taxable year of the partner is different from that of the partnership, the amount included in the partner's individual return is based on the income of the partnership for the taxable year of the partnership ending with or within the partner's taxable year.

● *Resident and nonresident partners and partnerships*

Nonresidents of Georgia who are individual members of a partnership that is engaged in business in Georgia are subject to tax on their share of the net profits of the partnership.

> **CCH Tip: Nonresidents' Income from Securities**
>
> Nonresidents of Georgia who are individual members of Georgia limited partnerships or other Georgia nontaxable entities that earn income exclusively from their transactions in and ownership of securities (but not as a broker) are not taxed on their distributive shares of the partnership's net income. Sec. 48-7-24(c), Code.

An individual resident of Georgia who is a partner of a partnership that is doing business outside Georgia must include on the individual return the partner's distributable share of the net income of the partnership for the taxable year. This applies regardless of whether the share is distributed.

● *Withholding*

For withholding requirements applicable to nonresident partners, see ¶ 610.

¶ 703 Limited Liability Companies

Law: Sec. 14-11-1104, Code (CCH Georgia Tax Reports ¶ 10-225, 15-135).

Comparable Federal: Secs. 701—761, 1361, 7701.

Georgia authorizes the formation of limited liability companies (LLCs), business entities that combine the corporate level characteristic of limited liability while preserving for members the pass-through tax advantages of partnerships. For purposes of the Georgia income tax, an LLC is classified as a partnership, unless otherwise treated under federal income tax law. Therefore, Georgia LLCs qualifying as partnerships are not subject to taxation. However, individual LLC members are taxed on their distributive share of LLC income as if they were partners in a partnership. See ¶ 702 for a discussion of the taxation of partners' distributive shares of income.

¶ 703

PERSONAL INCOME TAX

CHAPTER 8

ADMINISTRATION, DEFICIENCIES, PENALTIES, REFUNDS, APPEALS

¶ 801 Administration—In General
¶ 802 Deficiencies—Procedure
¶ 803 Interest on Deficiencies
¶ 804 Penalties
¶ 805 Statute of Limitations on Assessments
¶ 806 Jeopardy Assessments
¶ 807 Bankruptcy and Receivership
¶ 808 Transferee Liability
¶ 809 Overpayments and Refunds
¶ 810 Interest on Overpayments and Refunds
¶ 811 Abatement—Protest to Commissioner
¶ 812 Statute of Limitations on Refund Claims
¶ 813 Judicial Review
¶ 814 Settlements and Compromise of Tax

¶ 801 Administration—In General

Law: Secs. 48-2-1, 48-2-12(a) and (d), 48-2-35(b), Code (CCH GEORGIA TAX REPORTS ¶ 15-010, 89-010, 89-015, 89-510).

Georgia personal income tax is administered by the Georgia Department of Revenue Income Tax Division. For address information, see Chapter 32, "Georgia Resources."

The State Revenue Commissioner is the executive and administrative head of the Department. The Commissioner has the authority to administer and enforce the collection of taxes, approve or deny refund claims, and issue regulations.

For additional information, see ¶ 2901, Chapter 29, "Georgia Administration and Procedure."

¶ 802 Deficiencies—Procedure

Law: Secs. 48-2-46, 48-2-47, 48-2-48, 48-2-49(c), Code (CCH GEORGIA TAX REPORTS ¶ 17-701).

The State Revenue Commissioner may make a deficiency assessment if an improper or inadequate assessment of personal income tax has been made as a result of incorrect, misleading, false, or omitted statements on a return. Taxes collected by deficiency assessment bear interest from the date the

Commissioner advises the taxpayer in writing of the amount of taxes due until such taxes are paid. For the current rate of interest, see ¶ 3003.

● *Procedure for protest*

A taxpayer may contest a proposed assessment by filing a written protest with the Commissioner within 30 days from the date of notice of the assessment, or within another time limit specified by the notice of proposed assessment. The information contained in the protest and information submitted by the taxpayer will be considered in a conference or hearing. Upon making a final assessment, the Commissioner must notify the taxpayer of the decision.

● *Limitation period for making deficiency assessments*

In the absence of fraud, no assessment may be redetermined more than two years after the last date for filing the return without delinquency by the taxpayer. In the case of a false or fraudulent return or report filed with the intent to evade tax, or a failure to file a return or report, the personal income tax may be assessed at any time.

Procedures for judicial appeal of a deficiency assessment are discussed at ¶ 3101.

¶ 803 Interest on Deficiencies

Interest on deficiencies is discussed at ¶ 3003.

¶ 804 Penalties

Penalties are discussed at ¶ 3003.

¶ 805 Statute of Limitations on Assessments

Statutes of limitations on assessments are discussed at ¶ 3001.

¶ 806 Jeopardy Assessments

Jeopardy assessments are discussed at ¶ 3002.

¶ 807 Bankruptcy and Receivership

Law: Sec. 48-7-22(a) (3), Code (CCH GEORGIA TAX REPORTS ¶ 15-120).

Comparable Federal: Sec. 6012.

Trustees and receivers in bankruptcy are subject to tax as fiduciaries. The taxation of fiduciaries is discussed at ¶ 701.

¶ 808 Transferee Liability

Law: Sec. 48-7-128, Code (CCH GEORGIA TAX REPORTS ¶ 17-195).

Comparable Federal: Secs. 6013, 6901—6904 (U.S. MASTER TAX GUIDE ¶ 2743).

Forms: Form G-2RP, Withholding on Sales or Transfers of Real Property and Associated Tangible Personal Property by Nonresidents.

A purchaser or transferee of certain property sold by a nonresident is required to withhold personal income tax on the purchase and, if the transferee fails to withhold the tax, the transferee is personally liable for the tax (¶ 609).

¶ 803

> ***Practitioner Comment: Tax Clearance Letters***
> A purchaser or transferee of business assets may be liable for the unpaid withholding taxes of the seller unless he receives a tax clearance letter issued by the Department of Revenue, as discussed at ¶ 609.
>
> *Michael T. Petrik, Esq., Alston & Bird LLP*

¶ 809 Overpayments and Refunds

Overpayments and refunds are discussed at ¶ 3101.

¶ 810 Interest on Overpayments and Refunds

Interest on overpayments and refunds is discussed at ¶ 3003.

¶ 811 Abatement—Protest to Commissioner

Procedures for the abatement of taxes are discussed at ¶ 3101.

¶ 812 Statute of Limitations on Refund Claims

The statute of limitations on refund claims is discussed at ¶ 3101.

¶ 813 Judicial Review

Judicial review is discussed at ¶ 3101.

¶ 814 Settlements and Compromise of Tax

Settlements and compromise of tax are discussed at ¶ 3101.

PART III

CORPORATE INCOME TAX

CHAPTER 9

IMPOSITION OF TAX, RATES, EXEMPTIONS, CREDITS

¶ 901	Overview of Corporate Income Tax
¶ 902	Corporations Subject to Tax
¶ 903	Exempt Corporations
¶ 904	Tax Bases—In General
¶ 905	Tax Rate
¶ 906	Assignment of Credits to Affiliated Entities
¶ 907	Accounting Periods and Methods
¶ 908	Credits Against Tax—In General
¶ 909	Approved Retraining Programs Credit
¶ 910	Basic Skills Education Programs Credit
¶ 911	Credit for Employer-Provided Child Care
¶ 912	Consistent Net Taxable Income Growth Credit
¶ 913	Employment Increases (Job Tax Credits)
¶ 914	Transportation Fringe Benefits Credit
¶ 915	Clean Fueled Vehicles and Equipment Credits
¶ 916	Manufacturing and Telecommunications Facility Investment Credits
¶ 917	Research Expense Credit
¶ 918	Water Conservation Credits
¶ 919	Depository Financial Institutions Credit
¶ 920	Credits for Establishing Headquarters in Georgia
¶ 921	Cigarette Exports Credit
¶ 922	Low-Income Housing Credit
¶ 923	Credit for Employer-Provided Transportation
¶ 924	Credits for Increasing Port Traffic
¶ 925	Credit for Rehabilitation of Historic Property
¶ 926	Jobs Credit for New Manufacturing Facilities
¶ 927	Manufacturers' Credit for New Facilities

¶ 901 Overview of Corporate Income Tax

Law: Secs. 48-7-21(a), 48-7-25(a), 48-7-31, 48-7 128, Code.

Georgia corporate income tax is based on the federal income tax (¶ 904). Various adjustments are made to the federal base for Georgia tax purposes.

Current law is set forth in Title 48 of the Code of Georgia of 1981 as amended.

Corporate income tax is imposed on domestic and foreign corporations (¶ 902). Organizations that are exempt from federal income tax and insurance companies that pay gross premiums tax are exempt from corporate income tax (¶ 903).

The tax is imposed on taxable net income, *i.e.*, income from property owned and business done in Georgia (¶ 905). Several credits are available to taxpayers who qualify (¶ 908).

This chapter discusses the imposition of tax, rates, and exemptions. Chapter 10 covers computation of tax. Additions to the federal base are discussed in Chapter 11, and Chapter 12 deals with subtractions from federal base. Allocation and apportionment of income are covered in Chapter 13. Chapter 14 deals with returns, estimates, and payment of tax, while Chapter 15 discusses administrative provisions specific to corporate income taxes; however, general administrative provisions are covered in Chapter 29.

Corporate net worth (franchise) tax is discussed beginning with Chapter 16.

● *Internal Revenue Code references*

For taxable years beginning after 2003, Georgia conforms with the Internal Revenue Code as amended as of January 1, 2004. However, for Georgia corporate and personal income tax purposes, Georgia has not adopted the increased limits applicable to the expensing of assets under IRC Sec. 179 that were enacted by the federal Jobs and Growth Tax Relief Reconciliation Act (JGTRRA) (P.L. 108- 27).

Federal bonus depreciation: Georgia does not adopt the bonus depreciation provisions of IRC Sec. 168(k), nor the New York Liberty Zone provisions of IRC Sec. 1400L.

¶ 902 Corporations Subject to Tax

Law: Secs. 14-11-1104, 48-1-2(8) and (11), 48-7-1(l), 48-7-21(b)(7)(B), 48-7-31(a), Code; Reg. Sec. 560-7-7-.03 (CCH Georgia Tax Reports, ¶ 10-210—10-370).

Comparable Federal: Sec. 11 (U.S. Master Tax Guide ¶ 201).

The term "corporation" includes associations, professional associations, and insurance companies, as well as corporations.

● *Corporations doing business in Georgia*

A corporation engaging in any activity or transaction for the purpose of financial profit or gain within Georgia is doing business within Georgia. This is true regardless of whether the corporation qualifies to do business in Georgia, maintains an office or place of business within Georgia, or engages in any activity or transaction connected with interstate or foreign commerce.

¶ 902

Part III—Corporate Income Tax   **105**

● *Domestic or foreign corporations*

A corporation is domestic if it is created, organized, or domesticated in Georgia. A corporation is foreign if it is created or organized outside Georgia.

The current Business Corporation Act does not provide for the domestication of foreign corporations. However, foreign corporations domesticated before April 1, 1969, may retain their domesticated status until they are dissolved or otherwise cease to do business.

● *Banks and financial institutions*

Georgia adopts the federal income tax treatment of banks. A state occupation tax is also imposed on the gross receipts of depository financial institutions that conduct business or own property in the state (see Ch. 19). However, a dollar-for-dollar credit against corporate income tax liability is available to depository financial institutions in an amount equal to the occupation tax paid by the institution.

● *S corporations*

An election under IRC Subchapter S not to pay the federal income tax imposed on corporations, instead having the shareholders pay tax on their proportionate part of the corporation's taxable income, generally results in the same type of treatment for Georgia purposes.

● *Limited liability companies (LLCs)*

Georgia adopts the federal income tax treatment of limited liability companies (LLCs), as set out in the federal "check-the-box" regulations. For Georgia corporate income tax purposes, an LLC is classified as a corporation if it is classified as a corporation for federal income tax purposes. Georgia LLCs qualifying as partnerships are not subject to taxation; however, individual LLC members are taxed on their distributive share of LLC income.

● *DISCs and FSCs*

Georgia adopts the federal income tax treatment of domestic international sales corporations (DISCs) and foreign sales corporations (FSCs)

● *Corporate partners*

A C corporation is considered to own property or do business in Georgia if it is a limited or general partner in a partnership operating in Georgia.

● *Intangible property holding companies*

A common state tax planning method involves the creation of an affiliated corporate entity to hold intangible property, such as trademarks, trade names, service marks, or other intellectual property. The holding company subsidiary exists to own, manage, and protect the intellectual property. Licensing and royalty arrangements are used within this entity structure such that payments for the use of the intellectual property are made to the holding company for the rights to use the property. This company also may be referred to as a passive investment company (PIC).

¶ **902**

Holding company tax issues: Issues concerning a state's ability to tax the flow of value attributable to an intangible holding company have arisen in many states since the 1993 decision in *Geoffrey, Inc. v. South Carolina Tax Commission,* 313 S.C. 15, 437 S.E. 2d 13 (1993), cert. den. 510 U.S. 992, 114 S.Ct. 550, 126 L.Ed. 2d 451 (1993). In *Geoffrey,* the court determined that an out-of-state intangible holding company could be subject to tax in South Carolina based on its economic presence in the state, as well as the presence of the intangible property in the state. The primary rationale was that the licensing of intangibles for use in South Carolina and the receipt of income in exchange provided the minimal connection with the state required by the Due Process Clause. In addition, the court held that this business activity provided a substantial nexus with South Carolina and satisfied the requirements of the Commerce Clause.

Since the *Geoffrey* decision, many other states have addressed the issue of whether an affiliated out-of-state corporation licensing the use of intellectual property is subject to the taxing jurisdiction of the state. The U.S. Supreme Court has not provided a ruling on this issue.

Holding company tax issues arise in states where a corporation files its tax return on a separate return basis, typically because the payment made by the corporate parent to the PIC is taken as a deduction from the parent's income in the state. The issue does not arise if a combined report is filed including the parent and the holding company.

Georgia has not addressed the issue of intangible property holding companies.

¶903 Exempt Corporations

Law: Sec. 48-7-25, Code (CCH GEORGIA TAX REPORTS, ¶ 10-245).

Comparable Federal: Secs. 401, 501, 664 (U.S. MASTER TAX GUIDE ¶ 601—698).

Organizations that are exempt from federal income tax under IRC Secs. 401, 501(c), 501(d), 501(e), or 664 are exempt from Georgia corporate income tax in the same manner and to the same extent as for federal purposes.

● *Tax on unrelated business income*

An exempt organization that has unrelated business income from Georgia sources is subject to tax on such income.

● *Revocation of exempt status*

An organization's exempt status may be revoked if the IRS revokes the exempt status of the organization; the organization ceases to be organized or operated in the same manner as it was organized or operated when its exempt status was granted; the organization engages in any transaction prohibited by the IRC; or there is any material change in the organization's character, purpose, or mode of operation. A revocation is effective retroactively to the occurrence of the disqualifying event.

Part III—Corporate Income Tax   107

CCH Tip: *Procedure for Federally Exempt Organizations*

Organizations that had exempt status with the IRS on or before January 1, 1987, are not required to apply to the Georgia Income Tax Division for a tax exempt determination letter. Organizations that received IRS determination letters after that date and organizations desiring a Georgia income tax determination letter for any reason must apply using an Application for Recognition of Exemption (Form 3605). A nonprofit corporate charter does not constitute an exemption from corporate income tax (Georgia Corporate Income Tax Return Instructions, Form IT-611).

● *Insurance companies*

Insurance companies that pay gross premiums tax (¶ 2804) are also exempt.

¶ 904 Tax Bases—In General

Law: Sec. 48-7-21(a) and (b), Code (CCH GEORGIA TAX REPORTS ¶ 10-5050).

Comparable Federal: Sec. 63 (U.S. MASTER TAX GUIDE ¶ 214).

Foreign and domestic corporations must compute their Georgia corporate income tax on Georgia taxable net income, *i.e.,* taxable income from property owned or business done in Georgia, determined as follows:

—Start with the corporation's federal taxable income as defined in the IRC. Elections adopted for federal income tax purposes apply for Georgia income tax purposes except as provided for some S corporations.

—Make whatever adjustments are required under Sec. 48-7-21(b), *i.e.,* additions, subtractions, adjustments, net operating losses, credits, and exemptions (see Chapters 10 through 12).

—Allocate and apportion the taxable income after adjustments (see Chapter 13).

¶ 905 Tax Rate

Law: Secs. 48-7-21(a), 48-7-31(c) and (d), Code (CCH GEORGIA TAX REPORTS ¶ 10-380).

Comparable Federal: Sec. 11 (U.S. MASTER TAX GUIDE ¶ 33).

The tax is imposed at the rate of 6% on the basis of Georgia taxable net income, *i.e.,* the corporation's taxable income from property owned and business done in Georgia.

¶ 906 Assignment of Credits to Affiliated Entities

Law: Sec. 48-7-42, Code (CCH GEORGIA TAX REPORTS ¶ 12-001).

A corporation that receives any credit against Georgia corporate income tax may elect to assign that credit in whole or in part to one or more affiliated entities. An affiliated entity is a member of the corporation's "affiliated

¶ 906

group," as defined in IRC Sec. 1504(a) or an entity affiliated with the taxpayer that (1) owns or leases the land where a project is constructed, (2) provides capital for construction of the project, and (3) is the grantor or owner under a management agreement with a managing company of the project. If the assignor and recipient of a tax credit end their affiliation, any carryover is transferred back to the assignor. The assignor and recipient of the assigned credit are jointly and severally liable for any tax, interest, or penalties owed if the assigned credit is disallowed or recaptured.

¶ 907 Accounting Periods and Methods

Law: Secs. 48-7-1(4), 48-7-33, Code (CCH Georgia Tax Reports ¶ 10-520).

Comparable Federal: Secs. 446—482 (U.S. Master Tax Guide ¶ 1501—1577).

For Georgia corporate income tax purposes, the annual accounting period and the accounting method regularly employed in keeping the taxpayer's books are used in the computation of the taxpayer's net income. However, taxpayers may be required to use a method clearly reflecting income if no accounting method is employed or the method used does not clearly reflect income.

● *Calendar year*

Ordinarily, net income is computed on the basis of the calendar year. If a taxpayer does not have an accounting period or does not keep books, or if the taxpayer's accounting period is not a fiscal year, the taxpayer must compute net income on the basis of the calendar year.

● *Fiscal year*

An accounting period of 12 months ending on the last day of any month other than December is a fiscal year. If a year consisting of 52 to 53 weeks has been elected for federal income tax purposes, that year is a fiscal year.

With the State Revenue Commissioner's approval, a taxpayer using a fiscal year may return net income on the basis of its fiscal year.

● *Change in taxable year*

In changing its taxable year, a taxpayer may use the new taxable year to compute net income only if the Commissioner's approval was obtained at least 30 days before the close of the new taxable year.

● *Change in applicable law*

If it is necessary to compute the tax for a period beginning in one calendar year and ending in the following calendar year, and the applicable law has changed, the tax is computed by calculating the tax for each year involved as if that year's law applied to the entire amount, then taking the proportion of each year's total as the amount of the period falling in that year bears to the total period, and adding the two amounts together.

Part III—Corporate Income Tax

¶908 Credits Against Tax—In General

Georgia corporate income tax credits are authorized for many employment related purposes. In addition to the jobs tax credits for increasing employment (¶913), establishing headquarters in Georgia (¶920), and increasing port traffic (¶924), there are credits for approved retraining programs (¶909), basic skills education programs (¶910), child care provided by employers (¶911), federal qualified transportation fringe benefits (¶914), and employer-provided transportation (¶923). Other credits are available for consistent net taxable income growth (¶912), clean fueled vehicles (¶915), manufacturing and telecommunications facility investments (¶916), research expenses (¶917), water conservation (¶918), depository financial institutions (¶919), increasing cigarette exports (¶921), low-income housing (¶922), and rehabilitation of historic property (¶925).

Manufacturing facilities are encouraged by a credit for new jobs (¶926), and a credit for an existing Georgia manufacturer that builds new facilities costing at least $800 million. (¶927)

● *Tier-ranked counties*

Requirements and amounts for certain jobs credits may vary by the tier ranking of the various Georgia counties, as determined annually by the Commissioner of Community Affairs.

"Tier 1 counties" are the first through 71st least-developed counties, "tier 2 counties" are the 72nd through 106th least-developed counties, "tier 3 counties" are the 107th through 141st least-developed counties, and "tier 4 counties" are the 142nd through 159th least-developed counties.

● *Assignment of credits*

As discussed at ¶906, credits may be assigned to affiliated entities.

● *Priority of credits*

Georgia does not require that credits be claimed in a particular order.

¶909 Approved Retraining Programs Credit

Law: Sec. 48-7-40.5, Code (CCH Georgia Tax Reports ¶12-075a).

Employers that provide or sponsor an approved retraining program for employees may receive a credit against corporate income tax.

Credit amount: The credit amount is equal to one-half the costs of retraining or $500 per full-time employee, whichever is less, for each employee who has successfully completed an approved retraining program.

CCH Tip: Calculating the Retraining Credit

Separate calculations are required for classes costing less than $1,000 and those costing $1,000 or more. For example, if 10 employees take an approved class costing $250, a Form IT-RC would be prepared claiming a credit of $1,250 (half the cost of the

¶909

class for each employee). If two other employees take an approved class in the same tax year costing $5,000 each, a separate Form IT-RC would be prepared claiming a credit of $1,000 (the maximum credit of $500 for each employee). The amount of the retraining credit claimed on the return for the tax year would be the aggregate of the two forms, or $2,250 (Policy Statement IT-2001-12-1-1, Georgia Department of Revenue, December 1, 2001).

Limitations and carryovers: The credit may not exceed 50% of the amount of the taxpayer's income tax liability for the taxable year as computed without regard to this credit. An employer may not receive the credit if its employees are required to reimburse or pay the employer for the cost of retraining.

Unused credit amounts may be carried forward 10 years from the close of the taxable year when the credit was granted.

¶ 910 Basic Skills Education Programs Credit

Law: Sec. 48-7-41, Code (CCH GEORGIA TAX REPORTS ¶ 12-075).

Employers that provide approved basic skills education programs for their employees may receive a credit against corporate income tax. An approved basic skills education is employer-provided or employer-sponsored education that enhances reading, writing, or mathematical skills to the 12th grade level. Education costs include direct instructional costs, instructor salaries, materials, supplies, and textbooks.

Credit amount: The credit amount for each employee successfully completing an approved basic skills education program is the lesser of one-third of the cost per full-time equivalent student or $150 per full-time equivalent student.

Limitations: The credit may not exceed the amount of the tax liability for the tax year, and there is no provision for carryover of any excess credit. An employer may not receive the credit if the employee is required to reimburse or pay the employer for the education costs. The credit does not apply to costs associated with renting or securing space.

Filing requirements: The employer must certify the name of the employee, the course work successfully completed by the employee, the name of the approved basic skills education provider, and other information required to ensure that credits are granted only to employers that provide or sponsor approved basic skills education and only with respect to employees who successfully complete such approved basic skills education.

¶ 911 Credits for Employer-Provided Child Care

Law: Sec. 48-7-40.6, Code (CCH GEORGIA TAX REPORTS ¶ 12-110a).

Employers that provide or sponsor child care for their employees may receive a credit against corporate income tax based on their operational costs.

¶ 910

Part III—Corporate Income Tax

Credit amount: The credit amount is equal to 75% of the cost of operation to the employer, minus any amounts paid by the employees during a taxable year.

Limitations and carryovers: The credit may not exceed 50% of the amount of the taxpayer's income tax liability for the taxable year as computed without regard to any other credits.

Credit amounts claimed but not used may be carried forward for five years from the close of the taxable year when the cost was incurred.

● *Credit for placing qualified child care property into service*

An additional credit is available to employers for the cost of qualified child care property.

Qualified child care property: Qualified child care property includes tangible personal property and real property acquired or purchased on or after July 1, 1999. This property must be used solely for improving, expanding, constructing, or operating a child care facility operated by an employer with the following limitations: (1) the facility must be commissioned or licensed by the Department of Human Resources; (2) at least 95% of children using the facility must be the children of the taxpayer's employees, children of employees of joint and several owners of the facility, or children of employees of a corporation in the taxpayer's affiliated group; and (3) the taxpayer must not have claimed credit for operating costs of such a facility before taxable years beginning on or after January 1, 2000. Qualified child care property also includes funds spent on acquiring land, fixtures, improvements, buildings, equipment, building improvements, and furniture.

Credit amount: The credit amount equals 100% of the cost of the qualified property, to be claimed at 10% per year over 10 years, but may not equal more than 50% of the tax liability for a given year. An employer's Georgia taxable income must be increased by any depreciation deductions attributable to qualified child care property that are taken in determining the employer's federal taxable income.

Carryforward of credit: Any credit claimed but not used in a given tax year may be carried forward three years.

Recapture of credit: The credit is subject to recapture under certain circumstances.

CCH Tip: Filing Requirements

The taxpayer must attach a schedule to the return showing (1) a description of the facility, (2) amounts of qualified property acquired during the tax year and their cost, (3) the amount of the credit claimed for the tax year, (4) amounts and costs of qualified property acquired in previous tax years, (5) any tax credits claimed in previous tax years, (6) amounts of tax credit carried forward from previous years, (7) amounts of tax credits currently used, (8) the amount of tax credit being carried forward to subsequent years, and (9) a description of any recapture event that has occurred during the tax year, a calculation of the reduction in allowable tax

¶911

credits in the recapture and future tax years, and a calculation of the tax increase for the recapture year.

¶912 Consistent Net Taxable Income Growth Credit

Law: Sec. 48-7-40.13, Code (CCH GEORGIA TAX REPORTS ¶ 12-085b).

Eligibility and credit amount: A Georgia business with a current year net taxable income that exceeds the net taxable income of the prior year by 20% or more, and whose net taxable income for the previous two years exceeded the net taxable income of the prior years by 20% or more, may receive a credit against corporate income tax for the current year growth that exceeds 20% of current net taxable income.

Businesses eligible for the consistent net taxable income growth credit include those engaged in manufacturing, warehousing and distribution, processing, telecommunications, tourism, and research and development. Retail businesses are not eligible for the credit.

Limitations and carryovers: The credit may not exceed 50% of the business's Georgia net income tax liability after all other credits have been applied. The credit may not be applied if the total Georgia income tax liability, before the credit is applied, exceeds $1.5 million. Unused credit may not be carried backward or forward.

Practitioner Comment: Priority of Credits

While Georgia does not have formal rules regarding the order in which credits must be used, the statute does provide that, with respect to this credit and the research expense credit (see ¶ 917), the amount of the credit is limited to 50% of the enterprise's Georgia net income tax liability *after all other credits have been applied.* The Department interprets this language to require that these two credits be taken last.

Jeffrey C. Glickman, Esq., Alston & Bird LLP

¶913 Employment Increases (Job Tax Credits)

Law: Secs. 36-62-5.1, 48-7-40—48-7-40.4, 48-7-40.21, 48-7-40.22, Code; Reg. Sec. 560-7-8-.36 (CCH GEORGIA TAX REPORTS ¶ 12-070, 12-070a).

Certain businesses that increase their number of employees may receive a job tax credit against corporate income tax. Minimum qualifying increases depend on the county and year in which the jobs are created. The counties are ranked into tiers on the bases of their unemployment rate, per capita income level, percentage of residents below poverty level, and average weekly manufacturing wage, with the least developed counties designated as tier 1 counties and the most developed counties designated as tier 3 or 4 counties.

Eligible areas and businesses: In counties recognized and designated as the first through 40th least developed counties in the tier 1 designation, a

¶912

Part III—Corporate Income Tax 113

business of any nature may receive the credit. In other counties, only business enterprises, *i.e.*, any business or headquarters of a business engaged in manufacturing, telecommunications, warehousing and distribution, processing, tourism, or research and development, may receive the credit. The term "business enterprise" does not include retail businesses.

The Georgia Commissioner of Community Affairs is authorized to designate the following additional areas as less developed:

—any area comprised of one or more census tracts adjacent to a federal military installation where pervasive poverty is evidenced by a poverty rate of at least 15% as reflected in the most recent federal decennial census, and

—any area comprised of two or more contiguous census block groups with a poverty rate of at least 20% as determined from data in the most recent federal decennial census, if the area is also located within a state enterprise zone; a redevelopment plan has been adopted; and in the Commissioner's opinion the area displays pervasive poverty, underdevelopment, general distress, and blight.

In areas determined to be suffering from pervasive poverty, credits may be claimed by any lawful business and are not limited to business enterprises. Also, for credit eligibility purposes, new jobs created by a taxpayer are not required to be held by residents of less developed areas.

Allowance of credit: The job tax credit is allowed over a five year period for each new full-time job created above the minimum number required, provided that the job was created within seven years after the business first became eligible. The credit is claimed in years two through six after the creation of the job. The credit is not allowed during a year if the net employment increase falls below the number required in such tier, but any credit received for years prior to a year when the net employment increase falls below the minimum number of jobs required to earn the credit is not affected. The State Revenue Commissioner adjusts the credit allowed for each year for net new employment fluctuations above the minimum number.

The sale, merger, acquisition, or bankruptcy of any business enterprise does not create new eligibility for job tax credits in any succeeding entity, but any unused credits may be transferred and continued by any transferee of the business enterprise.

Credit amount: For tax years beginning on or after January 1, 2001, the amount of the annual credit is equal to the following for each new full-time job created: (1) $3,500 for a tier 1 business that increases employment by at least five employees; (2) $2,500 for a tier 2 business that increases employment by at least 10 employees; (3) $1,250 for a tier 3 business that increases employment by at least 15 employees; and (4) $750 for a tier 4 business that increases employment by at least 25 employees.

Limitation on credit: The maximum jobs credit amount that may be claimed by a taxpayer in a single taxable year is 100% of the taxpayer's Georgia corporate or personal income tax liability attributable to income derived from operations in Georgia during that taxable year.

¶913

The average wage of all new jobs created must exceed the lowest average wage of any county in Georgia.

Carryforward of credit: Unused credits may be carried forward for 10 years from the close of the taxable year when the qualified jobs were established.

Health insurance requirement: For tax years beginning on or after January 1, 2001, to qualify for the credit, employers must make health insurance coverage available to the employee filling the new full-time job. However, the employer is not required to pay for all or any part of such insurance coverage.

● *Additional credits*

Additional credits are available for a period of five years for qualified business enterprises that create additional new full-time jobs. Additional new full-time jobs are to be determined by subtracting the highest total employment of the business enterprise during years two through six. The State Revenue Commissioner adjusts the credit allowed in the event of employment fluctuations during the additional five years of credit.

Also, business enterprises that are located in one or more joint development authority jurisdictions qualify for an additional $500 credit for each new job created. A joint development authority is an active, bona fide joint authority created by two or more contiguous counties that has a board of directors, meets at least quarterly, and develops an operational business plan.

● *Jobs tax credit for increasing port traffic*

An additional job tax credit is available to business enterprises increasing their port traffic at in-state facilities (¶ 924).

● *Business expansion credit against withholding tax*

Effective for tax years beginning after 2000, an existing business enterprise, not including a retail business, that creates 500 new jobs and has a beneficial effect on the region for which it is planned may offset the jobs credit that it cannot use in the current year or that is carried over from prior years against the withholding tax liability of the business.

The credit is available only if the total credit exceeds 50% of the business' tax liability and may not exceed $5 million. The business may use this credit up to five years for each year that 500 new jobs are created. Any unused credit may be carried forward for ten years.

If the business does not meet the minimum job requirement, the credit is subject to recapture. Each employee whose employer receives a credit will also receive a credit against his or her Georgia personal income tax liability for the corresponding tax year for the full amount of the credit that the employer received for the employee's withholding taxes (¶ 125).

¶ 913

Part III—Corporate Income Tax

¶ 914 Transportation Fringe Benefits Credit

Law: Sec. 48-7-29.3, Code (CCH GEORGIA TAX REPORTS ¶ 12-125).

Comparable Federal: Sec. 132(f) (U.S. MASTER TAX GUIDE ¶ 863).

Taxpayers that provide federally qualified transportation fringe benefits to their employees may receive a credit against corporate income tax.

Credit amount: The credit amount is $25 for each employee who receives the benefit in addition to the employee's compensation.

Limitations and carryovers: The credit amount may not exceed the annual benefit expenditure or the taxpayer's total income tax liability.

Any unused credit may be carried forward for three successive years, but may not be used against liability from prior years.

¶ 915 Clean Fueled Vehicles and Equipment Credits

Law: Secs. 48-7-40.16, 48-7-40.19, Code; Reg. Sec. 391-3-25-.01 (CCH GEORGIA TAX REPORTS ¶ 12-080b, 12-080c).

A taxpayer that purchases or leases a new clean fueled vehicle (a low-emission vehicle or zero-emission vehicle) or converts a conventional vehicle to a clean fueled vehicle may receive a credit against corporate income tax if the vehicle is registered in Georgia.

Credit amount: The credit amount for each new low-emission vehicle is the lesser of 10% of the vehicle's cost or $2,500. The credit for a new zero-emission vehicle is the lesser of 20% of the vehicle's cost or $5,000.

For converted vehicles, the credit amount equals the cost of conversion, but no more than $2,500 for each converted vehicle.

Qualifying vehicles: The vehicle must be registered in Georgia. A low-emission vehicle must operate on alternative fuel and meet the emission standards set by the Georgia Board of Natural Resources. A zero-emission vehicle may have no tailpipe or evaporative emissions.

Low-speed vehicles designed to transport 10 passengers or less could qualify for the credit, but only if the low-speed vehicle was placed in service during 2001.

Carryforward of credit: The credit may be carried forward five years.

● Electric vehicle chargers

A business that purchases or leases an electric vehicle charger located in Georgia may receive a credit against corporate income tax.

Credit amount: The credit amount is equal to $2,500 per charger or 10% of the cost of the charger, whichever is less.

Limitations and carryovers: This credit may be claimed only by an ultimate purchaser or lessee of a new electric vehicle charger at retail. This credit may be carried forward five years.

¶ 915

● *Equipment to reduce diesel particulate emissions*

Taxpayers may receive a credit against corporate income tax for installing diesel particulate emission reduction technology equipment at a truck stop, depot, or other facility.

Credit amount: The credit amount is 10% of the cost of the equipment and installation.

Limitations and carryovers: The credit is allowed for the tax year when the taxpayer first places the equipment in use. This credit may not be carried forward.

¶916 Manufacturing and Telecommunications Facility Investment Credits

Law: Secs. 48-7-40, 48-7-40.2—48-7-40.4, 48-7-40.7—48-7-40.9, Code; Reg. Secs. 560-7-8-.37, 560-7-8-.40 (CCH GEORGIA TAX REPORTS ¶ 12-055a, 12-055b).

A taxpayer that operated a manufacturing facility, manufacturing support facility, telecommunications facility, or telecommunications support facility in Georgia for the three years immediately preceding the tax year and that purchases or acquires qualified investment property during the tax year may receive a regular investment tax credit or an optional investment tax credit against corporate income tax. "Qualified investment property" means all real and personal property purchased or acquired by a taxpayer for use in constructing an additional manufacturing or telecommunications facility in Georgia or expanding an existing manufacturing or telecommunications facility in Georgia, including amounts expended on land acquisition, improvements, buildings, building improvements, and machinery and equipment to be used in the manufacturing or telecommunications facility.

● *Regular investment credit*

Once the investment requirements discussed below are satisfied, the regular investment tax credit may be taken beginning with the tax year immediately following the tax year when the taxpayer purchases or acquires qualified investment property having an aggregate cost of more than $50,000.

Credit amount: The credit amount depends on the type of qualified investment property and the county where the facility is located. The counties are ranked into tiers on the bases of their unemployment rate, per capita income level, percentage of residents below poverty level, and average weekly manufacturing wage, with the least developed counties designated as tier 1 counties and the most developed counties designated as tier 3 or 4 counties (¶ 908). A greater credit amount is allowed in less developed counties and for property used for recycling, pollution control or prevention, or conversion from defense to domestic production.

For taxpayers in tier 1 counties, the credit amount is 8% of the cost of property used for recycling, pollution control or prevention, or conversion from defense to domestic production, or 5% of the cost of other property. For taxpayers in tier 2 counties, the credit amount is 5% of the cost of property used for recycling, pollution control or prevention, or conversion from defense to domestic production, or 3% of the cost of other property. For taxpayers in

Part III—Corporate Income Tax 117

tier 3 counties and tier 4 counties, the credit amount is 3% of the cost of property used for recycling, pollution control or prevention, or conversion from defense to domestic production, or 1% of the cost of other property.

Investment requirements: To qualify for the credit, taxpayers must purchase or acquire qualified investment property pursuant to a project plan, must have operated an existing manufacturing or telecommunications facility or related support facility in Georgia for three years, and must have previously filed any required state tax returns. Only qualified investment property purchased or acquired by taxpayers after the three year eligibility requirement is satisfied may be used to compute the credit. Taxpayers may not file an amended return to claim a credit for qualified investment property purchases or acquisitions before eligibility is established.

Application for credit: Taxpayers must submit a written application for approval of the project plan within 30 days of completing the project. Late applications require the Commissioner's express written approval.

Limitations and carryovers: The amount of credit taken in any one taxable year is limited to 50% of the taxpayer's state income tax liability that is attributable to income derived from operations in Georgia for the taxable year. However, unused credits may be carried forward up to ten years from the close of the taxable year of the acquisition, so long as the property remains in service.

Coordination with jobs credit: Generally, a taxpayer may not claim the investment credit for a given project in the same taxable year that it claims a job tax credit (¶ 913).

Succession to credit: The sale, merger, acquisition, or bankruptcy of the taxpayer does not create new eligibility for the investment tax credit in any succeeding entity, but any unused investment tax credit may be transferred and continued by any transferee of the taxpayer.

● Optional investment tax credit

As an alternative to the regular investment tax credit discussed above, taxpayers may receive an optional investment credit against corporate income tax that may be taken over a 10-year period. For purposes of this credit, qualified investment property must be first placed in service in the designated county and must remain in service throughout the 10-year period. Furthermore, an election to take this optional credit is irrevocable.

Optional credit amount: The annual optional credit amount is (1) 90% of the excess of the taxpayer's state income tax liability for the applicable tax year (without regard to any credit) over the taxpayer's base year average tax liability or (2) the excess of the taxpayer's aggregate credit amount allowed for the applicable year over the sum of the credits already used in the years following the base year, whichever is less. "Base year" means the taxable year when the qualified investment property is first placed in service. "Base year average" means the sum of the amount of tax owed by the taxpayer for the base year and for each of the two immediately preceding taxable years, without regard to any credits, divided by three.

¶ 916

Limitations and investment requirements: If the qualified investment property is first placed in service in a tier 1 county, the aggregate credit amount may not exceed 10% of the cost of all qualified investment property first placed into service during the taxable year and the property must have an aggregate cost exceeding $5 million. If the qualified investment property is first placed in service in a tier 2 county, the aggregate amount of the credit may not exceed 8% of the cost of the qualified investment property and the property must have an aggregate cost exceeding $10 million. If the qualified investment property is first placed in service in a tier 3 or tier 4 county, the aggregate amount of the credit may not exceed 6% of the cost of the qualified investment property and the property must have an aggregate cost exceeding $20 million.

Application for credit: To qualify for the credit, a taxpayer must purchase or acquire qualified investment property pursuant to a project plan and must submit a written application requesting approval of the plan within 30 days of completing the project. Late applications require the Commissioner's express written approval.

Coordination with jobs credit: A taxpayer that elects to take the optional investment tax credit may not claim either the job tax credit (¶ 913) or the regular investment tax credit (see above) for a given project.

Alternative investment tax credits available to businesses increasing their port traffic at in-state facilities are discussed at ¶ 924.

¶ 917 Research Expense Credit

Law: Sec. 48-7-40.12, Code; Reg. Sec. 560-7-8-.42 (CCH GEORGIA TAX REPORTS ¶ 12-065).

Comparable Federal: Sec. 41 (U.S. MASTER TAX GUIDE ¶ 1330).

Georgia businesses that are allowed a federal income tax credit for qualified research expenses also may receive a credit against Georgia corporate income tax. All wages paid and all purchases of services and supplies must be for research conducted within Georgia.

Eligible businesses: Eligible businesses include those engaged in manufacturing, warehousing and distribution, processing, telecommunications, tourism, and research and development. Retail businesses are not eligible for the credit.

Credit amount: The credit amount is equal to 10% of the excess over the base amount. The base amount is the taxpayer's Georgia taxable net income in the current taxable year multiplied by the average of the ratios of its aggregate qualified research expenses to Georgia taxable net income for the preceding three taxable years or 0.3, whichever is less. Therefore, in order to qualify for the credit, a business must have positive Georgia taxable net income for the preceding three tax years.

Limitations and carryovers: The credit in one year may not exceed 50% of the taxpayer's remaining Georgia net income tax liability after all other credits have been applied. Any unused credit can be carried forward for 10 years.

Part III—Corporate Income Tax   **119**

¶ 918   Water Conservation Credits

Law: Secs. 48-7-40.10, 48-7-40.11, Code (CCH GEORGIA TAX REPORTS ¶ 12-080, 12-080a).

Credits against corporate income tax are available to businesses that shift from using groundwater to using water from a qualified water conservation facility and that financially participate in qualified water conservation investments.

● *Shift to use of water from conservation facility*

Taxpayers that shift from using groundwater to using water from a qualified water conservation facility may receive a credit against Georgia corporate income tax. The credit is first available in the fourth taxable year following the shift. To qualify for the credit, a taxpayer must relinquish at least 10% of its groundwater usage and must instead purchase water from a qualified water conservation facility.

Documentation required: In the initial year in which the taxpayer claims the credit, a certificate of verification by the Department of Natural Resources must be submitted as proof that the taxpayer shifted from the groundwater usage. In addition, in every year in which the taxpayer claims the credit, a schedule must be attached to the taxpayer's income tax return stating (1) the amount of ground-water usage permitted to the taxpayer in the first permit issued after July 1, 1996, (2) the ground-water usage permitted to the taxpayer four years prior to the current tax year, (3) the ground-water usage permitted the taxpayer in the current year, and (4) the amount of the credit used by the taxpayer in the current year.

Credit amount: The credit amount equals $0.0001 for every gallon of groundwater relinquished and transferred from an annual groundwater permit that was issued to the taxpayer after July 1, 1996.

Limitations: The credit may not exceed 50% of the taxpayer's tax liability as determined before any other credits are applied and, if the annual permit for the same groundwater increases after a taxpayer is approved for the credit, the taxpayer's eligibility to use the credit will expire immediately.

● *Water conservation investment credit*

Taxpayers that financially participate in qualified water conservation investments in a modified manufacturing process or a new or expanded water conservation facility that is placed in service on or after January 1, 1997, may receive a credit against Georgia corporate income tax. A lease for five years or more of real or personal property resulting from a qualified water conservation investment qualifies as a water conservation investment by the lessee.

Documentation required: The first year the credit is claimed, the taxpayer must include a description of the project meeting the requirements and a copy of certification from the Department of Natural Resources. In each year that the credit is claimed, the taxpayer must attach a schedule to the income tax return stating the following: (1) amounts, dates, and nature of investments which have allowed the facilities to be placed in service in the prior taxable year; (2) amounts and dates of reductions in permitted groundwater usage because of this investment; (3) amount of tax credit claimed for

¶ 918

the current tax year; (4) amounts of the investments reported for tax years preceding the prior tax year; (5) amounts of tax credit used in prior tax years; (6) amounts of tax credits carried over from previous tax years; (7) amounts of tax credits used in the current tax year; and (8) amounts of tax credits to be carried over to subsequent tax years.

Credit amount: The credit amount is equal to a percentage of the taxpayer's qualified water conservation investment that is based on the cost of the project as follows: for projects costing between $50,000 and $499,999, the credit is 10% of the taxpayer's investment; for projects costing between $500,000 and $799,999, the credit is 8% of the taxpayer's investment; for projects costing between $800,000 and $999,999, the credit is 6% of the taxpayer's investment; and for projects costing $1 million and over, the credit is 5% of the taxpayer's investment.

Credit period: The credit becomes available the tax year following the year when either the modified manufacturing process or the new or expanded water conservation facility has been placed in service and when the taxpayer has initiated at least a 10% reduction in the permit by the relinquishment or transfer of annual permitted water usage from existing permitted groundwater sources. If the annual permit for water usage from the same groundwater source is increased, unused credits will immediately expire.

Limitations and carryovers: Regardless of any other credits, the amount of credit used in any tax year may not exceed 50% of that year's tax liability.

The credit may be carried forward for up to 10 years if the property remains in service and continues to be used by the taxpayer and if the reduction in the permit is maintained.

¶ 919 Depository Financial Institutions Credit

Law: Secs. 48-6-93, 48-6-95, 48-7-29.7 (CCH GEORGIA TAX REPORTS ¶ 14-050).

Comparable Federal: Sec. 381(a).

Depository financial institutions may deduct a dollar-for-dollar credit against their Georgia corporate income tax liability.

Deduction amount: The deduction amount is equal to the local business license tax and special state occupation tax paid.

Carryovers: Any unused credit arising due to an excess of the gross receipts and occupation taxes paid over the income tax liability may be carried forward for a period of five years from the tax year in which the unused credit arose.

Acquiring institution eligible for credit: If the assets of an institution are acquired by another institution in a corporate acquisition transaction described in IRC Sec. 381(a), the acquiring institution will be entitled to any unused credit of the distributor or transferor institution.

● *S corporations—Pass through of credit to shareholders*

For depository financial institutions that elected S corporation status, the dollar-for-dollar credit may be passed through on a *pro rata* basis to the institution's shareholders. The amount of passed through credit that exceeds

Part III—Corporate Income Tax

the shareholder's income tax liability may be carried forward five years, but may not be applied against the tax liability for a prior year.

¶ 920 Credits for Establishing Headquarters in Georgia

Law: Secs. 48-7-40.17, 48-7-40.18, Code; Reg. Sec. 560-8-7-.14 (CCH GEORGIA TAX REPORTS ¶ 12-085d).

A taxpayer that establishes or relocates its headquarters or, beginning in 2003, the headquarters of a subsidiary in Georgia may receive a credit against Georgia corporate income tax if the taxpayer (1) within one year after it first withholds wages, employs at least 50 persons at the headquarters in new full-time jobs (2) within one year after it first withholds wages, incurs within the state at least $1 million in construction, renovation, leasing, or other costs related to the establishment or relocation, and (3) elects not to receive other tax credits for the jobs.

The new jobs must pay at least the following wages:

—in Tier 1 counties, the average wage;

—in Tier 2 counties, 105% of the average wage;

—in Tier 3 counties, 110% of the average wage;

—in Tier 4 counties, 115% of the average wage;

Credit amount: The credit amount is $2,500 annually per eligible new full-time job, or $5,000 if the average wage of the new full-time jobs created is 200% or more of the average wage of the county in which the jobs are located.

Credit period: The credit may be taken for the first taxable year in which the taxpayer first becomes eligible for the credit and for the four succeeding taxable years, provided that the job was created within seven years of the taxpayer's first eligibility.

Carryovers: Unused credits may be carried forward for 10 years from the close of the taxable year in which the qualified jobs were established. Alternatively, the taxpayer may elect to apply the credit against its quarterly or monthly withholding tax payment. Form IT-JOBW is used for this purpose.

● *Additional credit*

A variation of the above credit is available for business enterprises, *i.e.*, businesses or business headquarters engaged in manufacturing, warehousing and distribution, processing, telecommunications, tourism, or research and development industries, that establish their headquarters in Georgia or relocate their headquarters to Georgia and enter into an allocation and apportionment agreement with the Georgia State Revenue Commissioner. This credit is not available to retail businesses. Eligibility for the credit begins in the tax year the business headquarters is established in Georgia.

Credit amount and applicability of credit: The credit is calculated in the same fashion as the credit described above, and in general, the same definitions, limitations, and carryforward provisions apply. However, in the first taxable year this credit is claimed, a business enterprise may apply all or part of the credit against its tax liability for the immediately preceding year by amending its returns for that year. In addition, the business enterprise may claim the credit for full-time jobs created before the taxable year when it establishes or relocates its headquarters, provided that the jobs are in excess of those in the business enterprise's allocation and apportionment agreement and are located at the headquarters. Such jobs are deemed to be created on the first day of the taxable year when the business enterprise establishes or relocates its headquarters.

Limitation: The total amount of credits available under this provision may not exceed $25 million.

¶ 921 Cigarette Exports Credit

Law: Sec. 48-7-40.20, Code (CCH GEORGIA TAX REPORTS ¶ 12-085c).

Cigarette manufacturing businesses that export cigarettes to foreign countries may receive a credit against Georgia corporate income tax.

Credit amount: The credit amount is determined by comparing the corporation's volume of exports in the year when the credit is claimed with the corporation's base year exportation volume, rounded to the nearest whole percentage. The amount of the credit per 1,000 cigarettes exported ranges from 40 cents for corporations with current year export volume of 120% or more of their base year volume to 20 cents for corporations with current year export volume of 50% to 59% of their base year volume.

Limitations and carryovers: Corporations with a current year export volume of less than 50% of base year volume are not eligible for the credit. The cumulative amount of the credit allowed in any tax year, including carryovers from previous tax years, may not exceed $6 million or 50% of corporate income taxes owed, whichever is less, reduced by the sum of all other allowable credits.

Unused portions of the credit may be carried forward for five years.

Expiration of credit: The credit expires on January 1, 2006.

¶ 922 Low-Income Housing Credit

Law: Sec. 48-7-29.6, Code (CCH GEORGIA TAX REPORTS ¶ 12-105).

Comparable Federal: Sec. 42 (U.S. MASTER TAX GUIDE ¶ 1334).

Taxpayers may receive a credit against Georgia corporate income tax for each Georgia housing project that qualifies as a low-income building under IRC Sec. 42 and that is placed in service after January 1, 2001.

Credit amount: The credit amount is equal to the federal low-income housing tax credit allowed with respect to the qualified project.

Limitations and carryovers: Credits claimed by a taxpayer may not exceed the taxpayer's liability for insurance taxes, but unused portions of the credit may be carried forward for a period of three years. Unused credits may not be carried back.

Allocation of credit: The credit may be allocated among some or all of the partners, members, or shareholders of the entity owning the project, regardless of whether such persons are allocated or allowed any portion of the federal housing tax credit with respect to the project.

Part III—Corporate Income Tax

Recapture of credit: If any portion of the federal housing tax credit is recaptured, the state tax credit must be recaptured proportionally. However, the Georgia credit is not subject to recapture if the federal recapture is due solely to the sale or transfer of any direct or indirect interest in the housing project by an exempt organization.

¶ 923 Credit for Employer-Provided Transportation

Law: Sec. 48-7-40.22, Code (CCH GEORGIA TAX REPORTS ¶ 12-055c).

A corporate income tax credit is available to any business located in a tier 1 or tier 2 county (¶ 908) that purchases or leases a new motor vehicle that is used exclusively for providing transportation for its employees.

Credit amount: A business located in a tier 1 county receives a $3,000 credit for each vehicle purchased or leased, and a business located in a tier 2 county receives a $2,000 credit for each qualified vehicle.

Planning considerations: The business must certify that each vehicle for which a credit is claimed has an average daily ridership of at least four employees. This credit may not exceed the business' income tax liability and may be carried forward for one year. Also, the taxpayer may not claim both this credit and the low-emission vehicle credit (¶ 915).

Recapture provisions: If the business enterprise sells this vehicle within:

—one year of receiving the credit, then the business must recapture the lesser of the credit amount or the net profit from the sale;

—two years of receiving the credit, then the business must recapture the lesser of two-thirds of the credit amount or the net profit from the sale; or

—three years of receiving the credit, then the business must recapture the lesser of one-third of the credit amount or the net profit from the sale.

However, these recapture provisions will not apply to:

—any sale by reason of death;

—any sale between spouses or incident to divorce;

—any transaction to which IRC Sec. 381(a) applies;

—any change in the form of conducting the taxpayer's trade or business, as long as the property is retained in the trade or business and the taxpayer retains a substantial interest in the trade or business; or

—any accident or casualty.

¶ 924 Credits for Increasing Port Traffic

Law: Sec. 48-7-40.15, Code (CCH GEORGIA TAX REPORTS ¶ 12-085, 12-085a).

Two corporate income tax credits are available for business enterprises that increase their port traffic at in-state facilities. The credits are tied to the jobs tax credit (¶ 913) and the manufacturer's and telecommunications investment credits (¶ 916). As is the case for those credits, business enterprises eligible for the port traffic credits are those engaged in manufacturing, warehousing and distribution, processing, telecommunications, tourism, or research and development, but not those engaged in retail businesses. The requisite increase in port traffic is determined on the basis of an enterprise's base year port traffic, which generally is the enterprise's port traffic during the 1997 calendar year, subject to a minimum traffic level.

● *Additional new jobs credit*

An additional new jobs tax credit is allowed for any business enterprise that increases its port traffic of products during the previous 12-month period by more than 10% above its base year port traffic and that is also qualified to claim the job tax credit for new full-time jobs created in any Georgia county after 1997.

Credit amount: The amount of the credit is $1,250. This credit is in addition to the credit amount available for creation of the job in the county (¶ 913).

Planning considerations: The credit is allowed only in tax years during which the port traffic remains above the minimum level, and the amount of the credit may not exceed 50% of the business' Georgia income tax liability for any one tax year. Any unused credit may be carried forward up to 10 years from the close of the tax year in which the qualified jobs were established, provided the requisite increase in port traffic remains above the minimum level.

● *Additional investment credit*

An increased investment credit is also allowed for most business enterprises that increase their port traffic of products during the previous 12-month period by more than 10% above their base year port traffic and that are also qualified to claim a manufacturer's and telecommunications investment tax credit or the optional manufacturer's and telecommunications investment tax credit upon qualified investment property added after 1997. A business may claim either the credit for increasing its port traffic of products or the investment or optional investment tax credit, but not both.

Credit amount: The credit is equal to the applicable percentage amount of either the investment tax credit or the optional investment tax credit for property placed in service in a tier 1 county. Thus, the primary benefit of the new credit applies to property placed in service in tier 2 or tier 3 counties, for which the applicable percentages are less under the existing credits than under the new credit. If a business claims the credit for increasing its port traffic instead of the investment tax credit, the amount of the credit may not exceed 50% of the business' Georgia income tax liability for any one tax year.

Planning considerations: Any unused credit may be carried forward up to 10 years following the tax year in which the qualified investment property was acquired or was first placed in service, provided the increase in port traffic remains above the minimum level and the qualified investment property remains in service.

● *Requirements for claiming both credits*

A business cannot claim both of the credits provided for increasing port traffic in any one tax year unless it has increased its port traffic of products

Part III—Corporate Income Tax 125

during the previous 12-month period by more than 20% above its base year port traffic, and has also created at least 400 new jobs after 1997, and purchased or acquired investment property after 1997 with an aggregate cost of over $20 million.

¶ 925 Credit for Rehabilitation of Historic Property

Law: Sec. 48-7-29.8, Code (CCH GEORGIA TAX REPORTS ¶ 12-090).

For taxable years beginning after 2003, a credit is available for taxpayers that substantially rehabilitate historic property.

A substantial rehabilitation is a rehabilitation of a certified structure for which the qualified rehabilitation expenditures exceed (1) for a historic home, the lesser of $25,000 or 50% of the adjusted basis of the property, or, in the case of a historic home located in a target area, $5,000, or (2) for any other certified structure, the greater of $5,000 or the adjusted basis of the property. At least 5% of the rehabilitation expenditures must be allocable to the exterior during a 24-month period (a 60-month period may be substituted under certain circumstances) selected by the taxpayer ending with or within the taxable year.

Credit amount: For a historic home, the credit is equal to 10% of the qualified rehabilitation expenditures, and if the home is located within a target area, an additional 5% of qualified expenditures. For any other certified historic structure, the credit is equal to 20% of the qualified rehabilitation expenditures. The credit may not exceed $5,000 in any 120-month period.

Planning considerations: To be eligible to receive the credit, the taxpayer must attach to the taxpayer's state tax return a copy of the Department of Natural Resources certification verifying that the improvements to the certified structure are consistent with the Department standards for rehabilitation.

The credit may be carried forward for 10 years, and may not be carried back. Furthermore, the credit may be transferred to subsequent purchasers of the property. However, if the property owner, other than a nonprofit corporation, sells the property within three years of receiving the credit, then the seller must recapture the credit and remit the applicable amount to the Department of Revenue.

The credit may be allocated among partners, members, or shareholders of flow-through entities.

¶ 926 Jobs Credit for New Manufacturing Facilities

Law: Sec. 48-7-40.24, Code (CCH GEORGIA TAX REPORTS ¶ 12-070b).

A credit is available for a business enterprise that plans a qualified project that creates at least 1,800 new full-time jobs with average wages that are 20% above the average wage for projects in Tier 1 counties, 10% above the average wage for projects in Tier 2 counties, and 5% above the average wage for projects in Tier 3 or Tier 4 counties.

Alternatively, the credit is available to any business enterprise that can demonstrate to a panel composed of the Commissioner of Community Affairs, the Commissioner of Industry, Trade and Tourism, and the Director of the

¶ 926

Office of Planning and Budget that its project has high growth potential based upon the prior year's Georgia net taxable income growth of over 20% from the previous year, if the business enterprise's Georgia net taxable income in each of the two preceding years also grew by 20% or more.

A "qualified project" is the construction of a new manufacturing facility in Georgia that requires an investment of at least $450 million. "Manufacturing facility" is defined as a single facility, including contiguous parcels of land, improvements to the land, buildings, building improvements, and any machinery or equipment used in the process of making, fabricating, constructing, forming, or assembling a product from components or from raw, unfinished, or semifinished materials, and any support facility.

Credit amount: The credit is equal to $5,250 annually for each new eligible, full-time job created for a period of five years, beginning with the year that the job is created. Any excess credit may be applied against quarterly or monthly withholding taxes. Each employee whose employer received a credit against the employer's withholding taxes would also receive a credit against his or her personal income tax.

Planning considerations: Jobs eligible for the credit must be created by the close of the seventh taxable year following the business enterprise's withholding start-date. The credit may not be claimed for more than 3,300 full-time jobs created by any one project.

In the event of a sale, merger, acquisition, or bankruptcy of any business enterprise claiming the credit, the successor entity would not retain eligibility for the credit. However, any unused credit is transferable to the successor entity.

The credit can be carried forward, but not back, for 10 years from the close of the taxable year in which the qualified job was established.

The business enterprise is required to file a report at the close of the sixth taxable year following the withholding start-date with the Commissioner of Revenue detailing the investment in the project and the jobs created. The credit is subject to recapture if the Commissioner determines at that time that the business enterprise failed to meet the investment or job creation requirements.

¶ 927 Manufacturers' Credit for New Facilities

Law: Sec. 48-7-40.25, Code (CCH GEORGIA TAX REPORTS ¶ 12-055).

A credit is available for any business enterprise that has operated an existing manufacturing facility in Georgia for the immediately preceding three years and that is planning on constructing a new manufacturing facility. To be eligible for the credit, the new manufacturing facility must be certified by a panel composed of the Commissioner of Community Affairs, the Commissioner of Industry, Trade and Tourism, and the Director of the Office of Planning and Budget that the new facility will have a significant beneficial economic effect on the region for which it is planned. Although the panel's certification may be based on other criteria, a project that meets the minimum job requirement of employing at least 1,800 employees, and the minimum investment requirement of $800 million, would have a significant beneficial economic effect on the region for which the construction of the new manufacturing facility is planned if:

> (1) wages would be 20% above the average wage for projects in Tier 1 counties;
>
> (2) wages would be 10% above the average wage for projects in Tier 2 counties;
>
> (3) wages would be 5% above the average wage for projects in Tier 3 or Tier 4 counties; or
>
> (4) the business enterprise could demonstrate that its project has high growth potential based upon the prior year's Georgia net taxable income growth of over 20% from the previous year, and if the enterprise's Georgia net taxable income in each of the two preceding years also grew by 20% or more.

Credit amount: The credit is equal to 6% of the cost of all qualified investment property purchased or acquired by the business enterprise in the taxable year. Any excess credit may be applied against quarterly or monthly withholding taxes. Each employee whose employer received a credit against the employer's withholding taxes would also receive a credit against his or her personal income tax. With respect to any one project, the credit could not be claimed for any amount in excess of $50 million in the aggregate.

Planning considerations: The credit can be taken beginning with the taxable year that the business enterprise has met both the investment requirement and the job requirement, and, for such first year, the credit may include qualified investment property purchased or acquired in prior years, but after March 31, 2003.

The credit can be carried forward, but not back, for 15 years from the close of the later of the taxable year that the qualified investment property was acquired or the taxable year that both the job requirement and investment requirement were satisfied.

In the event of a sale, merger, acquisition, or bankruptcy of any business enterprise claiming the credit, the successor entity would not retain eligibility for the credit. However, any unused credit is transferable to the successor entity.

The business enterprise is required to file a report at the close of the sixth taxable year following the withholding start-date with the Commissioner of Revenue detailing the investment in the project and the jobs created. The credit is subject to recapture if the Commissioner determines at that time that the business enterprise failed to meet the investment or job creation requirements.

¶927

Part III—Corporate Income Tax

CORPORATE INCOME TAX

CHAPTER 10

COMPUTATION OF TAXABLE NET INCOME

- ¶ 1001 In General
- ¶ 1002 Taxable Net Income
- ¶ 1003 Effect of Elections Made for Federal Purposes
- ¶ 1004 Special Rules on Adjustments
- ¶ 1005 Exempt Organizations—Unrelated Business Income
- ¶ 1006 Subchapter S Elections
- ¶ 1007 Depreciation of Business Property
- ¶ 1008 Reorganizations—Mergers and Acquisitions

¶ 1001 In General

Law: Sec. 48-7-21, Code.

Georgia taxable net income is computed by using federal taxable income as a starting point. The federal figure is adjusted for Georgia purposes by certain additions and subtractions, and allocated and apportioned in accordance with Georgia law.

¶ 1002 Taxable Net Income

Law: Secs. 48-1-2(14), 48-7-21, 48-7-29.4, Code (CCH GEORGIA TAX REPORTS ¶ 10-510).

Comparable Federal: Sec. 63 (U.S. MASTER TAX GUIDE ¶ 62, 214, 2301—2323, 2326—2340).

Practitioner Comment: IRS Conformity

Georgia conforms to the Internal Revenue Code of 1986 as *enacted* on or before January 1, 2004. Therefore, for the 2004 taxable year, Georgia will not conform to any federal tax legislation that is enacted after January 1, 2004 but otherwise effective for taxable years beginning on or after January 1, 2004. In addition, Georgia does not conform to IRC sections 168(k) (the 30% and 50% bonus depreciation provisions) and 1400L (relating to the New York Liberty Zone tax benefits). Further, Georgia treats IRC section 179(b) (the dollar limitations for expensing qualifying property placed in service) as it was in effect prior to the enactment of the Jobs and Growth Tax Relief Reconciliation Act of 2003 (P.L. 108-27). For more information, see the Georgia Department of

Revenue's website at http://www2.state.ga.us/departments/dor/inctax/inctax_legis.shtml

Jeffrey C. Glickman, Esq., Alston & Bird LLP

For both domestic and foreign corporations, Georgia taxable net income is the basis for computing Georgia corporate income tax. Georgia taxable net income is the corporation's taxable income from property owned or business done in Georgia, determined as follows:

(1) Start with the corporation's taxable income as defined in the Internal Revenue Code. In connection with this, note the following:

—Georgia incorporates by reference the provisions of the Internal Revenue Code of 1986 as of January 1, 2004 with certain exceptions (¶ 1007). References to the Internal Revenue Code as it existed on a specific date prior to that date, refer to the Internal Revenue Code of 1954 as it existed on the specific date. Provisions of the Internal Revenue Code of 1986 that were enacted into law as of January 1, 2004, but have not yet become effective, will be effective on the day the provision is effective under federal law.

—Elections adopted for federal income tax purposes apply for Georgia corporate income tax purposes, except as provided for some S corporations.

(2) Make the required addition and subtraction adjustments (Chapters 11 and 12). In addition, the following adjustments may be necessary:

—An adjustment may be made to replace real or tangible personal property located in Georgia with similar property, also located in Georgia, so that the gain or loss on its sale or exchange is not recognized.

—An adjustment to delete deductions and losses, including net operating losses, that occurred in a year when the taxpayer was not subject to tax in Georgia may be made under rules established by the State Revenue Commissioner.

CCH Tip: Net Operating Losses

Georgia treats net operating losses (NOLs) in the same manner as they are treated for federal tax purposes, except that Georgia did not adopt the provisions of the federal Job Creation and Worker Assistance Act (JCWAA) (P.L. 107-147), which extended the carryback period for net operating losses to five years for 2001 and 2002. Also, a deduction is not allowed for NOLs incurred in years in which the taxpayer was not subject to Georgia taxation, although carryovers of NOL deductions are permitted from years in which the taxpayer was subject to methods of Georgia taxation other than corporate income tax.

—An adjustment may be made with respect to previously reported income, losses, and deductions (¶ 1004).

¶ 1002

Part III—Corporate Income Tax 131

—An adjustment may be made for a portion of a qualified payment to minority subcontractors (¶ 1205).

—A dollar-for-dollar credit is allowed to depository financial institutions for local business license tax and special state occupation tax paid (¶ 919). Depository financial institutions that elect Subchapter S status may pass through the credit on a pro rata basis.

—Exemptions in other laws of the State of Georgia and exemptions provided by federal law or treaty are preserved.

(3) Allocate and apportion the result (Chapter 13).

CCH Tip: Impact of 2004 Federal Legislation

Because Georgia does not incorporate the Internal Revenue Code as amended to date, Georgia does not yet incorporate the federal amendments enacted by the Working Families Tax Relief Act (WFTRA) of 2004 (P.L. No. 108-311), or the American Jobs Creation Act (AJCA) of 2004.

Working Families Tax Relief Act (WFTRA) of 2004: In addition to extending the federal research credit (IRC Sec. 41) and numerous other federal credits through 2005, WFTRA extends the availability of the following deductions through the 2005 tax year. However, absent legislative action, Georgia does not allow these extended deductions and, therefore, addition modifications will be required on Georgia's returns for taxpayers that claim these deductions on their 2004 federal tax returns:

—the $250 above-the-line deduction for teachers' expenses (IRC Sec. 62(a)(2)(d));

—the enhanced charitable deduction for computer technology donated to schools and public libraries (IRC Sec. 170(e)(6)(g));

—the election to deduct environmental research expenses (IRC Sec. 198(h));

—the increased depreciation deduction resulting from the shortened MACRS recovery periods for Indian reservation property (IRC Sec. 168(j)(8)); and

—the increased depletion deduction resulting from the suspension of the taxable income limit on the percentage depletion allowance for oil and gas produced from marginal wells (IRC Sec. 613(A)(c)(6)(H)).

The WFTRA also eliminates the phase-out limitation for qualified clean-fuel vehicles placed in service in 2004 and 2005. As a result of this change, a taxpayer who purchases a qualified vehicle in 2004 and 2005 may claim 100 percent of the otherwise allowable deduction on their federal, but not their Georgia return (IRC Sec. 179A). Taxpayers claiming this deduction on their Georgia return must reduce the deduction by 25% during the 2004 tax year.

Finally, under the WFTRA a state that is approved by the Secretary of the Treasury may participate in a combined federal and

¶ 1002

state employment tax reporting program through December 31, 2005 (IRC Sec. 6103(d)(5)).

American Jobs Creation Act (AJCA) of 2004: The American Jobs Creation Act of 2004 makes extensive changes to the IRC—adding and amending over 300 IRC code provisions. The biggest changes that may affect the preparation of a taxpayer's Georgia 2004 tax returns are:

—Indexing the IRC Sec. 179 asset expense election allowing taxpayers to deduct up to $102,000 for property valued up to $410,000 during the 2004 tax year;

—Allowing a 15-year recover period for depreciation purposes for qualified leasehold improvements and restaurant property and extending the first year bonus depreciation deduction to restaurant property;

—Limiting the depreciation deduction for SUV vehicles;

—Tightening the eligibility rules for charitable contribution deductions for donations of vehicles and intellectual property.

¶1003 Effect of Elections Made for Federal Purposes

Law: Sec. 48-7-21(b)(7)(B), Code (CCH GEORGIA TAX REPORTS ¶10-515).

The elections made by corporate taxpayers under the Internal Revenue Code generally apply under Georgia law. However, elections involving consolidated corporate returns and S corporation elections may not apply.

¶1004 Special Rules on Adjustments

Law: Sec. 48-7-21(b), Code (CCH GEORGIA TAX REPORTS ¶10-600).

Comparable Federal: Sec. 1016.

The following special rules apply to adjustments made in computing a corporation's taxable net income:

Deductions or losses that occurred during any year when the taxpayer was not subject to Georgia tax may not be deducted from Georgia income.

Income, losses, and deductions used in computing Georgia taxable income at any time may never be used again in computing Georgia taxable income. Any necessary adjustments will be provided for by regulation.

● *Like-kind exchanges*

If the gain or loss on the sale or exchange of real or tangible personal property located in Georgia is not recognized because the taxpayer has received or purchased similar property, the nonrecognition is allowed for Georgia tax purposes only if the replacement property is also located in Georgia.

Other exemptions are preserved and the deductions are utilized by filing the appropriate forms.

¶1003

Part III—Corporate Income Tax

¶ 1005 Exempt Organizations—Unrelated Business Income

Law: Sec. 48-7-25(a) and (c), Code (CCH GEORGIA TAX REPORTS ¶ 10-245).

Comparable Federal: Sec. 512 (U.S. MASTER TAX GUIDE ¶ 655—685).

An organization that is exempt from Georgia income tax on the basis of its exemption from federal income tax is subject to tax on unrelated business income at the normal corporate rate. Unrelated business income is income derived from a trade or business that is not related to the organization's exempt purposes.

¶ 1006 Subchapter S Elections

Law: Sec. 48-7-21(b)(7)(B), Code (CCH GEORGIA TAX REPORTS ¶ 10-215).

Comparable Federal: Sec. 1362 (U.S. MASTER TAX GUIDE ¶ 301—349).

Form: 600 S-CA.

An election under IRC Subchapter S, providing that eligible closely held corporations do not pay federal income tax and the tax items of the corporation are attributed to the shareholders even if they are not distributed, applies for Georgia income tax purposes if all shareholders are subject to tax in Georgia. If there are nonresident shareholders, the election is effective if the nonresident shareholders pay Georgia income tax on their portion of the S corporation's income.

Practitioner Comment: Nonresident Shareholders

In order for the corporation to maintain its "S" corporation status in Georgia, each resident shareholder must file the S Corporation return, Form 600 S-CA (S Corporation Consent Agreement of Nonresident Stockholders) annually.

Jeffrey C. Glickman, Esq., Alston & Bird LLP

¶ 1007 Depreciation of Business Property

Law: Secs. 48-7-21(b)(12), 48-7-39, Code (CCH GEORGIA TAX REPORTS ¶ 10-670, 10-900).

Comparable Federal: Sec. 168 (U.S. MASTER TAX GUIDE ¶ 1201—1286).

Georgia adopts the federal treatment of depreciation with the exception of bonus depreciation under IRC Sec. 168(k).

Generally, federal law allows a deduction for depreciation of property used in a trade or business. The current system, Modified Accelerated Cost Recovery System (MACRS), uses statutory recovery periods and conventions, and either straight-line, 200%-declining, or 150%-declining methods. For most assets, there is no adjustment required for depreciation. However, depreciation on child care facilities must be added back under certain circumstances (¶ 911).

Bonus depreciation: Georgia has not adopted the 30% or 50% bonus depreciation allowed under IRC Sec. 168(k). Consequently, taxpayers who take the federal bonus depreciation must make a basis adjustment and prepare a separate Form 4562, marked "Georgia Form 4562." Both the federal Form 4562 and the Form prepared for Georgia should be attached to the Georgia return.

IRC Sec. 179 expensing: Georgia has not adopted the increased limits applicable to the expensing of assets under IRC Sec. 179 that were enacted by the federal Jobs and Growth Tax Relief Reconciliation Act (JGTRRA) (P.L. 108-27).

● *Pre-1987 property*

For property placed in service in tax years ending after March 11, 1987, Georgia adopts the federal depreciation provisions as in effect on the IRC tie-in date for the relevant tax year.

With respect to property placed in service in tax years ending before March 11, 1987, taxpayers could elect one of the following two options:

(1) continue to depreciate or otherwise recover the cost of certain property placed in service according to the same method used for Georgia income tax purposes for the taxable year the property was placed in service, making such adjustments to federal taxable income as required to reflect the effect of this election, or

(2) depreciate or otherwise recover the cost of property according to the method used for federal income tax purposes for the taxable year the property was placed in service. Taxpayers making this second election might never fully depreciate or recover the cost of the property for Georgia income tax purposes and in certain cases the taxpayer may be allowed to depreciate or recover more than the full cost of the property.

Note: If the taxpayer made no election, option (2) applies.

The election had to be made for a taxpayer's first taxable year ending on or after January 1, 1987. This election is an irrevocable choice applicable to all subsequent taxable years, and applies to both the determination of deductions for depreciation or the cost recovery of affected property and to the determination of gain or loss on the sale or other disposition of the property.

¶ 1008 Reorganizations—Mergers and Acquisitions

Law: Sec. 48-7-21(b)(7)(B), Code (CCH GEORGIA TAX REPORTS ¶ 10-540).

Comparable Federal: Secs. 358, 361, 381 (U.S. MASTER TAX GUIDE ¶ 2205—2247).

In most cases, the gain or loss recognized on a reorganization for Georgia corporate income tax purposes will be the same as the gain or loss recognized for federal tax purposes. Georgia uses federal taxable income as the starting point for the computation of its tax base, and there is no provision of Georgia law that modifies the federal recognition or nonrecognition rules applicable to reorganizations.

The amount of gain or loss reported for Georgia purposes may differ from the federal amount as a result of differences between the state and federal bases of the sellers' assets. For example, a basis difference may arise as a result of past differences between state and federal depreciation rules (¶ 1007).

IRC Sec. 338 elections: There is no provision of Georgia law that specifically indicates that IRC Sec. 338(h)(10) elections are inapplicable for Georgia tax purposes. Furthermore, all federal tax elections, except elections involving consolidated corporate returns and S corporation elections, apply for Georgia tax purposes. Accordingly, the federal tax consequences of IRC Sec. 338(h)(10) elections presumably also apply for Georgia purposes.

Georgia does not use the business/nonbusiness income concept in distinguishing between apportionable and allocable income. Rather, all gains recognized on a reorganization apparently constitute apportionable income under Georgia law. (Allocation and apportionment is discussed in Chapter 13.)

Net operating loss carryover: Georgia law does not specifically address the succession of net operating loss (NOL) carryovers. Accordingly, the federal rules presumably apply, subject to the state condition that the carryover must reflect in-state losses.

Capital loss and contribution carryovers: Georgia law does not specifically disallow the succession of capital loss and contribution to these carryovers, so the federal rules presumably apply.

¶ 1008

Part III—Corporate Income Tax

CORPORATE INCOME TAX

CHAPTER 11

ADDITIONS TO FEDERAL BASE

¶ 1101   In General
¶ 1102   Income from Government Obligations
¶ 1103   Income Taxes Deducted on Federal Return
¶ 1104   Depreciation of Certain Child Care Property

¶ 1101   In General

Law: Sec. 48-7-21(b), Code; Reg. Sec. 560-7-3-.06.

Georgia law requires corporate taxpayers to add to the federal base any income from obligations of governments, other than Georgia and its political subdivisions, to the extent that the income was excluded for federal tax purposes but is taxed by Georgia. A portion of certain liquidation gains, not recognized under federal law, are to be included in Georgia taxable income. Finally, employers claiming a credit for the cost of qualified child care property first placed into service in a taxable year must include depreciation deductions attributable to such property in their federal base.

Provisions applicable to special circumstances may require adjustments to the federal figure.

For additional information on additions, see ¶ 1002.

● *Other gains and losses*

Adjustments are also provided for the recognition of gain for replacement property not located in Georgia. No adjustment will be made for deductions or losses that occurred before the year when the taxpayer was subject to taxation in Georgia or for income, losses, or deductions previously reported. If such deductions are used in the computation of federal adjusted gross income or net income, the adjustment for state income tax can be made only as provided by regulation.

¶ 1102   Income from Government Obligations

Law: Sec. 48-7-21(b)(1)(A) and (B), Code (CCH Georgia Tax Reports ¶ 10-610).
Comparable Federal: Sec. 103.

Interest income derived from obligations of any state or political subdivision, except Georgia and political subdivisions of Georgia, must be added to taxable income to the extent that the interest income is not included in gross income for federal income tax purposes. Interest or dividends on obligations of any authority, commission, instrumentality, territory, or possession of the

¶ 1102

United States that are exempt from federal income tax but not from state income taxes must also be added to taxable income.

¶ 1103 Income Taxes Deducted on Federal Return

Law: Sec. 48-7-21(b)(2), Code (CCH GEORGIA TAX REPORTS ¶ 10-615).

Comparable Federal: Sec. 164 (U.S. MASTER TAX GUIDE ¶ 1021).

Any taxes imposed by any taxing jurisdiction except Georgia, that are imposed on or measured by net income or net profits paid or accrued within the taxable year, must be added to taxable income to the extent such taxes were deducted in determining federal taxable income.

CCH Tip: Michigan Single Business Tax

No addback to federal taxable income is required on the Georgia corporate return with regard to the Michigan Single Business Tax (*Letter to CCH from Mike O'Brien, Tax Conferee,* Georgia Department of Revenue, May 18, 1994).

¶ 1104 Depreciation of Certain Child Care Property

Law: Sec. 48-7-21(b)(13), 48-7-40.6, Code (CCH GEORGIA TAX REPORTS ¶ 10-670).

Employers that claim the credit against Georgia corporate income tax that is available with respect to qualified child care property first placed into service on or after July 1, 1999 (¶ 911), must add to their taxable income the amount of any depreciation deductions attributable to the property, to the extent that these deductions are used in determining federal taxable income.

Part III—Corporate Income Tax

CORPORATE INCOME TAX

CHAPTER 12

SUBTRACTIONS FROM FEDERAL BASE

¶ 1201 In General
¶ 1202 Income from Federal Obligations
¶ 1203 Dividends from Foreign Source or Affiliated Corporation
¶ 1204 Deductions Eliminated by Federal Jobs Credits
¶ 1205 Payments to Minority Subcontractors
¶ 1206 Federal Employer Social Security Credit

¶ 1201 In General

Law: Sec. 48-7-21(b), Code; Reg. Sec. 560-7-3-.06.

Corporate taxpayers are permitted to subtract the following from the federal base:

—income from federal obligations that is exempt from state taxation under U.S. law;

—dividends from sources outside the United States or from affiliates; and

—wage payments not deductible for federal purposes under the federal jobs tax credit provisions.

Other subtractions from the federal figure may be allowed by Georgia provisions that apply to special circumstances.

Practitioner Comment: Income Tax Refunds

Although Georgia law specifically provides that any income taxes paid during the taxable year to any jurisdiction other than Georgia must be added back to taxable income to the extent deducted on the federal return (see ¶ 1103), it does not directly address income tax refunds from jurisdictions other than Georgia. However, Sec. 48-7-21(b)(3), Code, provides generally that income previously used to compute Georgia taxable income shall not be used again to compute Georgia taxable income.

¶ 1201

Under this section, income tax refunds from jurisdictions other than Georgia should be subtracted from taxable income to the extent they were included in federal taxable income, because the tax that was refunded had been previously included in income for Georgia income tax purposes under the add-back provision.

Jeffrey C. Glickman, Esq., Alston & Bird LLP

¶ 1202 Income from Federal Obligations

Law: Sec. 48-7-21(b)(1)(B), Code (CCH GEORGIA TAX REPORTS ¶ 10-810, 10-815).

Comparable Federal: Sec. 3124(a).

Interest and dividends on obligations of the United States, its territories and possessions, or of any authority, commission, or instrumentality of the United States are subtracted from taxable income to the extent they are included in gross income for federal income tax purposes but are exempt from state income taxes under federal law. Any amount subtracted under this provision must be reduced by any expenses directly attributable to the production of the interest or dividend income.

¶ 1203 Dividends from Foreign Source or Affiliated Corporation

Law: Sec. 48-7-21(b)(8)(A) and (B), Code (CCH GEORGIA TAX REPORTS ¶ 10-810).

Comparable Federal: Sec. 243, 245 (U.S. MASTER TAX GUIDE ¶ 239, 241).

Dividends received by a corporation from sources outside the United States may be subtracted from taxable income. Amounts that may be subtracted include the following:

—Amounts treated as a dividend and income deemed to have been received under federal law;

—Qualified electing fund income;

—Subpart F income;

—Income attributable to an increase in United States property by a controlled foreign corporation.

The amount subtracted must be reduced by any expenses directly attributable to the dividend income.

Dividends received from affiliated corporations within the United States may also be subtracted from taxable income, to the extent they have been included in net income, if the corporation receiving the dividends is engaged in business in Georgia and is subject to Georgia corporate income tax. Dividends from affiliates also must be reduced by any expenses directly attributable to the dividend income.

¶ 1202

Part III—Corporate Income Tax   **141**

¶ 1204   Deductions Eliminated by Federal Jobs Credits

Law: Sec. 48-7-21(b)(9), Code; Reg. Sec. 560-7-7-.05 (CCH GEORGIA TAX REPORTS ¶ 10-855).

Comparable Federal: Secs. 45A, 51, 51A, 1396 (U.S. MASTER TAX GUIDE ¶ 1339A, 1340, 1342, 1343).

When a corporation takes a federal jobs credit, it is required by IRC Sec. 280C to reduce the federal deduction for salaries and wages corresponding to that credit. In calculating Georgia taxable income, the amount of the eliminated deductions is subtracted from federal taxable income. This subtraction is allowed with respect to each of the following federal jobs tax credits:

—IRC Sec. 45A credit for Indian employment;

—IRC Sec. 51 work opportunity credit;

—IRC Sec. 51A welfare-to-work credit;

—IRC Sec. 1396 empowerment zone employment credit.

¶ 1205   Payments to Minority Subcontractors

Law: Secs. 48-7-21(b)(11), 48-7-38(b)(1) and (c), Code (CCH GEORGIA TAX REPORTS ¶ 10-845).

A portion of the qualified payments made to minority subcontractors may be subtracted from taxable income. A qualified payment is a payment made for goods, personal property, or services furnished by a minority subcontractor to a taxpayer that, in turn, delivers the items or services to the state in furtherance of a state contract. The payment may not exceed the value of the goods, property, or services, and it must be made to a certified minority subcontractor during the taxable year for which the subtraction is claimed. The amount to be subtracted equals 10% of the qualified payments, but may not exceed $100,000 per year.

A minority is an individual who is a member of one of the following groups: African-American, Hispanic, Asian-Pacific American, Native American, or Asian-Indian American.

¶ 1206   Federal Employer Social Security Credit

Law: Sec. 48-7-28.2, Code (CCH GEORGIA TAX REPORTS ¶ 10-855).

Comparable Federal: Secs. 38, 45B(a) (U.S. MASTER TAX GUIDE ¶ 1341).

Employers electing to take a federal employer social security credit for portions of employer social security taxes paid with respect to employee cash tips are allowed a Georgia corporate income tax deduction equal to their federal employer social security credit.

¶ 1206

Part III—Corporate Income Tax

CORPORATE INCOME TAX

CHAPTER 13

ALLOCATION AND APPORTIONMENT

| ¶ 1301 | In General
| ¶ 1302 | Property Owned and Business Done Within and Outside Georgia
| ¶ 1303 | Allocation—Investment Income
| ¶ 1304 | Allocation—Special Cases
| ¶ 1305 | Apportionment—Three-Factor Formula
| ¶ 1306 | Special Definitions and Rules
| ¶ 1307 | Railroad and Public Service Corporations
| ¶ 1308 | Net Income of Subsidiaries and Affiliates
| ¶ 1309 | Returns Based on Books of Account
| ¶ 1310 | Revenue Commissioner's Power to Determine Income Attributable to Georgia

¶ 1301 In General

Law: Secs. 48-7-31, 48-7-34, 48-7-35, 48-7-58, Code; Reg. Sec. 560-7-7-.03 (CCH GEORGIA TAX REPORTS ¶ 11-505—11-540).

Georgia corporate income tax is imposed on business income derived from property owned or business done in Georgia (¶ 905, 1302). Under allocation and apportionment rules applicable to corporations having income derived from property owned or business done within and outside Georgia, tax is imposed on the portion of business income reasonably attributable to property owned and business done within Georgia. Investment income is generally allocated and business income is apportioned by use of a three-factor formula or by equitable apportionment.

An apportionment formula is used by corporations whose net income is derived principally from the manufacture, production, or sale of tangible personal property (¶ 1305). Corporations that have business income derived principally from business other than manufacturing, production, and sale of tangible personal property, or from the holding or sale of intangible property, apportion their income using special formulas (¶ 1306, 1307).

Corporations with books of account that provide a detailed allocation of receipts and expenditures that reflect income attributable to the state more clearly than the statutory process or formulas may, with permission from the State Revenue Commissioner, file on the basis of books of account (¶ 1309). Other corporations may request permission to use a method other than the statutory method (¶ 1310).

¶ 1301

● *Corporate partners*

A C corporation is deemed to own property or do business in Georgia if it is either a limited or general partner in a partnership operating in Georgia. A C corporation that is a limited partner in a business joint venture or in a business partnership operating in Georgia must include its pro rata share of partnership property, payroll, and gross receipts in its own three-factor apportionment formula.

¶ 1302 Property Owned and Business Done Within and Outside Georgia

Law: Sec. 48-7-31, Code (CCH GEORGIA TAX REPORTS ¶ 11-505).

If the business income of the corporation is derived in part from property owned or business done within Georgia and in part from property owned or business done outside Georgia, Georgia corporate income tax is imposed only on the portion of the business income that is reasonably attributable to the property owned and business done within Georgia.

CCH Tip: No Throwback Rule

A corporation deriving income from property owned or business done in another state may apportion its income to that state even if the corporation is not subject to the other state's taxing jurisdiction (*Habersham Mills, Inc.*, Georgia Supreme Court, January 28, 1975, 212 S.E.2d 337).

Unlike many other states, Georgia does not tax, *i.e.,* "*throw back*", income from out-of-state sales in which the seller is not taxable by the destination state.

¶ 1303 Allocation—Investment Income

Law: Sec. 48-7-31(c), Code (CCH GEORGIA TAX REPORTS ¶ 11-515).

Interest received on bonds held for investment, income from intangibles, and rentals from real estate are allocated either to Georgia or to another state. Interest on investment bonds and other income from intangible property, minus expenses attributable to such income, is allocated to Georgia if (1) the situs of the corporation is in Georgia or (2) the intangible property was acquired as income from property held in Georgia or as a result of business done in Georgia.

Rentals received from real estate held solely for investment and not used in the business are reduced for expenses connected with this income and are not subject to apportionment. Although the statute is not explicit on this point, this income should be allocated according to situs since the statute does provide that the net investment income from tangible property located in Georgia is allocated to Georgia.

¶ 1302

Part III—Corporate Income Tax

● *Gains from sales*

Even though gain results from the sale of tangible or intangible property not held, owned, or used in connection with the trade or business or held for sale in the regular course of business, the gain must be allocated to Georgia if the property sold is real or tangible personal property situated in Georgia, or if the property sold is intangible property having an actual situs or business situs within Georgia.

Any other gains are allocated outside Georgia.

¶ 1304 Allocation—Special Cases

Law: Sec. 48-7-35, Code (CCH GEORGIA TAX REPORTS ¶ 11-515).

If a corporation shows by any method of allocation other than the prescribed processes or formulas that another method more clearly reflects the income attributable to the trade or business within Georgia, the corporation may apply for permission to base the return upon the other method. The application must be accompanied by a statement showing the method the taxpayer believes will more nearly reflect its income from business within Georgia.

¶ 1305 Apportionment—Three-Factor Formula

Law: Sec. 48-7-31(d), Code; Reg. Sec. 560-7-7-.03 (CCH GEORGIA TAX REPORTS ¶ 11-520—11-535).

A corporation with net business income derived principally from the manufacture, production, or sale of tangible personal property uses the three-factor formula of property, payroll, and gross receipts to determine the corporation's net income attributable to property owned or business done in Georgia. The gross receipts factor is given double weight in the formula.

Practitioner Comment: Allocation and Appotionment

Both the Georgia Department of Revenue and the Georgia Attorney General's Office have taken the position that Georgia's apportionment provisions are broader and Georgia's allocation provisions are even more restrictive than UDITPA's. First, they note that, structurally, UDITPA defines "business income," and everything else is nonbusiness income, while the Georgia statute takes the opposite approach, defining in O.C.G.A. § 48-7-31(c) the limited types of income that can be allocated, with everything else being considered apportionable business income. They also put particular emphasis on the fact that while UDITPA uses the conjunctive "and" in describing business income ("income from tangible and intangible property if the acquisition, management, and disposition of the property constitute integral parts of the taxpayer's regular trade or business operations"), the Georgia statute uses the disjunctive "or:" gains from the sale of tangible or intangible property are allocable under 48-7-31(c)(3) only if they are "not held, owned, or used in connection with the trade or business of the corporation...." Also, UDITPA requires that the acquisition, management, and disposition of the tangible or intangible property be "integral" parts of the taxpayer's "regular" business operations, whereas Georgia merely requires that the tangible or intangible property be held, owned or used "in connection with" the trade or business of the taxpayer, without regard to whether those activities are "integral" to the taxpayer's business, or whether they were part of the taxpayer's "regular" business operations.

Accordingly, Georgia not only views the statutory language of O.C.G.A. § 48-7-31 as incorporating both the functional and transactional tests under UDITPA, but as being broader than UDITPA with respect to income that is apportionable. Of course, they will recognize (reluctantly) that even this broad statutory apportionment language is limited by constitutional restrictions of *Allied-Signal*, and that gains from intangible property that serve "an investment function" rather than an "operational" one may not be included in the apportionable base, regardless of the statutory apportionment language.

John L. Coalson, Jr., Esq., Alston & Bird

● *Property factor*

Real and tangible personal property are included in the property factor if the property is owned or rented and used in Georgia during the tax period in the regular course of the taxpayer's trade or business. Average values are used. The property factor uses a fraction with a numerator that reflects the taxpayer's Georgia real and personal property and a denominator that reflects all such property wherever it is located or rented and used. Real and tangible personal property includes land, buildings, machinery, stocks of goods, equipment, and other real and tangible personal property, but does not include coin or currency. Property used in the production of income subject to allocation is not included in the property factor. Property that is used both in the regular course of a taxpayer's trade or business and in the production of income subject to allocation must be included in the property factor only to the extent that the property is used in the regular course of business. Property that is actually used or is available for or capable of being used during the tax period in the regular course of the taxpayer's trade or business, such as reserves, standby facilities, or property held as a reserve source of materials, is included in the property factor.

Value of property: Property owned by a taxpayer is valued at its original cost. "Original cost" is defined as the original basis of the property for federal income tax purposes, before any federal adjustments, at the time of acquisition by the corporation and adjusted by any subsequent capital additions, improvements, or partial dispositions due to sale, exchange, or abandonment. Property rented by the taxpayer is valued at eight times the net annual rental rate, *i.e.,* the annual rental rate paid by the taxpayer minus any annual rental rate received by the taxpayer from subrentals.

Average value of property: Values at the beginning and end of the tax period are used to reach an average value of the property. However, the State

Part III—Corporate Income Tax

Revenue Commissioner may require averaging of monthly values in some cases.

● *Payroll factor*

The payroll factor relates to compensation. The numerator of the payroll factor reflects the total amount of compensation paid by the taxpayer in Georgia during the tax period and the denominator reflects total compensation paid everywhere during the tax period. Compensation includes wages, salaries, commissions, and any other form of remuneration paid directly or indirectly for personal services, including the value of board, rent, housing, lodging, and other benefits or services furnished to employees in return for their services, provided such amounts constitute income for federal income tax purposes. In general, an individual is an employee for payroll factor purposes if he or she has the status of an employee under common law rules. Payments to independent contractors and other persons are not taken into account.

Compensation paid in Georgia: Compensation is paid in Georgia if the employee's services are performed entirely within Georgia, or both within and outside Georgia if the service performed outside Georgia is incidental to the employee's service within Georgia. In addition, compensation is paid in Georgia if some of the service is performed in Georgia and either the base of operations, direction, or control is in Georgia or some of the service is performed in Georgia and the base of operations or the place from which the service is directed or controlled is not in any state in which some part of the service is performed, but the employee's residence is in Georgia.

CCH Tip: Employee Contributions to 401(k) Plans

Employees' direct contributions to a 401(k) Plan may be included in the payroll factor of the apportionment formula, while employers' contributions to such plans may not be included (*Letter,* Department of Revenue, Section Supervisor, Income Tax Division, October 20, 1988).

● *Gross receipts factor*

If the net business income of a corporation is principally derived from the manufacture, production, or sale of tangible personal property, the gross receipts factor is a fraction with a numerator equal to the total gross receipts from business done within Georgia during the tax period and a denominator equal to the total gross receipts from business done everywhere during the tax period.

Definitions of "gross receipts:" "Gross receipts" means all gross receipts derived from products shipped or delivered to customers in the regular course of the taxpayer's trade or business. If receipts are derived from products that are a combination of goods and services, gross receipts include the charge for services if the activity involved represents the business purpose of the taxpayer. If a taxpayer is engaged in manufacturing and selling or purchasing and reselling goods or products, "gross receipts" means gross sales minus returns and allowances, and includes all interest income, service charges,

¶ 1305

carrying charges, or time-price differential charges incidental to such sales. Federal and state excise taxes, including sales taxes, are included as part of the receipts if the taxes are passed on to the buyer or included as part of the selling price of the product. Finally, in the case of cost plus fixed fee contracts, such as the operation of a government owned plant for a fee, gross receipts include only the fee charged for operation of the plant.

Location of sales: Gross receipts from sales of tangible personal property are in Georgia if the property was delivered or shipped to a customer in the state or the shipment terminates in Georgia, even if it is subsequently transferred by the purchaser to another state. Also, if property being shipped by a seller from the state of origin to a consignee in another state is diverted while en route to a Georgia purchaser, the gross receipts will be deemed to be in Georgia. Property will be deemed to be delivered or shipped to a customer in Georgia if the recipient is in the state, even though the property was ordered from out of state or the Georgia customer picked up the property at the taxpayer's out of state place of business. However, if an out of state customer picks up the property at the taxpayer's Georgia place of business for transport out of state, the gross receipts from the sale are not in Georgia.

● *Calculation of apportionment ratio*

After the property factor, the payroll factor, and the gross receipts factor are separately determined, an apportionment fraction is calculated using the following formula:

—the property factor represents 25% of the fraction;

—the payroll factor represents 25% of the fraction; and

—the gross receipts factor represents 50% of the fraction.

The Georgia apportionment ratio is then computed by adding the weighted factor. If the denominator for either the property or payroll factors is zero, the weighted percentage for the other will be 33 1/3% and the weighted percentage for the gross receipts factor will be 66 2/3%. If the denominator for the gross receipts factor is zero, the weighted percentage for the property and payroll factors will be 50% each. Finally, if the denominators for any two factors are zero, the weighted percentage for the remaining factor will be 100%.

Business joint ventures and business partnerships: A corporation that is involved in a business joint venture or is a general partner in a business partnership must include its pro rata share of the joint venture or partnership property, payroll, and gross receipts values in its own apportionment formula.

CCH Tip: New or Expanding Facilities

Corporations that plan to develop new facilities or expand existing facilities in Georgia may enter into an agreement with the State Revenue Commissioner to establish, for a limited period of time, a different income allocation and apportionment method. These taxpayers must submit a proposal requesting permission and explaining why the proposal is being made. Also, a panel comprised of the Commissioner of Community Affairs; the Commissioner of Indus-

¶ 1305

Part III—Corporate Income Tax 149

try, Trade, and Tourism; and the Director of the Office of Planning and Budget must certify that the taxpayer's new facility or expansion will have a significant beneficial economic effect on the region where it will be located and that the benefits to the public from the new facility or expansion will exceed its costs to the public.

¶ 1306 Special Definitions and Rules

Law: Sec. 48-7-31(d), Code; Reg. Sec. 560-7-7-.03 (CCH GEORGIA TAX REPORTS ¶ 11-540).

For the purposes of apportionment, the term "sale" includes an exchange. The term "manufacture" includes the extraction and recovery of natural resources and all processes of fabricating and curing.

● *Income not derived from manufacture, production, or sale*

If the net business income of a corporation is derived principally from business other than the manufacture, production, or sale of tangible personal property, the formula is the same but the gross receipts factor is specially calculated.

Special calculation of gross receipts factor: In the special calculation, gross receipts are in Georgia if they are derived from customers within Georgia or if they are otherwise attributable to Georgia's marketplace. Examples of factors that may be used to measure the marketplace are: mileage, for transportation companies; audience, for advertising receipts of broadcasters; circulation, for advertising receipts of publishers; and product receipts, for royalty charges or franchise fees.

● *Petition to use other method of allocation and apportionment*

If the above allocation and apportionment provisions do not fairly represent the extent of the taxpayer's business activity in Georgia, the taxpayer may petition for a separate accounting; the exclusion of any one or more of the factors; the inclusion of one or more additional factors that will fairly represent the taxpayer's business activity within Georgia; or the employment of any other method to effectuate an equitable allocation and apportionment of the taxpayer's income.

A corporation must petition the State Revenue Commissioner and receive permission to depart from prescribed methods before filing a return. Permission will be extended for only one year unless otherwise specified by the Commissioner. Generally, a departure will be granted only if unusual fact situations that ordinarily will be unique and nonrecurring produce incongruous results under the standard provisions.

● *Income from transporting passengers or cargo in revenue flight*

When the business income of a corporation is derived from transporting passengers or cargo in revenue flight, the portion of the net income attributable to property owned or business done within Georgia is determined by taking

¶ 1306

the revenue air miles factor, tons handled factor, and the originating revenue factor and creating an apportionment fraction using the following formula:

—the revenue air miles factor represents 25% of the fraction;

—the tons handled factor represents 25% of the fraction; and

—the originating revenue factor represents 50% of the fraction.

The net income of the corporation is apportioned to the average fraction.

● *Income from processing credit card data and related services*

If more than 60% of a corporation's income is derived from the provision of credit card data processing and related services to Georgia banks and institutions, the income attributable to Georgia is determined by multiplying the corporation's net income by its gross receipts factor. The gross receipts factor is a fraction with a numerator equal to the corporation's total gross receipts during the tax period from its Georgia customers and a denominator equal to the corporation's total gross receipts from everywhere during the tax period from all customers.

● *Petroleum pipeline companies*

The portion of a petroleum pipeline company's net income derived from the interstate transportation of crude oil or refined petroleum products by corporations as common carriers that is attributable to property owned or business done in Georgia is determined by applying the following three-factor formula:

—*Property Factor:* The denominator is the average value of the real and tangible personal property owned or rented by the taxpayer and used everywhere during the tax period in the regular course of business. The numerator is the average value of the real and tangible personal property owned or rented by the taxpayer and used in Georgia during the tax period in the regular course of trade or business.

—*Payroll Factor:* The denominator is the total compensation paid everywhere during the tax period. The numerator is determined by multiplying the total amount of compensation paid everywhere by a fraction with a numerator equal to barrel miles in Georgia during the tax year and a denominator equal to total barrel miles everywhere during the tax year. "Barrel miles" means the movement of one barrel of crude oil or one barrel of refined petroleum product for a distance of one mile.

—*Gross Receipts Factor:* The denominator is the total gross receipts from business done everywhere during the tax period. The numerator is determined by multiplying the taxpayer's total gross receipts from business done everywhere by a fraction with a numerator equal to barrel miles in Georgia during the tax year and a denominator equal to total barrel miles everywhere during the tax year.

¶ 1307 Railroad and Public Service Corporations

Law: Sec. 48-7-32, Code (CCH GEORGIA TAX REPORTS ¶ 11-540).

Special apportionment provisions apply to corporations that operate a railroad, express service, telephone or telegraph business, or other form of

Part III—Corporate Income Tax

public service partly within and partly outside Georgia if the corporation keeps its records in accordance with the standard classification of accounts prescribed by the Interstate Commerce Commission. A similar maintenance of records is required if such a company is not required to make reports to the Commission.

A corporation that keeps records of operating revenues and operating expenses on a state basis may use those records to report net taxable income within Georgia if the records reflect intrastate and interstate business applicable to Georgia, although a corporation that is not required to keep such records, but does so anyway, must receive consent of the commissioner to use the records to report.

¶ 1308 Net Income of Subsidiaries and Affiliates

Law: Sec. 48-7-31(e), Code (CCH GEORGIA TAX REPORTS ¶ 11-520).

The net income of a domestic or foreign corporation that is a subsidiary of, or closely affiliated with, another corporation by stock ownership is determined by eliminating all payments made to the parent corporation or affiliated corporation in excess of fair value and by including fair compensation to the domestic business corporation for its commodities sold to or services performed for the parent or affiliated corporation. This has been interpreted as a mandatory rule. The State Revenue Commissioner has discretion to equitably determine the net income by reasonable rules of apportionment of the combined income of the subsidiary, its parent, and affiliates, or any combination of the subsidiary, its parent, and any one or more of its affiliates to the extent he or she is not limited by the rule just stated above.

Practitioner Comment: Authority of Commissioner

On its face, this section appears to authorize the Commissioner to require the filing of a combined return. However, the Georgia courts have recognized that the Commissioner's authority to require the filing of a combined return is limited. The Commissioner cannot require the filing of a combined return unless he finds that: (1) separate entity reporting does not reflect the true net income of the taxpayer, and (2) the statutory adjustments provided for in the first part of Section 48-7-31(e) do not adequately determine the taxpayer's net income (See *Blackmon v. Campbell Sales Co.*, 125 Ga. App 859, 189 S.E.2d 474 (1972), CCH GEORGIA TAX REPORTS ¶ 00483).

In addition, the statute requires that the apportionment of combined income be pursuant to reasonable rules (See *Polaroid Corp. v. Commissioner*, 393 Mass. 490, 472 N.E.2d 259 (1984) (interpreting a statute virtually identical to Georgia's, the Judicial Court of Massachusetts held that its revenue commissioner's determination requiring the filing of a combined return was invalid because it was not based on a rule or regulation)).

Jeffrey C. Glickman, Esq., Alston & Bird LLP

¶ 1309 Returns Based on Books of Account

Law: Sec. 48-7-34, Code (CCH GEORGIA TAX REPORTS ¶ 11-520).

A corporation that employs in its books of account a detailed allocation of receipts and expenditures that more clearly reflects the income attributable to the trade or business within Georgia than the process or formulas prescribed may apply for permission to base the return upon the its books of account. The application must be filed at least 60 days before the last day for filing the taxpayer's return and must be accompanied by a full and complete explanation of the method employed.

¶ 1310 Revenue Commissioner's Power to Determine Income Attributable to Georgia

Law: Secs. 48-7-31(d)(1) and (d)(3)(E), 48-7-58(a), Code; Reg. Sec. 560-7-7-.03 (CCH GEORGIA TAX REPORTS ¶ 11-520, 11-540).

The State Revenue Commissioner has the power to determine income if the amount of income or the amount attributable to Georgia is being distorted. This may involve situations such as price fixing or charges for services that result in income being arbitrarily assigned to one or another unit in a group of taxpayers carrying on business under a substantially common control.

The Commissioner may also determine income in situations involving sales of products, goods, or commodities to members, stockholders, or interested persons at less than the fair price or the creation of loss or improper net income in transfers of products between controlling and controlled corporations.

The Commissioner may permit by regulation the alteration of the three factor formula used to apportion the income of corporate taxpayers to more fairly represent a taxpayer's business activity within Georgia. The Commissioner may also alter the apportionment formula following a taxpayer's petition for relief.

CCH Tip: Finding Required for Discretionary Authority

The Commissioner may not use his or her discretionary authority in the absence of a finding that the income of the taxpayer cannot be adjusted in the manner prescribed (*Campbell Sales Company et al.*, Georgia Court of Appeals, March 15, 1972, 189 SE2d 474, CCH GEORGIA TAX REPORTS ¶ 00483).

● *Allocation and apportionment by agreement*

The Commissioner may enter into an agreement with corporate taxpayers planning to develop new facilities or expand existing facilities in Georgia to establish, for a limited period of time, a different income allocation and apportionment method. The taxpayer must submit a proposal requesting permission from the Commissioner to enter into an agreement and explaining why the proposal is being made.

Review of proposals: A review panel must first certify that the taxpayer's proposed new facility or expansion will have a significant beneficial economic effect on the region for which it is planned. The panel can only certify a proposal that meets at least two of the following criteria:

(1) the proposal creates new full-time jobs that are:

—20% above average wages for projects located in tier 1 counties;

—10% above average wages for projects located in tier 2 counties; or

—5% above average wages for projects located in tier 3 or tier 4 counties;

(2) the proposal invests in qualified investment property valued at:

—over $10 million in tier 1 counties;

—over $35 million in tier 2 counties; or

—over $75 million in tier 3 or tier 4 counties;

(3) the proposal creates at least:

—50 new full-time jobs in a tier 1 county;

—150 new full-time jobs in a tier 2 county; or

—300 new full-time jobs in a tier 3 or tier 4 county; or

(4) the proposal demonstrates high growth potential based upon the prior year's Georgia net taxable income growth of over 20% from the previous year, if the company's Georgia net taxable income in each of the two preceding years also grew by 20% or more.

Public records: Any proposal submitted by a taxpayer to enter into an allocation and apportionment agreement and any resultant agreement are public records open for inspection. However, all taxpayer information from any state or federal income tax return contained within these documents that would otherwise be privileged or protected from public disclosure will be deleted or redacted from the records made available for public inspection.

¶ 1310

CORPORATE INCOME TAX

CHAPTER 14

RETURNS, ESTIMATES, PAYMENT OF TAX

¶ 1401 Return—Time and Place for Filing
¶ 1402 Corporations Required to File
¶ 1403 Consolidated Returns
¶ 1404 Extensions of Time
¶ 1405 Estimated Tax Declarations
¶ 1406 Payment of Tax
¶ 1407 Forms

¶ 1401 Return—Time and Place for Filing

Law: Secs. 48-2-36, 48-2-39, 48-7-56(a), 48-7-58(a), 48-7-82(e), Code (CCH GEORGIA TAX REPORTS ¶ 89-102, 89-110).

Comparable Federal: Secs. 6071—6075, 6091 (U.S. MASTER TAX GUIDE ¶ 211—215).

Forms: Form 600; Form 600S (S corporations).

Annual Georgia corporate income tax returns (Form 600) are due by March 15, or by the 15th day of the third month after the close of a fiscal year.

If a filing due date or a payment due date falls on a Saturday, Sunday, or legal holiday, the filing of the return or the payment of the tax is timely if it is made on the next business day.

CCH Tip: Timely Filing by Mail

A return mailed by the due date is timely filed (*Letter from the Operations Manager,* Income Tax Division, April 16, 2001).

Corporate income tax returns (Form 600) should be mailed to:
  Georgia Income Tax Division
  P.O. Box 740397
  Atlanta, GA 30374-0397

S corporation income tax returns (Form 600S) should be mailed to:
  Georgia Income Tax Division
  P.O. Box 740391
  Atlanta, GA 30374-0391

A reasonable extension of time to file a return may be granted (¶ 1404).

¶ 1401

● *Federal change*

A taxpayer that is notified by federal taxing authorities that a final determination changes or corrects federal net income for any year has 180 days from the determination to file a return reporting the changed or corrected income for Georgia income tax purposes.

● *Possible shifting of income*

The State Revenue Commissioner may require a corporation to furnish facts necessary to correctly compute the entire net income or the amount attributable to Georgia if the Commissioner believes that a trade or business is being conducted in such a manner that income is being arbitrarily shifted. This may occur in cases involving price fixing, charges for service, etc. in businesses under substantially common control.

¶ 1402 Corporations Required to File

Law: Secs. 48-7-51, 48-7-52, Code (CCH GEORGIA TAX REPORTS ¶ 89-102).

Comparable Federal: Sec. 6011.

Every corporation subject to Georgia corporate income tax must file a return setting forth the items of its gross income and the deductions and credits allowed. The income from two or more corporations may not be included in a single return without the express consent of the State Revenue Commissioner. A receiver, trustee in bankruptcy, or assignee operating the property or business of a corporation must file returns for the corporation in the same manner and form as the corporation is required to file returns.

● *Corporations paying dividends*

Every corporation subject to Georgia corporate income tax must file a return showing its payments of dividends. The return must be verified under oath and must state, with respect to each shareholder who is a resident of Georgia, the name and address of each shareholder, the number of shares owned by the shareholder, and the amount of dividends paid to the shareholder.

¶ 1403 Consolidated Returns

Law: Secs. 48-7-21(b)(7)(A), 48-7-51, Code; Reg. Sec. 560-7-3-.13 (CCH GEORGIA TAX REPORTS ¶ 89-102).

Comparable Federal: Secs. 1501—1505 (U.S. MASTER TAX GUIDE ¶ 295, 297).

Form: Form 600, IT-CONSOL (Application for Permission to File Consolidated Georgia Income Tax Return).

The income of two or more corporations may not be included in a single return without the express consent of the State Revenue Commissioner. If corporations file their federal income tax return on a consolidated basis, they must also file consolidated returns for Georgia income tax purposes if all the corporations involved derive all of their income from sources within Georgia.

¶ 1402

Part III—Corporate Income Tax

Practitioner Comment: Computation of Income

[NOTE: The Georgia Department of Revenue adopted new consolidated return regulations applicable to all tax years beginning on or after January 1, 2002. This comment, therefore, applies only to tax years beginning prior to January 1, 2002.] It should be noted that, under the former consolidated return regulations applicable to tax years beginning prior to January 1, 2002, the computation of income more closely resembled a combined return computation approach. Under such an approach, each member of the Georgia consolidated return combines its income and computes one apportionment factor based on the combined factors of all the members. The result is the group's Georgia taxable net income. Under true consolidation, each member of the return computes its separate income and separate factors to determine its separate Georgia taxable net income. Each member's Georgia taxable net income is then combined to determine the group's consolidated Georgia income. The fact that the return is called a consolidated return is significant in that a consolidated return is filed on behalf of each member of the group, and each member is jointly and severally liable for the Georgia tax liability of the group. A combined return is technically the return of a single taxpayer even though it takes into account the income and factors of more than one corporation for computational purposes; however, the tax reported is the tax liability solely of the corporation on whose behalf the return is filed.

Jeffrey C. Glickman, Esq., Alston & Bird LLP

If affiliated corporations file on a consolidated basis for federal income tax purposes, but derive income from sources outside Georgia, they may seek prior approval from the Georgia Department of Revenue for filing on a consolidated basis for Georgia income tax purposes. The Department may require filing on such a basis.

Unless the Department of Revenue either requires or gives prior approval to the filing of a consolidated return for Georgia income tax purposes, affiliated corporations that file a consolidated federal income tax return, but derive income from sources outside Georgia, must file separate returns for Georgia income tax purposes.

Practitioner Comment: Requirements to File

[NOTE: The Georgia Department of Revenue adopted new consolidated return regulations applicable to all tax years beginning on or after January 1, 2002. This comment, therefore, applies only to tax years beginning prior to January 1, 2002.] Under the former consolidated return regulations applicable to tax years beginning prior to January 1, 2002, one of the requirements to file a Georgia consolidated return was that the corporations of the affiliated group must have transacted a substantial portion of their business in Georgia.

¶ 1403

Despite the fact that the first requirement did not expressly require that each corporation transact a substantial portion of its business in Georgia (only that the "corporations of the affiliated group"—taken as a whole—"transact a substantial portion of their business in Georgia"), the Department of Revenue's Income Tax Division interpreted the regulation as requiring that each corporation transact a substantial portion of its business in Georgia. In addition, the Division's position was that a corporation's business in Georgia is substantial only if the corporation has a Georgia apportionment percentage of 80% or more, although the Department of Revenue did, on occasion, negotiate a different standard on a taxpayer-by-taxpayer basis.

Jeffrey C. Glickman, Esq., Alston & Bird LLP

● *Permissive filing of consolidated return*

To request permission to file a consolidated return, a group of affiliated corporations must file an application with the Commissioner by at least 75 days prior to the earlier of the date the return is due or the date the return is actually filed. The Commissioner must grant permission if a consolidated return will clearly and equitably reflect the Georgia income of the corporations. However, the Commissioner may, as a condition of granting permission to file a consolidated return, require a consolidated group to exclude from the group's Georgia income interest expenses attributable to indebtedness incurred in connection with, or other expenses related to, the ownership of stock of any corporations that are not included in the Georgia consolidated return. Also, if the Commissioner determines that the inclusion of an otherwise eligible corporation in a Georgia consolidated return will not clearly and equitably reflect the consolidated group's Georgia income, the Commissioner may require that corporation to file a separate return or require an adjustment to the consolidated return.

Revocation of permisssion: The Commissioner may revoke permission to file a consolidated return, if the Commissioner determines that a consolidated return will not clearly and equitably reflect the group's Georgia income. The revocation applies prospectively to all tax periods beginning after the date of the Commissioner's written revocation notice. If the Commissioner determines that permission to file a consolidated return was based on an application that contained material omissions or misstatements of fact, the Commissioner may (1) retroactively revoke permission to file a consolidated return; (2) recalculate the tax liabilities of each member on a separate basis; and (3) assess additional tax, interest, and penalties.

● *Net worth tax*

Corporations that file a consolidated Georgia income tax return must report and pay Georgia net worth tax on a separate basis (¶ 1602).

● *Credits*

Corporations in a consolidated group must calculate their Georgia corporate income tax credits on a separate basis. If a credit is limited to 50% of a

¶ 1403

Part III—Corporate Income Tax 159

taxpayer's state income tax liability, this limit must also be computed on a separate basis. Assignment of credits is allowed in a consolidated return.

● *Net operating losses*

A consolidated NOL carryforward or carryback is allowed in a consolidated return, subject to certain restrictions. Reg. Sec. 560-7-3-.13 explains the rules governing NOL deductions for corporations that participate in a consolidated return with examples that illustrate the computation of NOL deductions. The regulation also explains how a corporation carrying over losses from a consolidated return year to a separate return year should apportion those losses.

¶ 1404 Extensions of Time

Law: Secs. 48-2-36, 48-7-56(a), Code (CCH GEORGIA TAX REPORTS ¶ 89-102).

Comparable Federal: Sec. 6081 (U.S. MASTER TAX GUIDE ¶ 2509).

Form: Form IT-611, Georgia Corporate Income Tax Return Instructions. IT-303.

The State Revenue Commissioner may grant an extension of time for filing a return. The maximum aggregate period of extensions of time, except as otherwise provided expressly by law, is six months. An extension of time for filing returns does delay the payment of tax unless a bond satisfactory to the Commissioner is posted. The filing of a tentative return is a condition of the extension.

● *Federal extension*

The Georgia Department of Revenue accepts federal extensions of time for filing returns. Taxpayers that receive a federal extension must attach a copy of the federal extension to the Georgia return.

¶ 1405 Estimated Tax Declarations

Law: Sec. 48-7-117, Code (CCH GEORGIA TAX REPORTS ¶ 89-104).

Comparable Federal: Sec. 6655 (U.S. MASTER TAX GUIDE ¶ 225—331).

Form: Form 602-ES.

Taxpayers are required to file declarations of estimated tax and make installment payments of estimated tax if the net income for the taxable year can reasonably be expected to exceed $25,000. "Estimated tax" means the estimated amount of income tax imposed minus the estimated sum of credits allowed by law against the tax.

A corporation may amend a declaration of estimated tax filed during the taxable year.

¶ 1405

¶ 1406 Payment of Tax

Law: Secs. 48-2-30, 48-2-32(a) and (f)(2), 48-2-36, 48-2-39, 48-7-80, 48-7-119, Code (CCH GEORGIA TAX REPORTS ¶ 89-104—89-108).

Comparable Federal: Secs. 6071—6075, 6151 (U.S. MASTER TAX GUIDE ¶ 5, 2529).

Forms: Form 600, Form IT-560-C (Payment of Income Tax and/or Net Worth Tax).

Corporations must pay the total amount of Georgia corporate income tax imposed by March 15 following the close of the calendar year, or by the 15th day of the third month following the close of the fiscal year if the return is filed on a fiscal year basis. If a payment due date falls on a Saturday, Sunday, or legal holiday, the payment of the tax may be postponed until the first day following that is not a Saturday, Sunday, or legal holiday.

The amount shown on the return as tax must be remitted with the return without further assessment, notice, or demand. Acceptance of the payment does not imply that the tax liability is satisfied; payments are accepted subject to a final determination as to tax liability. Special rules apply to payments received under authorized compromises and settlements.

● *Methods of payment*

The State Revenue Commissioner may accept tax payments through use of personal, company, and certified checks; treasurer's and cashier's checks; and bank, postal and express money orders, subject to whatever conditions the Commissioner reasonably prescribes. If a check or money order is authorized, it is considered to be paid at the time it is tendered and received by the Commissioner, provided it is duly paid when presented to the drawee.

Electronic funds transfers: Any person or business owing more than $10,000 of estimated tax must pay the tax by electronic funds transfer. Electronic funds transfers are discussed at ¶ 2902.

● *Estimated tax installment payments*

Estimated tax installment payments are due as follows:

	fourth month of the taxable year	sixth month of the taxable year	ninth month of the taxable year	twelfth month of the taxable year
Before the first day of the fourth month of the taxable year	25	25	25	25
After the last day of the third month and before the first day of the sixth month of the taxable year		33⅓	33⅓	33⅓
After the last day of the fifth month and before the first day of the ninth month of the taxable year			50	50
After the last day of the eighth month and before the first day of the twelfth month of the taxable year				100

¶ 1406

Part III—Corporate Income Tax

● *Receipt for payment*

A taxpayer may request a receipt for a tax payment. If payment is made in cash, the payor must demand that a written receipt be provided and the person receiving the payment must give the receipt in the form prescribed by the Commissioner as an official receipt of the Department. The receipt will be conclusive as to the transaction. The Commissioner is not required to give credit for a cash payment under any other circumstances.

● *Extension of time*

An extension of time for filing a return does not delay the payment of the tax unless a bond satisfactory to the Commissioner is posted.

● *Check or money order not duly paid*

If a check or money order is not duly paid, the person's tax liability continues and the person is subject to all legal penalties and additions that would have applied if the check or money order had not been tendered. Any delay by the Commissioner in presenting the check or money order for payment does not absolve this liability.

If a check has been certified, or if the payment is made with a treasurer's check, cashier's check, or money order, and this item is not duly paid, the person originally obligated continues to be liable. In addition, the state has a lien upon the assets of the drawee of the check or issuer of the money order.

¶ 1407 Forms

The following forms are in current use:

Form IT-CONSOL—Application for Permission to File Consolidated Georgia Income Tax Return

Form IT-CR—Composite Return for Non-resident Partners/Shareholders

Form IT-552—Corporation Application for Tentative Carry-Back Adjustment

Form IT-560-C—Payment of Income Tax and/or Net Worth Tax

Form IT-611—Corporation Income Tax Booklet

Form 600—Corporation Tax Return

Form 600S—S Corporation Tax Return

Form 600-T—Exempt Organization Unrelated Business Income Tax Return

Form 900—Financial Institutions' Business Occupation Tax Return

Form 3605—Application for Recognition of Exemption

Tax forms may be obtained at the Georgia Department of Revenue website, http://www2.state.ga.us/departments/dor/inctax/corporate_tax_index_page.shtml

For address information, see Chapter 32, "Georgia Resources."

¶ 1407

Part III—Corporate Income Tax

CORPORATE INCOME TAX

CHAPTER 15

ADMINISTRATION, DEFICIENCIES, PENALTIES, REFUNDS, APPEALS

¶ 1501 Administration—In General
¶ 1502 Deficiencies—Procedure
¶ 1503 Interest on Deficiencies
¶ 1504 Penalties
¶ 1505 Statute of Limitations on Assessments
¶ 1506 Jeopardy Assessments
¶ 1507 Bankruptcy and Receivership
¶ 1508 Transferee Liability
¶ 1509 Overpayments and Refunds
¶ 1510 Interest on Overpayments and Refunds
¶ 1511 Abatement—Protest to Commissioner
¶ 1512 Statute of Limitations on Claims for Refund
¶ 1513 Judicial Review
¶ 1514 Settlements and Compromise of Tax

¶ 1501 Administration—In General

Law: Secs. 48-2-1, 48-2-12(a) and (d), 48-2-35(b), Code.

Georgia corporate income tax is administered by the Georgia Department of Revenue. For address information, see Chapter 32, "Georgia Resources."

The State Revenue Commissioner is the executive and administrative head of the Department. The Commissioner has the authority to administer and enforce the collection of taxes, approve or deny refund claims, and issue regulations. For additional information on the Department of Revenue, see ¶ 2901.

¶ 1502 Deficiencies—Procedure

Law: Secs. 48-2-35(c), 48-2-45, 48-2-51, 48-2-54, 48-2-56(b), 48-2-58, 48-7-58, 48-7-59, 48-7-82(c), 48-7-120(d)(3), Code (CCH GEORGIA TAX REPORTS ¶ 89-162).

Comparable Federal: Secs. 6211—6215 (U.S. MASTER TAX GUIDE ¶ 2711, 2778).

The State Revenue Commissioner is authorized to make deficiency assessments. A notice of deficiency must be sent to the taxpayer. The taxpayer has the right to file a petition for redetermination.

● *Tax liens*

State tax liens are given priority. Property subject to a state tax lien may be released from the lien if the taxpayer provides sufficient security.

● *Tax executions*

If an income tax assessment has been made within the applicable limitation period, the tax may be collected by execution. The general provisions for tax executions are applicable.

● *Jeopardy assessments*

The Commissioner is authorized to make an arbitrary assessment whenever it appears that collection of the tax may be in jeopardy and, after notice, the Commissioner may bring suit to collect any unpaid tax.

● *State's right to a setoff*

The Commissioner may offset a taxpayer's refund against the taxpayer's unpaid tax liability for state taxes, including other state taxes.

● *Examination of federal returns*

The Commissioner may examine federal income tax returns and all statements, inventories, and schedules in support of the returns in order to properly audit the returns of the taxpayer.

● *Determination of a corporation's taxable income to avoid income shifting*

The Commissioner may determine a corporation's taxable income if it is believed that income is being arbitrarily shifted. Benefits to members or stockholders of the corporation or persons interested in the business through sales of products or services at less than a fair price, or creation of improper loss or net income among related corporations through disposal of products, may result in the Commissioner's determination of taxable income for one or more corporations.

● *Underpayment of estimated tax*

An addition to tax may be imposed if estimated tax is underpaid. An underpayment of estimated tax is equal to the excess of the amount of the installment payment that would be required if the estimated tax were equal to 70% of the tax shown on the return for the taxable year, or the tax for the year

Part III—Corporate Income Tax 165

if no return was filed, over the amount of any installment paid by the last day prescribed for payment.

The addition to tax may not be imposed if the total amount of all payments of estimated tax made by the installment payment deadline equals or exceeds the amount that would have to be paid by that date if the estimated tax were equal to the lesser of

—the tax shown on a return filed for the preceding taxable year, if the preceding taxable year was a 12-month taxable year,

—the tax computed on the basis of the facts and law of the preceding year using the rates and status of the current taxable year, or

—70% of the tax for the taxable year computed by annualizing the taxable income for the months in the taxable year ending the month before the installment is required to be paid.

CCH Tip: Annualizing Taxable Income

Taxable income is annualized by multiplying by 12 (or the number of months in the taxable year, if less than 12) the taxable income for the months in the taxable year ending before the month when the installment is to be paid and dividing the resulting amount by the number of months in the taxable year ending before the month in which the installment date falls. Any personal exemptions are then deducted, determined as of the last date prescribed for payment of the installment.

¶ 1503 Interest on Deficiencies

Interest on deficiencies is discussed at ¶ 3003.

¶ 1504 Penalties

Penalties are discussed at ¶ 3003.

¶ 1505 Statute of Limitations on Assessments

Statutes of limitations on assessments are discussed at ¶ 3001.

¶ 1506 Jeopardy Assessments

Jeopardy assessments are discussed at ¶ 3002.

¶ 1507 Bankruptcy and Receivership

Law: Sec. 48-7-51, Code (CCH GEORGIA TAX REPORTS ¶ 89-170).

Comparable Federal: Secs. 6871—6873.

A receiver, trustee in bankruptcy, or assignee operating the property or business of a corporation is required to make returns for the corporation in the same manner and form as the corporation is required to make returns. Any tax

¶ 1507

due on the basis of such a return is collected in the same manner as if collected from the corporation.

¶ 1508 Transferee Liability

Law: Secs. 48-7-83, 48-7-128, Code; Reg. Sec. 560-7-8-.35 (CCH GEORGIA TAX REPORTS ¶ 10-210).

Comparable Federal: Secs. 6901, 6902 (U.S. MASTER TAX GUIDE ¶ 2743).

Transferees in transactions involving transfers of property owned by nonresidents and corporate dissolutions may be required to withhold income tax imposed as a result of the transaction.

● *Property transfers by nonresidents*

Purchasers and transferees may be required to withhold tax imposed on certain transfers of real property and related personal property located in Georgia and sold by a nonresident. The tax is equal to 3% of the purchase price or consideration paid for the property sold or transferred. The transferee or purchaser remains personally liable for the tax. However, if the nonresident seller or transferor determines that an excess withholding would result, a signed affidavit under oath may be provided to the purchaser affirming the amount of gain to be recognized from the sale, and the purchaser or transferee must instead withhold 3% of the amount stated in the affidavit. In addition, when the amount otherwise required to be withheld exceeds the net proceeds payable to the seller or transferor, the buyer or transferee must withhold and pay over only the net proceeds otherwise payable to the seller or transferor.

If a nonresident seller transfers property in installment transactions, the buyer must withhold on each payment to the seller.

Purchasers and transferees required to deduct and withhold tax on transfers of nonresident-owned Georgia property must file a return and remit the payment by the last day of the month following the month when the sale or transfer occurred.

Exclusions from withholding requirement: The withholding requirement for nonresident property transfers does not apply if the property being transferred is

—the principal residence of the seller or transferor,

—the seller or transferor is a mortgagor conveying the mortgaged property to a mortgagee in a foreclosure, or in a transfer in lieu of foreclosure with no additional consideration,

—the transferor or transferee is an agency or authority of the United States, Georgia, the Federal National Mortgage Association, the Federal Home Loan Mortgage Corporation, the Government National Mortgage Association, or a private mortgage insurance company,

—the purchase price is below a minimum set by the State Revenue Commissioner, or

—a partnership, S corporation or other unincorporated organization certifies to the buyer or transferee that a composite return is being filed on behalf of the nonresident partners, shareholders, or members, and that

Part III—Corporate Income Tax 167

the tax on the gain has been paid on behalf of such nonresident partners, shareholders, or members.

Withholding is not required if the purchase price is less than $20,000. If the purchase price exceeds $20,000 and the tax liability is less than $600, the seller may submit an affidavit swearing to the gain and documentation of cost basis and selling expenses so that the buyer does not have to withhold.

● *Corporate dissolution*

Whenever a corporation has been dissolved, or the corporation's assets have passed entirely from control of the corporation into the possession of its former stockholders or other persons without the payment of income taxes due to Georgia, the State Revenue Commissioner has the right to bring action against any or all persons possessing the assets for the collection of any income taxes that may be due, up to the value of the assets. If the assets have come into the possession of more than one person, each person has the right to prorate the amount of the tax according to the value of the assets coming into each person's possession.

¶ 1509 Overpayments and Refunds

Overpayments and refunds are discussed at ¶ 3101.

¶ 1510 Interest on Overpayments and Refunds

Interest on overpayments and refunds is discussed at ¶ 3003.

¶ 1511 Abatement—Protest to Commissioner

Procedures for the abatement of taxes are discussed at ¶ 3101.

¶ 1512 Statute of Limitations on Claims for Refund

The statute of limitations on refund claims is discussed at ¶ 3101.

¶ 1513 Judicial Review

Judicial review is discussed at ¶ 3101.

¶ 1514 Settlements and Compromise of Tax

Settlements and compromise of tax are discussed at ¶ 3101.

PART IV

CORPORATE NET WORTH (FRANCHISE) TAX

CHAPTER 16

IMPOSITION OF TAX, RATES, EXEMPTIONS

¶ 1601 Overview
¶ 1602 Corporations Subject to Tax
¶ 1603 Exempt Corporations
¶ 1604 Tax Base
¶ 1605 Tax Rate

¶ 1601 Overview
Law: Secs. 48-13-72, 48-13-78, Code (CCH GEORGIA TAX REPORTS ¶ 5-001, 5-005).

Georgia corporate net worth (franchise) tax is essentially the type of levy commonly imposed by states on the privilege of doing business within their borders. The amount of the tax is based on a corporation's net worth. It is imposed on domestic (or domesticated) corporations for the privilege granted by Georgia charter, and on foreign corporations for the privilege of carrying on business in Georgia in a corporate form. The corporate net worth tax is imposed in addition to all other taxes imposed by law. The tax is administered by the State Revenue Commissioner through the Income Tax Division of the Georgia Department of Revenue.

¶ 1602 Corporations Subject to Tax
Law: Secs. 48-13-70, 48-13-72, Code (CCH GEORGIA TAX REPORTS ¶ 5-205, 5-210).

The corporate net worth (franchise) tax is imposed on both domestic corporations and foreign corporations doing business within Georgia, including associations and associations organized under the Georgia Professional Association Act.

● *Domestic corporations*

All corporations incorporated under the laws of Georgia and all domesticated foreign corporations are subject to tax. Domestic corporations are subject to tax as long as their charters are in existence, regardless of whether they are doing business. Provisions for domestication of foreign corporations were repealed in 1969.

A limited liability company (an LLC) is subject to net worth tax only if it is treated as a corporation for income tax purposes (*Frequently Asked Questions*, Georgia Department of Revenue, August 2004).

● *Foreign corporations*

Corporations incorporated or organized under the laws of any other state, territory, or nation that do business or own property in Georgia are subject to tax. The tax is imposed on such foreign corporations for the privilege of carrying on a business within Georgia in a corporate form.

¶ 1603 Exempt Corporations

Law: Sec. 48-13-71, Code (CCH GEORGIA TAX REPORTS ¶ 5-205, 5-210).

Nonprofit organizations and insurance companies are exempt from the corporate net worth (franchise) tax.

¶ 1604 Tax Base

Law: Secs. 48-13-73(a), 48-13-75(a), Code (CCH GEORGIA TAX REPORTS ¶ 5-305, 5-310).

The corporate net worth (franchise) tax is based on a corporation's net worth. Net worth includes the value of a corporation's issued capital stock, treasury stock, paid-in surplus, and earned surplus.

A foreign corporation is subject to corporate net worth (franchise) tax on the portion of its corporate net worth that is employed in Georgia. The taxable portion is determined by dividing the value of assets in Georgia plus receipts from business done in the state by the corporation's total assets and business receipts.

For additional information on the basis of tax, see Chapter 17.

Practitioner Comment: Apportionment

Although the net worth tax is minimal (the maximum is $5,000, see ¶ 1605), only foreign corporations (i.e., corporations formed under the laws of another state) are allowed to apportion their net worth for purposes of computing net worth subject to tax. Domestic (i.e., Georgia) corporations that do business both within and outside Georgia (and that are allowed to apportion for Georgia income tax purposes) are not allowed to apportion under the net worth tax. Therefore, unless there is a significant reason to be a Georgia corporation, taxpayers may be able to reduce their net worth tax liability by incorporating under the laws of a state other than Georgia.

Jeffrey C. Glickman, Esq., Alston & Bird LLP

¶ 1605 Tax Rate

Law: Sec. 48-13-73(a) and (b), Code (CCH GEORGIA TAX REPORTS ¶ 5-405).

The corporate net worth (franchise) tax is imposed at the following graduated rates on the full corporate net worth of domestic and domesticated corporations, and on the apportioned net worth of foreign corporations:

¶ 1603

Part IV—Corporate Net Worth (Franchise) Tax

Corporations with Net Worth Including Issued Capital Stock, Paid-in Surplus and Earned Surplus		Amount of Tax
Over	*But Not Over*	
.....	$ 10,000	$ 10
$ 10,000	25,000	20
25,000	40,000	40
40,000	60,000	60
60,000	80,000	75
80,000	100,000	100
100,000	150,000	125
150,000	200,000	150
200,000	300,000	200
300,000	500,000	250
500,000	750,000	300
750,000	1,000,000	500
1,000,000	2,000,000	750
2,000,000	4,000,000	1,000
4,000,000	6,000,000	1,250
6,000,000	8,000,000	1,500
8,000,000	10,000,000	1,750
10,000,000	12,000,000	2,000
12,000,000	14,000,000	2,500
14,000,000	16,000,000	3,000
16,000,000	18,000,000	3,500
18,000,000	20,000,000	4,000
20,000,000	22,000,000	4,500
22,000,000		5,000

● *Corporations initially taxable for less than six months*

When a corporation first becomes subject to tax for an initial period of less than six months, tax is imposed at one-half of the above rates for that period. The law does not provide for proration of the tax in any other circumstances, such as the termination or withdrawal of a corporation during its taxable year.

¶ 1605

CORPORATE NET WORTH (FRANCHISE) TAX

CHAPTER 17

BASIS OF TAX

¶ 1701   Corporate Net Worth
¶ 1702   Foreign Corporations—Apportionment of Net Worth

¶ 1701   Corporate Net Worth

Law: Secs. 48-13-73(a), 48-13-74, 48-13-75(a), Code; Georgia Corporate Income Tax Return Instructions, Form IT-611 (CCH GEORGIA TAX REPORTS ¶ 5-305).

Georgia corporate net worth (franchise) tax is a graduated tax that is based on a corporation's net worth. Net worth includes the value of a corporation's issued capital stock, treasury stock, paid-in surplus, and earned surplus.

Domestic and domesticated corporations are taxed on their full corporate net worth. In contrast, foreign corporations apportion the net worth figure to determine the amount subject to Georgia tax. A corporation's net worth is presumed to be the net worth shown on the corporation's books and reflected in its annual return. However, if the true net worth is not disclosed by the return or the books, the Commissioner may determine the value from information obtained from any source.

No-par-value stock: A foreign corporation's no-par-value stock is deemed to have a value as fixed by the Commissioner from the information given in the corporation's return or from any other available information.

¶ 1702   Foreign Corporations—Apportionment of Net Worth

Law: Sec. 48-13-75(a), Code (CCH GEORGIA TAX REPORTS ¶ 5-310).

A foreign corporation is subject to corporate net worth (franchise) tax on the portion of its corporate net worth that is employed in Georgia. The taxable portion is determined by dividing the value of assets in Georgia plus receipts from business done in the state by the corporation's total assets and business receipts. The resulting percentage is applied to total corporate net worth to find the amount subject to tax as shown in the rate table (¶ 1605).

Gross receipts: Only receipts from products shipped to customers in Georgia or delivered within Georgia to customers constitute gross receipts from business done in Georgia. Specifically excluded from Georgia receipts are those from sales negotiated or effected in corporate offices outside Georgia and delivered to out-of-state customers from storage in Georgia.

Part IV—Corporate Net Worth (Franchise) Tax

CORPORATE NET WORTH (FRANCHISE) TAX

CHAPTER 18

RETURNS AND PAYMENT OF TAX; ADMINISTRATION

¶ 1801 Returns—Time and Place for Filing
¶ 1802 Payment of Tax
¶ 1803 Period Covered by Tax Payment
¶ 1804 Administration

¶ 1801 Returns—Time and Place for Filing

Law: Secs. 48-13-76(b), 48-13-77, 48-13-78, 48-13-79(a), Code; Georgia Corporate Income Tax Return Instructions, Form IT-611 (CCH GEORGIA TAX REPORTS ¶ 6-005, 6-010, 6-015).

Forms: 600, 600-S, IT 303 (Application for Extension of Time for Filing State Income Tax Returns).

Every corporation subject to Georgia corporate net worth (franchise) tax must file a return sworn to by an officer of the corporation. The corporate net worth (franchise) tax and corporate income tax returns are combined on Form 600, or on Form 600S for small business corporations. See ¶ 1401 for mailing addresses.

Returns must be filed by the 15th day of the third calendar month following the beginning of the taxable period. Therefore, annual returns are due by March 15 in the case of calendar year corporations, and by an equivalent date in the case of companies operating on a fiscal year basis.

● *Short period return*

A return for a short initial taxable period of a corporation first becoming subject to tax, although made on the same form, will deal only with franchise tax, since the income tax law has no similar provisions.

CCH Tip: Computation of Net Worth on Short Period Return

Corporations filing a short period income and/or corporate net worth (franchise) tax return for any reason, other than initial or final return, must compute the corporate net worth (franchise) tax on net worth on the basis of the ending balance sheet of the short period return. The tax is then prorated on the basis of the number of months included in the short period return (*Letter from Income Tax Division,* April 20, 1987; CCH GEORGIA TAX REPORTS ¶ 200-126).

¶ 1801

Initial tax period and return due date: The initial tax period of a corporation coming into existence or becoming subject to tax for the first time begins on the date of incorporation or the date the corporation first becomes subject to tax. The first return for a new domestic corporation or a foreign corporation doing business or owning property in Georgia must be filed on or before the 15th day of the third calendar month after incorporation or qualification.

● *Consolidated returns*

Although two or more corporations may file a consolidated corporate income tax return, each subsidiary must file a separate corporate net worth (franchise) tax return. The parent corporation should file its net worth tax return in Schedule 2 of the consolidated corporate income tax return, using only the parent's net worth in computing the tax due.

● *Extension of time for filing return*

The State Revenue Commissioner may extend the time for filing a return if good cause is shown. The instructions for the franchise tax return state that application for an extension should be made on a prescribed form before the return is due.

Federal extension: If a taxpayer making a combined income/corporate net worth (franchise) tax return has obtained an extension of time for filing the federal income tax return, it is not necessary to apply for a similar Georgia extension. An extension is granted automatically if a copy of the approved federal request is attached to the Georgia return. However, if a taxpayer is filing only a corporate net worth (franchise) tax return, and no Georgia income tax return is due, a federal extension will not be applicable, and the taxpayer must apply for a Georgia extension.

In any case, extension of time for filing the return does not extend the time for paying the tax.

¶ 1802 Payment of Tax

Law: Sec. 48-13-78, Code (CCH GEORGIA TAX REPORTS ¶ 8-005, 8-010).

Forms: IT-560-C (Payment of Income Tax and/or Net Worth Tax).

The corporate net worth (franchise) tax must be paid by the 15th day of the third calendar month beginning with the first calendar month of the taxable period. In practice, the tax accompanies the return filed for an initial or annual taxable period unless the time for filing is extended.

There is no provision for extending the time for payment of the tax.

¶ 1803 Period Covered by Tax Payment

Law: Secs. 48-13-73(b), 48-13-76(a) and (b), Code (CCH GEORGIA TAX REPORTS ¶ 5-505, 5-510).

For a corporation that is subject to Georgia corporate income tax, the annual taxable period for the corporate net worth (franchise) tax is the calendar or fiscal year adopted for income tax purposes. Any corporation that does not file income tax returns is liable for corporate net worth (franchise) tax on a calendar year basis. In either case, the corporate net worth (franchise) tax

¶ 1802

Part IV—Corporate Net Worth (Franchise) Tax

is imposed and paid for the current year and liability accrues on the first day of the taxable year.

● *Initial taxable period*

The initial taxable period for domestic corporations begins on the date of incorporation. The initial taxable period for foreign corporations begins on the date of qualification. The initial period runs through the last day before the beginning of the regular annual taxable period. If the initial taxable period is less than six months, the tax is imposed at one-half of the regular rate.

¶ 1804 Administration

Law: Sec. 48-13-74, Code (CCH GEORGIA TAX REPORTS ¶ 7-005).

The corporate net worth (franchise) tax is administered by the State Revenue Commissioner. For information on generally applicable provisions concerning collection of tax, penalties, refunds, and appeals, see Part IX, "Administration and Procedure," beginning at Chapter 29.

● *Assessment or revision by Commissioner*

If the value of a corporation is not disclosed by its return or books, the State Revenue Commissioner may determine the true value from information obtained from any source. In the case of foreign corporations, the Commissioner may fix the value of no-par-value stock and may provide for an alternate method of apportionment if the standard formula does not accurately reflect the percentage of the corporation's total business attributable to Georgia.

PART V

BANKS AND FINANCIAL INSTITUTIONS TAX

CHAPTER 19

TAX ON DEPOSITORY FINANCIAL INSTITUTIONS

¶ 1901	Entities Subject to Tax
¶ 1902	Basis of Tax
¶ 1903	Rate of Tax
¶ 1904	Allocation of Local Business License Taxes
¶ 1905	Credit Against Corporate Income Tax
¶ 1906	Returns and Payments

¶ 1901 Entities Subject to Tax

Law: Secs. 48-6-90, 48-6-90.1, 48-6-91, 48-6-93, 48-6-95, Code (CCH GEORGIA TAX REPORTS ¶ 14-010).

Comparable Federal: Secs. 581—585 (U.S. MASTER TAX GUIDE ¶ 2383).

A state occupation tax is imposed on each depository financial institution that conducts business or owns property in Georgia. In addition, municipalities and counties may levy a business license tax on depository financial institutions having an office located within their jurisdictions.

The term "depository financial institution" refers to a bank or a savings and loan association. A "bank" is a financial institution chartered under federal law or state laws that is authorized to receive deposits in Georgia and that has a corporate structure authorizing the issuance of capital stock. A "savings and loan association" is any financial institution, other than a credit union, chartered under federal or state laws that is authorized to receive deposits in Georgia and that has a mutual corporate form.

Except as otherwise provided, depository financial institutions are subject to all forms of state and local taxation in the same manner and to the same extent as other business corporations in Georgia.

● *Exemption*

Domestic international banking facilities operating in Georgia under the Domestic International Banking Facility Act are not subject to state or local taxes.

¶ 1902 Basis of Tax

Law: Secs. 48-6-93, 48-6-95, Code (CCH GEORGIA TAX REPORTS ¶ 14-030).

The state occupation tax, as well as the local business license taxes, are based on Georgia gross receipts.

- *Items deducted from gross receipts*

The following amounts are deducted before determining gross receipts:

(1) interest paid on all liabilities for the period;

(2) income from authorized activities of a domestic international banking facility; and

(3) income from banking business with persons or entities outside the United States, its territories, or possessions.

To the extent that any deductions are made pursuant to (2) or (3) above, any deductions taken under (1) above will be reduced by the same proportion that the deductions in (2) and (3) above bear to the gross receipts of the depository institution as calculated before making any deductions pursuant to (1) through (3) above.

- *Gross receipts—banks*

The following items are included in the calculation of gross receipts with respect to banks:

—interest and fees on loans less any interest collected on those portions of loans sold and serviced for others;

—interest on balances with other depository financial institutions;

—interest on federal or correspondent funds sold and securities purchased under agreement to resell;

—interest on other bonds, notes, and debentures, excluding interest on obligations of the State of Georgia or its political subdivisions and obligations of the United States;

—dividends on stock;

—income from direct lease financing;

—income from fiduciary activities;

—service charges on deposit accounts;

—other service charges, commissions, and fees; and

—other income.

- *Gross receipts—savings and loan associations*

The following items are included in the calculation of gross receipts with respect to savings and loan associations:

—interest on mortgage loans, less any interest collected on those portions of loans sold and serviced for others;

—interest on mortgages, participations, or mortgage-backed securities;

—interest on real estate sold on contract;

Part V—Banks and Financial Institutions Tax

—discounts on mortgage loans purchased;

—interest on other loans, excluding interest on obligations of the State of Georgia or its political subdivisions and obligations of the United States;

—interest and dividends on investments and deposits;

—loan fees;

—loan servicing fees;

—other fees and charges;

—gross income from real estate owned operations;

—net income from office building operations;

—gross income from real estate held for investment;

—net income from service corporations and subsidiaries;

—miscellaneous operating income;

—profit on sale of real estate owned operations, investment securities, loans, and other assets; and

—miscellaneous nonoperating income.

● *Apportionment formula*

If a taxpayer conducts business both within and without Georgia, Georgia gross receipts are determined by multiplying gross receipts, as calculated above, by the taxpayer's gross receipts factor as used in the corporate income tax apportionment formula applicable to corporations whose net business is derived principally from business other than the manufacture, production or sale of tangible personal property (¶ 1306).

¶ 1903 Rate of Tax

Law: Secs. 48-6-93, 48-6-95, Code (CCH GEORGIA TAX REPORTS ¶ 14-020).

The state occupation tax is levied at the rate of 0.25% of the Georgia gross receipts of depository financial institutions.

● *Local taxes*

Municipalities and counties may levy and collect a business license tax from depository financial institutions within their jurisdictions at a rate not to exceed 0.25% of the Georgia gross receipts allocated to the locality. Municipalities and counties may provide that the minimum annual amount of the levy upon any depository financial institution may be no more than $1,000.

¶ 1904 Allocation of Local Business License Taxes

Law: Secs. 48-6-93, 48-6-95, Code (CCH GEORGIA TAX REPORTS ¶ 14-040).

A depository financial institution's Georgia gross receipts are allocated among each taxing jurisdiction in which the institution has an office as of December 1 of the year in which gross receipts are measured. Each jurisdiction is assigned the gross receipts attributable to the offices located within the jurisdiction.

In determining the amount of gross receipts attributable to each office, 20% of the institution's Georgia gross receipts are attributable to that institution's principal Georgia office, which, for this purpose, is the Georgia office to which the greatest amount of deposits by value are attributable. The remaining 80% of Georgia gross receipts are attributable to the institution's other Georgia offices, pro rata according to the number of offices.

¶ 1905 Credit Against Corporate Income Tax

Law: Secs. 48-6-93, 48-6-95, 48-7-29.4, Code (CCH GEORGIA TAX REPORTS ¶ 14-050).

Any state occupation or local license tax paid by a depository financial institution may be credited against any corporate income tax due the same tax year.

Additional details of this credit are discussed at ¶ 919.

¶ 1906 Returns and Payments

Law: Sec. 48-6-95, Code (CCH GEORGIA TAX REPORTS ¶ 14-060, 14-070).

Forms: Form 900 (Financial Institutions' Business Occupation Tax Return).

The tax is reported to the State Revenue Commissioner on Form 900 by March 1 of the year following the year in which the gross receipts are measured. The tax is to be paid at the time of filing the return.

For information on generally applicable provisions concerning collection of tax, penalties, refunds, and appeals, see Part IX, "Administration and Procedure," beginning at Chapter 29.

PART VI

SALES AND USE TAXES

CHAPTER 20

PERSONS AND TRANSACTIONS SUBJECT TO TAX

¶ 2001 Overview of Sales and Use Taxes
¶ 2002 Application of Sales Tax
¶ 2003 Out-of-State Dealers—Nexus Provisions
¶ 2004 Persons and Transactions Subject to Tax
¶ 2005 Taxable Services
¶ 2006 Use Tax

¶ 2001 Overview of Sales and Use Taxes

The Georgia Retailers' and Consumers' Sales and Use Tax Act was enacted in 1951.

Georgia sales and use taxes are imposed on the retail purchase, retail sale, rental, storage, use, or consumption of tangible personal property and certain services (¶ 2002).

Counties, municipalities, school districts, and political subdivisions of the state are prohibited from imposing or collecting sales and use taxes unless authorized by the General Assembly. Local taxes have been authorized; for further discussion, see ¶ 2103. Rates are listed at ¶ 2104.

The Department of Revenue administers and enforces the revenue laws of Georgia, under the direction of the State Revenue Commissioner. The Director of the Sales and Use Tax Unit of the Department of Revenue is directly responsible to the Commissioner for the administration of the sales and use tax.

Taxable transactions: Application of sales and use tax to selected transactions is discussed at ¶ 2004. Exemptions from tax are discussed at ¶ 2201 and ¶ 2202, and credits against tax are explained at ¶ 2203.

Taxation of services: Only specifically designated services are taxable, as discussed at ¶ 2005.

Returns, payments, and recordkeeping are discussed in Chapter 23, while collection issues, including business successor liability and penalties and interest are discussed in Chapter 24.

¶ 2002 Application of Sales Tax

Law: Secs. 48-8-1—48-8-3, 48-8-30, 48-8-38, 48-8-39(b), 48-8-65, Code (CCH GEORGIA TAX REPORTS ¶ 60-020, 60-510).

Georgia sales and use taxes are imposed on the retail purchase, retail sale, rental, storage, use, or consumption of tangible personal property and certain services. These taxes are intended to cover all such purchases, uses, and services as provided in the law to the extent permitted under the federal and state constitutions, with due regard being paid to the specific exemptions permitted by the sales and use tax provisions (¶ 2201).

● *Sales at retail*

"Retail sale" or "sale at retail" means a sale to a consumer or to any person other than for resale of tangible personal property or services taxable under the law, including transactions that the Commissioner finds to be in lieu of sales. Retail sales include the following:

—the sale of gas, oil, electricity, transportation, telephone services, beverages, and tobacco products;

—the sale or charges for rooms or lodging for less than 90 days;

—sales of tickets, fees, or charges for admission to, and voluntary contributions made to places of amusement;

—charges for the operation of coin-operated amusement devices; and

—charges for participation in games and amusement activities.

Sales of tangible personal property for resale to certain persons may be considered retail sales if it appears that the state will lose tax funds due to the difficulty of policing the business operations of such persons due to a number of factors, such as incomplete records (¶ 2306).

"Sale" means any transfer of title and/or possession, exchange, barter, lease, or rental, in any manner or by any means of tangible personal property for a consideration, and includes (1) the fabrication of tangible personal property for consumers who furnish the materials used, (2) the furnishing, repairing, or serving of tangible personal property consumed on the premises of the person furnishing, repairing, or serving, or (3) a transaction in which the possession of property is transferred but the seller retains title as security for payment.

"Lease or rental" means the leasing or renting of tangible personal property and the possession or use of property by the lessee or renter for a consideration without transfer of title.

"Tangible personal property" is personal property that can be seen, weighed, measured, felt, or touched, or that is perceptible to the senses. It does not include stocks, bonds, notes, insurance, or other obligations or securities.

● *Services*

Specific services are taxable. A person who has purchased or received any taxable service within Georgia is subject to tax on the gross charge or charges made for the purchase. This tax must be paid by the purchaser or recipient of

Part VI—Sales and Use Taxes

the service to the service provider. However, a sale of services is not taxable to the service provider if it is not taxable to the purchaser of the service.

The taxability of services is discussed in greater detail at ¶ 2005.

● *Incidence of tax*

The sales and use taxes are imposed on both the purchaser or lessee, the retail vendor or lessor, or the purchaser and provider of taxable services, but the measure of tax is different. The tax on the purchaser is imposed on the sales price, while the tax on the retail vendor is the greater of the tax based on the vendor's gross sales or the amount of taxes collected from the purchaser. No retail sale, lease, or rental is taxable to the retailer, dealer, or lessor which is not taxable to the purchaser at retail or to the person to whom property is leased or rented.

● *"Dealer" defined*

"Dealer" includes every person who:

—has sold at retail, used, consumed, distributed, or stored for use or consumption in Georgia tangible personal property and who cannot prove that tax has not been paid on the sale at retail or on the use, consumption, distribution, or storage of the property;

—imports tangible personal property for sale at retail, or for use, consumption, distribution, or storage for use or consumption in Georgia;

—is the lessee or renter of tangible personal property and who pays to the owner a consideration for the use or possession of the property without acquiring title;

—leases or rents tangible personal property for a consideration;

—maintains or has within the state, indirectly or by a subsidiary, an office, distributing house, salesroom, or house, warehouse, or other place of business;

—manufactures or produces tangible personal property for sale at retail or for use, consumption, distribution, or storage for use or consumption in the state;

—sells, offers for sale, or has in possession for sale at retail, or for use, consumption, distribution, or storage for use or consumption in the state tangible personal property; or

—solicits business by representatives or engages in the regular or systematic solicitation of a consumer market in Georgia by the distribution of catalogs, periodicals, advertising fliers, or other advertising, or by means of print, radio, or television media, by telegraphy, telephone, computer data base, cable optic, microwave, or other communication system.

● *"Retailer" defined*

"Retailer" means any person making sales at retail or for distribution, use, consumption, or storage for use or consumption in Georgia

¶ 2002

● *Presumption of taxability*

All gross sales of a retailer are subject to tax until the contrary is established. The person making the sale has the burden of proving that a sale is not a sale at retail unless a resale certificate is accepted from the purchaser.

● *Use of self-produced goods*

Self-produced goods are taxable when used by the processor or manufacturer—see ¶ 2101, "Basis of Tax."

● *Mobile Telecommunications Sourcing Act*

Georgia has adopted the provisions of the federal Mobile Telecommunications Sourcing Act (P.L. 106-252). Wireless telecommunications are sourced to the customer's primary place of use, which is the residential or primary business address of the customer located in the service provider's licensed service area. The jurisdiction in which the primary place of use is located is the only jurisdiction that may tax telecommunications services, regardless of the customer's location when an actual call is placed or received. The service provider may treat the address used for purposes of the mobile telecommunications tax for any customer under a service contract in effect on August 1, 2002, as that customer's place of primary use for the remaining term of the service contract or agreement, excluding any extension or renewal of the contract or agreement.

Address database: The service provider is held harmless for an error in assigning wireless services to a jurisdiction if it utilizes an electronic database provided by the state or a designated entity.

Bundled services: If taxable and nontaxable wireless services are bundled and sold for a single price, the service provider is not required to separately state the charges on the bill if it maintains sufficient books and records to support the nontaxable portion of the charge. A customer may only rely on the nontaxability of a service if the telephone service provider separately states the charge for the service, or the service provider elects, after receiving a written request from the customer, to provide verifiable data based upon the provider's books and records that reasonably identifies the amount charged for the nontaxable service.

Dispute resolution: Although not part of the federal Act, special taxpayer remedy provisions have been enacted for disputes arising from sourcing of wireless telecommunications. These provisions require customers who believe they have been erroneously taxed to seek relief from their service provider first, before proceeding to normal administrative or judicial methods. Any such taxpayer dissatisfied with the result may then proceed to normal relief procedures.

Local taxes: The application of a 911 service charge to a mobile telecommunications service is subject to the 2% limitation on local sales and use taxes.

¶ 2002

Part VI—Sales and Use Taxes 187

¶ 2003 Out-of-State Dealers—Nexus Provisions

Law: Secs. 48-8-2(3)(H), 48-8-30(b), (c.1), (d), (e.1), and (f), 48-8-32—48-8-35, Code; Reg. Sec. 560-12-1-.11 (CCH GEORGIA TAX REPORTS ¶ 60-020).

An out-of-state seller may be compelled to collect a state's use tax if it has certain minimum contacts, or "nexus," with the state. In 1967, the U.S. Supreme Court concluded that a mail order company could not be forced to collect Illinois use tax on sales made to customers in Illinois, because the corporation's only activity in Illinois consisted of soliciting sales by catalogs and flyers followed by delivery of the goods by mail or common carrier (*National Bellas Hess, Inc. v. Department of Revenue* (1967, US SCt) 386 US 753).

The *Bellas Hess* decision rested on both Due Process and Commerce Clause grounds. The position taken in *Bellas Hess* that physical presence is required to meet the requirements of the Commerce Clause was specifically reaffirmed by the High Court in *Quill Corporation v. North Dakota* (1992, US SCt) 504 US 298, 112 SCt 1904. However, *Quill* resolved the *Bellas Hess* due process objections, holding that physical presence is not required by the Due Process Clause before a state can compel an out-of-state mail-order company to collect its use tax. With the *Bellas Hess* due process objection removed, the Court noted that Congress is now free to decide whether, when, and to what extent the states may burden out-of-state mail-order concerns with a duty to collect use taxes.

Georgia appears to follow the *National Bellas Hess* and *Quill* cases, imposing the duty to collect tax on persons engaged as dealers in the sale at retail, or in the use, consumption, distribution, or storage for use or consumption in Georgia of tangible personal property. See the definition of a "dealer" at ¶ 2002. Dealers must collect sales and use taxes from purchasers or consumers at the time of sale or purchase and remit the tax to the Revenue Commissioner. The amount of tax is added to the sales price or charge.

Practitioner Comment: Use of Remote Seller

Businesses should consider forming special purpose entities to remotely sell products into a state. If an affiliate is doing business in the state, any relationship between the in-state affiliate and the remote seller should be minimized. Any agreements between the affiliates should be adequately documented and arm's-length fees should be paid for any services provided. If done properly, the remote entity will not have the obligation to collect and remit sales and use tax.

Alston & Bird LLP

● Voluntary disclosure

Georgia has a voluntary disclosure program administered through the Compliance Division. The program is often used to resolve nexus issues without exposing the taxpayer to excessive back taxes and may also avoid

¶ 2003

penalties and interest. The Department will determine taxpayer eligibility on a case-by-case basis. For additional information, see ¶ 3001.

• *Streamlined Sales Tax Project*

The Streamlined Sales Tax System for the 21st Century Project (SSTP) is an effort among the states to simplify and modernize sales and use tax laws and administration. A major goal of the project is to induce remote sellers to collect the tax of participating states. Incentives include tax amnesty for participating remote sellers, monetary collection incentives, and simplified registration, collection, and reporting. The project promotes the use of technology for calculating, collecting, reporting, and paying the taxes through tax calculation service providers certified by the states, with the states assuming the costs of the system. In addition, it proposes uniform definitions and standardized audit and administration procedures for adoption by the states.

Uniform Sales and Use Tax Administration Act: The Project has approved the Uniform Sales and Use Tax Administration Act and submitted it to the states for enactment. The Act authorizes an enacting state to enter into a multistate agreement that streamlines sales and use tax collection and administration in specified ways. The key features required in the multistate agreement include the following:

—*Uniform definitions within tax bases.* In deciding what to tax and exempt, legislatures would choose from a set of common definitions for key items in the tax base.

—*Simplified exemption administration for use- and entity-based exemptions.* Sellers would be relieved of the current good faith requirement and would not be liable for uncollected tax. Purchasers would be responsible for incorrect exemptions claimed.

—*Rate simplification.* States would have to simplify their tax rates and administer any local taxes. States and localities would have to restrict variances between their tax bases and assume responsibility for providing notice of local rate and boundary changes.

—*Uniform sourcing rules.* The states would have uniform sourcing rules for all property and services.

—*Uniform audit procedures.* Sellers who participate in one of the certified technology models discussed below would either not be subject to audit or would have a limited scope audit, depending on the technology model used.

—*Paying for the system.* States would assume responsibility for implementing the sales tax system.

The Act also authorizes an enacting state to establish with other states performance standards for multistate sellers and standards for certification of a certified service provider (an agent certified by the states to perform all of a seller's sales tax functions) and a certified automated system (software certified by the states to calculate the tax imposed, determine the amount to remit, and maintain a record of the transaction).

Under the Act, a seller that volunteers to collect tax for all states that sign the multistate agreement could register with a central electronic registration system without any inference of nexus arising. A seller wishing to take

¶ 2003

advantage of the uniform audit procedures would choose to participate in one of the following technology models:

—Certified service provider. If a seller contracts with a certified service provider, the provider would be the seller's agent and would be liable instead of the seller for any tax due on all transactions the provider processes for the seller, except in cases of seller fraud or misrepresentation. Absent probable cause to believe that the seller has committed fraud or made a material misrepresentation, the seller would not be subject to audit on transactions processed by a certified service provider. However, the states would be authorized to jointly perform checks to verify that the system is functioning properly and the extent to which the seller's transactions are being processed by the certified service provider.

—Certified automated system. A provider of a certified automated system would be liable to the states for underpayments of tax attributable to errors in the functioning of the system. However, a seller using a certified automated system would remain liable for reporting and remitting tax.

—Proprietary system. A seller using a proprietary system for determining the tax due that has signed an agreement establishing a performance standard for that system would be liable for the system's failure to meet the standard.

Sales and Use Tax Agreement: The Project also has approved the Streamlined Sales and Use Tax Agreement (SSTUA), which embodies the requirements for the multistate agreement authorized by the Uniform Sales and Use Tax Administration Act and the specific details necessary to satisfy those requirements. The Project continues to refine the Agreement and incorporate additional elements.

NCSL version of the Act and Agreement: The National Conference of State Legislatures (NCSL) has endorsed a modified version of the SSTP-approved Act and Agreement. The NCSL versions would allow states within a uniform base to levy a lower rate of tax (which could be zero) on food, clothing, electricity, gas, and other items specified in the multistate agreement. The NCSL version also eliminates as required elements of a multistate agreement all uniform definitions; uniform bad debt provisions; a uniform rounding rule; and limitations on caps, thresholds, and sales tax holidays for state and local governments. The NCSL version of the Act generally is known as the Simplified Sales and Use Tax Administration Act.

● *Participating states*

At press time, 42 states and the District of Columbia had enacted some version of the Uniform (Simplified) Sales and Use Tax Administration Act, and some 20 states have adopted the SSUTA. Legislation authorizing Georgia to enter into the Streamlined Sales and Use Tax Agreement was enacted in 2004 (H.B. 1437, Laws 2004). Georgia has now become a member of the Implementing States.

To comply with the Sales and Use Tax Agreement authorized by the Act, a state must conform its laws, regulations, and policies to the Agreement's terms. Georgia has not enacted the substantive changes to Georgia law

¶ 2003

necessary for the state to come into actual compliance with the Agreement. Subsequent legislation will be necessary to achieve that compliance.

The project maintains a website at http://streamlinedsalestax.org. The following states are listed as participants: Alabama, Arizona, Arkansas, California, Connecticut, District of Columbia, Florida, Georgia, Hawaii, Illinois, Indiana, Iowa, Kansas, Kentucky, Louisiana, Maine, Maryland, Massachusetts, Michigan, Minnesota, Mississippi, Missouri, Nebraska, New Jersey, New York, Nevada, North Carolina, North Dakota, Ohio, Oklahoma, Pennsylvania, Rhode Island, South Carolina, South Dakota, Tennessee, Texas, Utah, Vermont, Virginia, Washington, West Virginia, Wisconsin, Wyoming.

¶ 2004 Persons and Transactions Subject to Tax

Law: Secs. 48-1-10, 48-8-2, 48-8-3, 48-8-30, 48-8-38, 48-8-39.1, 48-8-40, 48-8-63, Code; Reg. Secs. 560-12-2-.01, 560-12-2-.02, 560-12-2-.06—560-12-2-.09, 560-12-2-.10, 560-12-2-.12—560-12-2-.15, 560-12-2-.17, 560-12-2-.18, 560-12-2-.19, 560-12-2-.21, 560-12-2-.23, 560-12-2-.24, 560-12-2-.26, 560-12-2-.28, 560-12-2-.30, 560-12-2-.32—560-12-2-.34, 560-12-2-.36, 560-12-2-.38, 560-12-2-.40, 560-12-2-.41, 560-12-2-.43, 560-12-2-.46, 560-12-2-.49, 560-12-2-.51, 560-12-2-.52, 560-12-2-.55, 560-12-2-.57, 560-12-2-.58, 560-12-2-.60, 560-12-2-.65—560-12-2-.67, 560-12-2-.72—560-12-2-.77, 560-12-2-.79(9), 560-12-2-.82, 560-12-2-.84, 560-12-2-.85, 560-12-2-.90, 560-12-2-.96, 560-12-2-.98, 560-12-2-.100, 560-12-2-.102 (CCH GEORGIA TAX REPORTS ¶ 60-230, 60-280, 60-285, 60-310, 60-330, 60-390, 60-400, 60-445, 60-460, 60-480, 60-550, 60-570, 60-580, 60-610, 60-630, 60-635, 60-640, 60-650, 60-660, 60-720, 60-740, 60-750, 60-760).

Application of the sales and use tax to specific persons, items, and selected transactions is discussed below. Taxable services are discussed at ¶ 2005, and exemptions are discussed at ¶ 2201 and 2202.

● *Admissions, entertainment, and dues*

Ticket sales, fees, charges made for admission, or voluntary contributions made to places of amusement, sports, or entertainment are included within the definition of "retail sale" and, therefore, are taxable (¶ 2002). Taxable places of amusement include billiard and pool rooms, bowling alleys, theaters, opera houses, moving picture shows, vaudeville, amusement parks, athletic contests, skating rinks, race tracks, public bathing places, public dance halls, and any other place at which any exhibition, display, amusement, or entertainment is offered to the public or where an admission fee is charged.

Charges made for participation in games, rides, and amusement activities are also taxable retail sales. Admission charges exceeding 10¢ for entering a place of amusement are taxable in accordance with the bracket system (¶ 2105).

Free passes: Free admission passes are exempt from the sales tax, but any service charge, donation, gratuity, or any other charge required for the issuance of the passes in excess of 10¢ is subject to tax.

Bazaars and school carnivals: Ticket sales, fees, charges for admission, and voluntary contributions made in lieu of admission charges to bazaars, school carnivals, and other similar amusement activities are subject to tax. The person or organization sponsoring the activity has the duty to collect and

¶ 2004

Part VI—Sales and Use Taxes

remit the tax. Also, charges for participation in games, amusement activities, and sales of tangible personal property are taxable notwithstanding the fact that the property sold may have been donated.

Public school events: Charges for admissions and voluntary contributions and donations in lieu of admission charges to public school entertainment, lectures, concerts, and similar activities are subject to tax. An exemption is provided for sales of tickets for admissions to certain school athletic events.

Golf and country clubs: Golf, country, and other social clubs must register as dealers and must collect and remit the tax on all sales at retail. Separate charges for swimming, green fees, and the like are taxable. Purchases of tangible personal property, such as seeds, equipment, plants, and fertilizer, for use or consumption for improvement and beautification of the clubs are subject to tax.

● *Advertising*

Charges for the professional services of an advertising agency for preparing and placing advertising in the media are not subject to sales tax. However, purchases by an advertising agency of tangible personal property (such as ink, paper, paint, office supplies, art work, engraver's charges, films, billboard posters, etc.) to be used or consumed in preparing and placing advertising in the media are subject to tax.

Charges for advertising in newspapers, magazines, radio, television, billboards, and other media are not taxable. Sales at retail of tangible personal property known as commercial advertising, such as catalogs, calendars, handbills, novelties, and the like are taxable.

Advertising display service: The furnishing of advertising displays under an advertising agreement that provides for a certain quantity of exposures in a general area is considered a service and is not subject to sales or use tax as a lease of tangible personal property. The same treatment is accorded to advertising agreements that require only an outdoor advertising company to display an advertiser's message. However, a person providing the services is a consumer of all tangible personal property, such as signs, posters, and other displays, used or consumed in displaying messages and must pay the tax at the time of purchase.

● *Agriculture*

Numerous sales and use tax exemptions apply to agriculture, as discussed at ¶ 2201.

● *Auctions*

Auctioneers, agents, or factors are liable for the collection and payment of sales tax when they sell tangible personal property. Sales tax is imposed on the gross sales price of each single sale without any deduction for commissions, service charges, or any other expenses.

¶ 2004

- *Computer hardware and software*

Sales tax is levied on the sale of canned or shelf software, but is not levied on the sale of "custom software," which is software that is uniquely written to a customer's specific need. A sale of custom software is considered a nontaxable personal service transaction unless it is deemed part of a sale of tangible personal property, such as computer hardware.

Practitioner Comment: Distribution of Software

The mode of distributing canned software can dictate its taxability. Software that is electronically transmitted to a customer is not subject to sales and use tax. However, if software is transferred in tangible form, *e.g.*, on a CD, the transaction will be subject to tax, absent any exemption. If a customer desires software on a tangible medium, the customer can receive software electronically and then create its own back-up on a tangible medium without incurring tax. In the alternative, a customer may avoid tax by sending the vendor a hard drive owned by the customer, having the vendor download any software electronically onto the hard drive, and then return the tangible medium to the customer.

Alston & Bird LLP

CCH Caution: Resale of Custom Software

Custom software, though not taxable on its initial sale, may become taxable if it is resold. The resale of such software may not qualify as a nontaxable personal service transaction, or it may become part of a sale of tangible personal property (*Letters to CCH*, Department of Revenue, April 18, 1991, and February 9, 1998; CCH GEORGIA TAX REPORTS ¶ 200-355).

Computer-related services such as consulting, training, support (telephone, on-site), hardware and software maintenance, and data processing are not subject to tax if the charges for such services are separately stated.

- *Construction*

A person who contracts to furnish tangible personal property and to perform services under a contract within Georgia is deemed to be the consumer of the tangible personal property and must pay the sales tax at the time of the purchase. Failure to pay the sales tax at the time of the purchase or at the time the sale is consummated outside the state renders the contractor liable for the payment of the sales or use tax. However, this does not relieve the dealer who made the sale from its duty to collect and remit the tax on the contractor's purchases.

Similarly, a person who contracts to perform services in Georgia, who is furnished tangible personal property for use under the contract by the person for whom the contract is to be performed, is considered to be the consumer of that property and must pay the sales or use tax if the person supplying the

¶ 2004

Part VI—Sales and Use Taxes

property fails to pay the tax. The contractor must pay a use tax on the basis of the fair market value of the property used, regardless of whether any right, title, or interest in the tangible personal property becomes vested in the contractor.

Subcontractors: General or prime contractors entering into contracts with subcontractors in which the aggregate amount of any single project is equal to or greater than $250,000 must a file an initial notice with the Commissioner of Revenue within 30 days on Form S&UT 214-1 that identifies each applicable subcontractor and the contract amount.

A subcontractor is liable for sales or use tax as a general or prime contractor. On contracts of $250,000 or more, a general or prime contractor is required to withhold a percentage of the payments due to a subcontractor in satisfaction of the sales and use tax. For withholding and surety bond requirements, see ¶ 2303.

Foreign and nonresident contractors: Foreign and nonresident contractors must file an Application for Authorization to Perform Contract (Form S&UT-348.1) for each contract of $10,000 or more and pay a $10 fee for each contract. A bond (Form S&UT-348.3) must also be executed in the amount of 10% of the contract price or compensation to be received.

Property used to construct aquariums: The sale of tangible personal property used to construct certain aquariums is exempt.

● *Food and grocery items*

Food sold for off-premises consumption is exempt from sales tax, as are purchases of eligible food and beverage items for home consumption that are made with food stamps or WIC Coupons. These and other exemptions are discussed at ¶ 2201, "Exemptions."

Sales of food are taxable when sold for "on-premises" or immediate consumption, such as food served in a restaurant, coffee shop, cafeteria, tavern, food cart, luncheonette, or vending machine. Tax also applies to the sale of hot foods, alcoholic beverages and tobacco products, as well as other items commonly available in grocery stores such as napkins, laundry detergents, vitamins and pet foods.

Beverages and Ice: The retail sale of beverages and ice are taxable, including ice for use in chilling fowl and other products in processing for market, and for chilling storage rooms, delivery trucks, etc. Ice is not taxable when it is used as a cooling ingredient and becomes part of a beverage for resale or when it is used as a packaging material.

Employee meals: Employers who sell meals to employees must add sales tax to the charge and remit the tax collected. The furnishing of meals to employees by an employer-operated eating facility without charge as part of the employees' compensation is a retail sale for the fair market value of the meal. If employees must take meals from employer-operated eating facilities without charge and not as compensation, the employer is the user or consumer of the meals and is subject to tax on the cost price (defined as the fair market value) of the meals.

¶ 2004

Carrier-provided meals, snacks, and beverages: In general, the taxation of food and beverages provided to passengers by common carriers depends upon whether the food and beverages are complimentary. If passengers are charged separately for food and beverages, there is a further distinction between charges incurred at the time the ticket for transportation is purchased and charges incurred when the food or beverage is served.

—*Complimentary food and beverages:* Carriers that provide complimentary meals, snacks, or other food and beverage items to passengers are considered the consumers of those items and must pay tax to the supplier of those items that are purchased by, or delivered to, the carrier in Georgia, regardless of where the food and beverage items are served. Food and beverage items are considered to be complimentary when (1) the carrier does not state a separate charge for the items and (2) the carrier does not normally reduce the price of transportation for passengers electing not to have food and beverage service.

—*Separate charge collected with ticket price:* If the charge for food and beverage items is stated separately and collected with the ticket price for transportation, then the carrier must collect sales tax on the food and beverage charges on all ticket sales that occur in Georgia, regardless of where the food and beverage items are served.

—*Separate charge collected at time of service:* If the charge for food and beverage items is stated separately and collected at the time the food or beverage is served to the passenger, then the carrier must collect sales tax on all food or beverage items sold or served in Georgia.

Restaurants, cafes, caterers: Retail sales of meals by restaurants, hotels, clubs, cafes, caterers, and others are taxable. Cover, minimum and room service charges, and mandatory tips and gratuities are part of the sales price and are taxable.

● *Funerals*

Tax is imposed on the retail sales price of all tangible personal property furnished in a funeral service, except that the tax does not apply to funeral merchandise, outer burial containers and cemetery markers when purchased with funds received from the Georgia Crime Victims Emergency Fund. The tax applies whenever a funeral director or undertaker conducts a funeral service in Georgia and furnishes tangible personal property delivered in the state, regardless of whether interment takes place in Georgia or in another state. In addition, equipment and supplies, including but not limited to ambulances, hearses, embalming materials, and chapel furnishings, are deemed purchases for use or consumption by undertakers and funeral directors and are taxable at the time of purchase.

Cemeteries and crematoriums: Sales of boxes, urns, markers, vases, flowers, and other tangible personal property by cemeteries and crematoriums are taxable. However, the sale of lots, crypts, and niches are real property transactions that are not subject to sales tax.

Memorial stones and monuments: Retail sales of memorial stones and monuments are subject to tax, without deduction for labor used in cutting and marking. Separately stated installation or erection charges are not taxable, but the purchase of materials for use in the installation are taxable.

¶ 2004

Part VI—Sales and Use Taxes   **195**

● *Gifts and promotional merchandise*

Purchases of tangible personal property to be given away by persons advertising their business or products or to be given away as premiums, door prizes, or for any other reason are subject to tax.

Samples: Tax is imposed on the cost price of samples of tangible personal property distributed by manufacturers and other dealers. Tax is imposed on the sales price of samples sold at retail after being used by a dealer.

Trading stamps: Amounts charged to a dealer by a trading stamp company for trading stamps for distribution to a dealer's customers, which stamps are redeemable by the trading stamp company in cash or premiums, are not subject to sales or use tax.

A trading stamp company must collect tax when it accepts trade stamps or trade stamps and money in exchange for premiums. The tax is based on the total value of the stamp book and cash paid. The trading stamp company does not pay the tax on the purchase of the premiums but should furnish resale certificates to its suppliers.

● *Government transactions*

The taxation and exemption of transactions with the federal, state, and local governments are discussed at ¶ 2201.

● *Internet/Electronic commerce*

Federal Internet Tax Freedom Act: The Federal Internet Tax Freedom Act (P.L. 105-277, 112 Stat 2681), as amended in 2001 by P.L. 107-75, barred state and local governments from imposing multiple and discriminatory taxes on electronic commerce, including taxes on Internet access until November 1, 2003. The moratorium did not apply to taxes that were imposed and enforced prior to October 1, 1998. As this book goes to press, legislation is pending in Congress that would make the moratorium permanent.

● *Industrial machinery and equipment*

Several exemptions are available for machinery, equipment, and materials directly used in manufacturing operations. These are discussed at ¶ 2201 under "Manufacturing machinery and equipment."

● *Leases and rentals*

The definition of a "sale" includes leases and rentals. A "lease or rental" means the leasing or renting of tangible personal property and the possession or use of the property by the lessee or renter for a consideration without transfer of the title to the property.

A person to whom tangible personal property in Georgia is rented or leased must pay sales tax to the lessor or renter of the property on the basis of the gross lease or rental charge. All persons who lease or rent tangible personal property to others are dealers and must remit the tax to the Revenue Commissioner. If the person to whom property is rented or leased is not taxable, then no tax is imposed on the person who leases or rents the property to that person.

¶ 2004

A lessee under a lease agreement containing a period of 10 or more years may discharge sales and use taxes by paying in a lump sum 4% of the fair market value of the property at the beginning of the lease agreement. A renewal of a lease is subject to tax.

Purchases for subsequent lease: No sales tax is imposed on purchases under certificates of exemption of tangible personal property to be used exclusively for lease or rental to others.

Option to purchase: A dealer is liable for tax during the term of the lease on the gross lease or rental charges and on the sales price at the time of sale.

Leases and rentals outside the state: A person to whom tangible personal property is leased or rented outside the state is considered to be a dealer when the property is first used in Georgia and is liable for tax on the rental charge paid to the out-of-state person who leased or rented the property, subject to credit for taxes paid another state. Tax is also imposed if property is delivered to a lessee in the state, even if later removed from the state.

Furnishing of machinery by contractor: A contractor who contracts to perform a service, the principal part of which is the furnishing of machinery that will not be under the contractor's exclusive control, must collect sales tax on the rental value of the machinery or on the entire contract price if labor and other charges are not separated from the rental charge.

Motion pictures and videotapes: The sale or rental of video tapes or motion picture films for private use is taxable. However, rentals of videotape or motion picture film to any person who charges an admission fee to view the film or videotape are exempt.

Common ownership: The lease or rental of property by a person who acquires the property from another person where both persons have under 100% common ownership of the property is exempt from tax if the sales or use tax was previously paid or credit was allowed for taxes paid to another state.

● *Laundry and cleaning services*

Services rendered by laundry and cleaning businesses are not taxable, but they must register as dealers and collect and remit tax on their sales of clothing and other property.

Receipts from coin-operated laundry and dry cleaning devices are not subject to tax.

Linen supply: Persons engaged in the business of periodically cleaning and laundering coats, caps, aprons, dresses, uniforms, smocks, towels, linens, diapers, and similar items and who furnish these items to barber shops, beauty parlors, workshops, and similar establishments and to individuals are deemed to be lessors of tangible personal property and must collect tax on the gross rental receipts. Purchases of items exclusively for rental purposes are exempt, but all other purchases for use in the rental business are taxable.

● *Lodging*

Charges for furnishing rooms, lodging, or accommodations by a hotel, inn, tourist camp, cabin, or any other place that regularly furnishes lodgings to

¶ 2004

Part VI—Sales and Use Taxes

transients for a consideration are subject to tax. Lodgings furnished for at least 90 consecutive days are not subject to tax.

Camps: Fees charged for attending a summer camp, such as scout, Y.M.C.A., church, and school camps, are exempt from sales and use taxes. However, operators of these camps are taxable on their purchases for use in their operations.

Trailer parks: No tax is imposed on charges for parking spaces in a trailer park.

● *Medical, dental, and optical supplies and drugs*

Retail sales of drugs, medicine, and medical supplies and equipment are generally taxable. Specific exemptions are discussed at ¶ 2201.

● *Motor vehicles*

Sales and use taxes generally apply to all retail sales, as well as leases, of motor vehicles in Georgia, except as discussed below.

Nonresidents: Sales of motor vehicles to nonresidents for immediate transportation to and use in another state where vehicles are required to be registered are exempt from sales and use taxes. The seller must obtain an affidavit from the purchaser that states the purchaser's name and address, the state in which the vehicle will be registered and operated, the make, model, and serial number of the vehicle, and any other information required by the Revenue Commissioner. Also, the purchaser must present a Nonresident Certificate of Exemption Purchase of Motor Vehicle (Form ST-8).

If delivery of a motor vehicle is made to a nonresident in another state, the sale is exempt if a certificate of exemption (Form ST-6) is presented.

Disabled veterans: Sales and use taxes are not imposed on the sale of a vehicle to a service-connected handicapped veteran who received a grant from the Veterans' Administration to purchase and adapt the vehicle.

Military personnel: Use tax is imposed on the cost price or fair market value of automobiles imported into Georgia by military personnel and others, with credit allowed for taxes paid to a reciprocating state.

Dealers: The withdrawal of a vehicle from inventory for use as a courtesy car, service car, etc., is taxed on the cost price to the dealer when removed from inventory. The use of a car that has been set aside as a demonstrator is taxable if used for more than six months.

Parts and component materials used to recondition a dealer-owned vehicle for resale are not taxable, but parts used to repair a customer's vehicle are taxable. Separately stated charges for labor are exempt, but if not billed separately, tax is imposed on the total charge. No tax is imposed on the exchange of parts under a warranty if no charge is made, but is imposed on any difference charged for parts exchanged.

Sales for resale to out-of-state dealers are exempt if a certificate of exemption (Form ST-4) is used.

¶ 2004

Leases and rentals: Lessors of motor vehicles must register as dealers and collect tax on the gross lease or rental charges, including service charges. Their purchases of cars, trucks, trailers, repair parts, tires, and accessories that become a part of a vehicle that is leased or rented are exempt. Purchases used in their operations, such as gasoline, grease, and tools, are subject to tax.

● *Nonprofit organizations, private schools, and churches*

Churches, religious, charitable, civic, and other nonprofit organizations generally are not exempt from sales and use taxes on their purchases. When such organizations engage in selling tangible personal property at retail, compliance with the law as to collection and remittance of sales tax is required. Certain exemptions are provided by law and are discussed below.

Raising funds for public libraries: Sales to or by federally exempt nonprofit organizations that have the primary purpose of raising funds for books, materials, and programs for public libraries are exempt from sales and use tax.

Nonprofit nursing homes; general or mental hospitals: Sales and use taxes are not imposed on sales of tangible personal property (including drugs, medicines, and medical supplies) and services to a nonprofit licensed nursing home, nonprofit licensed in-patient hospice, or a nonprofit general or mental hospital used exclusively in the performance of a general nursing home, in-patient hospice, hospital, or mental hospital treatment function in Georgia. The home, hospice, or hospital must be a tax-exempt organization under the Internal Revenue Code and have an exemption determination letter from the Revenue Commissioner.

Convalescent homes: Purchases of tangible personal property by homes for the care of children, the aged, or other persons are taxable, but receipts for the care of these persons are exempt (but see "Orphans' homes," below).

Nursing homes, sanitariums, and hospitals: Hospitals, sanitariums, and nursing homes generally must pay tax on their purchases for use or consumption in their operations, unless the institution is owned and operated by the federal government, state of Georgia, county, or municipality, or created under Sec. 88-1803, Georgia Health Code. They must register as dealers and collect and remit tax on their sales of tangible personal property.

Sales of tangible personal property and services to a tax-exempt nonprofit organization that primarily provides services to mentally disabled individuals are exempt. To qualify, the organization must obtain an exemption determination letter from the Commissioner of Revenue Services.

Religious institutions: Sales by religious institutions or denominations are exempt from sales and use taxes if (1) the sale results from a specific charitable fund-raising activity not exceeding 30 days in any calendar year; (2) no part of the gross sales or net profits from the sales inures to the benefit of any private person, and (3) the gross sales or net profit from the sales are used for the purely charitable purposes of relief to the aged, church-related youth activities, religious instruction or worship, or construction or repair of church buildings or facilities.

Pipe organs and steeple bells: Such items are exempt from sales and use taxes when sold to a tax-exempt religious organization.

¶ **2004**

Part VI—Sales and Use Taxes

Religious papers: Sales and use taxes are not imposed on sales of any religious paper in Georgia when the paper is owned and operated by religious institutions or denominations whose net profits do not benefit any private person.

Bibles: The sale or use of Holy Bibles, testaments, and similar books commonly recognized as being Holy Scripture is exempt from tax.

Orphans' homes: The sales and use taxes do not apply to sales of tangible personal property and services to orphans' homes located in the state and operated as nonprofit corporations.

Rock Eagle 4-H Center: An exemption from sales and use taxes is provided for sales of tangible personal property and fees and charges for services by the Rock Eagle 4-H Center.

Daughters of the American Revolution: A sale of personal property or services to any chapter of the Georgia State Society of the Daughters of the American Revolution that is a federal nonprofit organization is exempt.

Agricultural Commodities Commissions: Sales to any regulated agricultural commodities commission are exempt.

Blood banks: Sales and use taxes do not apply to sales made to blood banks that have tax-exempt status under IRC Sec. 501(c)(3).

Social and fraternal organizations: All retail sales of tangible personal property to social and fraternal organizations are taxable. An organization regularly engaged in the business of selling tangible personal property must register as a dealer and collect and remit sales and use taxes.

Private colleges and universities: Sales of tangible personal property and services to be used exclusively for educational purposes by private colleges and universities in the state whose academic credits are accepted as equivalents by the University System of Georgia and its educational units are exempt from sales and use taxes. To claim the exemption, the college or university must furnish each supplier of tangible personal property or services with a Letter of Authorization (Form ST-USC-1).

Examples of property and services that are exempt are books purchased for libraries and teachers; maintenance and instructional supplies; electricity and fuel; furniture and fixtures; office supplies and equipment; kitchen equipment, and laboratory equipment.

Private elementary and secondary schools: Sales and use taxes are not imposed on sales of tangible personal property and services to be used exclusively for educational purposes by bona fide private elementary and secondary schools approved by the Revenue Commissioner as organizations eligible to receive tax deductible contributions, if application for exemption is made to the Department of Revenue and proof of the exemption is established.

No exemption is available to sales made by parent-teacher associations, classroom mothers, student groups, and other school groups, or to sales on school property through vending machines, snack bars, or other outlets.

Sales of tangible personal property made by private schools are exempt from tax if all proceeds benefit the school or its students.

¶ 2004

School events: Sales made by concessionaires at, or tickets for admission to, a school event or function are exempt from tax. The exemption applies to any public or private school containing any combination of grades kindergarten through 12, and all proceeds must benefit the school or its students.

Vocational training schools: Persons operating vocational schools must pay tax on their purchases used, consumed, or furnished to students for use in the students' studies. A school must register as a dealer and collect tax on sales of equipment, tools, and other tangible personal property to students.

Foreign educational and cultural institutes: An educational or cultural institute is exempt on its sales or purchases of tangible personal property and services if the institute:

—is tax exempt under IRC Sec. 501(c)(3);

—furnishes at least 50% of its programs through universities and other institutions of higher education in support of their educational programs;

—is paid for by government funds of a foreign country; and

—is an instrumentality, agency, department, or branch of a foreign government operating through a permanent location in Georgia.

Employee organizations: Employee organizations must collect and remit tax on sales of tangible personal property to members or others.

● *Photography*

Sales and use taxes are imposed on sales of photographs, portraits, prints from camera film, including coloring and tinting charges, photostats, blueprints, frames, camera film, and other property. Purchases of cameras and other equipment by commercial photographers and others are taxable. Materials that become a component part of a finished photograph or print for sale and industrial materials coated upon or impregnated into the product for sale may be purchased under certificate of exemption.

Film developing charges and coloring and tinting charges on photographs furnished by customers are exempt if separately charged, but purchases of chemicals, paints, colors, and the like used in providing these services are taxable. Developing chemicals that are coated upon or impregnated into films in processing may be purchased under a certificate of exemption.

● *Printing*

A printer must collect and remit sales and use taxes on the total invoice charges made on sales of custom printing (production or fabrication of printed matter according to a customer's order or copy). The invoice charge includes charges made for engraved, lithoplated, or other photo-processed plate, die, or mat and charges for printing and imprinting if the customer furnishes the printing stock.

A printer's purchases of ink, printing stock, stapling wire, binding twine, glue, and other tangible personal property that become a component part of the printed matter, or are coated upon or impregnated into the property are considered purchases of industrial materials, which are exempt from tax if properly certificated. Purchases of engraved, photoprocessed, lithoplated, or

¶ 2004

Part VI—Sales and Use Taxes

other type of plate, die, or mat are exempt as purchases for resale if so certified. Purchases of typesetting are exempt as purchases of services.

● *Publishing and broadcasting*

Charges by radio and television stations for their services, including line charges, talent fees or charges, and the rental of motion picture film are not subject to sales or use taxes. The purchase, lease, or rental of machinery, equipment, or other tangible personal property such as records, blank video tapes or motion picture reels, costumes, make-up materials, lumber, transistors, condensers, transformers, etc., for use in producing radio or television broadcasts is taxable.

Publishers: Sales of newspapers, magazines, periodicals, etc., to persons other than registered dealers are subject to tax. Subscription sales are subject to sales tax on the subscription price.

Paper stock for catalogs: Sales and use taxes do not apply to the sale, use, storage, or consumption of paper stock manufactured in Georgia and incorporated into catalogs for delivery and use outside the state.

● *Resales*

The law specifically excludes sales for resale from the definition of "retail sale." A seller who in good faith takes a resale certificate from the purchaser is relieved from its burden of proving that a sale is not a retail sale. The purchaser must (1) be engaged in the business of selling tangible personal property, (2) hold a permit (certificate of registration), and (3) intend to sell the property in the regular course of business or be unable to ascertain at the time of the purchase whether the property will be sold or will be used for another purpose.

The resale certificate must be signed by and contain the name and address of the purchaser, indicate the permit (certificate of registration) number, and indicate the general character of the property sold by the purchaser in the regular course of business. Georgia Form ST-5 is used for various exemptions and for resales.

Sales for resale considered retail sales in certain cases: Sales for resale are considered retail sales when there is a likelihood that the state will lose tax funds because of the difficulty of policing the business operations of the taxpayer for any of the following reasons:

—the nature of the business or its operation;

—the turnover of independent contractors;

—the lack of a place of business in which to display a certificate of registration or keep records;

—the lack of adequate records;

—the persons are minors or transients;

the persons are engaged in essentially service businesses; or

—any other reasonable cause.

Commingled goods: When goods purchased under an exemption certificate are commingled with other similar goods so that the identity of the tax-

¶ 2004

exempt goods cannot be determined, sales from the mass of commingled goods are deemed to be of the tax-exempt goods until the quantity of goods purchased under the exemption certificate has been sold.

● *Services—Personal or professional*

Georgia sales tax is imposed only on certain specified services (¶ 2005). Professional or personal service transactions that involve sales as inconsequential elements for which no separate charges are made are not taxable.

● *Telecommunications*

The sale of local telephone services when made for purposes other than resale is a taxable retail sale. Sales tax is also imposed on the amount of guaranteed charges for semipublic coin-box telephone services. No tax is imposed on other communication services.

Interstate telecommunications: Georgia does not impose sales and use tax on interstate transmissions. Those states that do tax interstate communications may only impose the tax if the communication originates or terminates within the state and is either charged to a service address in the state or billed or paid within the state (*Goldberg v. Sweet,* No. 87-826 and No. 87-1101, 488 US 252 (1989)).

Cable television: Service charges for wired television services are nontaxable, but the purchase of machines, equipment, materials, and supplies used in providing those services is taxable.

Cellular telephone services: Cellular telephone services are taxable. The monthly access charge, special features such as call waiting, and the daily access portion of "roaming" charges are taxed. Airtime usage charges listed separately and voice mail services are not taxed.

A cellular service provider may either take a credit or provide an exemption certificate for taxes collected by the local exchange telephone carrier.

Georgia has adopted the federal Mobile Telecommunications Sourcing Act. Under this law, mobile telecommunications are sourced to the primary place of use within the taxing jurisdiction (home or business address).

Prepaid (debit) telephone cards: Prepaid telephone cards are not treated as tangible personal property subject to tax at the time of purchase (Response to Questionnaire to Georgia Department of Revenue from CCH, June 7, 1996). Telephone calls made with prepaid calling cards are not subject to tax as telephone services.

● *Transportation*

The sale of transportation services when made for purposes other than resale is a taxable retail sale. However, certain sales of transportation are exempt from taxation, as discussed below. Inclusion of transportation or delivery charges in the sales or use tax base is discussed at ¶ 2101. Transportation equipment is discussed at ¶ 2201.

¶ 2004

Part VI—Sales and Use Taxes   **203**

Public transit: Charges by counties, municipalities, public transit authorities, or urban transit systems for the transportation of passengers are exempt from sales and use taxes.

Transportation to another state: Sales and use taxes are imposed on charges by a common carrier for transporting persons between two points in Georgia, but not on charges for transporting persons from Georgia to another state.

See "Food and grocery items" above for a discussion of the taxability of food and beverages served by common carriers.

CCH Tip: Interstate Passenger Tickets

Federal law prohibits a state and its political subdivisions from collecting or levying a tax, fee, head charge, or other charge on: (1) a passenger traveling in interstate commerce by motor carrier; (2) the transportation of a passenger traveling in interstate commerce by motor carrier; (3) the sale of passenger transportation in interstate commerce by motor carrier; or (4) the gross receipts derived from such transportation (Sec. 14505, Title 49, U.S.C).

Transportation of goods: Charges made for the transportation of tangible personal property are exempt from sales and use taxes. This exemption includes charges for accessorial services such as refrigeration, switching, storage, and demurrage made in connection with interstate and intrastate transportation of the property.

Taxicabs: A taxicab owner and operator must register as a dealer and pay tax on its purchases of taxicabs, meters, accessories, tires, repair parts, gasoline, lubricants, tools, supplies, and other tangible personal property used or consumed in its operations. Furthermore, an owner and operator must collect tax on fares for providing transportation and remit it to the State Revenue Commissioner. Cars for hire are treated in the same manner as taxicabs.

● *Utilities*

Sales of natural or artificial gas, oil, electricity, steam, or solid fuel are taxable retail sales when made for purposes other than resale. Sales tax also applies to purchases of machinery and equipment, including meters, drums, cylinders, tanks, etc., by persons furnishing electricity, steam, gas, or fuels. Consumer deposits on meters, tanks, etc., are not subject to tax.

Privately or publicly owned public utilities must collect tax on sales of services, including gas, electricity, and steam, the furnishing of local telephone services, and the intrastate transportation of persons.

An exemption is provided for the sale of electricity used directly in the manufacture of a product if the cost of the electricity comprises a substantial portion of the cost of manufacturing the product. See "Manufacturing machinery and equipment" at ¶ 2201 for a discussion of the exemption.

¶ 2004

> *Practitioner Comment: Potential Use Tax Liability*
>
> The current trend in states moving to the deregulation of electricity is to tax generation, transmission, and distribution components of electric bills separately. Because out-of-state suppliers in most instances will not be obligated to collect sales tax from energy customers, companies who fail to pay use tax on any of these components risk being assessed use tax plus interest and penalties. In order to minimize the likelihood of a use tax deficiency, companies should review their energy usage for any available tax exemptions and maintain records of all interstate electricity purchases, as well as proof of tax payments on those purchases.
>
> Michael Granwehr, Utilities Management Consultants,
Wallingford, PA

Water: An exemption from sales and use taxes is provided for sales of water delivered through water mains, lines, or pipes.

- *Vending machine sales*

Sales of tangible personal property through vending machines are subject to tax; the owner of the machine is liable for the tax based on the gross receipts without deduction for commissions paid to a person on whose property the machine is located. If the seller leases the vending machine, the seller is a retail dealer and liable for tax on the gross receipts without deduction for the cost of the property sold, the rental charges, or for services performed by the renter. The owner or lessor of the machine must pay tax on the rental charges. When reporting vending machine sales, all sales made through any one vending machine are treated as a single sale, gross proceeds are treated as if tax was included in the sale, and taxable proceeds are net of the tax included in the sale.

Coin-operated amusement devices: An exemption applies to gross revenues generated from all bona fide coin-operated amusement machines that (1) vend or dispense music or are operated for skill, amusement, entertainment, or pleasure, (2) are in commercial use and provided to the public for play, and (3) are subject to the permit fee imposed by Sec. 48-17-9 Ga. Code.

¶ 2005 Taxable Services

Law: Secs. 48-8-2(9), 48-8-3(22), 48-8-30, Code; Reg. Secs. 560-12-2-.02, 560-12-2-.42, 560-12-2-.47, 560-12-2-.53, 560-12-2-.55, 560-12-2-.68, 560-12-2-.97 (CCH GEORGIA TAX REPORTS ¶ 60-665, 60-680).

The Georgia sales tax is imposed only on specified services. Because laundry services are not mentioned in the statute, for example, they are excluded from taxation. On the other hand, transportation and entertainment services are among those specifically subject to the tax. The taxability of specific services is discussed at ¶ 2004, "Persons and Transactions Subject to Tax."

¶ 2005

Part VI—Sales and Use Taxes

Transactions involving a service and a transfer of property: Generally, the law defines the taxable "sales price" of a purchase to include any services that are a part of the sale. However, there is a specific exception for services that are rendered in installing, applying, remodeling, or repairing the property sold. In addition, sales tax regulations concerning combined sale-service transactions illustrate how certain services may be excluded from the measure of tax if the charges are separately stated. For example, when an interior decorator makes a lump sum charge for both professional services and the furnishing of tangible personal property, tax is imposed on the total charge unless the charge for services is billed separately. A similar rule applies to florists: If a florist directs a wedding, furnishes flowers, decorations, refreshments, etc., for a flat charge, the total charge is subject to tax; if a separate charge is made for professional services, however, that charge may be excluded from the sales tax base.

If a professional, insurance, or personal service transaction involves a sale as an inconsequential element for which no separate charge is made, the transaction is exempt.

Practitioner Comment: Bundling Transactions

The current trend for many industries is to bundle services and property together for one lump-sum charge. This may result in sales tax being imposed on the entire charge, which includes both taxable and nontaxable items. If possible, companies should carefully group taxable items apart from nontaxable items and separately state the charge that relates to each in order to avoid unnecessary tax. This becomes complicated in a multistate context since different jurisdictions impose taxes on different categories of services.

Georgia has recently adopted an exception to the general bundling rule to allow local telephone service providers to bundle taxable and nontaxable services in one lump charge and impose and collect tax only on the taxable portion, provided proper records are maintained.

Alston & Bird LLP

Items purchased by service providers: Generally, a service provider must pay tax when purchasing property that he or she will use or consume in the business of providing a service, but if taxable items will also be sold to customers in the regular course of business, the service provider's initial purchases of those particular items will qualify as exempt purchases for resale. For example, tax applies to purchases by an advertising agency of tangible personal property (ink, paper, artwork, etc.) to be used or consumed in preparing advertising and placing it in newspapers, magazines, and other media. If an advertising agency goes beyond the rendition of professional services and sells tangible personal property, however, those sales are subject to tax, and registered agencies may purchase such property tax-free for resale by furnishing the supplier with a proper exemption certificate.

¶ 2005

● *Miscellaneous services*

This section covers miscellaneous services that are not discussed under the broad categories of services or service enterprises individually discussed at ¶ 2004, "Persons and Transactions Subject to Tax."

Furniture and storage warehousemen: Furniture and storage warehouse businesses that move, store, pack, and deliver tangible personal property belonging to other persons are providing nontaxable services. The purchases of crating, boxing, and packing materials used in performing such services are taxable.

Kennels, stables, and pet shops: Charges made for the keep of pets are not subject to sales tax. Purchases of tangible personal property for use in the operation of a kennel, stable, or pet shop are taxable. Retail sales of horses, dogs, animals, goldfish, and other pets are taxable.

Painters and paperhangers: Services rendered by painters and paperhangers are not subject to sales and use tax. However, their purchases of paint, wallpaper, supplies, and equipment are taxable.

Pilot training schools: Persons operating pilot training schools providing classrooms and ground and flight instruction, including a given number of hours of flight time for which no separate charge is made, are providing tax-exempt services but are subject to tax on their purchases of tangible personal property (including aircraft) used in providing those services.

If flight time is separately charged, the persons are engaged in providing services and the rental of property. When flight time is separately charged, those schools certificated by the FAA as pilot training schools or operating under FAR Part 61 with an established base of operations may elect to treat all aircraft flight time that is part of the training program as a rental of aircraft. Aircraft and accessories used exclusively in these operations may be purchased tax-free as sales for resale.

¶ 2006 Use Tax

Law: Secs. 48-8-2(10), 48-8-2(12), 48-8-2(13), 48-8-3(42), 48-8-30(c), 48-8-30(e), 48-8-34(b), Code (CCH GEORGIA TAX REPORTS ¶ 60-020).

Use tax is imposed on the use, consumption, distribution, and storage of tangible personal property within the state. The use, consumption, distribution, or storage for use or consumption in Georgia of tangible personal property is equivalent to a sale at retail.

● *Definitions*

"Use" means the exercise of any right or power over tangible personal property incident to the ownership of the property, including the sale at retail of the property in the regular course of business.

"Storage" means the keeping or retention in Georgia of tangible personal property for use or consumption in the state or for any purpose other than sale at retail in the regular course of business.

¶ 2006

Part VI—Sales and Use Taxes

● *Out-of-state transactions*

The owner or user of any tangible personal property that is purchased at retail outside Georgia is considered to be a dealer and is liable for a tax on the lesser of the cost price or fair market value of the property upon the first instance of use, consumption, distribution, or storage of the property in Georgia. Credit is allowed for taxes paid to other states.

A person who leases or rents tangible personal property outside of Georgia is considered to be a dealer when the property is first used within the state and the person is liable for a tax on the rental charge paid to the lessor.

● *Common ownership*

The use of property by a person who acquires the property from another person where both persons have under 100% common ownership of the property is exempt from tax if the sales or use tax was previously paid or credit was allowed for taxes paid to another state.

¶ 2006

Part VI—Sales and Use Taxes

SALES AND USE TAXES

CHAPTER 21

BASIS AND RATE OF TAX

¶ 2101	Basis of Tax
¶ 2102	Rate of Tax
¶ 2103	Local Taxes
¶ 2104	Local Tax Rate Chart
¶ 2105	Bracket Schedule

¶ 2101 Basis of Tax

Law: Secs. 48-8-2(2), 48-8-2(9), 48-8-3(3), 48-8-30, 48-8-39(b), 48-8-44, 48-8-45(c), 48-8-58, Code; Reg. Secs. 560-12-1-.02, 560-12-1-.06, 560-12-1-.14, 560-12-1-.17, 560-12-1-.19, 560-12-1-.25, 560-12-1-.27, 560-12-1-.34, 560-12-1-.35, 560-12-2-.09, 560-12-2-.45 (CCH GEORGIA TAX REPORTS ¶ 61-110—61-190).

Tax imposed on purchasers is based on the "sales price" of each purchase. On the first instance of use, consumption, distribution, or storage in Georgia of property purchased at retail out of state, tax is imposed on the owner or user on the basis of the lesser of the "cost price" or fair market value of the property. In the event of a lease or rental, the tax is imposed upon the gross charge. The tax on the purchase of services is based on the gross charge made for the purchase.

● *Incidence and measure of tax*

The sales and use taxes are imposed on both the purchaser or lessee, the retail vendor or lessor, or the purchaser and provider of taxable services, but the measure of tax is different. The tax on the purchaser is imposed on the sales price while the tax on the retail vendor is the greater of the tax based on the vendor's gross sales or the amount of taxes collected from the purchaser.

● *Definitions*

"Sales price" means the total amount valued in money for which tangible personal property or services are sold including, but not limited to, any services that are a part of the sale and any amount for which credit is given to the purchaser, and without any deduction for the cost of the property sold, the cost of materials used, labor or service costs, losses, or any other expenses of any kind.

"Cost price" means the actual cost of tangible personal property without deductions for the cost of materials used, labor costs, service costs, transportation charges, or other expenses of any kind.

¶ 2101

- *Use of self-produced goods*

A person in the business of processing, manufacturing, or converting industrial materials into articles of tangible personal property for sale is liable for sales tax on the use of its own self-produced article, other than retaining, demonstrating, or displaying it for sale. The use of the article constitutes a retail sale when first used, and the tax is based on the fair market value that is the deemed sales price of the article. If the sole use of the article, other than retaining, demonstrating, or displaying it for sale, is the rental of the article while holding it for sale, an election may be made to treat the rental charge as the sales price.

- *Withdrawal from inventory*

A dealer's conversion to its own use of stock in trade held for sale is subject to tax based on the cost price of the tangible personal property. Gifts of stock-in-trade are considered conversions and the dealer is liable for tax.

A dealer in the business of selling tangible personal property who withdraws tangible personal property from inventory for use in performing contracts (known as a dual operator) must collect and remit tax on the sales price of property sold at retail and pay tax on the fair market value of the property used in performing contracts. "Fair market value" means the fabricated cost of the article at the time of its first use in performing a contract. A dual operator should furnish its supplier with a certificate of exemption.

Practitioner Comment: Samples

Georgia Department of Revenue auditors frequently scrutinize the self-assessment of tax on items taken out of inventory and given as samples to potential customers. Companies that withdraw sample merchandise from their product inventories are advised to carefully document and self-assess tax at the time the property is removed from inventory in order to avoid the imposition of interest and penalties on audit.

As discussed above, the base of tax on such a deemed sale differs depending upon whether the company giving the sample is a dealer or a manufacturer. In 2003, the Georgia legislature enacted a provision governing the fair market value, and thus, the deemed sales price, of samples given by carpet manufacturers (H.B. 189, Laws 2003). To the extent that carpet samples are manufactured exclusively for commercial use, the fair market value of the sample is 1% of its total raw material cost. In all other instances, the fair market value of the carpet sample is equal to 21.9% of its total raw material cost. The distinction is based in part on a prior Department of Revenue audit practice that recognized that commercial sellers had an especially difficult time recovering the cost of samples by selling them.

Alston & Bird LLP

Part VI—Sales and Use Taxes

● *Bad debts*

A person using the accrual basis of accounting is allowed a bad debt deduction if a debt is worthless, uncollectible, and legal action would probably not result in its collection. A person deducting bad debts must attach a schedule to the return showing the amount of the debt, the name of the debtor, the date each debt was created, when they became due, efforts made to collect, and why they were determined to be worthless. If bad debts are collected after a deduction is taken, they must be included in gross sales when collected.

Credit card debt holders: Assignees of credit card debt purchased directly from a dealer without recourse and credit card banks that extend credit to customers under private label credit card programs that report on the accrual basis of accounting, may deduct the bad debts on the same basis that bad credit card debts are deductible from the state income tax.

Practitioner Comment: Financing Companies

A vehicle financing company was not entitled to claim a bad debt deduction, as defined by the Georgia statute, because the company did not qualify as a "person" entitled to take the deduction under the statute. See *General Motors Acceptance Corporation v. Jackson*, A00A1315, 247 Ga.App., 542 S.E.2d 538, 2000 Ga.App. 1366 (November 15, 2000), GEORGIA TAX REPORTS ¶ 200-411.

Alston & Bird LLP

● *Coupons, premiums, and cash discounts*

The sales price upon which tax is imposed does not include cash discounts that are allowed or taken on sales. A manufacturer rebate is not considered at cash discount, and does not reduce the taxable sales price.

Discount cards: Purchases made with discount cards (sometimes called purchase cards or scan cards) are taxed on the purchase price after the price deduction has been made by the retailer. Discount cards are issued by a retailer to a customer, free of charge, that allow the customer to purchase certain items at a lower price by presenting the card at the time of purchase (Response from Georgia Department of Revenue to CCH Survey, October 7, 1998).

● *Trade-ins*

Tax is imposed on the sales price of tangible personal property less the amount of credit allowed on tangible personal property taken in trade. This includes motor vehicles taken in trade on the sale of a motor vehicle.

● *Delivery charges and packing costs*

Freight, delivery, and transportation charges generally are not deductible from the sales price or cost price in determining the sales or use tax base if such charges are part of the sales transaction. See the definitions of "sales price" and "cost price," above.

¶ 2101

When tangible personal property is sold "F.O.B. shipping point" and the purchaser assumes the risks of ownership at that point, the cost of transportation paid by the purchaser is not taxable. If the seller has prepaid the transportation charges and those charges are on the invoice or separately stated, the tax applies to the total invoice charge unless the seller merely acted as the purchaser's agent in arranging the transportation. An "F.O.B. shipping point" sale in which the invoice allows a credit for transportation charges paid by the purchaser is subject to tax on the invoice charge after allowing the credit.

Tax is imposed on the total invoice charges on "F.O.B. destination" sales, even if the seller separately bills the purchaser for the freight charges.

A sale in which the seller delivers the property and makes a separate charge on the invoice, and the seller assumes the risk of loss during transit, is subject to tax on the total invoice price.

If only the use tax is involved, tax is imposed on the cost price without adding transportation charges paid to the carrier by the user or by the seller as the user's agent.

● *Federal, state, and local excise taxes*

The federal retailers' excise tax is excluded from the sales price or cost price when billed separately from the selling price of the property. The state motor fuel excise tax on gasoline and other motor fuel is also excluded from the sales or cost price. The federal excise taxes on (1) gasoline and diesel fuel, (2) tires, tubes, and accessories, and (3) cigarettes are not federal retailers' excise taxes and therefore are included in the sales or cost price.

The state excise tax on cigarettes is excluded from the sale or cost price.

● *Installment, lay-away, and conditional sales; finance charges*

Finance, carrying, and service charges, or interest under conditional sales contracts are excluded from the sales price. The tax on retail sales of motor vehicles is not imposed on finance, insurance, and interest charges for deferred payments billed separately.

● *Returns and repossessions*

If taxable property is returned to a seller for adjustment, replacement, or exchange under a warranty and new property is given free or at a reduced price, sales and use taxes are imposed on any additional amount paid to the seller for the new property.

If property is returned within 90 days from the date of sale and all or part of the sales price or cost price is refunded to the purchaser, the dealer may deduct from gross sales, in the return for the taxable period in which the refund was made, the amount refunded to the purchaser. If the property is returned more than 90 days from the date of sale, no credit is allowed except upon application for a credit memorandum (Form ST-16) for the tax imposed on the amount refunded to the purchaser. The application must be made within the time limit for filing refund claims (¶ 3001). The credit memoran-

¶ 2101

Part VI—Sales and Use Taxes   213

dum will be applied by the dealer to his or her liability for each succeeding taxable period until exhausted.

The sale of repossessed tangible personal property is subject to tax.

¶ 2102   Rate of Tax

Law: Sec. 48-8-30, Code; Reg. Secs. 560-12-1-.05, 560-12-1-.28 (CCH GEORGIA TAX REPORTS ¶ 60-110).

The state sales and use tax rate is 4% of the tax base.

The amount of tax imposed is determined by use of the bracket schedules, reproduced at ¶ 2105. However, the amount of tax required to be remitted to the state is the greater of 4% of gross sales or the amount collected under the bracket schedule (less compensation allowed to the vendor; see ¶ 2302). So, even though the bracket schedule requires no collection on sales of less than 11¢, a retail dealer still may be liable for 4% of the net taxable amount from sales of less than 11¢.

● *Representative conversion factor*

Upon proper application and approval by the Commissioner, a retail dealer may use a representative conversion factor to produce the equivalent tax required by the law and bracket system.

● *Sales tax holidays*

At press time, no sales tax holidays had been authorized in 2005. For the period July 29, 2004, through August 1, 2004, sales and use tax did not apply to certain school supplies (up to $20 per item), clothing and footwear (priced at $100 or less per article), and computers and computer-related accessories for noncommercial use (for a single purchase of $1,500 or less). A similar sales tax holiday was declared in 2003.

¶ 2103   Local Taxes

Law: Georgia Const. Art. VIII, Sec. VI, Para. IV; Secs. 48-8-6, 48-8-81—48-8-83, 48-8-85, 48-8-86, Sec. 48-8-92, 48-8-102, 48-8-103, 48-8-110—48-8-112, 48-8-141, Code (CCH GEORGIA TAX REPORTS ¶ 61-710, 61-735).

There are five local taxes authorized in Georgia, as discussed below. In addition, the cities of Atlanta and Columbus have been authorized to levy a special tax for water and sewer projects and costs. Effective October 1, 2004, transactions within the incorporated City of Atlanta (which includes part of DeKalb and Fulton counties) incur an additional 1% tax. The sale, lease, and rental of automobiles are exempt from this tax.

The joint county and municipal sales and use tax, the homestead option sales and use tax, the special county sales and use tax, and the educational local option sales and use tax are imposed at the rate of 1%. The Metropolitan Atlanta Rapid Transit Authority tax is imposed at the rate of 1% through June 30, 2047, and thereafter at the rate of .5%.

¶ 2103

● *Joint county and municipal sales and use tax*

The joint county and municipal sales and use tax provisions create 159 special districts whose boundaries are coterminous with those of the counties.

● *Special county sales and use tax*

Counties are authorized to impose a special 1% sales and use tax for a period not to exceed five years. The tax must be approved by a majority of the voters at an election called for the purpose of approving the tax; if disapproved the tax may not be voted upon until the next year.

● *Metropolitan Atlanta Rapid Transit Authority tax*

Fulton, DeKalb, Cobb, Clayton, and Gwinnett counties, as well as the City of Atlanta, are authorized, subject to voter approval, to impose a retail sales and use tax if they have entered into a final and binding contract with the Metropolitan Atlanta Rapid Transit Authority. The tax is imposed at the rate of 1% through June 2032, and thereafter at the rate of .5%, and corresponds, as far as is practicable, to the state sales and use tax.

● *Homestead option sales and use tax*

The homestead option sales and use tax creates 159 special districts corresponding with the boundaries of the counties. When the imposition of a local sales and use tax is authorized within a special district, the county corresponding to the district will levy a 1% sales and use tax. The tax subjects the same items and transactions to tax as the state sales and use tax, except that motor fuels are also subject to the local tax. The tax must be authorized by a majority vote in a referendum election, and is administered and collected by the State Revenue Commissioner.

The sales and use tax will only be levied in a special district following the enactment of a local act providing for a homestead exemption of an amount to be determined from the amount of the sales and use tax collected.

● *Educational local option tax*

The educational local option tax is a 1% sales and use tax imposed by county school boards and boards of education on taxable services and the sales, use, and lease of tangible personal property within the boards' taxing districts.

¶ 2103

Part VI—Sales and Use Taxes 215

¶ 2104 Local Tax Rate Chart

(CCH GEORGIA TAX REPORTS ¶ 61-735).

The following localities levy local sales and use taxes (rates are effective through March 31, 2005):

COUNTY	TOTAL RATE %	4% STATE	1% LOCAL OPTION	1% MARTA/ SPECIAL	1% EDUCATIONAL LOCAL OPTION
Appling	7	X	X	X	X
Atkinson	7	X	X	X	X
Bacon	7	X	X	X	X
Baker	6	X	X		X
Baldwin	7	X	X	X	X
Banks	7	X	X	X	X
Barrow	7	X	X	X	X
Bartow	7	X	X	X	X
Ben Hill	7	X	X	X	X
Berrien	7	X	X	X	X
Bibb	6	X	X		X
Bleckley	7	X	X	X	X
Brantley	7	X	X	X	X
Brooks	7	X	X	X	X
Bryan	7	X	X	X	X
Bulloch	7	X	X	X	X
Burke	6	X	X	X	
Butts	7	X	X	X	X
Calhoun	7	X	X	X	X
Camden	6	X	X	X	
Candler	7	X	X	X	X
Carroll	7	X	X	X	X
Catoosa	7	X	X	X	X
Charlton	7	X	X	X	X
Chatham	6	X	X	X	
Chattahoochee	7	X	X	X	X
Chattooga	7	X	X	X	X
Cherokee	6	X		X	X
Clarke	7	X	X	X	X
Clay	7	X	X	X	X
Clayton	7	X	X		X
Clinch	7	X	X	X	X
Cobb	5	X			X
Coffee	6	X	X	X	
Colquitt	7	X	X	X	X
Columbia	7	X	X	X	X
Cook	7	X	X	X	X
Coweta	7	X	X	X	X
Crawford	7	X	X	X	X
Crisp	7	X	X	X	X
Dade	7	X	X	X	X
Dawson	7	X	X	X	X
Decatur, Co.	7	X	X	X	X
Dekalb [1], [3]	7	X		X	X
Dodge	7	X	X	X	X
Dooly	7	X	X	X	X
Dougherty	7	X	X	X	X
Douglas	7	X	X		X
Early	7	X	X	X	X
Echols	6	X	X	X	
Effingham	7	X	X	X	X
Elbert	7	X	X	X	X
Emanuel	7	X	X	X	X
Evans	7	X	X	X	X

¶ 2104

COUNTY	TOTAL RATE %	4% STATE	1% LOCAL OPTION	1% MARTA/ SPECIAL	1% EDUCATIONAL LOCAL OPTION
Fannin	7	X	X	X	X
Fayette	5	X	X		
Floyd	7	X	X	X	X
Forsyth	7	X	X	X	X
Franklin	7	X	X	X	X
Fulton [3]	7	X	X	X	X
Gilmer	7	X	X	X	X
Glascock	7	X	X	X	
Glynn	6	X	X	X	
Gordon	7	X	X	X	X
Grady	7	X	X	X	X
Greene	7	X	X	X	X
Gwinnett	6	X	X	X	
Habersham	7	X	X	X	X
Hall	7	X	X	X	X
Hancock	6	X	X	X	
Haralson	7	X	X	X	X
Harris	7	X	X	X	X
Hart	7	X	X	X	X
Heard	7	X	X	X	X
Henry	7	X	X	X	X
Houston	7	X	X	X	X
Irwin	7	X	X	X	X
Jackson	7	X	X	X	X
Jasper	7	X	X	X	X
Jeff Davis	7	X	X	X	X
Jefferson	7	X	X	X	X
Jenkins	7	X	X	X	X
Johnson	7	X	X	X	X
Jones	7	X	X	X	X
Lamar	7	X	X	X	X
Lanier	7	X	X	X	X
Laurens	7	X	X	X	X
Lee	7	X	X	X	X
Liberty	7	X	X	X	X
Lincoln	7	X	X	X	X
Long	7	X	X	X	X
Lowndes	7	X	X	X	X
Lumpkin	7	X	X	X	X
Macon	7	X	X	X	X
Madison	7	X	X	X	X
Marion	7	X	X	X	X
McDuffie	7	X	X	X	X
McIntosh	7	X	X	X	X
Meriwether	7	X	X	X	
Miller	6	X	X	X	
Mitchell	7	X	X	X	X
Monroe	7	X	X	X	X
Montgomery	7	X	X	X	X
Morgan	6	X	X	X	
Murray	7	X	X	X	X
Muscogee	7	X	X	X	X
Newton	7	X	X	X	X
Oconee	7	X	X	X	X
Oglethorpe	7	X	X	X	X
Paulding	7	X	X	X	X
Peach	6	X	X	X	
Pickens	7	X	X	X	X
Pierce	7	X	X	X	X
Pike	6	X	X	X	

¶ 2104

Part VI—Sales and Use Taxes

COUNTY	TOTAL RATE %	4% STATE	1% LOCAL OPTION	1% MARTA/ SPECIAL	1% EDUCATIONAL LOCAL OPTION
Polk	7	X	X	X	X
Pulaski	7	X	X	X	X
Putnam	7	X	X	X	X
Quitman	7	X	X	X	X
Rabun	7	X	X	X	X
Randolph	6	X	X	X	
Richmond	7	X	X	X	X
Rockdale	6	X			X
Schley	7	X	X	X	X
Screven	7	X	X	X	X
Seminole	7	X	X	X	X
Spalding	6	X	X		X
Stephens	7	X	X	X	X
Stewart	7	X	X	X	X
Sumter	7	X	X	X	X
Talbot	7	X	X	X	X
Taliaferro	7	X	X	X	X
Tattnall	7	X	X	X	X
Taylor	7	X	X	X	X
Telfair	7	X	X	X	X
Terrell	7	X	X	X	X
Thomas	6	X	X		X
Tift	7	X	X	X	X
Toombs	6	X	X	X	
Towns [2]	7	X	X	X	X
Treutlen	6	X	X	X	
Troup	7	X	X	X	X
Turner	7	X	X	X	X
Twiggs	7	X	X	X	X
Union	7	X	X	X	X
Upson	7	X	X	X	X
Walker	7	X	X	X	X
Walton	7	X	X	X	X
Ware	7	X	X	X	X
Warren	7	X	X	X	X
Washington	6	X	X	X	
Wayne	6	X	X	X	
Webster	7	X	X	X	X
Wheeler	6	X	X		
White	7	X	X	X	X
Whitfield	7	X	X	X	X
Wilcox	7	X	X	X	X
Wilkes	7	X	X	X	X
Wilkinson	7	X	X	X	X
Worth	7	X	X	X	X

[1] Dekalb County imposes a 1% Homestead Option Sales and Use Tax. It is the only Georgia county to impose the tax.
[2] Towns County imposes a 1% 2nd Local Option Sales and Use Tax. It is the only Georgia county to impose the tax.
[3] Within the incorporated city limits of Atlanta only, a 1% tax to assist with funding renovations to the water and sewer system is imposed, in addition to all other local sales and use taxes. Parts of the City of Atlanta are located in DeKalb and Fulton counties. (The sale, lease, and rental of automobiles are exempt from this 1% tax.)

¶ 2104

For general information purposes, the following is a list of the most populous cities within the counties imposing the special 1% county tax. All cities in these jurisdictions are subject to the special 1% tax.

CITY	(COUNTY)	CITY	(COUNTY)
A		Banning	(Carroll)
		Barnett	(Warren)
Aaron	(Bulloch)	Barney	(Brooks)
Abba	(Irwin)	Barretts	(Lowndes)
Abbeville	(Wilcox)	Barwick	(Brooks)
Acree	(Dougherty)	Bath	(Richmond)
Adairsville	(Bartow)	Beach	(Ware)
Adrian	*(Emanuel)	Beacon Heights	(Morgan)
	(Johnson)	Beaulieu	(Chatham)
Ailey	(Montgomery)	Bellville	(Evans)
Airport Subdiv.	(Lowndes)	Bellville Bluff	(McIntosh)
Alapaha	(Berrien)	Bemiss	(Lowndes)
Albany	(Dougherty)	Benedict	(Polk)
Albion Acres	(Richmond)	Bentley Place	(Walker)
Allen City	(Gwinnett)	Berkeley Lake	(Gwinnett)
Allendale	(Gwinnett)	Berryton	(Chattooga)
Allenhurst	(Liberty)	Bethlehem	(Barrow)
Allentown	(Bleckley)	Between	(Walton)
	(Laurens)	Beverly Hills	(Walker)
	(Twiggs)	Bishop	(Oconee)
	(Wilkinson)	Blackshear Place	(Hall)
Allenwood	(Baldwin)	Blairsville	(Union)
Almon	(Newton)	Bland	(Bulloch)
Alston	(Montgomery)	Bloomingdale	(Chatham)
Altman	(Banks)	Blowing Springs	(Walker)
	(Screven)	Blythe	(Richmond)
Alto	(Banks)	Bogart	(Clarke)
	(Habersham)	Bolen	(Ware)
Alto Park	(Floyd)	Boneville	(McDuffie)
Amboy	(Turner)	Bonevolence	(Randolph)
Americus	(Sumter)	Boston	(Thomas)
Amsterdam	(Decatur Co.)	Bostwick	(Morgan)
Anderson City	(Worth)	Bowden Jct.	(Carroll)
Andersonville	(Sumter)	Bowdon	(Carroll)
Apalachee	(Morgan)	Bowman	(Elbert)
Arabi	(Crisp)	Boy Estate	(Glynn)
Aragon	(Polk)	Bradley	(Jones)
Aragon Park	(Richmond)	Bremen	(Haralson)
Arcade	(Jackson)	Brentwood	(Dougherty)
Arch City	(Gordon)	Brewton	(Laurens)
Armuchee	(Floyd)	Bridgeboro	(Worth)
Arnco Mills	(Coweta)	Brinson	(Decatur Co.)
Arnoldsville	(Oglethorpe)	Brockton	(Jackson)
Ashburn	(Turner)	Bronco	(Walker)
Ashintilly	(McIntosh)	Bronwood	(Terrell)
Athens	(Clarke)	Brooklet	(Bulloch)
Attapulgus	(Decatur Co.)	Brookton	(Hall)
Auburn	(Barrow)	Brunswick	(Glynn)
Augusta	(Richmond)	Buchanan	(Haralson)
Avalon	(Stephens)	Buckhead	(Morgan)
Axson	(Atkinson)	Buford	(Hall)
Ayersville	(Stephens)	Burford	(Gwinnett)
B		Bullard	(Twiggs)
		Burrows	(Chatham)
Baconton	(Mitchell)	Butler	(Taylor)
Baden	(Brooks)	Butler Subdv.	(Dougherty)
Bainbridge	(Decatur Co.)	Byromville	(Dooly)
Bairdstown	(Oglethorpe)	Byron	(Peach)
Ball Ground	(Cherokee)		

¶ 2104

Part VI—Sales and Use Taxes

CITY	(COUNTY)	CITY	(COUNTY)
C		Coverdale	(Turner)
		Covington	(Newton)
Cadwell	(Laurens)	Covington Mills	(Newton)
Calhoun	(Gordon)	Cox	(McIntosh)
Camak	(Warren)	Crandal	(Murray)
Camelot	(Clarke)	Crawford	(Oglethorpe)
Camilla	(Mitchell)	Crawfordville	(Taliaferro)
Campton	(Walton)	Crescent	(McIntosh)
Canton	(Cherokee)	Crossroads	(Liberty)
Carl	(Barrow)	Crystal Springs	(Floyd)
Carlton	(Madison)	Culverton	(Hancock)
Carnegie	(Randolph)	Cunning	(Forsyth)
Carnigan	(McIntosh)	Cuthbert	(Randolph)
Carrollton	(Carroll)	Cypress Mills	(Glynn)
Carsonville	(Taylor)		
Cartersville	(Bartow)	**D**	
Cary	(Bleckley)	Dacula	(Gwinnett)
Cash	(Gordon)	Daisy	(Evans)
Cassville	(Bartow)	Dakota	(Turner)
Cave Springs	(Floyd)	Dallas	(Paulding)
Cedar Creek Park	(Clarke)	Dalton	(Whitfield)
Cedartown	(Polk)	Damascus	(Gordon)
Center	(Bartow)	Danburg	(Wilkes)
Centralhatchee	(Heard)	Danielsville	(Madison)
Charling	(Taylor)	Danville	(Wilkinson)
Charlotteville	(Montgomery)	Danville	(Twiggs)
Chatsworth	(Murray)	Darien	(McIntosh)
Cherokee Forest	(Cherokee)	Dasher	(Lowndes)
Chestnut Mtn.	(Hall)	Dawson	(Terrell)
Chickamauga	(Walker)	Dawsonville	(Dawson)
Chicopee	(Hall)	Dearing	(McDuffie)
Cisco	(Murray)	Deenwood	(Ware)
Clarke Dale	(Clarke)	Demorest	(Habersham)
Clarkesville	(Habersham)	Denton	(Jeff Davis)
Clarksboro	(Jackson)	DeSoto	(Sumter)
Claxton	(Evans)	DeSoto Park	(Floyd)
Clayton	(Rabun)	Devereux	(Hancock)
Clem	(Carroll)	Dewberry	(Walker)
Clermont	(Hall)	Dewy Rose	(Elbert)
Cleveland	(White)	Dexter	(Laurens)
Climax	(Decatur Co.)	Dialtown	(Newton)
Clito	(Bulloch)	Dillard	(Rabun)
Cloudland	(Chattooga)	Dixie	(Brooks)
Clyattville	(Lowndes)	Dixie Union	(Ware)
Clyo	(Effingham)	Dock Junction	(Glynn)
Coal Mountain	(Forsyth)	Doles	(Worth)
Cobb	(Sumter)	Dooling	(Dooly)
Cobbtown	(Tattnall)	Doublegate	(Dougherty)
Cochran	(Bleckley)	Draketown	(Haralson)
Cohutta	(Whitfield)	Dry Branch	(Twiggs)
Colbert	(Madison)	Dublin	(Laurens)
Coleman	(Randolph)	Ducktown	(Forsyth)
College Hgts.	(Dougherty)	Dudley	(Laurens)
Collins	(Tattnall)	Duluth	(Gwinnett)
Comer	(Madison)	Dunn Store	(Murray)
Conyers	(Rockdale)		
Coolidge	(Thomas)	**E**	
Coopers	(Baldwin)	Eagle Cliff	(Walker)
Coosa	(Floyd)	East Boundary	(Richmond)
Cordele	(Crisp)	East Dublin	(Laurens)
Corinth	(Coweta)	East Juliette	(Jones)
Corinth	(Heard)	East Meadow	(Clarke)
Cornelia	(Habersham)	East Newman	(Coweta)

¶ 2104

CITY	(COUNTY)	CITY	(COUNTY)
Eastanollee	(Stephens)	Grantville	(Coweta)
Eastville	(Oconee)	Gratis	(Walton)
Echota	(Gordon)	Graves	(Terrell)
Eden	(Effingham)	Gray	(Jones)
Egypt	(Effingham)	Grayson	(Gwinnett)
Elberton	(Elbert)	Green Acres	(Clarke)
Eldora	(Bryan)	Greensboro	(Greene)
Eleanor Village	(Dougherty)	Gumbranch	(Liberty)
Emerson	(Bartow)	Guyton	(Effingham)
Emerson Park	(Ware)		
Enigma	(Berrien)	**H**	
Enterprise	(Oglethorpe)	Habersham	(Habersham)
Eson Hill	(Polk)	Haddock	(Jones)
Eton	(Murray)	Hagan	(Evans)
Euharlee	(Bartow)	Hahira	(Lowndes)
Eulonia	(McIntosh)	Haralson	(Coweta)
Everett	(Glynn)		*(Meriwether)
Everett Springs	(Floyd)	Hardwick	(Baldwin)
Evergreen	(Dougherty)	Hatley	(Crisp)
		Hazelhurst	(Jeff Davis)
F		Hebardville	(Ware)
Fairmount	(Gordon)	Helen	(White)
Fairview	(Walker)	Hepzibah	(Richmond)
Fantasy Hills	(Walker)	Hi Roc Shores	(Rockdale)
Farmington	(Oconee)	Hiawassee	(Towns)
Felton	(Haralson)	Hickory Flat	(Cherokee)
Findley	(Dooly)	Higgston	(Montgomery)
Fish Creek	(Polk)	High Point	(Walker)
Five Forks	(Gwinnett)	High Point	(Newton)
Fleming	(Liberty)	High Shoals	(Morgan)
Flemington	(Liberty)		(Oconee)
Flintside	(Sumter)		(Walton)
Flintstone	(Walker)	Highland Hgts.	(Lowndes)
Flovilla	(Butts)	Hill City	(Gordon)
Flowery Branch	(Hall)	Hilltonia	(Screven)
Folsom	(Bartow)	Hinesville	(Liberty)
Fort Gordon	(Richmond)	Hinkles	(Walker)
Fort Stewart	(Liberty)	Hinsonton	(Mitchell)
Fort Valley	(Peach)	Hiram	(Paulding)
Fowlstown	(Decatur Co.)	Holland	(Chattooga)
Franklin	(Heard)	Holly Springs	(Cherokee)
		Hollywood	(Habersham)
G		Homer	(Banks)
Gaillard	(Crawford)	Horseleg Estates	(Floyd)
Gainesville	(Hall)	Howard	(Taylor)
Gainesville Mills	(Hall)	Hulett	(Carroll)
Garden City	(Chatham)	Hull	(Madison)
Garden Lakes	(Floyd)	Hutchings	(Oglethorpe)
Gillsville	(Banks)		
	(Hall)	**I**	
Glenloch	(Heard)	Ideal	(Macon)
Glenn	(Heard)	Ila	(Madison)
Glenndale	(Richmond)	Indian Springs	(Butts)
Glennville	(Tattnall)	Industrial City	(Gordon)
Glenwood	(Floyd)	Irwinton	(Wilkinson)
Gloster	(Gwinnett)	Irwinville	(Irwin)
Glynco	(Glynn)	Isabella	(Worth)
Glynn Haven	(Glynn)	Isle of Hope	(Chatham)
Godfrey	(Morgan)	Ivey	(Wilkinson)
Good Hope	(Walton)		
Gorday	(Worth)	**J**	
Gordon	(Wilkinson)	Jackson	(Butts)
Gracewood	(Richmond)	Jake	(Carroll)

¶ 2104

Part VI—Sales and Use Taxes

CITY	(COUNTY)	CITY	(COUNTY)
James	(Jones)	Mansfield	(Newton)
Jamestown	(Ware)	Marlow	(Effingham)
Jeffersonville	(Twiggs)	Marshallville	(Macon)
Jenkinsburg	(Butts)	Martin	*(Franklin)
Johnson Corner	(Toombs)	Martin	(Stephens)
Jones	(McIntosh)	Mauk	(Taylor)
Jones Acres	(Jones)	Maxeys	(Oglethorpe)
Jonesville	(Carroll)	Mayfield	(Hancock)
Juno	(Dawson)	Maysville	(Banks)
		McGregor	(Montgomery)
K		McIntosh Mill V.	(Coweta)
Keller	(Bryan)	McIntyre	(Wilkinson)
Kildare	(Effingham)	Mechanicsville	(Gwinnett)
Kingsland	(Camden)	Meigs	(Thomas)
Kingston	(Bartown)	Meinhard	(Chatham)
Kirkland	(Atkinson)	Meldrin	(Effingham)
Kirkland	(Jeff Davis)	Mendes	(Tattnall)
Kite	(Johnson)	Menlo	(Chattooga)
Knoxville	(Crawford)	Meridian	(McIntosh)
		Merrillville	(Thomas)
L		Mesena	(Warren)
Lafayette	(Walker)	Metasville	(Wilkes)
Lake Capri Ests.	(Rockdale)	Metcalf	(Thomas)
Lake Lucerne	(Gwinnett)	Midway	(Liberty)
Lake Park	(Lowndes)	Midway-	
Lakeland	(Lanier)	Hardwick	(Baldwin)
Lakemont	(Richmond)	Mill Creek	(Whitfield)
Lakemount	(Rabun)	Milledgeville	(Baldwin)
Lakeview Ests.	(Rockdale)	Millen	(Jenkins)
Lanier	(Bryan)	Millwood	(Ware)
Lathentown	(Cherokee)	Milstead	(Rockdale)
Lawrenceville	(Gwinnett)	Mineola	(Lowndes)
Lax	(Irwin)	Minton	(Worth)
Lebanon	(Cherokee)	Modoc	(Emanuel)
Lee Pope	(Crawford)	Monroe	(Walton)
Leesburg	(Lee)	Montezuma	(Macon)
Leliaton	(Atkinson)	Montgomery	(Chatham)
Leslie	(Sumter)	Montivedio	(Hart)
Lexington	(Oglethorpe)	Montrose	(Laurens)
Lexsy	(Emanuel)	Moody AFB	(Lowndes)
Lilburn	(Gwinnett)	Moons	(Walker)
Lilly	(Dooly)	Moreland	(Coweta)
Lincolnton	(Lincoln)	Morganville	(Dade)
Lindale	(Floyd)	Morningside Hgts	(Hall)
Linton	(Hancock)	Morven	(Brooks)
Linwood	(Walker)	Mount Berry	(Floyd)
Little Miami	(Lowndes)	Mount Vernon	(Montgomery)
Loganville	(Gwinnett)	Mount Vernon	(Whitfield)
	(Walton)	Mountain City	(Rabun)
Lookout Mountain	(Walker)	Mountain Park	(Cherokee)
Lowell	(Carroll)	Mountain Park	(Gwinnett)
Lula	(Hall)	Mountain Park	(Fulton)
Luxonni	(Gwinnett)	Mountain View	(Walker)
Lyerly	(Chattooga)	Mt. Airy	(Habersham)
Lyons	(Toombs)	Mt. Zion	(Carroll)
		Murrayville	(Hall)
M		Musella	(Crawford)
Macedonia	(Cherokee)	Myrtie	(Irwin)
Madison	(Morgan)		
Madras	(Coweta)	**N**	
Magnet	(Rockdale)	Naomi	(Walker)
Manassas	(Tattnall)	Nashville	(Berrien)
Manor	(Ware)	National Hills	(Richmond)

¶ 2104

CITY	(COUNTY)	CITY	(COUNTY)
Naylor	(Lowndes)	Potterville	(Taylor)
Neco	(Richmond)	Poulan	(Worth)
Nelson	*(Pickens)	Powell Place	(Dougherty)
	(Cherokee)	Powelton	(Hancock)
Nevils	(Bulloch)	Powersville	(Peach)
New England	(Dade)	Princeton	(Clark)
New Holland	(Hall)	Putney	(Dougherty)
New Town	(Gordon)		
Newborn	(Newton)	**Q**	
Newington	(Screven)	Quitman	(Brooks)
Newnan	(Coweta)		
Nicholson	(Jackson)	**R**	
Noble	(Walker)	Rabun Gap	(Rabun)
Norcross	(Gwinnett)	Radium Springs	(Dougherty)
North Elberton	(Elbert)	Raines	(Crisp)
Norwood	(Warren)	Ranger	(Gordon)
O		Raoul	(Habersham)
Oak Grove	(Cherokee)	Ray City	(Berrien)
Oakfield	(Worth)	Rayle	(Wilkes)
Oakland Heights	(Bartow)	Raymond	(Coweta)
Oakman	(Gordon)	Red Rock	(Worth)
Oakwood	(Hall)	Redbud	(Gordon)
Ochard Hills	(Walker)	Register	(Bulloch)
Ochlocknee	(Thomas)	Reidsville	(Tattnall)
Ocilla	(Irwin)	Remerton	(Lowndes)
Oconee Heights	(Clarke)	Rentz	(Laurens)
Ogeecheeton	(Chatham)	Resaca	(Gordon)
Ogeecheeton Rd.	(Chatham)	Rest Haven	(Gwinnett)
Oglethorpe	(Macon)	Retreat	(Liberty)
Osierfield	(Irwin)	Reynolds	(Taylor)
Oxford	(Newton)	Riceboro	(Liberty)
		Richwood	(Dooly)
P		Ridgeville	(McIntosh)
Pace	(Newton)	Rincon	(Effingham)
Palmetto	(Oglethorpe)	Rising Fawn	(Dade)
Parkerville	(Worth)	Riverside	(Floyd)
Parrott	(Terrell)	Roberta	(Crawford)
Pavo	(Thomas)	Robertstown	(White)
Peach Orchard	(Richmond)	Robinson	(Taliaferro)
Pearson	(Atkinson)	Rochelle	(Wilcox)
Pelham	(Mitchell)	Rock Springs	(Walker)
Pendergrass	(Jackson)	Rockledge	(Laurens)
Penfield	(Greene)	Rockmart	(Polk)
Pepperton	(Butts)	Rocky Face	(Whitfield)
Perkins	(Jenkins)	Rocky Ford	(Screven)
Philomath	(Oglethorpe)	Rome	(Floyd)
Phoenix	(Putnam)	Roopville	(Carroll)
Pine Harbor	(McIntosh)	Roosterville	(Heard)
Pine Log	(Bartow)	Roscoe	(Coweta)
Pine Valley	(Richmond)	Rosemont Park	(Floyd)
Pinehurst	(Dooly)	Rossville	(Walker)
Pineora	(Effingham)	Round Oak	(Jones)
Pineview	(Wilcox)	Rupert	(Taylor)
Pittman	(Gwinnett)	Russell	(Barrow)
Pitts	(Wilcox)	Rutledge	(Morgan)
Plains	(Sumter)	Rydal	(Bartow)
Plainville	(Gordon)		
Point Peter	(Oglethorpe)	**S**	
Pooler	(Chatham)	Sale City	(Mitchell)
Port Wentworth	(Chatham)	Sanborn	(Dougherty)
Portal	(Bulloch)	Sandalwood	(Dougherty)
Porterdale	(Newton)	Sandfly	(Chatham)
		Sandy Cross	(Oglethorpe)

¶ 2104

Part VI—Sales and Use Taxes

CITY	(COUNTY)	CITY	(COUNTY)
Santa Claus	(Toombs)	Sycamore	(Turner)
Sapelo Island	(McIntosh)	Sylvania	(Screven)
Sapps Still	(Coffee)	Sylvester	(Worth)
Sargent	(Coweta)		
Sasser	(Terrell)	**T**	
Sautee-Nacoochee	(White)	Tallapoosa	(Haralson)
Savannah	(Chatham)	Tallulah	(Jackson)
Scott	(Johnson)	Talmo	(Rabun)
Sea Island	(Glynn)	Tarboro	(Camden)
Senoia	(Coweta)	Tarrytown	(Montgomery)
Seville	(Wilcox)	Taylorsville	(Bartow)
Shannon	(Floyd)	Temple	(Carroll)
Sharon	(Taliaferro)	Tennga	(Murray)
Sharpsburg	(Coweta)	Thomasville	(Thomas)
Shawnee	(Effingham)	Thomson	(McDuffie)
Shellman	(Randolph)	Thyatvia	(Jackson)
Shellman Bluff	(McIntosh)	Tiger	(Rabun)
Sherwood Forest	(Floyd)	Tignall	(Wilkes)
Sherwood Forest	(Coweta)	Tilton	(Whitfield)
Shields Crossroad	(Walker)	Toccoa	(Stephens)
Shingler	(Worth)	Toccoa Falls	(Stephens)
Silk Mills	(Elbert)	Toomsboro	(Wilkinson)
Siloam	(Greene)	Townsend	(McIntosh)
Silver Creek	(Floyd)	Town &	
Sky Valley	(Rabun)	Ctry Acrs	(Dougherty)
Smithsonia	(Oglethorpe)	Tree	(Towns)
Smithville	(Lee)	Trenton	(Dade)
Snellville	(Gwinnett)	Trion	(Chattooga)
Social Circle	(Walton)	Tunnel Hill	(Whitfield)
South Nellieville	(Richmond)	Turin	(Coweta)
South Newport	(McIntosh)	Turnerville	(Habersham)
Spain	(Brooks)	Twin Lakes	(Lowndes)
Sparta	(Hancock)		
Spencer Hills	(Walker)	**U**	
Springfield	(Effingham)	Unadilla	(Dooly)
Spring Place	(Murray)	Union Point	(Greene)
Springvale	(Randolph)	Upton	(Coffee)
Stansville	(Newton)	Uvalda	(Montgomery)
Stark	(Butts)		
Starrsville	(Newton)	**V**	
Statesboro	(Bulloch)	Valdosta	(Lowndes)
Statham	(Barrow)	Valley View	(Walker)
Stephens	(Oglethorpe)	Valona	(McIntosh)
Sterling	(Glynn)	Van Wert	(Polk)
Stevens Pottery	(Baldwin)	Varnell	(Whitfield)
Stilesboro	(Bartow)	Veazey	(Greene)
Stillwell	(Effingham)	Vesta	(Oglethorpe)
Stilson	(Bulloch)	Victoria	(Cherokee)
Stockton	(Lanier)	Victory	(Carroll)
Stockwood	(Cherokee)	Vidalia	(Toombs)
St. Mary	(Camden)	Vidalia	(Montgomery)
St. Simons Isl.	(Glynn)	Vienna	(Dooly)
Subligna	(Chattooga)	Villa Rica	(Douglas)
Suches	(Union)	Villanow	(Walker)
Sugar Hill	(Gwinnett)		
Sugar Valley	(Gordon)	**W**	
Sumac	(Murray)	Waco	(Haralson)
Summerville	(Chattooga)	Waleska	(Cherokee)
Sumner	(Worth)	Wallaceville	(Walker)
Sumter	(Sumter)	Walnut Grove	(Walton)
Sunnyside	(Ware)	Walthourville	(Liberty)
Suwanee	(Gwinnett)	Waresboro	(Ware)
Swords	(Morgan)	Waresville	(Heard)

¶ 2104

CITY	(COUNTY)	CITY	(COUNTY)
Waring	(Whitfield)	Winder	(Barrow)
Warren Terrace	(Walker)	Winona Park	(Ware)
Warrenton	(Warren)	Winterville	(Clarke)
Warwick	(Worth)	Woodbine	(Camden)
Washington	(Wilkes)	Woodcliff	(Screven)
Watkinsville	(Oconee)	Woodland Hills	(Walker)
Waverly	(Camden)	Woodstock	(Cherokee)
Wax	(Floyd)	Woodville	(Greene)
Waycross	(Ware)	Worth	(Turner)
Wayside	(Jones)	Wray	(Irwin)
Weber	(Berrien)	Wrightsville	(Johnson)
Wenona	(Crisp)		
Wesley	(Emanuel)	**Y**	
Westgate Park	(Clarke)	Yorkville	(Paulding)
White	(Bartow)	Young Harris	(Towns)
White Hall	(Clarke)	Youth	(Walton)
White Oak	(Camden)		
White Plains	(Greene)	**Z**	
Whitesburg	(Carroll)	Zenith	(Crawford)
Wildwood	(Dade)	Zetto	(Clay)
Wiley	(Rabun)		
Willacoochee	(Atkinson)		

* Denotes jurisdictions not imposing the 1% special tax.

¶ 2105 Bracket Schedule

Law: Secs. 48-8-31, 48-8-141, Code; Reg. Sec. 560-12-1.05 (CCH GEORGIA TAX REPORTS ¶ 60-130).

The Georgia Department of Revenue has determined the following brackets for the collection and remittance of Georgia state and local sales and use taxes (effective October 1, 2004).

Transactions taxable at the rate of 1%:

Amount of Sale	Tax
.01 - .49	no tax
.50 - 1.00	.01

For a taxable transaction of more than $1.00, 1¢ is charged on each dollar of the sales price, plus the tax amount due on any fractional part of $1.00.

Transactions taxable at the rate of 2%:

Amount of Sale	Tax
.01 - .24	no tax
.25 - .74	.01
.75 - 1.00	.02

For a taxable transaction of more than $1.00, 2¢ is charged on each dollar of the sales price, plus the tax amount due on any fractional part of each additional dollar.

Transactions taxable at the rate of 3%:

Amount of Sale	Tax
.01 - .16	no tax
.17 - .49	.01
.50 - .83	.02
.84 - 1.00	.03

For a taxable transaction of more than $1.00, 3¢ is charged on each dollar of the sales price, plus the tax amount due on any fractional part of each additional dollar.

¶ 2105

Part VI—Sales and Use Taxes

Transactions taxable at the rate of 4%:

Amount of Sale	Tax
.01 - .12	no tax
.13 - .37	.01
.38 - .62	.02
.63 - .87	.03
.88 - 1.00	.04

For a taxable transaction of more than $1.00, 4¢ is charged on each dollar of the sales price, plus the tax amount due on any fractional part of each additional dollar.

Transactions taxable at the rate of 5%:

Amount of Sale	Tax
.01 - .09	no tax
.10 - .29	.01
.30 - .49	.02
.50 - .69	.03
.70 - .89	.04
.90 - 1.00	.05

For a taxable transaction of more than $1.00, 5¢ is charged on each dollar of the sales price, plus the tax amount due on any fractional part of each additional dollar.

Transactions taxable at the rate of 6%:

Amount of Sale	Tax
.01 - .08	no tax
.09 - .24	.01
.25 - .41	.02
.42 - .58	.03
.59 - .74	.04
.75 - .91	.05
.92 - 1.00	.06

For a taxable transaction of more than $1.00, 6¢ is charged on each dollar of the sales price, plus the tax amount due on any fractional part of each additional dollar.

Transactions taxable at the rate of 7%:

Amount of Sale	Tax
.01 - .07	no tax
.08 - .21	.01
.22 - .35	.02
.36 - .49	.03
.50 - .64	.04
.65 - .78	.05
.79 - .92	.06
.93 - 1.00	.07

For a taxable transaction of more than $1.00, 7¢ is charged on each dollar of the sales price, plus the tax amount due on any fractional part of each additional dollar.

Transactions taxable at the rate of 8%:

Amount of Sale	Tax
.01 - .06	no tax
.07 - .18	.01
.19 - .31	.02
.32 - .43	.03
.44 - .56	.04
.57 - .68	.05
.69 - .81	.06
.82 - .93	.07
.94 - 1.00	.08

For a taxable transaction of more than $1.00, 8¢ is charged on each dollar of the sales price, plus the tax amount due on any fractional part of each additional dollar.

¶ 2105

SALES AND USE TAXES

CHAPTER 22

EXEMPTIONS AND CREDITS

¶ 2201	Exemptions
¶ 2202	Exemptions—Interstate Transactions
¶ 2203	Credits Against Tax

¶ 2201 Exemptions

Law: Secs. 48-8-3—48-8-5, 48-8-38, 48-8-39(b), 48-8-63, Code; Reg. Secs. 560-12-1-.07, 560-12-1-.08, 560-12-2-.03, 560-12-2-.04, 560-12-2-.17, 560-12-2-.19, 560-12-2-.21, 560-12-2-.23, 560-12-2-.25, 560-12-2-.28, 560-12-2-.30—560-12-2-.35, 560-12-2-.37, 560-12-2-.40, 560-12-2-.41, 560-12-2-.48, 560-12-2-.50—560-12-2-.52, 560-12-2-.54, 560-12-2-.56, 560-12-2-.61—560-12-2-.64, 560-12-2-.71, 560-12-2-.78—560-12-2-.81, 560-12-2-.87—560-12-2-.89, 560-12-2-.91, 560-12-2-.106, 560-12-2-.107, 560-12-2-.109, 560-12-3-.13 (CCH Georgia Tax Reports ¶ 60-240, 60-250, 60-270, 60-300, 60-310, 60-390, 60-420, 60-490, 60-510, 60-520, 60-560, 60-590, 60-600, 60-620, 60-645, 60-740, 61-010, 61-020).

Exemptions to sales and use taxes are expressed in several ways: (1) explicitly; (2) as exceptions to the definition of a taxable sale or tangible personal property; or (3) as exclusions from a taxable category of transactions. Exemptions may be granted on the basis of the nature of the product (such as food), the type of transaction (such as a purchase for resale), or the nature of the entity selling or buying the product (such as a charitable organization).

Sales and use tax exemptions applicable to specific goods, services, transactions, taxpayers, or businesses are explained below in alphabetical order. Interstate transactions are discussed at ¶ 2202. See also the discussions of selected transactions at ¶ 2004, and taxable services at ¶ 2005.

● *Exemption claims*

All sales are subject to tax until the contrary is established. To claim exemption, the purchaser ordinarily furnishes the seller with the appropriate exemption certificate. Under some circumstances, however, the tax must be paid at the time of sale and an application made to the Commissioner of Revenue for a refund of the exempt portion. No exemption certificate is needed for the following sales:

—sales in interstate commerce if the seller ships the property by common carrier to a point outside the state (see ¶ 2202);

—professional, insurance, or personal service transactions;

—sales of water;

—school lunches;

—sales of religious papers;

—sales of drugs for livestock, fish, or poultry if the purchaser raises livestock, fish, or poultry for profit; and

—sales of Bibles and Holy Scripture.

With the exception of the sales listed above, a dealer must have on file and ready for inspection one of the following certificates of exemption in order to be relieved of tax liability:

—Form ST-4 (out-of-state dealers purchasing property in Georgia for resale in another state);

—Form ST-5 (Georgia purchasers or dealers);

—Form ST-6 (Georgia dealers for deliveries outside the state);

—Form ST-7 (purchases of fuel and supplies by ships);

—Form ST-8 (motor vehicles purchased by nonresidents);

—Form ST-M2 (machinery for new or expanded industry);

—Form ST-M2B (tangible personal property for new or expanded industry);

—Form ST-M8 (pollution control machinery and equipment);

—Form ST-A1 (agricultural certificate of exemption);

—Form ST-NH2 (nonprofit nursing homes; general or mental hospitals);

If a taxpayer does not obtain and use a Georgia sales and use tax exemption certificate or determination letter prior to purchasing tangible personal property, any refund on that purchase does not include interest. (H.B. 1239), Laws 2004.)

Georgia purchasers or dealers: Georgia Form ST-5 is used to claim the exemption for a sale for resale. The form also is used for the following:

—exemption for materials for further processing, manufacture or conversion into articles of tangible personal property for resale which will become a component part of the property for sale;

—machinery used directly in the manufacture of tangible personal property for sale purchased as additional, replacement, or upgrade machinery to be placed into an existing plant;

—use by the federal government, Georgia, or any Georgia county or municipality, and hospital authorities;

—direct pay permit holders;

—aircraft, watercraft, motor vehicles and other transportation equipment manufactured or assembled, sold and delivered for use exclusively outside the state; and

—aircraft, watercraft, railroad locomotives, rolling stock, and motor vehicles that will be used to cross the state borders to transport passengers or cargo by common carriers.

¶ 2201

Part VI—Sales and Use Taxes

● *Agriculture*

The sales and use taxes do not apply to the sale of seed; fertilizers; insecticides; fungicides; rodenticides; herbicides; defoliants; soil fumigants; plant growth regulating chemicals; desiccants such as shavings and sawdust from wood, peanut hulls, fuller's earth, straw, and hay; and feed for livestock, fish, or poultry when used either directly in tilling the soil or in animal, fish, or poultry husbandry.

Sales of feed, minerals, drugs, medicine, and antibiotics to producers of poultry and livestock for sale are exempt.

It is presumed that sales of feed for commercial fisheries, poultry, mules, swine, and ruminant animals such as dairy cattle, beef cattle, sheep, and goats are exempt, and no exemption certificate is required. However, it is presumed that feed for horses that are not a part of an agricultural pursuit or animal husbandry engaged in for profit is taxable. A dealer selling feed for horses that are exempt must secure an exemption certificate from the purchasers.

Seeds: The sale of seeds for the purpose of growing agricultural products for sale is not taxable, but is taxable if for use on lawns, golf courses, or in residential or commercial projects.

Animals for breeding purposes: The sales and use taxes do not apply to the sale of cattle, hogs, sheep, horses, poultry, or bees when sold for breeding purposes.

Machinery: Sales of agricultural machinery and equipment used for the following purposes are exempt:

—*Irrigation:* machinery and equipment that is sold to persons engaged primarily in producing farm crops for sale and that is used exclusively to irrigate farm crops;

—*Poultry and egg production:* machinery and equipment sold for use on a farm in the production of poultry and eggs for sale;

—*Hatching and breeding:* machinery and equipment sold for use in hatching and breeding poultry and the breeding of livestock;

—*Milk production:* machinery and equipment sold for use on a farm in producing, processing, and storing fluid milk for sale;

—*Livestock production:* machinery and equipment sold for use on a farm in the production of livestock for sale;

—*Harvesting farm crops for feed:* machinery and equipment used by a producer of poultry, eggs, fluid milk, or livestock to harvest farm crops as feed for poultry and livestock;

—*Direct use in tilling soil or in animal husbandry:* machinery directly used in tilling the soil or in animal husbandry when the machinery is (1) incorporated for the first time into a new farm unit engaged in tilling the soil or in animal husbandry, (2) incorporated as additional machinery for the first time into an existing farm unit already engaged in tilling the soil or in animal husbandry, or (3) bought to replace machinery in an existing farm unit already engaged in tilling the soil or in animal husbandry;

¶ 2201

—Tractors and harvesting equipment: Rubber-tired farm tractors and attachments used exclusively in tilling, planting, cultivating, and harvesting farm crops, and equipment used exclusively in harvesting farm crops or in processing onion crops that are sold to persons engaged primarily in producing farm crops for sale;

—Pecan harvesting: pecan sprayers, pecan shakers, and other equipment used to harvest pecans that are sold to persons engaged in the growing, harvesting, and production of pecans;

—Off-road timber equipment: Off-road equipment and related attachments that are sold to, or used by, a person engaged primarily in the growing or harvesting of timber and used exclusively in site preparation, planting, cultivating, or harvesting timber.

All sales of machinery and equipment are presumed taxable unless the dealer secures a certificate of exemption from the purchaser (Form ST-A1).

Fuel for heating structures: The sale of liquefied petroleum gas or other fuel used to heat a poultry structure or a structure in which plants, seedlings, nursery stock, or floral products are raised primarily for resale is exempt from sales and use taxes.

Use of self-produced goods: Use tax is not imposed on the use by a farmer or members of the farmer's family of livestock, livestock products, poultry, poultry products, farm products, and agricultural products produced by the farmer.

Agricultural products not sold as finished product: An agricultural commodity sold by a nonproducer to a person who purchases not for direct consumption but for the purpose of acquiring raw products for use or for sale in the process of preparing, finishing, or manufacturing the commodity for the ultimate retail consumer trade is exempt from sales and use taxes, except when the commodity is sold as a marketable or finished product to the ultimate consumer.

Electricity: The sale of electricity for the operation of an irrigation system that is used on a farm exclusively for the irrigation of farm crops is exempt from sales and use tax.

● *Art and artifacts*

An exemption applies to sales of art and sales of anthropological, archaeological, geological, horticultural, or zoological objects or artifacts and other similar property, to, or for the use by, a museum or tax-exempt organization under IRC Sec. 501(c)(3). The property must be displayed or exhibited in a museum in Georgia that is open to the public and that has been approved by the Revenue Commissioner as an organization eligible to receive tax deductible contributions.

● *Coins, currency, and bullion*

Sales of coins, currency, and gold, silver, or platinum bullion, alone or in combination, are exempt from sales and use tax. Dealers must maintain proper documentation to identify each exempt sale.

¶ 2201

Part VI—Sales and Use Taxes

● *Commercial fishing*

Crab bait: Sales of crab bait to, and the use of crab bait by, licensed commercial fishermen are exempt from sales and use tax.

Dyed diesel fuel: Sales of dyed diesel fuel exclusively used to operate vessels or boats in the commercial fishing trade by licensed commercial fishermen are exempt from sales and use tax. Any person making a sale of dyed diesel fuel to a commercial fisherman must collect the tax unless the purchaser provides a certificate issued by the State Revenue Commissioner certifying that the purchaser is entitled to purchase the dyed diesel fuel without paying the tax.

● *Computer equipment*

Sales or leases to high-tech companies: The sale or lease of computer equipment to certain high-technology companies for use in a Georgia facility is exempt from sales and use tax if the sales price of the equipment exceeds $15 million or the fair market value of leased equipment exceeds $15 million in any calendar year. To be eligible for the exemption, any entity that qualifies for the exemption and is affiliated in any manner with a nonqualified entity must conduct a majority of its business with entities with which it has no affiliation.

The term "computer equipment" means any individual computer or organized assembly of hardware or software, such as a server farm, mainframe or midrange computer, mainframe-driven high speed print and mailing devices, and workstations connected to those devices via high bandwidth connectivity such as a local area network, wide area network, or any other data transport technology that performs one of the following functions: storage or management of production data, hosting of production applications, hosting of application systems development activities, or hosting of applications systems testing. The term does not include telephone central office equipment or other voice data transport technology, or equipment with imbedded computer hardware or software that is primarily used for training, product testing, or in a manufacturing process.

Practitioner Comment: Facilities Exemption

The Department of Revenue has issued a policy statement that the eligibility requirement for a high-technology company to be doing a majority of its business with nonaffiliated entities shall not apply to any exemption issued on a company facility basis. A business entity can qualify for the exemption on the purchase of computer equipment if its data processing or other qualifying technology department is located at a separate qualifying facility and meets the general requirements for exemption.

Alston & Bird LLP

The purchaser must furnish an exemption certificate to the seller; the seller must collect the tax if the certificate is not furnished.

¶ 2201

● *Construction*

Tourist attractions: Until December 31, 2007, sales of tangible personal property to, or used in or for the new construction of, an eligible corporate attraction are exempt from Georgia sales and use taxes. "Corporate attraction" means any tourist facility constructed on or after May 17, 2004, dedicated to the history and products of a corporation that (1) has costs that exceed $50 million; (2) has greater than 60,000 square feet of space; and (3) has associated facilities, including parking decks and landscaping owned by the same owner as the corporate attraction. For purposes of this exemption, a seller must collect tax unless the purchaser furnishes the seller with an exemption determination letter certifying that the purchase is exempt.

Symphony hall: Effective May 5, 2004, until September 1, 2009, sales of tangible personal property used in direct connection with the construction of a new symphony hall facility owned or operated by a federally exempt organization are exempt. To qualify, the aggregate construction cost of the facility must be $200 million or more. (Act 456 (H.B. 1511), Laws 2004.)

See also "Repair, installation, and warranties," below.

● *Food and grocery items*

Sales of eligible food and beverages for off-premises human consumption are exempt. The term "eligible food and beverages" includes food that is a staple product for home consumption, including meat, poultry, bread, milk, candy, canned soft drinks, etc. It does not include alcoholic beverages, tobacco products, items sold hot or intended to be heated at a store, immediate consumption products (fountain drinks), vitamins and minerals. The food exemption does not include sales made by vending machines or seeds and plants used to grow food. The exemption does not apply to the 1% special county sales and use tax (see ¶ 2103, "Local Taxes").

The state sales tax and all applicable local county taxes apply to the sale of food sold for "on-premises" or immediate consumption, such as food served in a restaurant, coffee shop, cafeteria, tavern, food cart, luncheonette, or vending machine (¶ 2004). It also applies to the sale of hot foods, alcoholic beverages and tobacco products, as well as on other items commonly available in grocery stores such as napkins, laundry detergents, vitamins and pet foods.

Food stamps: All purchases made with food stamps or WIC coupons are exempt from sales and use taxes.

Public school lunches: An exemption is provided for school lunches sold and served to public school students or employees. Food and drink that become component parts of these lunches are exempt and may be purchased under certificates of exemption.

Private school meals: Private elementary and secondary schools approved by the Revenue Commissioner as organizations eligible to receive tax-deductible contributions are exempt from tax on sales of food to their students and employees for consumption on the premises.

College meals: Purchases of food by a private college or university that is furnished to students as part of a single charge for room, board, and tuition are

Part VI—Sales and Use Taxes

exempt. The sale of meals to students by a private college or university is taxable when the meal is not provided as part of the room, board, and tuition.

Fraternities and sororities: Meals furnished to members by a student fraternity or sorority are exempt from tax. However, meals furnished to fraternities and sororities by caterers and others are taxable.

Girl Scout cookies: Sales of Girl Scout cookies to and by member councils of the Girl Scouts of the U.S.A. are exempt from tax.

Ice: The sale or use of ice for chilling poultry or vegetables in processing for market and for chilling poultry or vegetables in storage rooms, compartments, or delivery trucks is not subject to Georgia sales and use tax, effective July 1, 2004. (H.B. 1409), Laws 2004.)

● *Government transactions*

Sales to the United States government or any of its departments are exempt by statute when paid for directly to the seller by warrant on appropriated government funds. In addition, the Supremacy Clause (Article VI) of the U.S. Constitution declares that the U.S. Constitution and laws are the supreme law of the land, and the U.S. Supreme Court held early that this clause invalidated a state tax imposed directly on a federal instrumentality (*McCulloch v. Maryland* (1819, US SCt) 17 US 316).

Government contractors: Contractors purchasing tangible personal property or taxable services under a contract with the U.S. government are the consumers of the property or services and must pay the tax when they purchase the property or services. However, where a contractor was merely acting as a purchasing agent for the federal government and the latter took title to the property, the contractor was held not subject to a gross receipts tax (*Kern-Limerick, Inc. v. Scurlock* (1954, US SCt) 347 US 110, 74 SCt 403).

The sales and use taxes do not apply to any transaction in which tangible personal property is furnished by the U.S. Government to any person who contracts to install, repair, or extend any public water, gas, or sewage system when the particular property is installed for general distribution purposes. No exemption is granted if tangible personal property is installed to serve a particular property site.

Federal areas: The federal Buck Act (4 U.S.C. 105—110) provides that state sales tax can be collected in federal areas, such as military reservations, although not from the government itself. A Georgia regulation also provides that such sales are taxable.

Sales to persons in the armed services and to civilian employees of those services are taxable except when made to them as authorized purchasers for a service organization operating exclusively within a U.S. military reservation and authorized by the Secretary of Defense. No tax is imposed on sales to officers' clubs and post exchanges organized, operated, and controlled under Department of Defense regulations and operated exclusively in a functional area of the command of which they are a part.

Government employees: Sales to U.S. government employees for their own use or consumption are taxable.

¶ 2201

Military equipment: The sale of major components and repair parts installed in military craft, vehicles, and missiles is exempt.

Overhead materials used by certain U.S. agencies: Until January 1, 2007, a sales tax exemption applies for overhead material sold to, or used by, a government contractor in the performance of a contract with the U.S. Department of Defense or the National Aeronautics and Space Administration.

State and local transactions: Sales to the state, a county or municipality, or department of these governments are exempt from sales and use taxes when paid for directly to the seller by warrant on appropriated government funds.

Coliseums: Effective July 1, 2002, sales to any local governmental authority are exempt from sales and use tax if the local government's principal purpose is to construct or operate a coliseum and related facilities for public entertainment including, among other things, athletic contests, trade fairs, expositions, conventions, agricultural events, and theatrical and musical performances.

Hospital authorities: Sales to public hospital authorities are exempt.

Public transit systems: Sales by a county or municipality arising from its operation of a public transit facility, and sales by public transit authorities are exempt from tax.

Housing authorities: Sales to housing authorities organized under Georgia law are exempt from sales and use tax.

Public school transactions: A sale of tangible personal property to public schools, public school principals, teachers, officers, employees, organizations, and students is exempt if an exemption certificate is presented (Form ST-5) and if the purchase is made pursuant to an official purchase order to be paid for out of public funds.

Sales of tangible personal property and services to the University System of Georgia and its educational units are exempt.

Sales by schools of tangible personal property, concessions, or tickets for admission to a school event or function are exempt from tax. The exemption applies to any public or private school containing any combination of grades kindergarten through 12, and all proceeds must benefit the school or its students.

Parent-teacher organizations: Sales by any parent-teacher organization exempt from federal taxation under IRC Sec. 501(c)(3) are exempt from state sales and use taxation.

- *Lottery and gambling*

The sale of lottery tickets authorized by Georgia law is exempt from the state sales and use tax.

- *Manufacturing machinery and equipment*

Various exemptions are available for the sale or purchase of certain manufacturing machinery and industrial materials, as discussed below.

¶ 2201

Part VI—Sales and Use Taxes

Exemption for manufacturing machinery: Sales of machinery used directly in the manufacture of tangible personal property that is bought to replace or upgrade machinery in an existing Georgia manufacturing plant, and sales of machinery components purchased to upgrade machinery used directly in the manufacture of tangible personal property in a manufacturing plant, are exempt from sales and use tax. Before 2001, this exemption applied to sales of machinery and components directly used in the manufacture of tangible personal property if the machinery or component replaced or upgraded machinery in an existing manufacturing plant.

In addition, machinery used directly in the manufacture of tangible personal property is exempt if the machinery is incorporated for the first time into a new manufacturing plant located in this state. Machinery used directly in the manufacture of tangible personal property is exempt if the machinery is incorporated as additional machinery for the first time into an existing Georgia manufacturing plant.

To obtain the exemption for machinery purchased for a new plant, the purchaser must present a certificate of exemption (Form ST-M2) to the seller. To obtain the certificate, the purchaser must file an application (Form ST-M1) with the Commissioner and include a schedule of the machinery to be purchased, a description of the machinery's use in the manufacturing operation, and the cost of each item.

CCH Caution: Regulations May Not Reflect Current Law

Although replacement or upgrade machinery is currently eligible for a statutory exemption, regulations continue to reflect the former procedure that required the tax to be paid but permitted refunds of taxes paid on qualifying sales (Reg. Sec. 560-12-3-.63). This regulation continues to apply to qualifying purchases or leases made prior to July 1, 1994. The refund procedures also presumably apply to a purchaser that has paid the tax on a purchase of machinery even though the machinery qualified for exemption.

Manufacture of tangible personal property: "Manufacture of tangible personal property" consists of an operation or series of separate operations at a fixed location whereby, through the application of machines and labor to raw materials or materials at any stage of becoming finished tangible personal property, the form or composition of the material or materials is significantly changed. It includes the assembly of finished units of tangible personal property into a new unit or units of tangible personal property; packaging when it is a part of a continuous manufacturing operation and the package or container becomes a part of the tangible personal property as such unit is customarily offered for sale by the taxpayer to another manufacturing operation or to the retail trade; and delivery of raw materials and work in process or finished units directly from one manufacturing operation to another in the same plant facility. However, the term does not include storage, delivery to or from the plant, or delivery to or from storage within the plant; repairing or maintenance of facilities; research or testing; and crating or packaging for shipment.

¶ 2201

Directly used in manufacturing: Both new and replacement machinery must have the character of machinery when purchased, it must be used to manufacture tangible personal property for sale, and it must also be used directly in the manufacturing operation. There is no exemption for machinery indirectly used in the manufacturing operation or for auxiliary equipment and appurtenances or materials to be incorporated into real estate construction.

Machinery and equipment incorporated into telecommunications manufacturing facilities: The sale of machinery and equipment used directly in the manufacture of tangible personal property to improve the air quality in advanced technology clean rooms of Class 100,000 or less by incorporating them into a telecommunications manufacturing facility are exempt from sales and use tax.

Electricity used in manufacturing: Electricity used directly in the manufacture of a product is exempt if the cost of the electricity exceeds 50% of the cost of all materials used in the product.

Repair or replacement parts, machinery clothing, molds, dies, and tooling: A phased-in exemption is allowed for the sale or use of repair or replacement parts, machinery clothing or replacement machinery clothing, molds or replacement molds, dies or replacement dies, and tooling or replacement tooling for machinery used directly in the manufacture of tangible personal property in a Georgia manufacturing plant. The parts must restore the machinery to its original condition.

The exemption applies to the portion of the sale price of each part or item not exceeding $150,000. The exemption is allowed in a percentage amount of the total sale price or use value as follows: 20% for the calendar year beginning January 1, 2001; 40% for the calendar year beginning January 1, 2002; 60% for the calendar year beginning January 1, 2003; 80% for the calendar year beginning January 1, 2004; and 100% for calendar years beginning on or after January 1, 2005.

Clean room equipment: The sale of machinery, equipment, and material incorporated into and used in the construction or operation of a clean room of class 100 or less is exempt from sales and use tax if the clean room is used directly in the manufacture of tangible personal property. This exemption does not include the building or any permanent, nonremovable component of the building that houses the clean room.

Primary material handling equipment: Sales of primary material handling equipment, such as conveyors, carousels, lifts, cranes, hoists, automated storage and retrieval systems, and forklifts, are exempt from tax if used directly for the handling and movement of tangible personal property in a warehouse or distribution facility located in Georgia. To qualify, less than 15% of the facility's revenues may be from retail sales to the general public. Furthermore, the equipment must be either (1) part of an expansion worth $10 million or more to an existing warehouse or distribution facility or (2) part of the construction of a new warehouse or distribution facility where the total value of all real and personal property purchased or acquired by the taxpayer for use in the warehouse or distribution facility is worth $5 million or more.

Industrial materials: An exemption applies to the sale, use, storage, or consumption of (1) industrial materials for future processing, manufacture, or

Part VI—Sales and Use Taxes

conversion into articles of tangible personal property for resale when the industrial materials become a component part of the finished product or (2) industrial materials (excluding machinery and machinery repair parts) that are coated upon or impregnated into the product at any stage of its processing, manufacture, or conversion. Chemicals used or consumed as industrial materials are exempt.

The term "industrial materials" does not include gas, oil, gasoline, electricity, solid fuel, ice, or other materials used for heat, light, power, or refrigeration in any phase of the manufacturing, processing, or converting process.

Fabrication: The definition of "sale" includes the fabrication of tangible personal property for consumers who furnish the materials used. An operation that changes the form or state of property is one of fabrication; however, the restoration of a used or worn piece of tangible personal property is a service and separately stated labor charges are not taxable.

A person regularly engaged in the fabrication or production of tangible personal property for sale at retail must collect the tax on the sales price, or if the property is converted to the fabricator's own use, on the fair market value. The sales price includes fabrication labor even if separately stated.

Equipment and fuel: Purchases of equipment, tools, and supplies by manufacturers, processors, and other businesses are subject to tax. Sales of oxygen, acetylene, hydrogen, and other gases to manufacturers, processors, refiners, welders, and others for use as fuel or illumination are also taxable.

Aircraft engine remanufacturing: Machinery and equipment used directly in the remanufacture of aircraft engines, engine parts or components at a Georgia remanufacturing facility are exempt. Sellers of such equipment must collect sales tax unless the purchaser provides a certificate certifying the purchaser's entitlement to the exemption.

● *Medical, dental, and optical supplies and drugs*

Specific exemptions are provided for the following:

—the sale of drugs dispensed by prescription and prescription eyeglasses and contact lenses;

—the sale of insulin, insulin syringes, and blood glucose level monitoring strips dispensed without a prescription and, effective July 1, 2000, the sale of blood measuring devices, other monitoring equipment, and insulin delivery systems;

—the sale of oxygen prescribed by a licensed physician;

—the sale or use of hearing aids; and

—the sale or use of any durable medical equipment or prosthetic device as defined under Titles XVIII and XIX of the federal Social Security Act.

¶ 2201

> **CCH Caution: *Regulation Does Not Reflect Current Law***
>
> Reg. 560-12-2-.30(4)(b), which provides that sales of drugs, medicine, and medical equipment to Medicare and Medicaid recipients are taxable, was promulgated prior to the adoption of Sec. 48-8-3(54), Code, which provides an exemption for certain purchases of durable medical equipment and prosthetic devices under Medicare or Medicaid programs, as discussed above.

Free samples: The sale of prescription eyeglasses and contact lenses distributed by a manufacturer to licensed dispensers as free samples not intended for resale is exempt.

Ophthalmic drug samples purchased by the manufacturer out-of-state for delivery as samples in Georgia were subject to use tax because the manufacturer did not intend to resell the drugs, but rather to give them away as customer samples. (*CIBA Vision Corp.*, Georgia Court of Appeals, No. A00A2123, March 21, 2001, CCH GEORGIA TAX REPORTS, ¶ 200-417.)

Government purchases: Sales of drugs, medicines, and medical equipment to the federal government, the state, any county, municipality, or department of such governmental entities are exempt when paid for directly by warrant on appropriated government funds.

Hospitals: Sales of drugs, medicines, and medical equipment to certain nonprofit nursing homes and hospitals are exempt.

Dental labs and supply houses: Sales of dentures and other tangible personal property by dental laboratories to dentists and other consumers are subject to tax. Tax must be paid on tangible personal property used to make repairs on dentures and other property and on purchases of machinery, equipment, and supplies purchased for use.

Industrial materials that become a component part of the finished product for sale, or are coated upon or impregnated into the product at any stage of its processing, manufacture, or conversion, may be purchased under a Certificate of Exemption (Form ST-5).

- *Motor fuels*

Sales of motor fuels are exempt from the first 3% of the sales and use taxes, but are subject to the remaining 1% of the sales and use taxes. This exemption does not apply to motor fuel (other than gasoline) purchased for purposes other than propelling motor vehicles on public highways.

Fuel for ships: The sales and use taxes do not apply to the sales of fuel for use or consumption aboard ships on the high seas, either in intercoastal trade between ports in Georgia and of other states of the United States or its possessions, or in foreign commerce between ports in Georgia and of foreign countries. Purchasers may claim this exemption by presenting the dealer a certificate of exemption (Form ST-7).

Part VI—Sales and Use Taxes   239

Fuel for common carriers: Sales and use taxes are imposed on the purchase and delivery of fuel within Georgia by or to any common carrier and on the purchase of fuel outside the state and stored in Georgia, regardless of where the fuel is subsequently used.

● *Nonprofit organizations, private schools, and churches*

Churches, religious, charitable, civic, and other nonprofit organizations generally are not exempt from sales and use taxes on their purchases. When such organizations engage in selling tangible personal property at retail, compliance with the law as to collection and remittance of sales tax is required. However, certain exemptions provided by law are discussed at ¶ 2004.

Child care organizations and maternity homes: Sales of tangible personal property and services to or by a child-caring institution, a child-placing agency, or a maternity home are exempt if the entity is engaged primarily in providing child services and is a nonprofit exempt organization under IRC Sec. 501(c)(3). The entity must obtain an exemption determination letter from the Commissioner. (Act 727 (H.B. 1744), Laws 2004.)

● *Occasional sales and mergers*

Sales and use taxes are not imposed on casual sales. A "casual sale" is defined as a sale of tangible personal property (1) which property was not acquired or held by the seller for use in the operation of a business or for resale, (2) acquired or held by the seller for use in the operation of a business, and not acquired or held for resale, if the total selling price of the sale and all such sales made during that calendar month and the preceding 11 calendar months does not exceed $500, or (3) which property was acquired or held by the seller for use in the operation of a business, and not acquired or held for resale, if the sale is made in a complete and bona fide liquidation of the seller's business.

The following transactions are not considered exempt casual sales:

—sales of tangible personal property through an agent, broker or other person who is regularly engaged in making sales of tangible personal property, either as a principal or agent; and

—sales by an individual who is employed by or associated with another person who is regularly engaged in the business of selling the same type of tangible personal property.

Practitioner Comment: Occasional Sales of Going-Concern Businesses

The casual sale exemption can apply on a location-by-location basis. Although it is possible to sell one business or division of an entity while retaining others and still qualify for the exemption, be careful when the different businesses are located in the same location—the sale may not be construed as a complete liquidation and thus not qualify for the exemption.

The term "a complete and bona fide liquidation" refers to "the sale of all the assets of such business conducted over a period of time not

¶ 2201

exceeding thirty days from the date of the first sale of such assets, or a longer time if approved by the Commissioner." The Department of Revenue has approved time periods of up to one year. Because it is not clear whether approval must be obtained in advance, such advance approval is advisable.

Alston & Bird LLP

Mergers, consolidations, and acquisitions: An exemption from sales and use taxes is provided for sales, transfers, or exchanges of tangible personal property pursuant to a business reorganization if the owners, partners, or stockholders of the old business maintain the same proportionate interest in the new business.

- *Packaging*

The sales and use taxes do not apply to the sale, use, storage, or consumption of materials, containers, labels, sacks, or bags that are used solely for packaging tangible personal property for shipment or sale, and that may not be purchased for reuse. Examples of nontaxable containers are cans in which goods, paint, and other commodities are contained; medicine bottles; boxes in which jewelry, candy, and clothes are delivered to customers; tooth paste tubes, etc.; wrapping paper; twine; cotton baling wire; ice cream cartons; milk bottle caps; crating; packing cases; excelsior insulating material and the like when used in connection with the packaging for shipment or sale of tangible personal property; and labels or name plates affixed to products manufactured or processed.

The purchase of containers for use as equipment in the operation of a business is taxable even though the containers may be used in connection with the shipment or sale of property. These equipment-type containers are purchased by a shipper or seller for reuse and include storage tanks, truck bodies, shopping carts, delivery crates, dispensers, and dishes.

Returnable containers: Purchases of returnable containers are taxable. Examples of returnable-type containers are milk and beer bottles, soft drink bottles, and crates, bread boxes, banana boxes, chicken coops, wine barrels, chemical carboys, gas cylinders, and other similar items.

Labels and tags: Purchases (not for reuse) of labels, name plates, or tags are exempt from tax if used solely for packaging tangible personal property for shipment or sale. No tax is imposed on items providing information on the nature, quality, maker, price, size, operation, maintenance, or destination of the packaged property, but tax is imposed if the items are inserts, invoices, packing slips, etc.

Ice: The sale of ice used as a packaging material in a disposable package that contains perishable tangible personal property for shipment or sale is exempt from tax.

- *Pollution control and cleanup equipment*

Exemptions are provided for sales of machinery and equipment for use in reducing, eliminating, or combating air and water pollution, including indus-

¶ 2201

Part VI—Sales and Use Taxes

trial material bought for further processing or industrial material or by-product thereof that becomes a wasteful product contributing to pollution problems and that is used up in a recycling or burning process.

A certificate of exemption (Form ST-M8) must be furnished by the purchaser. An application for a certificate of exemption may be made on Form ST-M7 with the State Revenue Department.

A contractor must pay tax on purchases for use in performing a contract (see "Construction" at ¶ 2004), and if a contractor purchases machinery and equipment certified by the Environmental Protection Division as being necessary and adequate for pollution control, the ultimate owner of the property may file a claim for refund of the tax paid.

For a discussion of the sales and use tax treatment of machinery and equipment used directly in the manufacture of property to improve air quality in telecommunications facilities, see "Manufacturing, processing, assembling, or refining," above.

● *Repair, installation, and warranties*

Repair services for which a separate charge is made are exempt from sales and use taxes. If no separate charge is made for labor by a dealer, tax is imposed on the total charge for materials and labor. Separately stated charges for parts, materials, and supplies used or consumed by a dealer in the repair work are subject to tax. Installation charges are exempt if separately stated.

Dealers who are engaged in the business of repairing tangible personal property may purchase materials and supplies for resale under a certificate of exemption. Repair businesses not required to register as dealers must pay tax on purchases of tangible personal property. The purchase of chemicals is taxable.

Warranties and service contracts: Factory warranties that are purchased together with property are considered to be part of the sales price and are subject to sales tax. However, optional warranties that are separately stated on the invoice are not subject to tax. Optional warranties are defined as warranties that are not required for the purchase of property and that are sold at an additional separately stated charge. The person repairing the property under an optional warranty contract is responsible for the tax on any parts used in the repair.

The charge for a maintenance or service contract (a contract to repair, improve, or service property) is not subject to tax if it is separately stated on the invoice or billing statement. However, the repairer must pay tax on any parts used in making a repair under the contract.

● *Services—Personal or professional*

Professional or personal service transactions that involve sales as inconsequential elements for which no separate charges are made are not taxable. See also ¶ 2005, "Taxable Services."

¶ 2201

● *Telecommunications, broadcasting, and film production*

Digital broadcast equipment sold or leased to, or used by, federally licensed commercial or public radio or television broadcast stations, cable network and cable distributors is exempt. "Digital broadcast equipment" means equipment for the origination or integration by cable, satellite, or fiber optic line that uses or produces an electronic signal generated, stored, and processed as strings of binary data. Eligibility for dual-use equipment (digital and analog), is determined by the equipment's use. To be eligible for the exemption, the equipment must use a digital signal and the equipment must be used as an essential part of a process to originate or integrate a digital signal for transmission or broadcast.

Eligible digital equipment for commercial or public television or cable distributors is limited to antennas, transmission lines, towers, studio-to-transmitter links, digital routing switchers, character generators, Advanced Television Systems Committee video encoders and multi-plexers, monitoring facilities, cameras, terminal equipment, tape recorders, and filer servers.

Eligible digital equipment for radio broadcasters is limited to transmitters, digital audio processors, and diskettes.

The exemption does not apply to repair or replacement parts, or new equipment purchased to replace equipment for which a digital broadcast equipment exemption was previously claimed; any equipment purchased after a television station or cable network or distributor has ceased analog broadcasting, or purchased after November 1, 2004, whichever occurs first; or any equipment purchased after a radio station has ceased analog broadcasting, or purchased after November 1, 2008, whichever occurs first.

Film production equipment or services: A certified film producer or film production company's purchase or lease of production equipment or services for use in Georgia is eligible for an exemption from sales and use tax if the equipment or services are used for "qualified production activities," defined as the production or post-production of film or video projects that are intended for nationwide distribution.

Production equipment includes, but is not limited to, cameras, camera supplies, camera accessories, lighting equipment, cables, wires, generators, motion picture film and videotape stock, cranes, booms, dollies, and teleprompters.

Production services include, but are not limited to, digital or tape editing, film processing, transfers of film to tape or digital format, sound mixing, computer graphics services, special effects services, animation services, and script production. Some items not covered by the exemption that remain taxable include, but are not limited to, office supplies and furniture, catered food, transportation services, hotel rooms and lodging, and repairs to equipment.

Prior to applying for an exemption certificate from the Department of Revenue (Form ST-PE1), film producers and production companies must obtain prior written approval from the Georgia Film and Videotape Office of the Department of Industry, Trade, and Tourism. Upon approval of the

¶ 2201

Part VI—Sales and Use Taxes 243

application, the DOR will issue an exemption certificate (Form ST-PE2), which must be presented to suppliers at the time of purchase.

- *Transportation equipment*

Exempted from sales and use taxes are sales of aircraft, watercraft, railroad locomotives and rolling stock, motor vehicles, and their major components to be used principally in transporting passengers or cargo in interstate commerce by common carriers or by carriers who hold common carrier and contract carrier authorization. Replacement parts installed by carriers and that become an integral part of the craft, equipment, or vehicle are also exempt.

To claim the exemption, a common carrier must furnish each supplier with an exemption certificate (Form ST-5). Common carriers may purchase component and replacement parts for inventory under a certificate of exemption even when some of its vehicles do not qualify for exemption. Tax is imposed on the cost price of parts when withdrawn from inventory and applied to taxable vehicles.

Contract and private carriers must pay tax on tangible personal property, not otherwise exempted, used, or consumed in their operations whether or not their craft or vehicles cross Georgia borders. Tax is also imposed on purchases for use, consumption, or storage in Georgia of tangible personal property used in constructing, repairing, or maintaining permanent structures such as garages, repair shops, hangers, railroad bridges, railroad tracks, landing and communication equipment, tools, equipment, and other tangible personal property not specifically exempt.

Practitioner Comment: Taxable Moment Theory

Because aircraft generally must be registered by a state, states invariably enforce use taxes as part of the registration process. Historically, taxpayers have successfully avoided both sales and use tax by taking delivery of the airplane in a state without a sales (or use) tax and then immediately dedicating the airplane to an interstate activity before hangaring the aircraft in its true home state. Courts have traditionally refused to allow the state where the property is situated or hangared to impose a use tax on the grounds that there existed no "taxable moment" where the item was not dedicated to interstate commerce. See *Southern Pacific Co. v. Gallagher,* 306 U.S. 167 (1939), ; see, e.g., *Grundle v. Iowa Department of Revenue* (Iowa Supreme Court 1-24-90, IOWA TAX REPORTS ¶ 200-520) for a recent application of this doctrine. First New Jersey, then Pennsylvania and most recently Missouri have rejected the traditional "taxable moment" approach and have applied use taxes to aircraft used in interstate commerce, based on the analysis that the four-prong test of *Complete Auto Transit* is satisfied. *K S S Transport Corp. v. Baldwin,* 9 N.J. Tax 273 (1987), NEW JERSEY TAX REPORTS ¶ 201-390; *H.K. Porter Co. v. Commonwealth,* 534 A.2d 169 (Pa. Commw. 1987), PENNSYLVANIA TAX REPORTS ¶ 201-814; *Director of Revenue v. Superior Aircraft Leasing Co.,* 734 S.W.2d 504 (Mo. 1987), MISSOURI TAX REPORTS

¶ 2201

¶ 201-094. The *Superior Aircraft* case is especially notable because, in that recent case, the Missouri Supreme Court found sufficient flights in Missouri to create nexus for taxation, even though the plane was hangared and repaired in Ohio. The Georgia Department of Revenue position on this issue is not completely clear.

Alston & Bird LLP

Aircraft sales and rentals: An aircraft sales and service dealer may purchase for resale, without paying tax, aircraft, accessories, tires, repair parts, fuels, and lubricants. Persons using aircraft to provide services to customers must pay tax on purchases unless otherwise exempt. Persons who both sell or lease aircraft and use aircraft to provide services may make purchases without paying tax (upon the Revenue Commissioner's approval) when it cannot be determined at the time of purchase whether the property will be resold or used in providing services. When property is allocated to personal use or use in providing services, tax must be remitted on the purchase or cost price.

Aircraft parts: Sales tax is not imposed on the purchase of aircraft parts if (1) the delivery terms are FOB buyer's aircraft in Georgia, (2) the parts are delivered by the seller directly on board the purchaser's aircraft for immediate exportation outside the United States pursuant to an export license, and (3) the parts are actually transported outside the United States as soon as practicable after being loaded onto the aircraft without diversion to another state. Tax is imposed on parts installed on or in an aircraft while in Georgia and on parts used in repairing or servicing an aircraft in Georgia.

Cargo containers used for storage: Sales and use taxes do not apply to the use of cargo containers and their related chassis that are owned by, or leased to, persons engaged in the international shipment of cargo by ocean-going vessels. The cargo containers and related chassis must be used directly for the storage and shipment of tangible personal property in intrastate or interstate commerce. Sales and use taxes are imposed on sales of dunnage and other shoring materials.

Supplies for ships: The sale of supplies for use aboard ocean-going ships in intercoastal trade between ports in Georgia and ports in other states or in foreign commerce between Georgia ports and foreign countries is exempt. The purchaser must furnish a certificate of exemption (Form ST-7) to the supplier.

- *Utilities*

The sale of natural or artificial gas used directly in the production of electricity that is subsequently sold is exempt from state sales and use tax. This exemption does not apply to local sales and use tax.

- *Wheelchairs*

The sale or use of wheelchairs and certain related equipment to or by permanently disabled individuals is exempt from sales and use tax.

¶ 2201

Part VI—Sales and Use Taxes 245

¶ 2202 Exemptions—Interstate Transactions

Law: Secs. 48-8-1, 48-8-3(19), 48-8-3(31), 48-8-3(32), 48-8-30(c), 48-8-34(b), Code; Reg. Secs. 560-12-2-.54 (CCH GEORGIA TAX REPORTS ¶ 60-340, 60-450).

The federal Constitution reserves to Congress the power to regulate commerce among the states, with foreign nations, and with Native American tribes (U.S. Const., Art. I, Sec. 8, Cl. 3). In *Complete Auto Transit, Inc. v. Brady* (1977, US SCt) 430 US 274, 97 SCt 1076, the U.S. Supreme Court established a four-part test to determine the constitutionality of a tax on multistate transactions:

(1) The tax must be applied to an activity having a substantial nexus with the taxing state;

(2) The tax must be fairly apportioned;

(3) The tax must not discriminate against interstate commerce; and

(4) The tax must be fairly related to services provided by the taxing state.

In addition to the four-part test, in *Japan Line, Ltd. v. County of Los Angeles* (1979, US SCt) 441 US 434, 99 SCt 1913, the High Court ruled that a tax affecting foreign or international commerce must not create a substantial risk of multiple taxation or prevent the federal government from "speaking with one voice" regarding foreign trade.

The High Court determined in *Itel Containers International Corporation v. Huddleston* (1993, US SCt), 113 SCt 1095, that Tennessee's imposition of sales tax on leases of cargo containers delivered to lessees in the state and used in international commerce satisfied the requirements of *Complete Auto Transit* and *Japan Lines* and did not violate the Supremacy, Commerce, or Import-Export Clauses of the U.S. Constitution.

In addition, in *Oklahoma Tax Commission v. Jefferson Lines, Inc.* (1995, US SCt) 514 US 175, 115 SCt 1331, the U.S. Supreme Court found that an Oklahoma sales tax imposed on the full purchase price of an interstate bus ticket sold by a Minnesota-based interstate carrier also satisfied the requirements of Complete Auto Transit because the taxable event, the actual sale of the ticket, could only happen in Oklahoma, and was thus fairly apportioned to that state.

However, effective January 1, 1996, federal law prohibits states and political subdivisions thereof from imposing a tax on interstate passenger tickets (Sec. 14505, Title 49 USC).

● *Interstate transactions*

It is the intent of the Georgia General Assembly to tax all sales and services described in the law except to the extent prohibited by both the state and U.S. Constitutions.

Sales and use taxes are imposed on all retail sales of tangible personal property delivered in Georgia, even if subsequently put in interstate commerce, and on the first use in Georgia of tangible personal property (that has become a part of the mass of the property in Georgia) purchased out-of-state that would have been taxable had it been purchased in Georgia. Credit is

¶ 2202

allowed for taxes paid to another state if that state grants a credit for like taxes paid to Georgia.

No tax is imposed on (1) deliveries outside Georgia in the seller's vehicle or by an independent trucker hired by the seller if a certificate of exemption (Form ST-6) is secured, (2) deliveries to a common carrier or the post office for transportation outside the state, and (3) purchases for resale and immediate transportation outside Georgia by a registered dealer in another state if a certificate of exemption (Form ST-4) is secured by the Georgia seller.

- *Drop shipments*

A drop shipment is a shipment of tangible personal property from a seller directly to the purchaser's customer, at the direction of the purchaser. These sales are also known as third-party sales because they require that there be, at arm's length, three parties and two separate sales transactions. Generally, a retailer accepts an order from an end purchaser/consumer, places this order with a third party, usually a manufacturer or wholesale distributor, and directs the third party to ship the goods directly to the end purchaser/consumer. Drop shipments are examined as two transactions (1) the sale from the primary seller to the purchaser, and (2) the sale from the purchaser to the purchaser's customer.

Georgia's treatment of drop-shipment sales: When all the parties are located in the state, the retailer furnishes a resale certificate to the primary seller, rendering the first sale a nontaxable transaction. The retailer then collects sales tax on behalf of the state on the secondary sale to its customer. However, different considerations arise when one or more of the parties are not within the state.

Georgia exempts the primary sale, *i.e.*, the sale to an out-of-state retailer by a Georgia manufacturer who drop ships the product to the retailer's customer, if the retailer furnishes a resale exemption from its state. The secondary sale by the retailer to its Georgia customer is an exempt interstate sale when the retailer lacks any Georgia nexus. When that is the case, the customer is subject to the use tax because no sales tax has been paid.

- *Manufacture or assembly for export*

The sale of tangible personal property manufactured or assembled in Georgia for export is exempt from sales and use taxes if delivery is taken out of state.

Sales of aircraft, watercraft, motor vehicles, and other transportation equipment manufactured or assembled in Georgia for use exclusively outside the state are exempt from sales and use taxes if the purchaser takes possession from the manufacturer or assembler within the state for the purpose of removing it from the state under its own power when the equipment cannot reasonably be removed by other means.

- *Dealer use of imported property*

The use by a dealer of tangible personal property imported from outside the state by that dealer is subject to tax as if the property had been sold at retail for use in the state.

¶ 2202

Part VI—Sales and Use Taxes   **247**

● *Nonresidents moving to Georgia*

Tangible personal property that was purchased outside the state by nonresidents of Georgia who later became domiciled in Georgia is not subject to sales and use taxes if brought into the state for the first time as a result of the change of domicile, provided that the property is not for use in a trade, business, or profession.

¶ 2203   Credits Against Tax

Law: Sec. 48-8-42, Code; Reg. Sec. 560-12-1-.32 (CCH GEORGIA TAX REPORTS ¶ 61-270).

The use, consumption, distribution, or storage of tangible personal property in Georgia is not subject to tax if a similar tax has been paid in another state that grants credit for a like tax paid in Georgia. When the other state's tax is less than Georgia's, the difference must be paid to Georgia. Credit will be allowed for tax paid to a nonreciprocating state up to the amount of the Georgia tax only with respect to the use in the other state of tangible personal property by a manufacturer or fabricator in fulfillment of a contract to furnish the property and perform services relative to the property in the other state when the property was manufactured or fabricated in Georgia exclusively for use by the manufacturer or fabricator in fulfillment of the contract.

No credit is allowed for tax levied by a political subdivision of a state.

Credit is also allowed to dealers for the tax on amounts refunded to purchasers on returned merchandise.

Part VI—Sales and Use Taxes

SALES AND USE TAXES

CHAPTER 23

RETURNS, PAYMENTS, AND RECORDS

¶ 2301 Remittance of Tax
¶ 2302 Returns, Payments, and Due Dates
¶ 2303 Prepayment of Tax; Withholding
¶ 2304 Vendor Registration
¶ 2305 Direct Payment Permits
¶ 2306 Recordkeeping Requirements

¶ 2301 Remittance of Tax

Law: Secs. 48-8-2(4), 48-8-30, 48-8-33—48-8-36, Code; Reg. Secs. 560-12-1-.05, 560-12-1-.11 (CCH GEORGIA TAX REPORTS ¶ 61-210).

Purchasers must pay sales tax to the retailer on retail sales of tangible personal property. The retailer remits the tax to the Revenue Commissioner. Similarly, persons to whom property is leased or rented pay tax to the lessor, and the lessor then remits the tax to the Revenue Commissioner. Persons purchasing or receiving services in Georgia that are retail sales pay tax to the service provider, and the tax is then remitted to the Revenue Commissioner. The amount of tax required to be remitted is the greater of (1) the amount of taxes actually collected from purchasers or (2) the current rate of tax (¶ 2102) multiplied by gross sales or gross charges.

"Gross sales" means the total retail sales of tangible personal property or services, without any deduction of any kind except as otherwise provided by law. It includes charges on sales of telephone service, made for local exchange telephone service, except local messages that are paid for by inserting coins in coin-operated telephones, but including the total amount of the guaranteed charge for semipublic coin box telephone services.

The tax must be collected on each single sale, *i.e.,* the total of all sales made to a customer in one visit to a place of sale.

The tax is a debt from the purchaser to the dealer until paid and may be recovered in the same manner as other debts are recovered.

• *Absorption of tax*

A retailer may not advertise or represent to the public that it will absorb all or any part of the tax or that the purchaser is relieved from paying all or any part of the tax.

¶ 2301

¶ 2302 Returns, Payments, and Due Dates

Law: Secs. 48-2-30—48-2-33, 48-2-36, 48-2-39, 48-2-45, 48-2-46, 48-2-49—48-2-51, 48-2-58, Code; Reg. Secs. 560-12-1-.06, 560-12-1-.13, 560-12-1-.19, 560-12-1-.22, 560-12-1-.33, 560-12-2-.26, 560-12-2-.44, 560-12-3-.04, 560-12-3-.09 (CCH GEORGIA TAX REPORTS ¶ 61-220).

Forms: Form ST-3, Sales and Use Tax Report.

Each dealer, contractor, and subcontractor normally files returns on or before the 20th of each month with the Revenue Commissioner showing the gross sales and purchases arising from all taxable sales and purchases during the preceding month. Returns must be filed on a calendar-month basis, but permission may be granted for returns to be filed for fiscal periods other than on a monthly basis after the dealer has been registered for six months.

The Commissioner will provide all necessary forms (ST-3) for filing returns, and instructions. Amended returns are filed on Form ST3AR. Failure of a dealer to secure the forms does not relieve the dealer from the timely payment of the tax.

A dealer must include on its return the dealer's certificate of registration number, the registration numbers for each sales location or affiliated entity of the dealer, and the dealer's master number (provided such a number has been assigned by the Department of Revenue). In general, an "affiliated entity" is an entity that the dealer owns, is owned by, or is otherwise related to the dealer by common ownership or control.

● *Quarterly, annual, and special period returns*

Any dealer whose monthly sales and use tax liability has averaged less than $200 for six consecutive months may file returns on a quarterly basis on or before the 20th day of the month following the close of each quarter, covering the three calendar months ending on the last day of March, June, September, and December.

Any dealer whose monthly sales and use tax liability has averaged less than $50 for six consecutive months may file returns on an annual basis on or before the 20th day of the month following the close of each year, covering the twelve calendar months ending on the last day of the calendar year.

Any dealer who submits a written request showing reasonable grounds and who is given permission by the Commissioner may file on a special period basis. Any dealer permitted to file on a special period basis must notify the Department on November 1 of each year of the exact reporting period for the next calendar year.

A dealer may be required to return to a monthly basis by the Commissioner if its tax liability exceeds quarterly or annual filing limitations or if the Commissioner determines a loss of revenue may result if a dealer continues to file a quarterly or annual return. Failure to timely file a quarterly, annual, or special period return or make remittance of the tax due thereon is a ground for returning a dealer to a monthly or quarterly basis.

Part VI—Sales and Use Taxes

● Payment

The amount of tax shown on a return must be remitted with the return. Payment may be made in cash, check, or postal, bank, or express money orders. Upon request, the Commissioner will give a receipt for sums collected.

● Electronic funds transfer

Sales and use tax payments of $10,000 or more must be made by electronic funds transfer (EFT). For additional information, see ¶ 2902.

● Estimated tax payments

If the estimated tax liability of a dealer for any taxable period exceeds $2,500, the dealer must file a return and remit to the Commissioner, on or before the 20th day of the period, at least 50% of the estimated tax liability.

Payment of estimated tax is credited against the amount due on the dealer's return covering the preceding reporting period. Estimated tax payments are not required unless, during the prior fiscal year, the dealer's monthly payments exceeded $2,500 per month, excluding local sales taxes, for at least three consecutive months.

● Extension of time for filing returns

The Commissioner has the discretion to grant extensions, upon written application, to the end of the calendar month in which any tax return is due. An extension is valid only for a period of not more than 12 consecutive months. However, the taxpayer must remit, by the date the tax would otherwise become due, an amount that, when added to the estimated tax previously paid, equals at least 100% of the taxpayer's payment for the corresponding period of the preceding tax year. Interest and penalties will not be charged, assessed, or collected by reason of the granting of an extension.

Extensions for good cause: The Commissioner may, for good cause and upon written application, extend the time for making any return for not more than 30 days. Extensions granted for good cause are limited to a period of not more than 12 consecutive months or four calendar quarters. The taxpayer must remit, by the date the tax would otherwise be due, an amount equal to at least 100% of the taxpayer's payment for the corresponding period of the preceding tax year. Interest will not be imposed during the first ten days of the extension period but will be imposed thereafter on the unpaid balance.

Required forms: The taxpayer must prepare Sales and Use Tax Remittance Form ST-3EXT each reporting period and mail it along with the remittance on or before the 20th of the month following the period of the report to the Sales and Use Tax Division. Also, Sales and Use Tax Report Form ST-3 must be prepared each reporting period and mailed with the remittance on or before the extended filing date.

Providential cause: The Commissioner may, for providential cause and upon a signed affidavit, grant an extension of ten days. An extension is limited to a reporting period of one calendar month or quarter.

Form ST-76 extends the time for filing returns.

¶ 2302

- *Final returns*

A dealer who sells its business or quits the business must prepare a final return and remit all taxes due within 15 days after the date of selling or quitting the business. See also ¶ 2407, concerning successor liability for tax.

- *Foreign vendors*

A person outside Georgia who engages in business in Georgia as a dealer must register, collect, and remit the tax on all taxable tangible personal property sold or delivered for storage, use, or consumption in Georgia. Monthly sales and use tax reports must be filed unless otherwise authorized.

- *Consolidated returns*

Upon the Commissioner's written approval, a person with four or more places of business in Georgia may file one return for each reporting period showing the consolidated sales and use tax due for all the places of business in the state. The consolidated return (Form ST-3) must show the Certificate of Registration number for each location, the gross sales, taxable sales, itemized allowable exemptions, tax collected and sales and use tax due for each location in Georgia.

Certain dealers having four or more sales locations and/or affiliated entities must file consolidated returns in order to claim the collection discount, as discussed below.

- *Method of accounting*

Taxpayers having both cash and credit sales may report the sales on either the cash or accrual basis of accounting. An election must be made on the first return filed and is irrevocable unless the Commissioner grants written permission. Taxpayers on an accrual basis must report and remit tax due on all transactions during the reporting period.

Taxpayers reporting on a cash basis must include in each return all cash sales made during the period covered by the return and collections made in any period on credit sales of prior periods and must pay the tax on the sales at the time of filing the return. A dealer who sells, discounts, or disposes of accounts receivable must include in its report for the current month the amount of the original sales regardless of the sales price of the accounts.

- *Payment or return date falling on holiday or weekend*

If the date prescribed for filing a return or paying tax is on a Saturday, Sunday or legal holiday, the return or payment may be made on the next day that is not a Saturday, Sunday, or legal holiday, i.e., through the next business day.

- *Collection discounts*

A dealer that timely files its sales and use tax return and pays the tax due is entitled to a deduction as compensation for reporting and paying the state and local sales and use taxes. For each certificate of registration number reported on a return, the deduction is an amount equal to 0.5% of the

¶ 2302

Part VI—Sales and Use Taxes

combined amount of all sales and use taxes reported due for each location. For collection allowances applicable to motor fuel taxes, see ¶ 2805.

Consolidated filing requirement: To claim the deduction, a dealer that consists of four or more sales locations and/or affiliated entities must file a consolidated return for the group, while a dealer that consists of fewer than four sales locations and/or affiliated entities must file a separate return for each location and entity. In general, an "affiliated entity" is an entity that the dealer owns, is owned by, or is otherwise related to the dealer by common ownership or control. A consolidated return must identify separately the reporting and paying of the tax due for each sales location or affiliated entity.

Disallowance of deduction: The deduction is not allowed if the dealer fails to file on the proper basis (consolidated or separate) or if the dealer fails to include the requisite certificate of registration numbers or master number on the return.

● *Leased departments*

A lessee who keeps its own records and makes its own collections on retail sales from a leased department must make separate monthly returns and remittances. When a lessor of a leased department keeps the records and makes the collections, the lessor may request in writing to the Commissioner that it be allowed to be the lessee's agent and make returns and pay the taxes due. A lessee is not relieved of liability if the lessor does not make the returns or pay the tax.

¶ 2303 Prepayment of Tax; Withholding

Law: Sec. 48-8-57, Code; Reg. Sec. 560-12-2-.26 (CCH GEORGIA TAX REPORTS ¶ 61-230).

Georgia has no provisions concerning prepayment of taxes. See ¶ 2302 for the payment of estimated taxes by dealers.

A dealer who is chronically delinquent or in default may be required to file with the Commissioner a bond or legal securities in an amount of not less than $1,000 and not more than $10,000. Any security deposited with the Commissioner may be sold to recover any tax, penalty, and interest due.

● *Withholding by contractors*

General or prime contractors entering into contracts with subcontractors in which the aggregate amount on any single project is equal to or greater than $250,000 are required to withhold 2% of the payments due the subcontractor, unless the subcontractor filed an approved surety bond with the Commissioner.

Surety bond: Subcontractors are required to hold a surety bond according to the following schedule: anticipated annual gross receipts of less than $250,000 do not require a bond; anticipated annual gross receipts of $250,000 to $500,000 require a $5,000 bond; anticipated annual gross receipts of $500,000 to $750,000 require a $20,000 bond; anticipated annual gross receipts of $750,000 to $1 million require a $30,000 bond; and anticipated annual gross receipts over $1 million require a $50,000 bond.

¶ 2304 Vendor Registration

Law: Secs. 48-8-59—48-8-62, Code; Reg. Secs. 560-12-1-.09, 560-12-1-.10, 560-12-1-.31, 560-12-2-.26(1), 560-12-2-.39, 560-12-2-.70, 560-12-2-.86, 560-12-3-.02, 560-12-3-.03 (CCH GEORGIA TAX REPORTS ¶ 61-240).

Forms: Form CRF-002 (State Tax Registration Application), Form CRF-004 (State Tax Registration Application Additional Ownership/Relationship Form), Form ST-2 (Certificate of Registration).

Any person who desires to engage in or conduct business as a seller or dealer in Georgia must file with the Commissioner an application for a certificate of registration (Forms CRF-002, CRF-004) for each place of business. When the application is approved, the Commissioner must issue to the applicant a separate certificate of registration (Form ST-2) for each place of business in the state. Each certificate must be conspicuously displayed at the place of business for which issued. A certificate is not transferable and may be used only at the place designated in the certificate.

Each person whose business extends into more than one county is required to secure only one certificate of registration. The certificate covers all operations of the company throughout the state.

There is no fee for the original certificate, but a $1 fee is charged for the renewal or issuance of a suspended or revoked certificate.

A dealer must apply for a new certificate and return the old one if it discontinues business, changes location from one county to another, or changes the type of business. If the trade name is changed or the business changes location within the same county, the old certificate of registration must be returned and a new one reflecting the changes will be issued.

● *Contractors*

Persons contracting to perform services and furnish tangible personal property in constructing, altering, repairing, or improving real property must file an application for a certificate of registration (Forms CRF-002, CRF-004) as a contractor before engaging in construction activity in the state.

● *State contractors*

Any nongovernmental vendor or an affiliate bidding on a state agency contract that exceeds $100,000 per year is required to register with the state and to collect and remit Georgia sales and use taxes on all retail sales occurring in Georgia.

● *Special certificates*

A certificate of registration bearing the symbol "SR" after the certificate number may be issued to a person not regularly engaged in making retail sales for the purpose of buying tangible personal property tax exempt for resale or further processing. The dealer to whom the certificate is issued is relieved from filing tax returns for months in which no tax is due.

Part VI—Sales and Use Taxes

● *Importing dealers*

Dealers who import tangible personal property from other states for use or consumption or for storage for use or consumption in Georgia must obtain a certificate of registration if not already registered as dealers.

● *Successors in business*

A successor in business to another dealer must file an application for a certificate of registration. The successor must inform the Commissioner of the acquisition and furnish the name and certificate number of the previous dealer.

● *Farmers and market masters*

Farmers, market masters, and others engaged in selling tangible personal property must file applications for certificates of registration, regardless of whether the places of business are located on private, state, county, or municipal land.

● *Peddlers and street vendors*

All persons engaged in retail selling of tangible personal property in any manner must file applications for certificates of registration. However, peddlers, street merchants, and other persons making sales at retail from other than established places of business are not issued certificates of registration, but their vendors (persons selling to them for resale) must collect tax from them on the retail price to be charged by them.

● *Trustees, receivers, and administrators*

Trustees, receivers, executors, and administrators who operate, manage, or control a business engaged in making retail sales of tangible personal property must apply for a new certificate of registration unless the corporate business continues to exist as a legal entity.

● *Revocation or suspension*

The Commissioner may revoke or suspend any one or more of the certificates of registration held by a person in case of failure to comply with the law or the Commission's regulations. The person is given ten days notice specifying the time and place for a hearing at which the person may show cause why a certificate should not be revoked or suspended. It is illegal to engage in business after a certificate has been suspended or revoked.

¶ 2305 Direct Payment Permits

Law: Reg. Sec. 560-12-1-.16 (CCH GEORGIA TAX REPORTS ¶ 61-250).

When the State Revenue Commissioner deems it impractical or inequitable for a taxpayer to pay sales and use tax separately because of the operation of his or her business, the taxpayer may be given a direct payment permit. The direct payment permit will be issued only upon written application. In such cases, the taxpayer reports and pays tax directly to the Department of Revenue on all taxable purchases of property or services. The taxpayer

¶ 2305

furnishes each seller of tangible personal property or taxable services with a photographic copy of the permit or Certificate of Exemption bearing the registration number. The placement of such registration number on the taxpayer's purchase orders is sufficient to relieve the sellers or dealers from collecting the sales or use tax due.

¶ 2306 Recordkeeping Requirements

Law: Secs. 48-8-30(h), 48-8-52, 48-8-53, Code; Reg. Secs. 560-12-1-.15, 560-12-1-.23 (CCH GEORGIA TAX REPORTS ¶ 61-260).

Dealers must keep and preserve for three years following each taxable transaction adequate records necessary to determine tax liability. Records of the following must be kept: daily records of all cash and credit sales, the amount of merchandise purchased (bills of lading, invoices, purchase orders), all deductions and exemptions claimed in filing returns, all tangible personal property used in the conduct of the business, and inventory of stock on hand.

All books, invoices, and other records required to be kept must be open to examination at all reasonable hours by the Commissioner.

● *Wholesalers and jobbers*

Records of all sales of tangible personal property made in the state must be kept by every wholesale dealer or jobber in Georgia, whether the sales are for cash or credit. The records must include the name and address of the purchaser, the date of the purchase, the article purchased, and the sales price. The records must be kept for three years and must be open to the inspection of the Commissioner at all reasonable hours during the day.

● *Separate books by retailer-wholesaler*

A person engaged in business both as a retailer and wholesaler or jobber pays the tax imposed on the gross proceeds of the retail sales of the business when proper books are kept showing separately the gross proceeds of sales for each business. If the books are not kept separately, the tax must be paid as a retailer or dealer on the gross sales of the business.

Practitioner Comment: Centralized Procurement

An entity dedicated to procurement may enhance a corporation's ability to effectively centralize the procurement process and make accurate tax decisions on the purchase of its capital assets and consumable supplies. Centralization allows the company to manage all of the purchasing needs of its affiliates, resulting in economies of scale. In addition, the company has control over all the phases of the procurement process—from the initial purchase and tax determination to the ultimate filing of the return and tax payment. By maintaining control of the decision of whether to tax or not, a company is provided with greater assurance that the appropriate sales tax is paid to the state.

Daniel L. Thompson, PricewaterhouseCoopers LLP, San Francisco, CA

SALES AND USE TAXES

CHAPTER 24

COLLECTION OF TAX, REFUNDS

¶ 2401	Deficiency Assessments
¶ 2402	Audit Procedures
¶ 2403	Jeopardy Assessments
¶ 2404	Consumer Liability
¶ 2405	Seller Liability
¶ 2406	Corporate Officer's Personal Liability
¶ 2407	Business Successor Liability
¶ 2408	Reciprocal Tax Enforcement
¶ 2409	Tax Liens and Warrants
¶ 2410	Levy and Sale of Taxpayer's Property
¶ 2411	Collection; Refunds
¶ 2412	Statute of Limitations
¶ 2413	Penalties and Interest

¶ 2401 Deficiency Assessments

Law: Secs. 48-2-37, 48-2-48, 48-8-51(b), 48-8-52, 48-8-55, Code; Reg. Secs. 560-12-3-.20, 560-12-3-.21 (CCH GEORGIA TAX REPORTS ¶ 61-410).

If a dealer fails to make a return and pay the required tax, or makes a grossly incorrect return or a return that is false or fraudulent, the Commissioner will assess and collect the tax, interest, and penalty, as accrued, based on the Commissioner's estimates for the taxable period of retail sales of the dealer, gross proceeds from rentals or leases of tangible personal property by the dealer, and the cost price of all articles of tangible personal property imported by the dealer for use, consumption, distribution, or storage for any use or consumption in Georgia. The assessments are considered prima facie correct and the dealer has the burden to show otherwise.

Notices of assessment for errors made in reporting taxes are made on Forms 51A and 53A.

If any return is not filed, the Commissioner may make the return, which is deemed correct and sufficient for all legal purposes.

No invoice or invoice inaccurate: When a dealer has imported tangible personal property and fails to produce an invoice showing the cost price of each article that is subject to tax or if the invoice does not reflect the true or actual cost price, the Commissioner will assess and collect the tax with interest and penalties on the true cost price. The assessment is considered prima facie correct and the dealer must prove otherwise.

¶ 2401

Incorrect report of rentals: If the Commissioner believes the consideration reported from a lease or rental of tangible personal property does not represent the true or actual consideration, the Commissioner may fix the true or actual consideration and assess and collect the tax.

● *Notice to appear*

A dealer who fails to submit a return within the time required or submits a return that is false or fraudulent or otherwise fails to comply with the law is given ten days' written notice to appear before the Commissioner. The dealer must then produce the books, records, and papers required by the Commissioner that relate to the business of the dealer for the taxable period. An assessment thereafter made by the Commissioner is prima facie correct.

See ¶ 3001 for the statute of limitations on assessments.

Practitioner Comment: Checking Proposed Assessment

After a revenue agent has presented your corporation with workpapers and a proposed assessment, be sure to review five areas.

(1) **Nonrecurring items.**—Frequently, a sample will be selected for the assessment of purchases subject to use tax and the results projected. Review the detail of the larger purchase adjustments and prove to the agent that they are nonrecurring and should be removed from the sample.

(2) **Accrual accounts.**—Check some of the larger items that your company has accrued sales taxes on for the same period of time the above sample was selected from. Many times tax has erroneously been accrued. The agent should allow you to project these items as offsets. Also check some period of the larger fixed asset items. If you find errors on larger items, you may want to review progressively smaller items.

(3) **Proper test period cutoff.**—Examine the dates of several invoices from the beginning and end of the test periods to ensure none are incorrectly included in the sample.

(4) **Sales.**—Run the numbers to see if you would be better off removing a customer from projected sales errors and using actual customer data.

(5) **Overlapping audits.**—Find out if a revenue agent has also conducted an audit of the supplier or customer of any of the items listed as proposed adjustments. Most states have policies to correct double taxation if you bring it to their attention and have documentation.

The final result will be a greatly reduced assessment, and sometimes, a refund.

Brent M. Stratton, CPA, Esq., Law Office of David E. Marmelstein, Suffield, CT

¶ 2401

Part VI—Sales and Use Taxes

¶ 2402 Audit Procedures

Audit procedures are discussed at ¶ 3001.

¶ 2403 Jeopardy Assessments

Law: Sec. 48-2-51, Code (CCH GEORGIA TAX REPORTS ¶ 61-430).

The Commissioner may declare the taxable period of a taxpayer terminated and demand immediate payment of tax due if the taxpayer gives evidence of an intention to (1) leave the state, (2) remove property from the state, (3) conceal property or person, (4) discontinue business, or (5) do any other act to prejudice or render ineffective proceedings to compute, assess, or collect tax. The Commissioner may immediately make an arbitrary assessment and collect the tax or require the taxpayer to file a bond as security for payment.

¶ 2404 Consumer Liability

Law: Sec. 48-8-30(c), (e), and (g), Code (CCH GEORGIA TAX REPORTS ¶ 61-440).

Forms: Form ST-3USE (Consumer Use Tax Reporting Form).

The owner or user of any tangible personal property that is purchased at retail outside Georgia is considered to be a dealer and is liable for a tax on the lesser of the cost price or fair market value of the property upon the first instance of use, consumption, distribution, or storage of the property in Georgia. A person who leases or rents tangible personal property outside Georgia is considered to be a dealer when the property is first used within the state and is liable for a tax on the rental charge paid to the lessor.

A purchaser of tangible personal property, a lessee or a renter of property, or a purchaser of services who does not pay the tax to the retailer, lessor, or dealer involved in the taxable transaction is considered a dealer, and the Commissioner may assess and collect the tax directly from the purchaser, lessee, or renter, unless it is shown that the retailer, lessor, or other dealer involved in the transaction has remitted the tax to the Commissioner. Payment received directly from the purchaser will not be collected a second time from the retailer, lessor, or dealer involved.

¶ 2405 Seller Liability

Law: Secs. 48-8-2(3)(II), 48-8-30(b), (c.1), (d), (e.1), and (f), 48-8-33, 48-8-34(a), Sec. 48-8-35, Code; Reg. Secs. 560-12-1-.11, 560-12-1-.30 (CCH GEORGIA TAX REPORTS ¶ 61-450).

Dealers must collect sales and use taxes from purchasers or consumers at the time of sale or purchase and remit the tax to the Revenue Commissioner. The amount of tax is added to the sales price or charge.

A dealer who neglects, fails, or refuses to collect the tax on a retail sale of tangible personal property subject to tax is liable for and must pay the tax. A dealer is also liable for taxes collected from purchasers that are stolen, misplaced, or lost before being remitted to the state, even though the dealer was without fault.

See ¶ 2002 for the definition of "dealer."

¶ 2405

¶ 2406 Corporate Officer's Personal Liability

Law: Secs. 48-2-52, 48-8-60, Code (CCH GEORGIA TAX REPORTS ¶ 61-460).

An officer or employee of a corporation who controls or supervises the collection of tax from purchasers or others or who controls or supervises the accounting for, and paying over of, the tax to the Commissioner, and who willfully fails to collect the taxes, fails to truthfully account for and pay over the taxes to the Commissioner, or willfully attempts to evade or defeat any obligation imposed under the law, is personally liable for an amount equal to the amount evaded, not collected, not accounted for, or not paid over.

The liability imposed above will be paid upon notice and demand by the Commissioner and will be assessed and collected in the same manner as the tax.

Each corporate officer is guilty of a misdemeanor if the corporation engages in business as a seller without a certificate of registration.

¶ 2407 Business Successor Liability

Law: Secs. 48-8-46, 48-8-48, Code; Reg. Sec. 560-12-1-.31 (CCH GEORGIA TAX REPORTS ¶ 61-470).

A dealer's successors and assigns must withhold an amount from the purchase price to cover unpaid taxes, interest, and penalties due from the former owner absent a receipt from the Commissioner showing that the amount has been paid or a certificate from the Commissioner stating that no taxes are due. Failure to withhold the required sum renders the successor personally liable for the unpaid sales and use taxes, penalties, and interest. The successor's liability may not exceed the amount of the total purchase money, but the property transferred remains subject to the tax lien arising from the former owner's delinquencies.

Anyone violating these provisions is guilty of a misdemeanor.

Practitioner Comment: Get Tax Clearance

Many states have statutory provisions regarding successor liability and bulk sales. Purchasers should remain aware of these potential liabilities and obtain tax clearance certificates from sellers for all jurisdictions where the purchased assets are located. Georgia will act on tax clearance requests made by a seller prior to the sale of the business.

Alston & Bird LLP

¶ 2408 Reciprocal Tax Enforcement

Reciprocal tax enforcement is discussed at ¶ 3002.

¶ 2409 Tax Liens and Warrants

Tax liens and warrants are discussed at ¶ 3002.

¶ 2406

Part VI—Sales and Use Taxes

¶ 2410 Levy and Sale of Taxpayer's Property
The levy and sale of property is discussed at ¶ 3002.

¶ 2411 Collection; Refunds
Collection of tax is discussed at ¶ 3002. Refunds are discussed at ¶ 2907.

¶ 2412 Statute of Limitations
Statutes of limitations are discussed at ¶ 3001.

¶ 2413 Penalties and Interest
Penalties and interest are discussed at ¶ 3003.

PART VII

ESTATE TAX

CHAPTER 25

IMPOSITION OF TAX AND RATES

¶ 2501	In General
¶ 2502	Rates
¶ 2503	Additional Estate Tax
¶ 2504	Taxable Transfers
¶ 2505	Settlement of Domiciliary Disputes
¶ 2506	Property Subject to Tax
¶ 2507	Return and Assessment
¶ 2508	Payment and Refund
¶ 2509	Notice and Waivers

¶ 2501 In General

Georgia estate tax is imposed by Chapter 12, Title 48, 1981 Georgia Code, as amended.

¶ 2502 Rates

● *Estates of decedents dying on or after November 1, 1982*

It is provided that the state tax on a decedent's estate shall be an amount equal to the maximum credit allowable under the federal estate tax. The following is a table of the maximum federal credits:

Maximum Federal Credit

Adjusted Taxable Estate (After $60,000 Exemption) From	To	Credit =	+	%	Of Excess Over
$ 0	$ 40,000	$ 0	0	$ 0
40,000	90,000	0	0.8	40,000
90,000	140,000	400	1.6	90,000
140,000	240,000	1,200	2.4	140,000
240,000	440,000	3,600	3.2	240,000
440,000	640,000	10,000	4.0	440,000
640,000	840,000	18,000	4.8	640,000
840,000	1,040,000	27,600	5.6	840,000
1,040,000	1,540,000	38,800	6.4	1,040,000
1,540,000	2,040,000	70,800	7.2	1,540,000
2,040,000	2,540,000	106,800	8.0	2,040,000

2,540,000	3,040,000	146,800	8.8	2,540,000
3,040,000	3,540,000	190,800	9.6	3,040,000
3,540,000	4,040,000	238,800	10.4	3,540,000
4,040,000	5,040,000	290,800	11.2	4,040,000
5,040,000	6,040,000	402,800	12.0	5,040,000
6,040,000	7,040,000	522,800	12.8	6,040,000
7,040,000	8,040,000	650,800	13.6	7,040,000
8,040,000	9,040,000	786,800	14.4	8,040,000
9,040,000	10,040,000	930,800	15.2	9,040,000
10,040,000	....	1,082,800	16.0	10,040,000

Practitioner Comment: Situs of Property

For estates of Georgia residents, the Georgia estate tax is equal to the maximum credit for state death taxes allowable against the federal estate tax. If the decedent owned property with situs in another state that imposes a tax on property that qualifies for the federal credit for state death taxes, the Georgia estate tax is reduced by an amount that bears the same ratio to the total allowable federal credit for state death taxes as the value of the property taxable in the other state bears to the total gross estate for federal estate tax purposes.

If the estate of a Georgia nonresident includes real property located in Georgia or personal property with situs in Georgia, the Georgia estate tax is an amount which bears the same ratio to the total allowable federal credit for state death taxes as the value of the property taxable in Georgia bears to the total gross estate for federal estate tax purposes.

R. Mark Williamson, Alston & Bird LLP

¶ 2503 Additional Estate Tax

The Georgia estate tax law is designated to absorb the credit allowed by the federal estate tax law, and does not, therefore, provide for an additional estate tax.

¶ 2504 Taxable Transfers

● *Residents*

Transfers are taxable when made by:

—will;

—intestate law;

—grant or gift in contemplation of death;

—grant or gift intended to take effect in possession or enjoyment at or after death; or

—revocable trust.

¶ 2503

Part VII—Estate Taxes

Special types of property interests are treated as follows:

—dower and curtesy are subject to tax;

—jointly held property is taxable to the extent of the decedent's contribution to the property;

—the exercise of a power of appointment is subject to tax;

—proceeds of life insurance are taxable if vested in the executor;

—life insurance proceeds with respect to which decedent possessed, at his death, any incidents of ownership, exercisable either alone or in conjunction with any person, are taxable upon vesting in the beneficiary; and

—the value of an annuity to the extent of decedent's payment of cost.

● *Nonresidents*

Transfers of real property located in Georgia and tangible and intangible personal property that has acquired a business situs in Georgia are subject to tax, in an amount equal to the proportion of the federal credit allowable for death taxes that the Georgia property bears to the property of the entire estate.

¶ 2505 Settlement of Domiciliary Disputes

There is no provision for compromise and arbitration of state death taxes in cases where there is a dispute over the question of the decedent's domicile.

¶ 2506 Property Subject to Tax

The Georgia estate tax is not based on a Georgia taxable estate or on Georgia deductions. Instead, the tax is based entirely on the federal credit for state death taxes (as described at ¶ 2504), based on the gross estate and deductions as determined for federal estate tax purposes.

¶ 2507 Return and Assessment

● *Jurisdiction*

The Ordinary of the County where the estate is being administered has jurisdiction of tax matters.

● *Returns*

A duplicate of the federal estate tax return is to be filed with the State Revenue Commissioner within the time required for the filing of the federal estate tax return including extensions of time received from the federal authorities. This is usually within 9 months of the date of the decedent's death.

● *Final determination*

Upon final determination of the federal estate tax, the personal representative must file a copy of the determination with the State Revenue Commissioner within 30 days of the federal adjustment. The Commissioner may require that other documentation be filed within the same time period.

If there is an adjustment to the federal estate tax return that increases or decreases the credit for state death taxes, a copy of the relevant documentation must be filed with the Department of Revenue and additional Georgia estate tax must be paid or a refund will be received, as the case may be.

¶ 2508 Payment and Refund

● *Time for payment*

The tax is to be paid to the state on or before the date of the filing of the return, usually within 9 months of the decedent's death.

● *Interest and discount*

If not paid within that time the tax shall bear interest at the rate of 1% per month until paid. There is no discount for early payment. A 10% penalty must be paid by the personal representative for failure to file a duplicate return or for failure to pay the tax within 30 days after notice of the amount due from the State Revenue Commissioner.

● *Refunds*

If the federal authorities should decrease the amount of federal estate tax, the state will refund to the estate its proportion of the decrease. If any tax is erroneously or illegally assessed and collected, a written claim for refund must be made within 3 years after the date of payment to the state.

● *Reciprocal enforcement of domiciliary taxes.*

Provision is made for reciprocity with other states in the collection of taxes imposed by the state of domicile.

¶ 2509 Notice and Waivers

There are no provisions or rules specifying that the consents or waivers must be had for the transfer of property of a resident decedent. Administrative practice does not require any waivers.

¶ 2508

PART VIII

PROPERTY TAXES

CHAPTER 26

PROPERTY TAXES

¶ 2601	Scope of Chapter
¶ 2602	Imposition of Tax
¶ 2603	Property Subject to Tax
¶ 2604	Exemptions
¶ 2605	Valuation, Assessment, and Equalization
¶ 2606	Returns and Payment of Tax
¶ 2607	Collection of Tax
¶ 2608	Penalties and Interest
¶ 2609	Taxpayer Remedies

¶ 2601 Scope of Chapter

This chapter is intended to be a general survey of the property taxes and is not intended to provide detailed coverage. It outlines primarily the property subject to taxation, the assessment procedure, the basis and rate of the tax, and the requirements for making payments.

¶ 2602 Imposition of Tax

Law: Art. VII, Sec. I, Pars. 2 and 3, Ga. Const., Art. VIII, Sec. VI, Par. I, Ga. Const.; Secs. 48-5-32.1, 48-5-220, 48-5-299, 48-5-350, 48-5-351, Code (CCH GEORGIA TAX REPORTS ¶ 20-080, 20-103, 20-665, 21-910, 21-930).

Counties may levy and collect taxes on real property for public purposes. Municipalities have constitutional authority to levy a school tax of not more than 20 mills upon the assessed value of all taxable property within the territory served by the school system.

The state of Georgia has the constitutional authority to levy ad valorem taxes on tangible property. The tax is limited to ¼ mill on each dollar of the assessed value of the property, except for defending the state in an emergency.

● *Tangible personal property*

The tax millages applicable to real property are also levied on the assessed value of tangible personal property, except that the prior year's rates are applied to motor vehicles. For example, the motor vehicle millage rates for 2005 equal the real and personal property tax rates for 2004.

● Millage rates; rate increases

A millage rate of one mill produces a tax of $1 for each $1000 of property value. A mill is expressed as .001 in decimal format.

Uniform procedures provide guidance on certifying and increasing local Georgia millage rates for Georgia real property tax and for providing notice of millage rate increases.

Rollback rates: An increase in a local millage rate must take into account increases in property value from a reassessment. The local millage rate applied against original assessed property value produces a certain amount of expected property tax revenues. When property value is increased from a reassessment, additional tax revenues are due after the millage rate is applied to the increased value. However, when original assessed value is combined with increased value, the millage rate applied against the combined value is effectively reduced to produce the same property tax revenues that were initially expected from applying the millage rate only against original assessed value. This reduced millage rate, called the rollback rate, must be regarded as the starting point of a millage rate increase.

When a local taxing authority proposes to increase the local millage rate for Georgia property tax over the rollback rate, three public hearings must be held, the proposed increase must be advertised in a newspaper of general circulation one week prior to each hearing, and a press release must be issued. If the proposed increase is further increased, the notice process must be reinvoked. A taxing authority proposing to adopt a millage rate below the rollback rate need only hold a single public meeting that must be advertised in a newspaper of general circulation at least two weeks prior to the rate's adoption.

● Uniformity of rate

The Georgia Constitution provides that all taxes must be levied and collected under general laws and for public purposes only and must be uniform upon the same class of subjects within the territorial limits of the authority levying the tax.

The General Assembly is given the power to classify property and establish different rates and methods for the different classes. Equalization of valuations is required by statute to ensure uniformity of assessment of property for taxation.

Property located within a municipality whose boundaries extend into more than one county must be uniformly assessed with other properties located within the municipality but outside the county where the property is located. Any adjustments made to a property's valuation to ensure uniformity apply only to the assessment used for municipal property tax purposes within the applicable county.

¶ 2602

¶ 2603 Property Subject to Tax

Law: Secs. 48-5-7.1—48-5-7.4, 48-5-10—48-5-12, 48-5-16, Code; Reg. Sec. 560-11-2-.20 (CCH Georgia Tax Reports ¶ 20-105, 20-107).

Real and tangible personal property subject to Georgia property tax is taxed at its value, classification, and location on January 1 of the tax year.

There are ten classes of property, which are described below. They are subject to differing assessment rates, which are discussed at ¶ 2605.

● *Residential*

Residential classification applies to all land used or best suited to be used as a single family homesite, its residential improvements, and other nonresidential improvements on the property. Duplexes and triplexes are also considered to be single residential improvements. This classification also applies to all personal property owned by individuals that has not acquired a business situs elsewhere and is not otherwise used for agricultural, commercial or industrial purposes.

● *Residential transitional*

Residential transitional classification applies to the residential improvement of up to a maximum of five acres of land underneath the improvement and comprising the homestead, the value of which is influenced by its location in a transitional area and which is receiving a current use assessment.

● *Agricultural*

Agricultural classification applies to all real and personal property used or best suited to be used as an agricultural unit, including the single family homestead that is an integral part of the unit, the residential improvement, nonresidential homesite improvements, nonhomesite agricultural land, and production and storage improvements.

Agricultural classification also includes all personal property not connected with the agricultural unit but that has not acquired a business situs elsewhere, and the personal property connected with the agricultural unit which includes machinery, equipment, furniture, fixtures, livestock, products of the soil, supplies, minerals, and off-road vehicles.

● *Preferential*

Preferential classification applies to all land and improvements primarily used for *bona fide* agricultural purposes and receiving preferential treatment as such.

● *Conservation use*

Conservation use classification applies to all land and improvements primarily used in the good faith production of agricultural products or timber and receiving current use assessment.

- *Environmentally sensitive*

    This classification applies to all land certified as environmentally sensitive property by the Georgia Department of Natural Resources and receiving current use assessment as such.

- *Commercial*

    Commercial classification applies to all real and personal property used or best suited to be used as a business unit primarily for the exchange of goods and services at either the wholesale or retail level, including multi-family dwelling units of four or greater.

- *Historic*

    Historic classification applies to up to two acres of land and improvements designated as rehabilitated historic property or landmark historic property and receiving preferential treatment as such.

- *Industrial*

    Industrial classification applies to all real and personal property used or best suited to be used as a business unit primarily for the manufacture or processing of goods destined for wholesale or retail use.

- *Utility*

    This classification applies to the property of companies that are required to file property tax returns with the State Revenue Commissioner, and includes all real and personal property of railroad companies and public utility companies. It also includes the flight equipment of airline companies.

- *Subclasses*

    In addition to the classification above, real property is further stratified as follows: (1) improvements; (2) operating utility; (3) lots; (4) small tracts; (5) large tracts; (6) production, storage, auxiliary; and (7) other real property.

    Personal property is further stratified as follows: (1) aircraft; (2) boats; (3) inventory; (4) freeport inventory; (5) furniture, fixtures, machinery, equipment; and (6) other personal property.

- *Situs of property*

    As a general rule, real property is taxed and returned to the tax commissioner or tax receiver in the county where the property is located. Personal property, however, is taxed in the county where the owner is domiciled. All real and personal property of nonresidents is taxed by the county where the property is located. Business tangible personal property is taxed in the county where the business is located. In general, the location and status of property on January 1 each year determines taxability.

¶ 2603

Practitioner Comment: Out-of-State Property

Counties have attempted to assess property taxes against property, typically movable in nature, that has a tax situs outside the state. These efforts have been rejected by the Georgia Supreme Court, which has held that imposing property taxes on property located outside of Georgia is a violation of the Due Process Clause of the United States Constitution.

Mary T. Benton, Esq., Alston & Bird LLP

¶ 2604 Exemptions

Law: Art VII, Sec. II, Par. 3, Ga. Const.; Secs. 36-88-1—36-88-10, 36-89-3, 36-89-4, 48-5-4, 48-5-5, 48-5-40—48-5-45, 48-5-47, 48-5-47.1, 48-5-48.1, 48-5-48.2, 48-5-52, 48-5-71—48-5-74, 48-5-356, 48-5-440, 48-5-470.1, 48-5-471, 48-5-472, 48-5-478.2, Code; Atlanta Urban Enterprise Zone Act (Act 981, Laws 1998); Reg. Sec. 560-11-2-.54 (CCH GEORGIA TAX REPORTS ¶ 20-113, 20-122, 20-140, 20-146, 20-164, 20-167, 20-176, 20-179, 20-206, 20-212, 20-218, 20-224, 20-236).

The following discussions concern property that is specifically exempt from property tax. See also the discussions of preferentially valued property at ¶ 2605.

● *Agricultural property*

In addition to the preferential assessment of agricultural land, discussed at ¶ 2605, the following exemptions relating to agricultural property are allowed:

—fertilizer used on land that has been properly returned for taxation;

—agricultural products that have a planting-to-harvest cycle of 12 months or less and that are customarily cured or aged for a period of more than one year after harvesting and before manufacturing and are held in Georgia for manufacturing or processing; and

—agricultural products and livestock (and products of livestock) that are grown in Georgia and brought into or sold in the municipality by the producer within 90 days after introduction into the municipality are exempt from municipal taxation.

All qualified farm products grown in Georgia including livestock, crops, fruit or nut bearing trees, bushes, plants, Christmas trees, and plants and trees grown in nurseries for transplantation elsewhere, produced and held by a family-owned qualified farm products producer are exempt from tax. However, standing timber is specifically excluded from the exemption.

Farm equipment: The exemption also includes farm equipment owned and used by family-owned qualified farm products producers.

Effective January 1, 2004, self-propelled farm equipment owned by a dealer and held in inventory for resale is exempt.

¶ 2604

- *Cemeteries*

All burial grounds in Georgia are exempt from ad valorem taxes.

- *Nonprofit charitable, educational, and religious organizations*

Specific exemptions are provided for the following types of property:

—all places of religious worship;

—property owned by religious groups and used for single family residences, when no income is derived from the property;

—all institutions of purely public charity;

—all property of nonprofit hospitals that do not have stockholders and that have no income or profit that is distributed to or for the benefit of any private person. Property is not exempt if it is held primarily for investment purposes or if it is used for purposes unrelated to providing patient care, providing and delivery of health care services, or the training and education of physicians, nurses, and other health care personnel;

—all buildings erected for and used as a college, incorporated academy, or other seminary of learning;

—all funds or property held or used as endowment by colleges, nonprofit hospitals, incorporated academies, or other seminaries of learning when the funds or property are not invested in real estate;

—public library property;

—books, philosophical apparatus, paintings, and statuary kept in a public place and not held for sale or gain;

—property of nonprofit homes for the aged that qualify as exempt organizations under IRC Sec. 501(c)(3) and Code Sec. 48-7-25 and that have no stockholders and no income or profit distributed to or for the benefit of any private person;

—all property that is owned by and used exclusively as the headquarters, post home, or similar facility of a veterans organization; and

—property that is owned by an historical fraternal benefit association and that is used exclusively for charitable, fraternal, and benevolent purposes.

Exempt purposes: To qualify for one of the above exemptions, the property may not be used for the purpose of providing private or corporate profit. Rather, any income from such property must be used for religious, educational, and charitable purposes and for the purpose of maintaining and operating the religious, educational, and charitable institutions. The exemptions do not apply to real estate or buildings that are rented, leased, or otherwise used to primarily secure income. Further, the exemptions do not apply to real estate or buildings that are not used for the operation of religious, educational, and charitable institutions. The exemption for colleges, nonprofit hospitals, incorporated academies, or other seminaries of learning apply only to those that are open to the general public.

¶ 2604

> ### Practitioner Comment: Property Exempt During Construction Period
>
> Georgia courts have drawn the distinction between property that is actually used for the exempt purpose of an organization from property that is held primarily for investment purposes. Thus, there is a strong argument that property otherwise qualifying for an exemption should obtain the exemption during a period of construction as it is being used for the exempt purpose of the organization during the construction stage and is not held for an impermissible purpose, such as investment.
>
> Mary T. Benton, Esq., Alston & Bird LLP

Handicapped or disabled persons: Motor vehicles owned by exempt schools or educational institutions and used primarily for transporting persons with disabilities or disabled students to or from schools or educational institutions are exempt from ad valorem taxes.

● *Energy systems or facilities*

There are no statutory provisions in Georgia regarding exemptions or special treatment for solar, wind, or other alternative energy systems, energy conversion or energy conservation equipment.

● *Enterprise zone property*

Georgia law authorizes the designation of enterprise zones in the state under certain circumstances. Additionally, special state law provisions govern the designation of urban enterprise zones by the city of Atlanta.

Enterprise Zone Employment Act: Local governments can designate areas as enterprise zones and grant them the authority to offer qualifying business or service enterprises property tax exemptions, abatements or reductions in their occupational taxes, regulatory fees, and business inspection fees.

To qualify, businesses must create a minimum of five new full-time job equivalents within the enterprise zone and it is recommended that at least 10% of the new employees be low-income or moderate-income individuals. The new enterprises must also provide additional economic stimulus to the surrounding area, the quality and quantity of which will be determined on a case-by-case basis by the local government that designated the zone.

Qualifying business and service enterprises are exempt from state, county, and municipal ad valorem taxes at a rate of 100% for the first five years, 80% for the sixth and seventh years, 60% for the eighth year, 40% for the ninth year, and 20% in the 10th year. If an enterprise zone designation terminates, the tax exemptions will continue to apply to qualified enterprises that maintain a minimum of five new jobs.

Atlanta Urban Enterprise Zone Act: The Atlanta city council is authorized to designate areas as urban enterprise zones and provide tax exemptions from city and county ad valorem tax for inventories of goods and real

¶ 2604

property. Real property exemptions within a zone apply to the underlying land if the taxable value of the improvements made to the land is at least three times greater than the taxable value of the land at the time of the zone's creation. Additionally, only improvements to real property during a year in which the area has an enterprise zone designation are exempt.

Enterprise zones may be created for 10-year periods for qualifying areas used for various purposes (industrial/commercial/residential). Qualifying real property within a zone is exempt from ad valorem taxes at a rate of 100% for the first five years, 80% for the sixth and seventh years, 60% for the eighth year, 40% for the ninth year and 20% in the 10th year. Inventories within an industrial or mixed-use industrial/commercial zone are totally exempt from ad valorem taxes for 10 years.

In zones created for residential purposes, the exemption for rehabilitated property is only for the value of improvements, unless the value of improvements is eight times or more greater than the value of the land, making both the land and the improvements eligible for exemption.

● *Governmental and public property*

As a general rule, all public property is exempt from ad valorem property taxation. However, government property used for proprietary activities is subject to taxation to the same extent as privately owned property. Further, public property that is located outside the territorial limits of the political subdivision is not exempt unless (1) it is less than 300 acres, (2) at least 25% of the area is improved and used for public or governmental purposes, (3) it is located within the county, or (4) it has been designated a watershed by the United States Soil and Water Conservation Service.

Exemptions for property of governments, to the extent granted, apply to property used for governmental purposes. Thus, property owned within Georgia by a corporation organized under the laws of the United States, or owned or possessed by an agency of the United States, engaged in proprietary activities is subject to property taxation at the same rate and in the same manner as the property of private corporations engaged in similar activities.

● *Homesteads*

A homestead exemption is available for homes occupied by owners who are in possession of and reside upon the property as of January 1 of the taxable year. The exemption also applies to land immediately surrounding the residence that is owned by the taxpayer. The statewide exemption is $2,000 and applies to state, county and school taxes, except school taxes levied by municipalities and except to pay interest on and to retire bonded indebtedness. The exemption does not apply to taxes levied by municipalities.

Many counties provide a homestead exemption that is greater than the $2,000 exemption provided by the state. Many municipalities also provide exemptions.

¶ 2604

Part VIII—Property Taxes 275

CCH Example: Calculation of Tax on a Homestead
To calculate the property tax on a home, use the following example: A taxpayer owns a home with a fair market value of $100,000 in an unincorporated area of a county that has a millage rate of 40 mills. Multiply $100,000 by 40% to arrive at the assessed value of $40,000. Subtract the $2,000 homestead exemption to arrive at $38,000. Multiply $38,000 by 0.04 (the millage rate), which calculates to $1,520 as the amount of tax.

Homestead property includes any of the following situations:

—a homestead that is destroyed by flood, fire, storm, or other unavoidable accident or is demolished or repaired so that the owner is compelled to reside temporarily in another place and continues to be a homestead for a period of one year after the occurrence;

—a building that is occupied primarily as a dwelling;

—a homestead occupied by the children of deceased or incapacitated parents when one of the children is an applicant; or

—the permanent place of residence of an individual in the armed forces.

A person's absence from the dwelling for health reasons does not constitute a waiver for purposes of applying for a homestead exemption if all other qualifications are met.

Applications for homestead exemption: Until June 1, 2005, applications generally must be filed by June 1, or in counties that collect the tax in installments, by May 1, or as otherwise established by local law. The owner of a homestead that is actually occupied by the owner as a residence and homestead need not apply for the exemption more than once so long as the owner remains in continuous occupation of the residence as a homestead. A deed showing actual ownership of the property for which an applicant seeks a homestead exemption must be filed with the county recorder of deeds prior to filing the application for the exemption.

Effective June 1, 2005, an applicant seeking a homestead exemption may file a written application and schedule at any time during the calendar year subsequent to the property becoming the applicant's primary residence up to and including March 1 of the following year. The failure to file an application and schedule by March 1 of a calendar year in which taxes are due constitutes a waiver of the homestead exemption for that year.

Military personnel: A member of the U.S. armed forces serving outside the continental United States may file the member's initial or renewal application for special property tax assessment at any time within six months following the member's return to the continental United States.

For discussions of exemptions for senior citizens and veterans, see those topics below. For the homeowner's incentive adjustment, see "Specially valued property," at ¶ 2605.

¶ 2604

- *Household goods; tools*

All personal clothing and effects, household furniture, furnishings, equipment, appliances, and other personal property used within the home, if not held for sale, rental, or other commercial use, is exempt from ad valorem taxation. All tools and implements of trade of manual laborers are exempt up to $2,500 in actual value. Domestic animals are exempt up to $300 in actual value.

- *In-transit property*

Foreign merchandise in transit is not subject to property tax imposed by a political subdivision in which the port of original entry or port of export is located because the merchandise acquires no situs in such ports. There is no tax situs by reason of the property being held in a warehouse where it is assembled, bound, joined, processed, disassembled, divided, cut, broken in bulk, relabeled, or repackaged.

- *Inventory*

The Georgia Constitution authorizes counties and municipalities to exempt from property taxation inventories of goods in the process of manufacture or production and inventories of finished goods ("Freeport exemption").

Specifically, the exemption applies to the following:

—inventories of finished goods in the process of manufacture or production, including partly finished goods and raw materials;

—inventories of finished goods manufactured or produced in Georgia and held by the original manufacturer or producer for a period not exceeding 12 months; and

—inventories of finished goods that are, on January 1, stored in a public or private warehouse, dock or wharf and destined for shipment outside of Georgia within a period of 12 months.

The amount of the exemption can be set at 20%, 40%, 60%, 80%, or 100% of the inventory value.

Practitioner Comment: Valuation of Inventory

If a taxpayer who has previously applied for and been granted a Freeport exemption is audited, and the value of his inventory is increased as a result of the audit, the taxpayer is entitled to a proportional increase in the Freeport exemption. For example, if 50% of the taxpayer's property had been granted a Freeport exemption initially, then 50% of the increased value of the inventory would also receive the Freeport exemption.

Mary T. Benton, Esq., Alston & Bird LLP

Application for Freeport exemption: Any person, firm, or corporation seeking the exemption for inventory must file a written application and complete a schedule of the inventory with the county board of tax assessors on

Part VIII—Property Taxes

forms furnished by the board on or before April 1 of the tax year in most counties. If the freeport exemption has been granted to a taxpayer for a taxable year, the county board of tax assessors must issue a notice of renewal to the taxpayer for the following taxable year by January 15 of that year.

Practitioner Comment: Freeport Exemption Application

Pursuant to Act 515 (S.B. 393), Laws 2004, if a taxpayer has applied for a Freeport exemption in the preceding year, the county now has an obligation to send renewal notices to the taxpayer by January 15. The taxpayer still has the obligation, however, to timely file its Freeport application for the current taxable year.

Mary T. Benton, Esq., Alston & Bird LLP

Practitioner Comment: Documenting the Exemption

The documentation requirements for the Freeport exemption vary from one jurisdiction to another. If, however, the taxpayer does not have at least minimal proof that the inventory has left the state, the exemption is likely to be disallowed. The more information to substantiate one's claim for a Freeport exemption the better. Detailed documentation of quantities and their destination will be a good start to a successful claim. Of course, a knowledge of local rules and statutes should provide the taxpayer with the background necessary to complete a successful application for a Freeport exemption.

Joseph J. Calvanico, KPMG, Chicago, IL

Motor vehicle inventory exemption: Motor vehicles that are owned by a dealer and held in inventory for sale or resale are exempt. Such vehicles are not required to be reported on the dealer's property tax return. The exemption is limited to vehicles designed primarily for use upon the public roads.

Personal property exemption: All personal property is subject to tax, except for the first $7,500 of the actual fair market value of the total amount of tangible personal property, excluding motor vehicles, trailers and mobile homes, as determined by the board of tax assessors.

- *Pollution control equipment*

All property used in, or that is a part of, any facility installed or constructed at any time for the primary purpose of eliminating or reducing air or water pollution is exempt. The facilities must be certified by the Department of Natural Resources as necessary and adequate for the purposes intended.

- *Senior citizens*

Persons 62 years of age or over, whose net family income does not exceed $10,000 a year, may qualify for an exemption from taxes levied for school purposes within the independent or county school district. The exemption is

¶ 2604

$10,000 of the homestead's assessed value, although it may be increased by local option. To qualify for the exemption, the senior citizen must file an affidavit by April 1 in the first year for which the exemption is sought showing the applicant's age as of January 1, total income from all sources, and the income of each individual member of the applicant's family residing within the homestead.

Tax deferrals: Any individual 62 years of age or older who is entitled to claim a homestead exemption may elect to defer payment of all or part of the ad valorem taxes levied on his or her homestead for state, county, or school purposes. Municipal ad valorem taxes imposed for municipal purposes may also be deferred. An annual application for tax deferral must be filed with the tax collector or tax commissioner by April 1. The deferral applies only to the taxes on the first $50,000 of assessed value. The applicant may not have gross household income in excess of $15,000 in the immediately preceding calendar year and the total amount of the deferred taxes and interest, when added to all other unsatisfied liens on the homestead, may not exceed 85% of the homestead's value.

Individuals aged 62 or older, living in a county with a population of at least 550,000, may claim a homestead exemption and may elect to defer payment of all or any part of the property taxes levied on the individual's homestead that exceeds 4% of their gross household income for the preceding year.

All persons applying for homestead tax deferrals must provide proof of fire and extended coverage insurance in an amount that exceeds the sum of all outstanding liens and deferred taxes and interest with a loss payable clause to the tax collector or tax commissioner.

Increased homestead exemption: A person who is 65 years of age or older whose Georgia net income, together with the income of his or her spouse, does not exceed $10,000 (excluding Social Security and pension income) for the immediately preceding taxable year may qualify for an increased homestead exemption from state and county ad valorem taxes in the amount of $4,000. This exemption also may be increased by local option.

Individuals 62 or older with income less than $30,000: Residents 62 years of age or older, whose family income does not exceed $30,000 for the preceding tax year, are eligible for an exemption from all state and county ad valorem taxes, except taxes related to the payment of interest on and retirement of bonded indebtedness. The exemption equals the amount of the assessed value of a homestead that exceeds the assessed value of that homestead for the tax year immediately preceding the tax year in which this exemption is first granted. A homestead includes only the primary residence and not more than five contiguous acres of land immediately surrounding such residence.

● *Veterans*

Disabled veterans who are residents and citizens of Georgia are granted an exemption from all ad valorem taxation for state, county, municipal and school purposes on homesteads they own and actually occupy as residences. The amount of the exemption is the greater of $32,500 or the maximum amount that may be granted to a disabled veteran under 38 USC § 2102, *i.e.,*

Part VIII—Property Taxes

$50,000 as of January 1, 2004. The value of the property in excess of the exemption amount is taxable.

Each disabled veteran may file for the exemption in his or her county of residence. The exemption is automatically renewed unless the county board of tax assessors requires a substantiation of continuing eligibility for the exemption.

Surviving spouse: The exemption is also available to the unremarried surviving spouse or minor children at the time of the veteran's death so long as they continue to occupy the home as a residence and homestead. If a qualified disabled veteran dies or becomes incapacitated to the extent that he or she cannot personally file for such exemption, the unremarried surviving spouse or the minor children at the time of the disabled veteran's death can file for the exemption.

Exemption for certain veterans: A single motor vehicle owned or leased by a veteran who has been awarded the Purple Heart citation is exempt from personal property tax. The veteran must be a citizen and resident of Georgia and must place on the vehicle a license plate received from the state.

A motor vehicle owned by or leased to a veteran who has been awarded the Medal of Honor is exempt from all Georgia property taxes, provided that the vehicle bears special Georgia license plates.

Veterans' organizations: Effective January 1, 2005, a motor vehicle owned by or leased to a veterans organization is exempt from all state and local property taxes (Act 497 (H.B. 1446), Laws 2004).

- *Vehicles owned by nonresident armed forces members*

A motor vehicle owned by a nonresident U.S. Armed Forces member temporarily stationed in Georgia as a result of military orders is exempt from personal property tax. The exemption applies to only one motor vehicle jointly owned by the armed forces member and the member's nonresident spouse and does not apply to motor vehicles that are used in the conduct of a business.

¶ 2605 Valuation, Assessment, and Equalization

Law: Art. IX, Sec. II, Par. VII, Ga. Const.; Secs. 48-5-1, 48-5-2, 48-5-7, 48-5-7.1, 48-5-7.2, 48-5-7.4, 48-5-10, 48-5-260—48-5-261, 48-5-269, 48-5-342, 48-5-420, 48-5-423, 48-5-441.1, 48-5-442(b), 48-5-443, 48-5-491, 48-5-540—48-5-543, 48-5-511, 48-5-519, 48-5-520, Code; Reg. Sec. 560-11-2-.22, 560-11-4-.03, 560-11-6-.03 (CCH GEORGIA TAX REPORTS ¶ 20-113, 20-129, 20-140, 20-161, 20-221, 20-227, 20-615—20-700).

Fair market value is the starting point when computing the tax on property. The market value is multiplied by an assessment ratio (usually 40%), to arrive at the assessed value. The assessed value (less any applicable exemption) is then multiplied by the tax rate to compute the tax. The intent of the legislature is to have all property returned at the value that would be realized from a cash sale, but not a forced sale, of the property.

¶ 2605

● *"Fair market value" defined*

Fair market value is the amount a knowledgeable buyer would pay for property and a willing seller would accept for the property at an arm's length, *bona fide* sale. Where no ready market exists for equipment, machinery and fixtures, fair market value may be determined by any reasonable, relevant and useful information available to the appraiser and assessor. Original cost, depreciation, and inflation may be factors in valuation.

CCH Tip: Excessive Depreciation

It is clearly in the taxpayer's interest to note, and substantiate, any instances of greater than usual depreciation: machines running nonstop for three shifts, for example, or molds warehoused because of a discontinued product line.

● *Valuation methods*

Fair market value is most often determined by application of standard appraisal methods. The most commonly used methods, both throughout the country and by Georgia, are the cost method, the income method, and the market data method.

Practitioner Comment: Mergers and Acquisitions

Ad valorem property taxes may be adversely affected through mergers and acquisitions, if the acquiring company is not familiar with the methodology taxing jurisdictions employ in determining annual real estate assessments.

Real estate assessments are typically assessed on the basis of a correlation of the cost approach, income approach, and sales comparison approach to value. However, because assessors often view the sale of the real property as the best reflection of fair market value, the sales comparison approach often receives the greater weight.

Because assessors often obtain sales data through a review of recent deed and transfer tax recordations, the failure to adequately segregate non-realty components (*i.e.,* personal property and intangible assets) from the real estate valuation may result in an assessment in excess of fair market value.

To avoid this pitfall, many companies often employ the services of purchase price allocation firms to ensure that tangible and intangible assets are properly segregated.

D. Glenn Williams, KPMG, LLP, Atlanta, GA

¶ 2605

Part VIII—Property Taxes 281

● *Assessed value*

All taxable property is assessed at 40% of its fair market value, unless special valuation provisions apply.

● *Specially valued property*

Certain property is valued using special methods or considerations, either because the property is unique and difficult to value, or because special valuation furthers tax policy goals (*e.g.*, use valuation of conservation property reduces economic pressure to develop the property).

Property that is subject to special valuation is discussed below.

Airline companies: Each type and model of flight equipment owned by airline companies is separately returned, valued, and apportioned for taxation. The valuation of aircraft apportioned to Georgia is, for each type and model of aircraft, that portion of the total valuation of each type or model of aircraft as the ratio of plane hours in Georgia bears to the total system plane hours, for each type and model of aircraft. The apportionment among the tax jurisdictions in Georgia is based as nearly as practicable upon plane hours. Plane hours means all hours in flight and all hours on the ground, including, but not limited to, time associated with overhaul, maintenance, flight testing and training.

Agricultural land: Real property that is primarily used for the commercial production of agricultural products is assessed at 75% of the value at which other real property is assessed, which is to say that the property is assessed at 30% of fair market value rather than 40%. The term agricultural products is defined to include horticultural, floricultural, forestry, dairy, livestock, poultry, and apiarian products and all other forms of farm products.

The preferential assessment applies only to the first $100,000 of fair market value and only to a maximum of 2,000 acres. The entire value of a residence located on such agricultural property is excluded from preferential treatment.

To qualify for the preferential assessment, the owner of the property must agree by covenant with the appropriate taxing authority to maintain the eligible property in *bona fide* agricultural purposes for a period of at least 10 years. The covenant is renewable at the expiration of any 10-year covenant period.

Brownfield property: A preferential assessment is applied to property classified as brownfield property by the Georgia Department of Natural Resources. Property is categorized as brownfield property if:

(1) there has been a release of hazardous waste, hazardous constituents, and hazardous substances into the environment;

(2) the Director of the Environmental Protection Division of the Department of Natural Resources has approved the prospective purchaser's corrective action plan or compliance status report for the property;

¶ 2605

(3) the Director of the Environmental Protection Division of the Department of Natural Resources has issued a limitation of liability certificate for the prospective purchaser; and

(4) the Environmental Protection Division of the Department of Natural Resources has certified eligible costs of remediation.

Property classified as brownfield property is assessed at the preferential rate of 40% of its fair market value. To receive the preferential assessment rate, the property owner must file an application with the county board of tax assessors and include the required certifications from the Department of Natural Resources with the application.

Property will remain classified and assessed as brownfield property for 10 years, unless prior to the 10-year period:

(1) the taxpayer provides written notice to the local taxing authority to remove the preferential classification;

(2) the property is sold or transferred to an exempt taxpayer;

(3) the Department of Natural Resources revokes the limitation of liability; or

(4) the tax savings accrued on the property equal the eligible brownfield costs certified by the Environmental Protection Division of the Department of Natural Resources.

Eligible brownfield costs are costs incurred after July 1, 2003, and directly related to the receipt of a limitation of liability from the Department of Natural Resources.

Brownfield property owners must annually report the tax savings realized for that year to the local taxing authority. The report must also include:

(1) the number of years that the preferential tax treatment has been received;

(2) the total eligible brownfield costs;

(3) any tax savings realized to date;

(4) transfers of eligible brownfield costs, if any; and

(5) any eligible brownfield costs remaining.

A qualified brownfield property may be transferred, subdivided, or leased and continue to receive preferential tax treatment if certain circumstances are met.

Community redevelopment programs: Counties and municipalities may establish community redevelopment property tax incentive programs. Under the amendment, communities can increase tax on properties maintained in a blighted condition and decrease tax for rehabilitated properties. Tax incentive programs developed by communities will not be subject to uniformity requirements under the Georgia Constitution.

Conservation use or residential transitional property: Tangible real property that qualifies as *bona fide* conservation use property, or *bona fide* residential transitional property, is assessed and taxed at 40% of its current use value. Assessment increases are limited to 3% annually.

¶ 2605

"Bona fide conservation use property" means real property consisting of no more than 2,000 acres, belonging to a single owner, with the primary purpose of good faith production, including, but not limited to, subsistence farming or commercial production of agricultural products or timber, subject to certain qualifications. The term also includes up to 2,000 acres of environmentally sensitive property maintained in its natural condition, and, effective January 1, 2004, certified storm-water wetlands of the free-water surface type.

Effective July 1, 2004, "bona fide conservation use property" includes land used for the production of fish or wildlife by maintaining no less than 10 acres of wildlife habitat either in its natural state or under management. Effective January 1, 2005, the term also includes land within buffer zones adjacent to rivers or perennial streams within which land-disturbing activity is prohibited by state or local law.

"Bona fide residential transitional property," limited to five acres of real property owned by a single owner, is private, single-family residential owner-occupied property located in an area that is changing from single-family residential use to agricultural, commercial, industrial, office-institutional, multifamily or utility use, or any combination. To qualify as residential transitional property, the valuation must reflect a change in value attributable to the property's proximity to or location in a transitional area.

In order for property to qualify for current use assessment, the property owner must enter into a renewable covenant with the taxing authority agreeing to maintain the property in *bona fide* qualifying use for ten years. The owner of bona fide conservation use property may enter into a renewal contract in the ninth year of a covenant period so that the contract for maintaining the property as conservation use property is continued without a lapse for an additional 10 years.

Going business: In determining the fair market value of a going business, equipment, machinery and fixtures may be valued to reflect accurate market value as a whole. In general, the following criteria may be used to determine fair market value: (1) existing zoning of property; (2) existing use of property, including any restrictions or limitations on the use of property resulting from federal or state law, or rules or regulations adopted pursuant to the authority of state or federal law; (3) existing covenants or restrictions; and (4) other pertinent factors.

Low income housing: In determining the fair market value of low income housing property, the assessor may not consider federal or state income tax credits that may apply with respect to the property.

Homeowner's incentive adjustment: The Georgia Constitution provides for an annual homeowner's incentive adjustment on the tax return of each taxpayer claiming the homestead exemption. The adjustment may be in an amount up to $18,000 of the assessed value of the property, or the ad valorem tax liability on the property, whichever is less.

Historic property: The fair market value of rehabilitated historic property and landmark historic property is computed as follows:

—for the first eight years, in which the property is classified as rehabilitated historic property or landmark historic property, the value is

¶ 2605

equal to the greater of the acquisition cost or the appraised fair market value according to the county tax digest at the time of certification;

—for the ninth year, the value is equal to the above formula plus one-half of the difference between that value and the current fair market value; and

—for the 10th and following years, there is no special valuation of rehabilitated historic property and landmark historic property.

The county board of tax assessors is required to grant preferential assessment if the owner of rehabilitated property can document rehabilitation expenditures equal to or greater than specified percentages of fair market value. Costs incurred for preserving specimen trees on rehabilitated historic property are included in the amount of rehabilitation expenditures that qualify the property for required preferential assessment.

Motor vehicles: The State Revenue Commissioner prepares and publishes a manual of uniform motor vehicle assessments each year. The uniform evaluation must reflect the average of the current fair market value and the current wholesale value for all motor vehicles.

The valuation of a commercial vehicle for property tax purposes is determined by multiplying the vehicle's gross capital cost by a percentage factor representing the remainder of the vehicle's value after depreciation according to a depreciation schedule distributed by the Commissioner. The resulting value of the commercial vehicle will be assessed at 40% of its value.

All antique, hobby, or special interest motor vehicles are deemed to have a fair market value of $100.

Public utilities: Each class or species of public utility property is separately valued. Each chief executive officer must apportion, under rules and regulations promulgated by the Commissioner, the fair market value of the public utility's properties to Georgia, if the public utility owns property in states other than Georgia, and among the several tax jurisdictions in Georgia. Factors that may be considered are (1) location, (2) gross or net investment in the property, (3) any other factor reflecting the utility's investment in the property, (4) pertinent business factors, (5) pertinent mileage factors, and (6) any other reasonable factors.

Railroads: A railroad equipment company, as distinguished from a railroad company operating a railroad, is taxed on the basis of the car-wheel mileage in Georgia as compared to the car-wheel mileage everywhere in the country. This value is then apportioned to the local jurisdictions on the basis of the track mileage in each jurisdiction as compared to the total track mileage in Georgia. The rolling stock of a railroad company operating a railroad is taxed on as much of the whole value of the rolling stock and appurtenant personal property as the length of the railroad in Georgia bears to the whole length of the railroad.

Special franchises: A tax is levied on special franchises at the same rate as on other property. The tax is based upon the value of the special franchise as returned unless the value is not accepted by the State Revenue Commissioner. If not accepted, the tax is based upon the value of the franchise as determined by the county board of tax assessors.

¶ 2605

Part VIII—Property Taxes   **285**

A special franchise includes the following:

—the power of eminent domain;

—the use of public highways and streets;

—the land above or below any highway or street;

—the construction and operation of railroads;

—the common carrying of passengers or freight;

—the construction and operation of plants for sale of gas, water, electric lights, electric power, steam heat, or refrigerated air;

—the construction and operation of telephone and telegraph plants;

—the right to conduct a wharfage, dockage, or cranage business and the right to conduct an express business or a sleeping, palace, dining, or chair car;

—the construction and maintenance of canals, toll roads, and toll bridges; or

—the right to carry on the business of equipment companies, navigation companies, freight depots, and passenger depots.

Timber: Standing timber with no merchantable value will have no fair market value for ad valorem tax purposes. When determining the merchantable stumpage value of standing timber, the tax assessor must consider (1) comparable stumpage sales within the United States Forest Service survey unit classification in which the county is located, and (2) any other factors deemed pertinent.

● *Assessment date*

Property is assessed for taxation on January 1 of the taxable year. However, new mobile homes in transit and not actually in a dealer's inventory on January of each year are not subject to taxation for that year.

Practitioner Comment: Personal Property
Statute of Limitations

Pursuant to Act 518 (S.B. 453), Laws 2004, if a taxpayer has filed a personal property return, taxes must be assessed within three years from the date the original tax bill was paid. The previous statute of limitations had been dictated by case law and was seven years. The statute of limitations does not apply if the taxpayer filed a false or fraudulent return.

Mary T. Benton, Esq., Alston & Bird

● *Equalization*

County appraisal staffs are charged with the duty of creating a comprehensive system for the equalization of taxes on real property within Georgia. Among their duties is to provide for adjustments and equalizations of property valuations in certain instances. For purposes of administration, counties are placed in classes, ranging from Class I (counties having less than 3,000 parcels

¶ **2605**

of real property), to Class VIII (counties having at least 100,000 or more parcels of property).

The State Revenue Commissioner examines the tax digests of the counties office to determine if the valuations of property for taxation purposes are reasonably uniform and equalized between counties and within counties.

¶ 2606 Returns and Payment of Tax

Law: Secs. 48-3-9, 48-4-2, 48-5-9—48-5-18, 48-5-23, 48-5-24, 48-5-127, 48-5-148, 48-5-150, 48-5-444, 48-5-473, 48-5-494, Code; Reg. Sec. 560-11-9-.03 (CCH GEORGIA TAX REPORTS ¶ 21-010—21-030, 21-801, 21-803).

Taxes are generally paid by the owner of the property to the tax collector. If the owner is not known, the taxes are charged against the specific property. Life tenants and those owning and enjoying the property are charged with the taxes on the property.

Taxes not paid by the due date are delinquent and are subject to interest penalties (¶ 2608). However, discounts are not authorized for the early payment of taxes. There are no provisions for the extension of time for payment of taxes.

● *Due dates*

As a general rule, taxes payable to the state or any county are due by December 20. However, the governing authority of any county, with the approval of the tax collector or tax commissioner, may provide by resolution that all unpaid state or local taxes be due on either November 15 or December 1 annually. Taxes are delinquent when not paid by the due date.

After notices of taxes due are sent, the taxpayer is allowed 60 days from the date of the postmark to pay the taxes in full before interest is imposed.

Owners of mobile homes must pay the tax due by May 1, or at the time of the first sale or transfer before May 1.

● *Returns*

All property subject to taxation must be returned by the taxpayer to either the tax commissioner or the tax receiver. Real property of a resident is returnable to the tax commissioner or tax receiver of the county where the property is located. Personal property of a resident, in contrast, is returnable to the tax commissioner or tax receiver of the county where the individual maintains a permanent legal residence.

Nonresident returns: All real and personal property of nonresidents is returnable to the tax commissioner or tax receiver of the county where the property is situated.

Taxable lands: Improved and unimproved taxable lands must be returned by the owner to the tax commissioner or tax receiver of the county where the land lies.

Personal business property: Persons who conduct a business enterprise on real property that is not taxable in the county of the person's residence or where the person's office is located must file a return for the tangible personal

Part VIII—Property Taxes 287

property of the business with the tax commissioner or tax receiver of the county in which the real property is taxable.

A taxpayer who does not file a return for its real property is deemed to have returned its property at the previous year's value. And when property is sold, the transfer tax declaration is deemed to be the return for the year immediately following the sale. Thus, it is really only necessary to file a return if a taxpayer wishes to make a change in the previous year's value or the value reflected on the transfer tax declaration.

● *Time for filing tax returns*

The books of the tax commissioner or tax receiver are open for tax returns between January 1 and April 1 in most counties. However, the time for filing is different in certain counties.

Motor vehicles: Property taxes are not collected during the initial registration of motor vehicles, and there is no requirement that motor vehicles be returned for taxation during that time period.

Mobile homes owned by residents must be returned to the county where the owner claims a homestead exemption or, if no such exemption is claimed, then in the county of the owner's domicile. If the vehicle is used in business in another county, the vehicle is returned to the county where the business is located. Nonresidents file the return for motor vehicles in the county where the motor vehicle is located.

● *Installment payments*

Counties and municipalities are authorized to provide for payment of ad valorem taxes on tangible property (other than motor vehicles) in two installments. Generally, due dates for installment payments are August 15 and November 15 of each year.

¶ 2607 Collection of Tax

Law: Secs. 48-3-1, 48-3-3, 48-3-8, 48-3-9, 48-3-19, 48-3-21, 48-4-1, 48-4-2, 48-4-6, 48-4-20—48-4-22, 48-4-40—48-4-48, 48-4-61, 48-4-64, 48-4-65, 48-4-76—48-4-81, 48-5-28, 48-5-299, Code (CCH GEORGIA TAX REPORTS ¶ 21-110—21-150).

The State Revenue Commissioner, a tax collector or a tax commissioner has the authority to issue tax executions when property taxes become delinquent. After proper notice has been made to the owner, the advertisement and sale of the property occurs. Rights of redemption exist for the owner of property sold under a tax execution.

Counties and municipalities may adopt an ordinance or resolution to authorize the use of judicial *in rem* tax foreclosures for delinquent taxes.

● *Tax liens*

Assessment of taxes constitutes a lien for taxes against the property. The property returned, the property held at the time of returning property, and the property held after the time of returning property is also subject to a lien for taxes.

¶ 2607

● *Tax executions*

The State Revenue Commissioner may issue an execution for any money owed to the state. In addition, all tax collectors and tax commissioners are authorized to issue executions for the nonpayment of taxes. On the due date for payment of taxes, the tax collector or tax commissioner must notify the taxpayer in writing that a delinquency has occurred and that unless paid, an execution will be issued. However, notice is not required for taxes due on personal property and the execution can be issued on the day following the due date for the tax.

When a levy is placed on any real property, the sheriff must give 20 days notice to the record owner of the property and any record owner of each security deed and mortgage on the property before the sheriff can advertise the property for sale.

● *Tax sales*

The sale of real or personal property under a tax execution is made in the same manner as provided for judicial sales. However, in addition to other notice that may be required by law, the defendant must be given 10 days written notice by registered or certified mail of a sale under a tax execution. The deed or bill of sale made by the sheriff to a purchaser at a tax sale is as valid as if made under an ordinary execution issued from the superior court.

Unknown owner: When property that has not been returned by anyone is assessed for taxes, the tax collector or tax commissioner issues an execution against the property as soon as it is assessed for the amount due and costs. The sheriff then advertises the property for sale in a newspaper in which sheriffs' sales are advertised once a week for four weeks before the day of sale. If the taxes are not paid by the day of the sale, the property is sold, but only if renting or leasing the property will not bring the required amount. The true owner can claim the property within four years.

Authority of counties to purchase: The governing authority of any county can purchase and hold any property sold under a tax execution. However, the governing body is only authorized to bid on the property when other bids do not cover the amount of the tax execution and costs.

● *Redemption of property sold under tax execution*

Whenever land is sold under an execution for the collection of taxes, the delinquent property owner or any other person with an interest in the property may redeem the property from the sale by payment of the redemption price within 12 months of the sale and at any time after the sale until the right to redeem is foreclosed by the giving of required notice.

Redemption by creditor without lien: If the property is redeemed by a creditor of the delinquent taxpayer who does not possess a lien, the creditor holds a claim against the property for the amount paid to redeem the property if there is any sale of the property after the redemption under a judgment in favor of the creditor and if the quitclaim deed is properly recorded.

Notice of foreclosure of right to redeem: The purchaser of property at a tax sale may foreclose the right to redeem by notifying the delinquent owner of

¶ 2607

Part VIII—Property Taxes

foreclosure after 12 months from the date of the tax sale. Within the county in which the property is located, notice must be served to the delinquent taxpayer if that person resides within the county, as well as any occupants of the property, and anyone having of record any right, title, interest or lien in the county in which the property is located. If the owner resides outside the county, notice is by registered or certified mail and publication once a week for four consecutive weeks.

Amount payable for redemption: The redemption price for property sold for taxes is the sum of (1) the amount paid for the property at the tax sale, (2) any taxes paid on the property by the purchaser after the sale for taxes, (3) any special assessments on the property, and (4) a premium of 20% of the amount for each year or fraction of a year that has elapsed between the date of the sale and the date on which the redemption payment is made. If redemption is not made until after the required notice has been given, the following amounts are added to the amount payable for redemption: (1) the sheriff's cost in connection with serving the notice; (2) the cost of publication of the notice, if any; and (3) an additional 20% of the amount paid for the property at the sale to cover the cost of determining the persons upon whom notice should be served. The total amount due must be paid to the purchaser at the tax sale or to the purchaser's successors.

Ripening of tax deed title: A title under a tax deed properly executed at a valid and legal sale ripens by prescription after four years from the recordation of that deed in the land records in the county in which the property is located.

● *Judicial tax foreclosure*

Counties and municipalities may authorize the use of judicial *in rem* tax foreclosures for delinquent taxes. Tax commissioners and tax collectors must wait a period of 12 months following the date on which taxes became delinquent before commencing a judicial *in rem* foreclosure.

Redemption of property: Any interested party may redeem the property from the sale by payment of the redemption amount at any point prior to the moment of sale. Payment must be made to the petitioner. Following receipt of payment, the petitioner must file for dismissal of the proceedings.

● *Acquisition of tax-delinquent land by land bank authority*

One or more cities and the county in which the city or cities are located may enter into an interlocal cooperation agreement or adopt a resolution to form land bank authorities for the purpose of acquiring tax delinquent properties to provide housing, new industry and jobs for the county's residents.

A land bank authority may act on behalf of any party of the authority who obtains a judgment for taxes against any tax delinquent property within the county and may tender one bid at a tax sale and obtain a deed to the property if there are no other bidders. The authority can foreclose the right to redeem property at any time after the 12-month redemption period has expired.

¶ 2607

● *Statute of limitations*

The statute of limitations on tax executions is seven years from the date of issuance or the time of the last entry in the execution docket.

¶ 2608 Penalties and Interest

Law: Secs. 48-2-40, 48-2-44, 48-5-7.1, 48-5-7.4, 48-5-7.5, 48-5-23, 48-5-84, 48-5-148, 48-5-150, 48-5-242, 48-5-299, 48-5-451, 48-5-493, 48-5-507, 48-5-513, 48-5-519, 48-5-541, Code (CCH GEORGIA TAX REPORTS ¶ 21-410, 21-415).

Penalties are imposed as follows:

Property devoted to agricultural or conservation use: Penalties are imposed for a breach of covenant on property devoted to bona fide agricultural purposes or conservation use. The penalty is computed by multiplying the amount by which the preferential assessment has reduced taxes otherwise due for the year in which the breach occurs times (1) a factor of five if the breach occurs in the first or second year of the covenant period, (2) a factor of four if the breach occurs during the third or fourth year of the covenant period, (3) a factor of three if the breach occurs during the fifth or sixth year of the covenant period, or (4) a factor of two if the breach occurs in the seventh, eighth, ninth, or 10th year of the covenant period.

Standing timber: The penalty for failure to file a report or disclosure of standing timber is equal to 50% of the tax due. However, if the failure to comply is unintentional and the report or disclosure is filed within 12 months after the due date, the penalty is equal to 1% per month for each month or fraction thereof for which the report or disclosure is late.

Late installment payments: Generally, installment payments, where permitted, become delinquent on the day following the due date and are subject to a penalty of 5%. That part of the entire tax bill that is unpaid after December 20 is subject to interest at the rate of 1% per month from December 20 until the tax is paid.

Tax deferrals: The penalty for filing incorrect information for a tax deferral is equal to 25% of the total amount of taxes and interest deferred.

Assessment of property by county board of tax assessors: A penalty of 10% of the tax due (minimum $10) is imposed when unreturned property is assessed by the county board of tax assessors.

Motor vehicles and mobile homes: Failure to file a return or pay the tax due on a motor vehicle or mobile home results in a penalty of 10% of the tax due or $5, whichever is greater.

For failure to attach and display a decal on a mobile home, the penalty is not less than $25 nor greater than $200. However, the penalty is $25 if proof of purchase of the decal is furnished prior to the issuance of the summons.

A person who transports or moves a mobile home without a decal that evidences possession of a mobile home location permit is guilty of a misdemeanor. The penalty ranges from $200 to $1,000 or imprisonment for not more than 12 months, or both.

¶ 2608

Part VIII—Property Taxes   **291**

The penalty for failure to pay tax due on a heavy-duty equipment vehicle is equal to 10% of the tax due.

Railroad equipment companies: The penalty for failure to file a return or pay tax by a railroad equipment company is equal to 10% of the tax due plus interest if not paid within 60 days of the mailing of the tax bill.

Airline flight equipment: For failure to file an annual property tax return for airline flight equipment on or before March 1 each year, airline companies must pay a penalty of 10% of the amount of subsequent taxes due.

Public utilities: For failure to file a timely return on or before March 1, public utilities are subject to a penalty of 10% of the amount of the taxes for which they are liable. In addition, the public utility's charter or permit to do business in Georgia may be revoked.

● *Interest*

Any person who willfully fails to file a property tax return or who fails to pay the amount due is liable for interest on the unpaid amount. Taxes bear interest at the rate of 1% per month from the due date until the date the tax is paid. Any period of less than one month is considered to be a month.

As a general rule, interest is assessed from December 20 until the time of payment on the amount due. However, certain counties are entitled to charge interest from an earlier date.

● *Waiver of penalties and interest*

A local tax collector or tax commissioner may waive a property tax penalty or any applicable interest with the written approval of the county governing authority. The delay in the payment of taxes must have been due to reasonable cause and not due to gross or willful neglect or disregard of the law.

¶ 2609   Taxpayer Remedies

Law: Secs. 48-1-9, 48-5-311, 48-5-380, Code (CCH GEORGIA TAX REPORTS ¶ 21-505—21-545).

An assessment of the county board of tax assessors may be appealed to the county board of equalization. An appeal is instituted by filing a timely notice of appeal with the local board of tax assessors stating the grounds for appeal.

Upon review, the county board of tax assessors may change the valuation or decision in question and send notice of the change or correction to the taxpayer. The notice must explain the taxpayer's right to appeal to the county board of equalization if the taxpayer is dissatisfied with the charges or corrections.

If no changes or corrections are made, the county board of tax assessors must send written notice to the taxpayer and the county board of equalization. Such notice perfects the taxpayer's appeal to the county board of equalization without the necessity of the taxpayer's filing any additional notice of appeal.

If changes or corrections are made by the county board of tax assessors, the board must notify the taxpayer in writing of the changes, including a

¶ 2609

statement of the grounds for rejecting the taxpayer's position on the value of property. If the taxpayer desires to appeal the changes or corrections, the taxpayer must, within 21 days of the date of mailing of the change notice, institute an appeal to the county board of equalization by mailing to or filing with the county board of tax assessors a written notice of appeal. A notice of appeal that is mailed is considered to be filed as of the date of the United States Postal Service postmark on the notice. The county board of tax assessors must then send the notice of appeal and all necessary papers to the county board of equalization.

● *Time for filing appeal*

Taxpayers must file a notice of appeal or arbitration within 45 days from the date the county board of equalization notifies the taxpayer of any changes in the return. When counties or municipal corporations provide for collection and payment in installments, the time for filing the notice of appeal is shortened to 30 days. Within 15 days of the taxpayer's notice, the county board of equalization must set a date for a hearing and notify the taxpayer. The hearing takes place within 30 days of such notification, but not earlier than 20 days.

Practitioner Comment: Appeal Deadlines

The deadline for appeal is based off the day the county mailed the notification to the taxpayer. Counties are not required to send notices of assessment or board of equalization decisions by certified mail, and Georgia courts have held that a county does not have to prove that the taxpayer actually received notification of its assessment but only that the county mailed the notification to the taxpayer. Even when a taxpayer did not receive its notification in time to file an appeal within the deadline, courts have disallowed the taxpayer's appeal filed after the deadline on the basis that it was untimely. (See "Refunds" below for a possible alternative remedy).

Mary T. Benton, Esq., Alston & Bird LLP

Military personnel: If an individual is absent from his or her residence because of duty in the U.S. armed forces, the deadline for filing a property tax notice of appeal or notice of arbitration is tolled for 90 days. During that period, a family member or friend of the individual may notify the taxing authority of the individual's absence due to military service and submit written notice of representation for the limited purpose of the appeal. Upon receipt of this notice, the taxing authority will initiate the appeal (Act 515 (S.B. 393), Laws 2004).

● *Arbitration*

Taxpayers have the option to appeal assessment decisions of the county board of tax assessors by arbitration. The county board of tax assessors must certify to the clerk of the superior court the notice of arbitration and any other papers specified by the person seeking the arbitration including, but not

¶ 2609

Part VIII—Property Taxes

limited to, the staff information from the file used by the county board of tax assessors. Within 15 days of the filing of the certification to the clerk of the superior court, the judge must issue an order authorizing the arbitration and appointing a referee.

If both parties agree, the matter is submitted to a single arbitrator. If the parties do not agree to a single arbitrator, then three arbitrators hear the appeal. If one or both parties are unable to select an arbitrator, the appeal is heard by a single arbitrator who is appointed by the judge of the superior court. Within 30 days after appointment, the arbitrator or arbitrators must render a decision. The decision may be appealed to the superior court in the same manner as a decision of the county board of equalization.

● *Burden of proof*

When a taxpayer appeals an assessment of Georgia property tax by a county board of assessors to a county board of equalization, an arbitrator, or a superior court, the county board of assessors has the burden of proving property valuation and proposed assessments by a preponderance of the evidence. Taxpayers are entitled to make audio recordings of their meetings with local Georgia property tax officials during assessment, appeal, or arbitration.

Questions of fact: Determinations by the county board of assessors as to questions of fact are *prima facie* correct in any appeal to the county board of equalization. The county board of equalization determines all questions presented to it on the basis of the best information available to it. A taxpayer may appear before the board during an appeal either in person or by his authorized agent or representative, or both.

● *Valuation; underpayments; overpayments*

If the county tax digest for the year in question is prepared, and tax bills are issued before the county board of equalization renders its decision, the county board of tax assessors must use the higher of the undisputed amount of the valuation of that property, or the previous year's valuation in compiling the tax digest. The tax bills must be based on that value.

In instances when the final determination of value is less than the valuation used in compiling the tax digest, the taxpayer receives a deduction, plus interest, not exceeding $150. Interest accrues from the date the tax was due or paid, whichever is later.

The taxpayer is liable for the increase in tax, plus interest, when the final determination of value is greater than the valuation used in compiling the tax digest. Interest, which may not accrue for more than 180 days, accrues from the date the taxes would have been due minus the appeal, to the date the additional taxes are paid.

● *Refunds*

Counties and municipalities may refund taxes that are determined to have been erroneously or illegally assessed and collected, or that have been voluntarily or involuntarily overpaid. Taxpayers have three years after the date of payment of the tax to file a claim for refund with the governing body

¶ 2609

of the county or municipality. If the claim is denied or not acted upon within one year, the taxpayer has one year to bring an action in superior court for the refund.

Practitioner Comment: Valuation Disputes

The Georgia Supreme Court has held that the refund provision in the Georgia property tax statute is not available to taxpayers disputing property taxes on the basis of valuation who must instead use the direct appeal procedure in O.C.G.A. Sec. 48-5-311. However, if the taxpayer did not receive a notice of assessment, in order to initiate an appeal, the Court of Appeals has indicated that the refund procedure may be available.

Mary T. Benton, Esq., Alston & Bird LLP

Practitioner Comment: Class Action Lawsuits

In March 2003, the Georgia Supreme Court reversed three decades of precedents that prohibited taxpayers from pursuing class action refund claims. The Georgia General Assembly promptly amended the refund claim statute for taxes administered by the state revenue commissioner to reverse this decision. The Legislature, however, did not amend O.C.G.A. Sec. 48-5-380, which provides for refund claims for taxes and fees administered by local tax officials. Accordingly, this option may now be available for refund claims involving local ad valorem property taxes.

Timothy J. Peaden, Esq., Alston & Bird LLP

● *Appeal to the Superior Court*

Taxpayers and county boards of tax assessors may appeal decisions of the county board of equalization, the arbitrator, or arbitrators, to the superior court of the county in which the property is located. An appeal by a taxpayer is effected by mailing to or filing with the county board of tax assessors a written notice of appeal. An appeal by a county board of tax assessors is effected by giving notice to the taxpayer. In either case, a notice must be mailed or filed within 30 days from the date on which the decision of the county board of equalization was mailed, or within 30 days from the date on which the arbitration decision is rendered.

Hearings before a jury are held at the first term following the filing of the appeal unless continued by the court upon a showing of good cause. Non-jury hearings are held within 40 days following the filing of the appeal.

If a superior court determines that the value of commercial property is 80% or less of the value set by a county board of equalization, or is 85% or less of the value set for other kinds of property, the taxpayer may recover litigation costs and reasonable attorney's fees. Recovery of litigation costs and attorney's fees is not allowed for taxpayers who have failed to submit a property tax return reporting their property.

¶ 2609

Practitioner Comment: Attorneys' Fees

The law providing for attorneys' fees states that "[t]his act shall become effective on January 1, 2000, and shall be applicable to all assessments and proceedings commenced on or after that date." A court of appeals decision has held that an appeal to superior court is actually a continuation of the appeal filed with the board of equalization and consequently, the provision for attorneys' fees was only applicable to assessments and appeals initiated in their entirety after January 1, 2000. (*Morrison v. Cobb County Bd. of Tax Assessors,* 258 Ga. App. 697 (2002), CCH GEORGIA TAX REPORTS ¶ 200-444.)

Mary T. Benton, Esq., Alston & Bird LLP

● *Taxpayer Bill of Rights*

The Taxpayer Bill of Rights requires the State Revenue Commissioner to prepare a statement setting forth: (1) the rights of taxpayers and the obligations of the Commissioner during any tax audit or examination; (2) procedures for appeal of unfavorable opinions by the Commissioner; (3) procedures for prosecuting refund claims and taxpayer complaints; and (4) procedures for enforcing Georgia's revenue laws, including the filing and enforcement of liens.

Taxpayers must also be informed that they will receive fair and courteous treatment in all dealings with the Department of Revenue, prompt and accurate responses to questions and requests for tax assistance, and fair and timely hearings on disputes of any tax liability.

The Commissioner must provide this statement upon a taxpayer's request; when he or she deems it appropriate; when a proposed assessment is made against a taxpayer; or when the Department of Revenue requests an examination of a taxpayer's records, whichever is earlier.

For additional information on taxpayers' rights, see ¶ 3101.

PART IX

MISCELLANEOUS TAXES

CHAPTER 27

UNEMPLOYMENT INSURANCE

¶ 2701	Scope of Chapter
¶ 2702	Coverage
¶ 2703	Tax Rates
¶ 2704	Returns and Reports
¶ 2705	Benefits

¶ 2701 Scope of Chapter

This chapter discusses briefly the Georgia unemployment insurance law. Its purpose is to give a general idea of the impact of the employer's tax and of the principal provisions. It is not intended to provide a detailed analyis of the law or regulations. It covers, generally, the questions of who is subject to the tax, who is exempt, the base and rate of tax, and the benefits payable.

The Georgia Employment Security Law is administered by the Department of Labor under the supervision of the Commissioner of Labor, 148 International Blvd., N.E., Sussex Place, Atlanta, Georgia 30303-1751.

¶ 2702 Coverage

● *Employer*

An employer is one who makes a payment of $1,500 or more in any calendar quarter in either the current or preceding year, or employs at least one individual for some portion of a day in each of 20 calendar weeks in either the current or preceding calendar year. Generally, an employer subject to the FUTA is automatically subject to the Georgia law.

● *Employment*

"Employment" is defined as service, including service in interstate commerce, performed for wages or under any contract of hire, written or oral, express or implied. Services by any officer of a corporation, by certain agent-drivers or commission-drivers and traveling or city salesmen are covered. Also covered is service on an American vessel or aircraft operating outside the United States if the employee's contract of service was entered into within the United States and if, while the employee is employed on such vessel or aircraft, it touches a port in the United States.

¶ 2702

Services performed by individual for wages is deemed "employment" unless and until it is shown that such individual is:

(a) free from direction or control, both under the contract of service and in fact; and

(b) performing such service outside the usual course of an employer's business, or outside all places of an employer's business; and

(c) customarily engaged in an independently established trade, occupation, profession, or business.

Except for covered nonprofit organizations or governmental employing units, individuals performing services for an employee leasing company are its employees, but individuals performing services for temporary help contracting firms are not. An employee leasing company is an independently established business entity that engages in the business of providing leased employees to any other employing unit under specified conditions. A temporary help contracting firm is any person who is in the business of employing individuals and, for compensation from a third party, provides those individuals to perform work for the third party under the general or direct supervision of that third party.

- *Exemptions*

Exemptions include:

—Services not in the course of an employer's trade or business.

—Commission agents performing services for common carriers in disseminating information for sale of transportation and in maintaining certain facilities, provided such agents are independent contractors, are remunerated solely by way of commissions, are free from control, and do not render services in the waiting rooms or storage rooms of the carrier.

—Insurance agents or solicitors solely on a commission basis.

—Interns.

—Maritime employees on other than American vessels.

—Newspaper and shopping news carriers under 18 years of age.

—Organizations that are exempt from income tax, with respect to services performed in calendar quarter if: (a) the remuneration does not exceed $50; or (b) such service is for a school, college or university by a student in regular attendance, or by the spouse of that student if the spouse's employment is under a program of assistance to the student; or (c) services by a student enrolled in a full-time work study program, but this exemption does not apply if the program was established for an employer or group of employers.

—Railroad employees and employee representatives covered by the Railroad Unemployment Insurance Act.

—Real estate salesmen, licensed, reimbursed solely on a commission basis, unless their services are performed for a nonprofit organization or state hospital or institution of higher education.

—Relatives, *i.e.,* services performed in employ of a son, daughter or spouse, and services performed by a child under 21 in the employ of a parent.

¶ 2702

Part IX—Miscellaneous Taxes

—Services covered by the federal system providing for the payment of unemployment benefits.

—Student nurses.

● *Agricultural and domestic employers*

Services performed in agricultural labor are covered if they are performed for an employer who employed 10 or more workers in such services for 20 different weeks in the current or preceding calendar year or paid cash remuneration of $20,000 or more for such services in any quarter of the current or preceding calendar year. When agricultural labor is provided by a crew leader, the employing unit for which the services are performed is the employer of the crew members, unless the crew leader is registered under the Farm Labor Contractor Registration Act of 1963, or substantially all of the crew members operate or maintain certain equipment that is provided by the crew leader. In either of these instances, the crew leader is the employer.

Domestic service in a private home, local college club or local chapter of a college fraternity or sorority is covered if it is performed for an employer that paid cash remuneration of $1,000 or more in any quarter of the current or preceding calendar year for such service.

● *Government and nonprofit employers*

Coverage is required for most services performed for state governmental entities, including political subdivisions. Other government services are not covered.

Mandatory coverage is required for tax-exempt, nonprofit organizations employing four or more individuals for some portion of a day in each of 20 weeks within either the current or preceding calendar year.

Services for nonprofit organizations and the state do not include the following:

—A church or an organization operated primarily for religious purposes which is controlled by a church.

—Religious duties of a minister or a member of a religious order.

—Patients performing services in a rehabilitation facility or sheltered workshop.

—Individuals receiving unemployment work-relief or work-training under program financed by federal agency, or an agency of a state or political subdivision.

—Inmates of penal or correctional institutions.

—Elected officials.

—Members of a legislative body or the judiciary.

—Members of the National Guard or Air National Guard.

—Individuals in certain major nontenured policymaking or advisory positions.

Nonprofit organizations and state governmental entities have the choice of financing the payment of benefits by either the regular contributions or the

¶ 2702

reimbursement method. Payments under the reimbursement method are equal to the full amount of regular benefits plus one half (full for governmental entities) of the amount of extended benefits paid to claimants.

Bills must be paid not later than 30 days after they were mailed. A cash deposit or surety bond or, in lieu thereof, a deposit of securities may be required by reimbursement employers. No cash deposit or surety bond will be required from a private nonprofit institution of higher education.

- *Wages*

Wages are all remuneration for personal services, including commissions, bonuses and the cash value of all remuneration paid in any medium other than cash, except:

—Renumeration over $8,500 paid by an employer to an individual during any calendar year with respect to employment. Wages paid by an employer's predecessor may be included in the wage base.

—Payments to or on behalf of employees under a plan or system established on account of sickness or accident disability (but only if paid under a workers' compensation law), medical or hospitalization expenses, or death.

—Payments made upon the termination of an employee's employment relationship because of death, retirement or disability, other than a payment that would have been paid if the employment relationship had not been terminated.

—Remuneration in any medium other than cash for agricultural labor or services not in the course of the employer's trade or business.

—Any payment on account of sickness or accident disability, medical or hospitalization expenses made by the employer after the expiration of 6 calendar months following the last month in which the employee worked for the employer.

—Payments made from, under, or to a trust, annuity plan, simplified employee pension plan, annuity contract, exempt governmental deferred compensation plan, supplemental pension benefits plan or trust, or cafeteria plan, as defined under the IRC.

—Payments made by an employer to a survivor or the estate of a former employee after the calendar year in which the employee died.

—Payments by an employer to an employee under an agreement, contract, trust, etc., for supplementation of unemployment benefits, provided that the such recipient meets certain conditions.

—Payment of employees' FICA tax without deduction from wages; this is applicable to agricultural and domestic workers only.

—Payments made as a commission by a real estate broker to a licensed real estate salesman exclusively for the sale of real property; such payments constitute wages if such individuals were employed by a nonprofit organization or state hospital or institution of higher education.

—Payments for a temporary layoff, if such payments are made out of a 100% vested account in the name of the employee under a pension or profit-sharing plan or trust that is qualified under IRC Sec. 501(a).

¶ 2702

Part IX—Miscellaneous Taxes

The term "common paymaster" means one of two or more related corporations that concurrently employ the same individual and is designated to remunerate the individual for services performed for all of the related corporations. The common paymaster is considered the employer of the individual and is responsible for contributions due on wages paid. Each of the related corporations is considered to have paid as remuneration to such individual only the amounts actually disbursed by it to the individual and is not considered to have paid amounts actually disbursed to the individual by the common paymaster.

Notwithstanding the above provisions, the term "wages" includes any remuneration subject to federal tax if the employer is subject to the Federal Unemployment Tax Act.

¶ 2703 Tax Rates

● *Standard rate*

The standard rate is 5.4%. The maximum possible basic rate is 5.4%. There is no employee tax.

● *Experience rates*

The employer's rate for any calendar year can be reduced below 2.62% for the period of January 1, 2000 through December 31, 2005, if: (1) its account was chargeable with benefits throughout the 36 months ending on the computation date, and (2) its total contributions paid by the end of the month following the computation date exceed the total benefits charged to its account and paid by the computation date. The computation date is the June 30th preceding the rate year.

If an employer fails to file all required contribution and wage reports by the end of the month following the computation date, or by 30 days from the date of notice to the employer that the required reports or payments are due and have not been received, whichever is later, it will be assigned a special rate for the next year. Such an employer is assigned the maximum applicable rate for its classification (positive or negative balance) in effect for the year (subject to the increases and decreases discussed below). Under certain conditions, a delinquent employer may be enjoined from employing individuals in Georgia employment.

Rates are based on the excess of contributions over benefits, divided by the employer's average annual payroll for the last three 12-month periods ending on the computation date (or for lesser periods in the case of newly subject employers and those qualifying under the 12-month provisions discussed above). The resulting percentage is applied to the applicable table of rates.

Rates for employers with positive reserve accounts range from 0.04% to 2.16% for the periods *before* April 1, 1987 and *after* December 31, 2005. Rates for employers with deficit reserve accounts range from 2.2% to 5.4% for the same periods.

Rates for employers with positive reserve accounts range from 0.025% to 2.110% for the period of January 1, 2000 through December 31, 2005. Rates

¶ 2703

for employers with deficit reserve accounts range from 2.15% to 5.4% for the same period.

The Governor has the authority to suspend by executive order any future portion of the reduction in calculated rates provided above in the event he or she determines, upon the recommendation of the Commissioner, that suspension of the reduction is in the best interests of the state.

State-wide reserve ratio (SWRR): If the SWRR is 2.4% or more for any calendar year, each employer who does not have a deficit reserve balance will have its rate reduced by (1) 25% if the SWRR equals or exceeds 2.4% but is less than 2.7%, or (2) 50% if the SWRR is 2.7% or greater.

When the SWRR is less than 1.7%, each employer whose rate is computed under a rate table, whether or not it has a deficit percentage balance, will have its rate increased by (1) 25% if the SWRR equals or exceeds 1.5% but is less than 1.7%, (2) 50% if the SWRR equals or exceeds 1.25% but is less than 1.5%, (3) 75% if the SWRR equals or exceeds 0.75% but is less than 1.25% or (4) 100% if the SWRR is under 0.75%.

Note that, for the period of January 1 through December 1, 2005, the overall increase in the rate above also will be suspended, except in the event the SWRR, as calculated above, is less than 1%; then the Commissioner will have the option of imposing an increase in the overall rate of up to 35%, as of the computation date, for each employer whose rate is computed under a rate table.

Note that for any calendar year with respect to which the SWRR equals or exceeds 2.0%, contribution rates will be further reduced for the succeeding calendar year by a percentage that will be computed in the following manner:

(A) The dollar amount by which the Unemployment Trust Fund exceeds the dollar amount that equates to a SWRR of 2.0% will be divided by the total of contributions collected attributable to wages paid during the preceding calendar year, excluding penalty and interest, as of the computation date.

(B) The resulting percentage will be used to reduce all experience-rated contribution rates by that same percentage; provided, however, that the resulting reduction will not reduce contribution rates below the level that will produce a contribution rate of 5.4% for maximum deficit reserve accounts. This reduction in contribution rates will be valid for the succeeding calendar year only.

(C) Accounts that are not eligible for a computed contribution rate will not receive the reduction in rates.

● *Administrative assessment*

For the period of January 1, 2000 through December 31, 2005, each contributing employer except an employer who, after application of the state-wide reserve ratio, has been assigned the minimum positive reserve rate or the maximum deficit reserve rate, must pay an administrative assessment equal to 0.08% of all wages paid.

New employers are also subject to the assessment, which is due and payable by each employer and must be reported on the employer's quarterly

Part IX—Miscellaneous Taxes

tax and wage report. However, reimbursing employers are not required to pay the assessment. Note that these assessments must not be deducted, in whole or in part, from the wages paid to individuals employed by the employer.

For rate year 2004, rates be determined from the following tables. The rates do not include the 0.08% administrative tax where applicable (this tax is not payable by employers paying the minimum rate or the maximum rate).

If the Excess Percentage Equals or Exceeds	But is Less Than	Employer Rate
0.00	0.86	2.82
0.86	1.17	2.72
1.17	1.48	2.61
1.48	1.79	2.51
1.79	2.10	2.40
2.10	2.41	2.30
2.41	2.72	2.20
2.72	3.04	2.09
3.04	3.35	1.99
3.35	3.65	1.88
3.65	3.97	1.78
3.97	4.29	1.68
4.29	4.60	1.57
4.60	4.91	1.47
4.91	5.22	1.36
5.22	5.53	1.26
5.53	5.84	1.16
5.84	6.15	1.05
6.15	6.47	0.95
6.47	6.77	0.84
6.77	7.08	0.74
7.08	7.40	0.64
7.40	7.71	0.53
7.71	8.02	0.43
8.02	8.33	0.32
8.33	8.64	0.22
8.64	8.95	0.12
8.95 and over		0.03

If the Deficit Percentage Equals or Exceeds	But is Less Than	Employer Rate
0.00	0.5	2.88
0.5	1.5	3.14
1.5	2.5	3.40
2.5	3.5	3.66
3.5	4.5	3.92
4.5	5.5	4.18
5.5	6.5	4.44
6.5	7.5	4.70
7.5	8.5	4.96
8.5	9.5	5.22
9.5	10.5	5.48
10.5	11.5	5.74
11.5	12.5	6.00
12.5	13.5	6.26
13.5	14.5	6.52
14.5	15.5	6.78
15.5 and over		7.02

● *Voluntary payments*

Voluntary contributions may be made and used in the computation of reduced rates if paid within 30 days following the date upon which a notice is mailed, stating that such payments may be made with respect to a calendar year. In no event may such payments be made later than the expiration of 120 days after the beginning of the year for which the rates are effective. Voluntary payments are not refundable.

¶ 2704 Returns and Reports

The contribution and wage report, Form DOL-4, is due quarterly on or before last day of the following month. Reports that are postmarked by midnight of the due date are deemed to be timely filed. Unless a different format is specifically required, employers are encouraged to use the preprinted Form DOL-4 but may use their own forms with prior written approval of its format from the department. Reports submitted by magnetic tape media must be in a format prescribed by the department or approved by the department in writing prior to approval.

For all quarterly reporting periods after December 31, 2003, employers with more than 100 employees, if not reporting by Internet filing, must

¶ 2704

submit reports by magnetic media in a format approved or provided by the department. Employers with 100 employees or less who do not elect to file Internet reports but prefer to file by magnetic media, instead of using Form DOL-4, may submit reports by magnetic media in a format approved or provided by the department.

Wage reports: Detailed quarterly wage reports are required on Form DOL-4, as noted above.

● *New hires*

Employers must report newly hired persons living or working in the state, as well as those returning to work after being laid off, furloughed, separated, granted leave without pay, or terminated from employment. The report may be made by fax or mail on the new hire reporting form, Form W-4, printed list, computer disk, tape or cartridge or by calling the New Hire Reporting Center. The report must be submitted within 10 days of an employee's hiring, rehiring, or return to work.

● *Reports for separated employees*

An employer must furnish a separation notice (DOL-800) to any employee who leaves its employ. This notice must contain detailed reasons for the employee's separation, and the employee must give such notice to the claims center at the time of filing a claim for benefits.

Within 48 hours after separation of 25 or more workers at same time and for same reason, the employer must furnish the employment office with Forms DOL 402 and DOL 402a.

In the case of a labor dispute, the employer must file Form DOL 402 within 48 hours after such unemployment first occurs. Within four business days after such request, the employer must furnish agency names and social security numbers of the workers involved.

At least seven days prior to a layoff for any scheduled unpaid vacation period, the employer must submit Form DOL 406, showing the name, social security number, and vacation beginning and ending date for each worker.

● *Low earnings*

A Weekly Report of Low Earnings (DOL-408) must be filed by an employer with respect to any complete pay-period week during which an otherwise full-time employee works less than full time, due to lack of work only, and either earns less than the current maximum weekly benefit amount plus $30.00 or an amount not exceeding the employee's weekly benefit amount plus $30.00. Both the employer and the worker must sign the form.

¶ 2705 Benefits

● *Base period*

The base period is the first 4 of last 5 completed quarters preceding first day of benefit year.

¶ 2705

Part IX—Miscellaneous Taxes 305

● *Benefit year*

The benefit year is the one-year period beginning with first day of first week with respect to which valid claim is filed.

● *Weekly benefit amount*

An individual's weekly benefit amount is computed by dividing wages paid in the two highest quarters of the base period by 46. However, total wages in the base period must equal or exceed 150% of high-quarter base period wages or the weekly benefit amount is computed by dividing the highest single quarter of base period wages paid by 23. Under this alternative method, wages must have been paid in at least two quarters of the base period and total base period wages must equal or exceed 40 × the weekly benefit amount. Beginning July 1, 2002, the minimum weekly benefit amount is $40. Beginning July 1, 2003, the maximum weekly benefit amount is $300.

Note, however, that for the period on or after January 1, 2000, whenever the state-wide reserve ratio is 1.25% or less, no future increase in the weekly benefit amount will be effective until the it is once again over 1.25%.

Benefits are reduced by earnings in excess of $50. Any fraction of $1 is disregarded.

● *Maximum total benefit*

The maximum total benefit is the lesser of 26 × the weekly benefit amount or ¼th of base-period wages, adjusted to the nearest multiple of the weekly benefit amount. In addition, during certain periods of high unemployment, extended benefits may be paid at the claimant's weekly benefit amount.

● *Benefit eligibility*

A claimant is eligible for unemployment insurance benefits if the claimant:

(a) is paid wages in at least two quarters of the base period and paid total base period wages of at least 150% of high quarter wages or alternatively, paid wages in at least two quarters of the base period and paid total base period wages of at least 40 × the weekly benefit amount;

(b) is able and available for work and actively seeking work;

(c) performed services and earned insured wages, since last benefit year, equal to at least 10 × the weekly benefit amount; and

(d) participated in reemployment services if so required.

Notwithstanding the availability for work requirement and the disqualification for refusal of suitable work without good cause, no benefits may be denied to an individual in approved training.

Educational institution employees: Benefits may not be paid to instructors, researchers, and certain administrators of any educational institution during school vacation periods or paid sabbatical leaves based on service with such institution.

Benefits may not be paid to nonprofessional employees of any educational institution during periods between academic years or terms if there is reasona-

¶ 2705

ble assurance of reemployment in the second year or term. If no opportunity to work is given in the second year or term, retroactive payments of benefits may be claimed.

A between-terms disqualification also applies if there is reasonable assurance of reemployment to an individual performing services in an educational institution while in the employ of an educational service agency.

Professional athletes: Benefits are not payable to a professional athlete for any period between sport seasons if there is reasonable assurance that he or she will perform services in both such seasons.

Aliens: Benefits may not be paid to an alien unless he or she has been lawfully admitted for permanent residence, is lawfully present for the purposes of performing services, or is otherwise permanently residing in the United States under color of law.

Vacations: The claimant is unavailable and ineligible for unemployment insurance benefits if the claimant is: (1) on vacation or leave of absence at his or her own request, (2) on vacation pursuant to employment contract, or collective bargaining agreement, or (3) on vacation, in the absence of an employment contract, or collective bargaining agreement, pursuant to established employer custom or practice; except that a claimant on unpaid vacation under (2) or (3) will not be held ineligible for more than two weeks if eligible for benefits otherwise.

Armed services members: The wage credits and benefit rights of persons who enter the armed services of the U.S. during a national emergency are preserved for the period of actual service and six months thereafter.

Temporary layoff or change in assignment: An individual who is laid off with a scheduled return-to-work date within six weeks from the date of separation is attached to the employer and exempt from seeking work. If he or she has not returned to work at the end of that period, he or she must meet the seeking-work requirement.

An individual is not employed in any week in which he or she refuses an intermittent or temporary assignment without good cause when the assignment is comparable to previous work or meets the conditions of employment previously agreed to between the individual and the employer.

● *Disqualification period*

An individual will be disqualified from receiving unemployment compensation benefits under the following circumstances:

—The individual is discharged or suspended from work with the most recent employer for failure to obey orders, rules, or instructions or failure to discharge duties of employment. The disqualification lasts until the individual is reemployed and has earned insured wages of at least (10 × his or her weekly benefit amount.

—If an individual is discharged for cause from his or her most recent employment for intentional conduct that results in: (1) physical assault upon or bodily injury to the employer, fellow employees, customers, patients, bystanders, or the eventual consumer of products; or (2) the employee being discharged for, and limited to, theft of property, goods, or

¶ 2705

Part IX—Miscellaneous Taxes

money valued at $100 or less. The disqualification lasts until employment is secured and at least 12 × the weekly benefit amount is earned in insured wages.

—If an individual is discharged for cause for intentional conduct that results in: (1) property loss or damages amounting to $2,000 or more; or (2) the employee being discharged for, and limited to, theft of property, goods, or money valued at over $100, sabotage, or embezzlement. This disqualification lasts until employment is secured and at least 16 × the weekly benefit amount is earned in insured wages. If an individual is separated from approved training due to his or her own failure to abide by rules of the training facility, he or she will be disqualified under the misconduct disqualification.

—An individual is discharged or suspended for violation of an employer's drug-free workplace policy. This disqualification lasts until individual has earned at least 10 × the weekly benefit amount in subsequent employment.

—The individual voluntarily leaves without good cause connected with the most recent work. The disqualification lasts until employment is secured, at least 10 × the weekly benefit amount is earned in insured wages, and the claimant is unemployed through no fault of his or her own. Voluntarily leaving an approved training course is also cause for disqualification under the foregoing provision; however, benefits are not denied for a separation pursuant to a labor-management contract or agreement or an established employer plan, program, policy, layoff, or recall that permits the individual, because of lack of work, to accept a separation.

—In addition, an employee of a temporary help contracting firm, an employee leasing company or a professional employer organization will be presumed to have voluntarily left employment without good cause if he or she fails to contact the firm, company or organization for reassignment upon an assignment's completion. However, failure to contact the firm, company or organization will not be considered a voluntary departure, absent advice in writing of the obligation to do so upon completion of assignments with a warning that benefits may otherwise be denied.

—An individual refuses suitable work without good cause. The disqualification lasts until employment is secured and at least 10 × the weekly benefit amount is earned in insured wages.

—The individual is not working because of a labor dispute (not including lockouts). This disqualification lasts for the duration of such unemployment caused by the dispute.

—The individual makes a misrepresentation to obtain benefits. This disqualification lasts through the quarter in which the act occurred and the following four quarters.

—The individual receives wages in lieu of notice, terminal leave pay, severance pay, separation pay, or dismissal payments or wages by whatever name, regardless of whether the remuneration is voluntary or required by policy or contract. In this case, the weekly benefit amount is reduced by the amount of such payment.

—The individual receives temporary partial or temporary total disability benefits under the workers' compensation law of any state or

¶ 2705

the federal government and receives unemployment compensation under another state or federal law. This disqualification lasts during the period for which such payments are received.

—The individual receives a governmental or other pension, retirement or retired pay, annuity or other similar payment based on previous work. In this case, the weekly benefit is reduced by the amount of the payment. As required by federal law, such reduction will apply only to pension plans contributed to by base period or chargeable employers, and the amount of such reduction will be determined by taking into account contributions made to the plan by the individual. An individual who, while working, contributed 50% or more toward such a plan is not subject to reduction.

¶ 2705

Part IX—Miscellaneous Taxes

MISCELLANEOUS TAXES

CHAPTER 28

OTHER STATE TAXES

¶ 2801	Scope of Chapter
¶ 2802	Alcoholic Beverages Taxes
¶ 2803	Cigarettes and Tobacco Taxes
¶ 2804	Insurance Taxes
¶ 2805	Motor Fuel Taxes
¶ 2806	Motor Vehicles
¶ 2807	Rental Vehicles
¶ 2808	Motor Carriers
¶ 2809	Environmental Taxes
¶ 2810	Realty Transfer and Recording Taxes
¶ 2811	Utilities
¶ 2812	Lodgings Taxes

¶ 2801 Scope of Chapter

This chapter deals with the Georgia taxes that have not been given detailed treatment elsewhere in the Guidebook. The purpose is merely to indicate in general terms the persons subject to the tax, the basis and rate of the tax, and the payments and reports due.

¶ 2802 Alcoholic Beverages Taxes

Law: Secs. 3-2-6, 3-4-2, 3-4-60, 3-5-60, 3-5-61, 3-5-90, 3-6-3, 3-6-50, 3-6-70, 3-6-71, Code (CCH GEORGIA TAX REPORTS ¶ 65-010, 65-105 *et seq.*).

Taxes are imposed in the form of license and excise taxes on manufacturers, wholesalers, and retailers of malt beverages, wines, and alcoholic liquors.

● *Exemptions*

The excise tax on malt beverages is not applicable to the following:

—sales to persons outside the state for resale or consumption outside the state; and

—sales to stores or canteens in U.S. military reservations.

A head of household producing up to 200 gallons of domestic wine annually is not subject to the excise tax.

Also, the tax does not apply to the following:

—sales to and use by established and recognized churches and synagogues for use in sacramental services only;

¶ 2802

—sales that are exempt from taxation by the state under the U.S. Constitution; and

—wine sold to persons outside the state for resale or consumption outside the state.

The tax on alcoholic liquors does not apply to ethyl alcohol when used

—for scientific, chemical, mechanical, industrial, medicinal, or culinary purposes,

—by persons authorized for tax-exempt use, and

—in the manufacture of products, syrups, or flavoring extracts unfit to drink.

● *Rates of tax*

Malt beverages: Malt beverages are taxed at the rate of $10 for each container of not more than 31 gallons, and 4.5¢ on each 12-ounce container. Taxes on malt beverages in excess of 1,440 ounces or five standard cases of 12-ounce size are imposed at the same rates as imposed for other such beverages. Malt beverages that contain less than 1/2 of 1% alcohol by volume are not subject to tax.

Wines: A tax of 11¢ per liter is imposed on the first sale, use, consumption, or final delivery within Georgia of table wines, and a tax of 29¢ per liter is imposed on the importation of table wines for use, consumption, or final delivery into Georgia. A tax of 27¢ per liter is imposed on the first sale, use, consumption, or final delivery into Georgia of dessert wines, and a tax of 40¢ per liter is imposed on the importation of dessert wines for use, consumption, or final delivery into Georgia. Wines that contain less than 1/2 of 1% alcohol by volume are not subject to tax.

Distilled spirits: A tax of 50¢ per liter is imposed on the first sale, use, or final delivery within Georgia of distilled spirits, and a tax of an additional 50¢ per liter is imposed on the importation of distilled spirits for use, consumption, or final delivery into Georgia. A tax of 70¢ per liter is imposed on the first sale, use, or final delivery within Georgia of alcohol, and a tax of an additional 70¢ per liter is imposed on the importation of alcohol for use, consumption, or final delivery into Georgia.

● *Payments and reports*

Licensed wholesalers are required to file monthly reports no later than the 20th day of the month following the month of purchase. The report must indicate the total disposition of malt beverages during the report period. The proper tax remittance must be attached to the report.

Monthly reports are required of wholesale dealers, importers, and brokers detailing wine sales for the month. The excise tax due must be remitted with the report. Licensed manufacturers, wineries, producers, shippers, importers, and brokers shipping wines into the state must file monthly reports showing the total quantity of wine transported. All reports are filed with the State Revenue Commissioner by the 15th day of the month following sale or shipment.

Each licensee must file a report itemizing for the preceding calendar month, by size and type of container, the exact quantities of distilled spirits

¶ 2802

Part IX—Miscellaneous Taxes 311

sold in Georgia. The tax must be remitted to the State Tax Commissioner by the 10th day of month following the month of sale.

¶ 2803 Cigarettes and Tobacco Taxes

Law: Secs. 48-11-2, 48-11-3, 48-11-5, 48-11-8, 48-11-10, 48-11-11, 48-11-13, 48-11-14, Code (CCH GEORGIA TAX REPORTS ¶ 55-005, 55-205, 55-210, 55-215, 55-220, 55-310, 55-315, 55-405, 55-410, 55-415, 55-605, 55-615, 55-620, 55-625, 55-805, 55-820, 55-825).

Georgia levies an excise tax on the sale, receipt, purchase, possession, consumption, handling, distribution, or use of cigars and cigarettes in the state. This applies as well to the purchase or use of cigars or cigarettes by the state, or any of its departments, institutions, or agencies. The tax on a group of cigars or cigarettes applies at the time of the first taxable transaction involving that group, regardless of whether or not that transaction involves the ultimate purchaser or consumer of the group.

All distributors and sellers are required to pay the tax on a given group of cigars or cigarettes to the Commissioner. They are responsible for collecting the tax from the purchaser or consumer of the group, and remitting the tax to the Commissioner. The tax may only be collected once on any given group of cigars or cigarettes.

Persons other than distributors who receive out-of-state shipments of cigars or cigarettes are considered to be distributors, and are responsible for paying tax on the cigars or cigarettes to the Commissioner. However, the Commissioner may license out-of-state shippers or manufacturers to affix tax stamps on behalf of their in-state customers who would ordinarily be liable for collection and payment of the tax.

All persons who use, consume, or store cigars or cigarettes in the state on which the excise tax has not been paid are subject to a tax measured in accordance with the volume of cigars or cigarettes used, consumed, or stored.

● *Exemptions*

Exemptions from the cigar and cigarette tax are granted for the following:

—cigars or cigarettes purchased exclusively for use by patients at the Georgia War Veterans Home and the Georgia War Veterans Nursing Home; and

—cigars or cigarettes acquired by a distributor that are already stamped or tax-paid.

The tax imposed on persons who use, consume, or store cigars or cigarettes on which the excise tax has not been paid contains the following exemptions:

—cigars or cigarettes in the hands of a licensed distributor or dealer;

—cigars or cigarettes in the possession of a carrier complying with the invoicing requirements of Code Sec. 48-11-22;

—cigars or cigarettes stored in a public warehouse;

—cigarettes in an amount not exceeding 200 cigarettes, or cigars in an amount not exceeding 20 cigars, that have been brought into the state on the person.

¶ 2803

● *Basis and rates of tax*

Cigars are taxed on the basis of their retail price, little cigars are taxed on the basis of weight, and cigarettes are taxed on the number of cigarettes in a package.

The rate of tax on cigars, little cigars, and cigarettes is as follows:

—cigars are taxed at the rate of 23% of the wholesale cost price, exclusive of any discounts or allowances;

—little cigars weighing not more than three pounds per thousand are taxed at the rate of 2.5 mills each;

—cigarettes are taxed at the rate of 37¢ per pack of 20 cigarettes.The same rate is applied, pro rata, to other size packages.

The tax imposed on persons who use, consume, or store cigars or cigarettes on which the excise tax has not been paid is measured by and graduated according to the volume of cigars and cigarettes used, consumed, or stored as set forth in Code Sec. 48-11-2.

The rate applicable to loose or smokeless tobacco is 36% of the wholesale price.

● *Payments and reports*

The cigar and cigarette tax is collected and paid by licensed distributors through the use of stamps sold by the State Revenue Commissioner. In lieu of these stamps, the tax on cigars and little cigars may be collected and paid by an alternate method as prescribed by regulations promulgated by the Commissioner.

Since the tax is to be collected only once on the same cigars and cigarettes, the amount of tax advanced and paid by the distributor is then added to and collected as part of the sales price. The amount of tax is to be separately stated from the price of the cigars or cigarettes.

The alternate method of paying tax on cigars and little cigars is the filing of monthly reports accompanied by payment of the proper tax on all cigars or little cigars sold, used, or otherwise disposed of during the report period. The report must be filed on or before the 10th day of each month on a form provided by the Commissioner. The report must disclose the number of cigars on hand on the first and last days of the calendar month immediately preceding the month in which the report is made. It must also contain the number of cigars purchased, sold, or disposed of during the report period, and be accompanied by a certified or cashier's check or money order for the total tax value of taxable cigars sold, used, or otherwise disposed of during the report period.

Persons liable for the tax on the use, consumption, or storage of cigars or cigarettes on which the excise tax has not been paid must pay this tax when they file their monthly report with the Commissioner.

¶ **2803**

Part IX—Miscellaneous Taxes

Licensed distributors must file reports with the State Revenue Commissioner on or before the 10th day of each month, specifying

—the number of cigars or cigarettes on hand on the first and last days of the month immediately preceding the month in which the report is filed,

—required information about the amount of stamps purchased, used, and on hand during the report period, and

—any other information required by the Commissioner for the report period.

In lieu of the monthly report, distributors, dealers, and manufacturers may furnish copies of all invoices covering shipments of cigars or cigarettes from outside the state.

In general, dealers are not required to file reports with the Commissioner. However, dealers who come into possession of cigars or cigarettes that do not bear proper tax stamps or other evidence of the tax must report the cigars or cigarettes to the Commissioner before displaying, selling, using, or otherwise disposing of them.

Nonresident manufacturers and distributors of cigars and cigarettes making shipments by common carrier or other means to Georgia distributors or dealers must make reports of the shipments to the Commissioner as he requires. Additionally, as a condition to being licensed as nonresident distributors, such persons must agree to submit all books, accounts and records for examination by the Commissioner.

Persons subject to the tax on the use, consumption, or storage of cigars or cigarettes on which the excise tax has not been paid are required to report to the Commissioner on or before the 10th day of the month following the month in which the cigars or cigarettes were acquired. The amount of tax due must accompany the report.

Common carriers and warehousemen may be required to file reports with the Commissioner with respect to cigars and cigarettes delivered to or stored at any point in the state.

The Commissioner is also authorized to examine the books and records of any common, contract, or private carrier, or any public or private warehouse.

¶ 2804 Insurance Taxes

Law: Secs. 33-5-31, 33-5-33, 33-5-35, 33-7-1, 33-7-9, 33-8-4, 33-8-5, 33-8-6, 33-8-7, 33-8-8.1, 33-8-8.2, 33-8-8.3, 33-15-28, 33-21-2, 33-40-5, 33-41-22, 47-7-61, Code (CCH GEORGIA TAX REPORTS ¶ 88-110, 88-115, 88-120, 88-125, 88-210, 88-215, 88-310, 88-315, 88-320, 88-323, 88-330, 88-345, 88-510, 88-515, 88-520, 88-525).

The state imposes a tax on gross premiums collected by all foreign, alien, and domestic insurers and surplus line brokers authorized to do business in Georgia. The kinds of insurance authorized cover all of the common forms, including marine, surety, and title insurance.

A health maintenance organization (HMO) subject to gross premiums insurance tax must be organized domestically as a stock, mutual, or nonprofit

¶ 2804

corporation in order to be authorized to do insurance business in Georgia under a certificate of authority.

A tax is also imposed on persons obtaining independent coverage from an unauthorized insurer. Fire insurance companies, corporations, or associations that conduct business in Georgia and write fire, lightning, extended coverage, inland marine, allied lines, or windstorm insurance policies for risks in Georgia are subject to an additional tax to be paid into the Firefighter's Pension Fund.

● *Exemptions*

Companies paying the premiums tax are not required to pay income or corporation franchise taxes.

Farmers' mutual fire insurance companies and fraternal benefit societies are exempt from premium taxes. However, the farmers' mutual companies must pay taxes on real property and fraternal benefit societies are subject to taxes on real estate and office furniture. Gross premiums received from policies covering property served by fire suppression facilities that are rated less favorably than class nine under the rating services published by the Insurance Services Office or its successor, or less than a rating that the board of regulation determines is substantially equivalent under rating standards published by an organization performing similar rating functions, are excluded from the assessment of the tax. The amount of the exclusion must be reported on tax returns that are filed with the board of trustees.

The following types of insurance are exempt from provisions of the surplus lines insurance law:

—reinsurance;

—insurance on subjects located outside the state, including vehicles and aircraft principally garaged outside the state;

—insurance on the property or operation of railroads engaged in interstate commerce;

—insurance on aircraft, cargo, or liability for aircraft owned by aircraft manufacturers or operated in interstate flight.

Annuity considerations are exempt from tax.

County and municipal premiums taxes: A county tax is imposed on the gross direct premiums of each life insurance company doing business within the unincorporated area of a Georgia county. Municipalities, where their charters permit, may impose a gross premiums tax on each life insurance company doing business within municipal limits.

Counties and municipalities are authorized to levy a tax upon the gross direct premiums of all foreign, alien, and domestic insurance companies, other than life insurance companies, doing business in Georgia.

The county and municipal premiums tax on life insurance companies does not apply to gross direct premiums of a company that qualifies for the 1¼% or ½ of 1% state premiums tax because of investments in Georgia state, city or county bonds, Georgia property, or Georgia loans. The tax also does not apply to annuity considerations.

Captive insurance companies: All chartered and licensed captive insurance companies are taxed under the provisions of Chapter 8 of Title 33, and

¶ 2804

Part IX—Miscellaneous Taxes

any other provisions of law in the same manner as other domestic insurance companies.

Risk retention groups: All premiums paid for coverage within Georgia to risk retention groups are subject to taxation on all premiums paid or due and payable during the preceding quarter, less return premium. Risk retention groups are subject to interest, fines, and penalties for nonpayment or nonreporting as provided in Code Section 33-5-32 for surplus lines brokers.

- *Basis of tax*

The insurance tax is imposed by the state on the gross direct premiums received during the preceding calendar year by all foreign, alien, and domestic insurance companies, surplus line brokers and independently procured coverages.

Generally, no deductions are permitted for premium abatements of any kind, for reinsurance, for cash surrender values paid, or for any losses or expenses. However, deductions are allowed for return premiums or assessments including policy dividends, refunds and similar returns paid or credited to policyholders, provided they are not used as premium for additional or extended life insurance. The gross premiums tax may be reduced if the company has sufficient investments in Georgia bonds, property, or loans.

The tax on surplus line brokers is imposed on a quarterly basis but is not levied on return premiums and sums collected to pay state or federal taxes for the preceding quarter. Surplus line policies covering risks or exposures not wholly within the state are taxed only on that portion of the premium allocable to risks or exposures located in Georgia.

- *Rates*

The rate of tax on all foreign, alien, and domestic companies is 2¼% on the gross direct premiums received by the company.

Fire insurance companies, corporations, or associations that conduct business in Georgia and write fire, lightning, extended coverage, inland marine, allied lines, or windstorm insurance policies for risks in Georgia are taxed an additional 1% on gross premiums written by the company. The additional tax is paid into the Firemen's Pension Fund.

Surplus line brokers and independently procured coverages (including risk retention groups) are taxed at the rate of 4% on gross premiums paid or payable. However, surplus line policies covering risks or exposures partly within and partly without the state are taxed only on that portion of the premium allocable to in-state coverage.

All premiums paid for coverage within Georgia to risk retention groups are subject to taxation at the rate of 4% on all premiums paid or due and payable during the preceding quarter, less return premium.

A company that has invested one-quarter of its total assets in the following classes of property may reduce the premiums tax to 1¼%. If three-fourths of a company's total assets are invested in the following assets, not including direct obligations of the United States, the tax is reduced to 0.5%:

—general obligation bonds;

¶ 2804

—revenue bonds or revenue anticipation certificates of a county, municipality or political subdivision;

—revenue bonds or revenue anticipation certificates of a public corporation or authority;

—real estate located in and taxable by the state;

—tangible personal property located in and taxable by the state;

—loans obtained through liens on real estate;

—loans against life insurance policies of residents of Georgia;

—intangible property with a tangible situs in the state;

—shares in a Georgia corporation in which the insurance company is authorized to invest.

Insurance companies that issue policies on fire, lightning, extended coverage, and windstorm coverage on property within Georgia are allowed to deduct any retaliatory taxes paid to another state during the year from their taxes due for that year.

Credits—low-income housing: Insurers may take a credit against insurance gross premiums tax for each Georgia housing project that qualifies as a low-income building under the Internal Revenue Code and that is placed in service after January 1, 2001. The amount of the credit is the same as the federal credit under IRC Sec. 42.

Local taxes: A 1% tax is imposed on gross direct premiums of each life insurance company doing business within the unincorporated area of a Georgia county. Incorporated municipalities are authorized, in accordance with their charters, to impose a tax on life insurance companies for the privilege of operating within the municipality. Taxes paid to a county or municipality may be deducted from taxes payable to the state.

Counties and municipalities are authorized to levy a tax at a rate not to exceed 2.5% on the gross direct premiums of all foreign, alien, and domestic insurance companies, other than life insurance companies, doing business in Georgia.

● *Payments and reports*

The annual premium tax on foreign, alien, and domestic companies is paid to the Insurance Commissioner by March 1. Companies whose annual premium tax is $500 or more are required to estimate the tax due for each quarter and pay that amount in installments by the 20th day of March, June, September, and December. The final payment is made when the annual return is filed on March 1. There are no statutory provisions relating to delinquency or extension of time.

The 4% tax on surplus line brokers must be paid to the Insurance Commissioner in installments, by the 15th day of April, July, October, and January, at the same time that quarterly affidavits are submitted. The tax is considered delinquent if not paid within 30 days of the due date. However, the Commissioner may authorize an extension of time for paying the tax.

Individuals procuring independent coverage must pay the 4% tax to the Insurance Commissioner within 30 days after the coverage is procured, continued, or renewed. Payment of the tax coincides with filing the report. The

¶ 2804

Part IX—Miscellaneous Taxes   **317**

report must contain the name and address of the insured and the insurer, the subject insured and a description of the coverage, the amount of premium paid and any other information the Commissioner may reasonably request. There are no specific provisions regarding delinquency or extension of time.

Fire insurance companies, corporations, or associations that conduct business in Georgia and write fire, lightning, extended coverage, inland marine, allied lines, or windstorm insurance policies for risks in Georgia must remit an additional 1% tax on premiums written and must file a report with the secretary-treasurer of the Firefighter's Pension Fund by April 1 of each year. The tax is delinquent if not paid by the due date. There are no provisions concerning extension of time for payment.

¶ 2805   Motor Fuel Taxes

Law: Secs. 48-8-33, 48-9-2, 48-9-3, 48-9-8, 48-9-9, 48-9-14, 48-9-19, 48-9-30—48-9-34, 48-9-37, Code; Reg. Secs. 560-9-2.02, 560-9-2.04, 560-9-2.06—560-9-2.08, 560-9-2.10—560-9-2.12 (CCH Georgia Tax Reports ¶ 40-205—40-505, 40-550, 40-705—40-730, 40 750, 40 755).

Persons subject to tax: The motor fuel tax is imposed on distributors who sell or use motor fuel within the State of Georgia. Other persons subject to tax are consumer distributors and, to a limited extent, aviation gasoline dealers.

The fuels subject to taxation include the following:

—motor fuel;

—gasoline;

—fuel oils;

—special fuels; and

—aviation gasoline.

The political subdivisions of the State of Georgia are prohibited from levying any fee, license or other excise tax on a per gallon basis upon the sale, purchase, storage, receipt, distribution, use, consumption, or other disposition of motor fuel. However, such entities may levy license fees or taxes upon business that sell motor fuel.

Additional tax: In addition to the motor fuel excise tax, licensed motor fuel distributors must also collect, effective January 1, 2004, a Prepaid State Tax, comprising the Second Motor Fuel Excise Tax and the 1% state sales and use tax on the sale or use of motor fuel.

Road tax: The "road tax" is imposed on every motor carrier for the privilege of using the streets and highways of the State of Georgia. The tax is calculated on the amount of motor fuel used by the motor carrier in its operations within the state. Except as a credit against certain taxes, the motor carriers road tax is in addition to taxes imposed on the motor carriers by any other statute.

Georgia became a member of the IFTA on January 1, 1996.

¶ 2805

● *Exemptions*

Certain sales made by duly licensed distributors are exempt from the motor fuel tax. These exemptions generally reflect

—a limitation on the power of the state to impose the tax, as in the exemption for sales of motor fuel intended for export from the State of Georgia, and

—a legislative clarification to avoid taxing an exempt person, as in the exemption for bulk sales of motor fuel to other licensed distributors.

Bulk sales made by one duly licensed distributor to another licensed distributor are exempt from the motor fuel tax.

Fuels not sold by the gallon: Exports from Georgia of motor fuels not commonly sold by the gallon will not be recognized as being exempt from tax unless the exporter informs the seller and the terminal operator of the intention to export and sets out certain minimum information on the bill of lading, or equivalent documentation under which the motor fuel is transported. If the motor fuel is delivered to any point other than that indicated on the bill of lading or equivalent documentation, the legal incidence of the tax must continue to be imposed exclusively on the exporter who caused the documentation to be issued. No exemption will be recognized until suitable proof of exportation has been provided to the State Revenue Commissioner.

Sales of motor fuel to a licensed distributor for export from Georgia are exempt from the motor fuel tax.

Sales of motor fuel to the United States for the exclusive use of the United States are exempt from the motor fuel tax when the motor fuel is purchased and paid for by the United States.

The sale of aviation gasoline to a licensed aviation gasoline dealer is exempt, except for 1¢ per gallon of the motor fuel tax, and all of the tax imposed by the "second motor fuel tax."

Bulk sales of fuel oils, compressed petroleum gas, or special fuel to a licensed consumer distributor are exempt from the motor fuel tax.

Sales of fuel oils, compressed petroleum gas, or special fuel to a consumer who has no highway use of the fuel at the time of the sale and does not resell the fuel are exempt from the motor fuel tax. Consumers of fuel oils, compressed petroleum gas, or special fuel who have both highway and nonhighway use of the fuel and resellers of the fuel must be licensed as a distributor in order for sales to be exempt. Each type of motor fuel is to be considered separately under this exemption.

The sale of fuel oils, compressed petroleum gas, or special fuel directly to an ultimate consumer to be used for heating purposes only, is exempt from the motor fuel tax. Delivery must be made directly into the storage receptacle of the heating unit. Further, the storage receptacles may not be equipped with any secondary withdrawal outlets for the motor fuel.

Sales of dyed fuel oils to a consumer for other than highway use are exempt from the motor fuel tax.

Every purchaser of fuel oil (other than dyed fuel oils) who buys 25 gallons or more for use in operating equipment for nonhighway purposes may claim a

¶ 2805

Part IX—Miscellaneous Taxes 319

refund (without interest) of the motor fuels tax paid on the fuel oils, effective July 1, 2004. Refund applications must be filed within 18 months from the date the fuel oil was purchased.

Exemptions from the "second motor fuel tax" are the same as those for persons and fuels subject to the motor fuel tax.

Compressed natural gas: When determining tax on fuels not sold by the gallon, the gallon equivalent of compressed natural gas must not be less than 110,000 British thermal units, notwithstanding any provision contained in the National Bureau of Standards Handbook or any other national standard that may be adopted by law or regulation. "Compressed natural gas" is a mixture of hydrocarbon gases and vapors, consisting principally of methane in gaseous form, that has been compressed for use as motor fuel.

● *Rates*

The rate of tax imposed on motor fuel is 7½¢ per gallon.

The rate for the second motor fuel tax is 3% of the retail sale price less the 7½¢ per gallon tax levied by Code Sec. 48-9-3 upon the sale, use, or consumption of motor fuel in the State of Georgia. Although 3% of the retail sales tax is designated a second motor fuel tax, the sale of motor fuel is still subject to the remaining 1% of the 4% sales tax. It is levied, administered and collected in the same manner as the sales and use tax. Suppliers are required to collect the tax as a prepaid state tax and pay the tax over to the Commissioner of Revenue on a separate schedule. The tax must be separately invoiced throughout the chain of distribution until it reaches the dealer who makes the retail sale.

The prepaid state tax rates are published on the Georgia Department of Revenue's Internet website within 60 days prior to January 1 and July 1 of each year. Different methods of calculation are used for (a) gasoline except aviation gasoline and (b) all other types of motor fuel, including aviation gasoline.

The following prepaid tax rates are effective for the period from July 1, 2004, through December 31, 2004.

Motor Fuel Type	3% Prepaid State Tax Rate (State, County & Municipalities Only)	4% Prepaid State Tax Rate (All Other Motor Fuel Sales)
1. Gasoline	$0.050 Per/Gal.	$0.066 Per/Gal.
2. Diesel (Clear/Dyed)	$0.040 Per/Gal.	$0.054 Per/Gal.
3. Aviation Gasoline	$0.078 Per/Gal.	$0.104 Per/Gal.
4. L.P.G.	$0.035 Per/Gal.	$0.046 Per/Gal.
5. Special Fuel*	$0.037 Per/Gal.	$0.050 Per/Gal.

* Includes Compressed Natural Gas (CNG).

Source: *Georgia Motor Fuel Bulletin*, Department of Revenue, May 2004.

The rate of motor fuel tax imposed on sales of aviation gasoline is 1¢ per gallon.

¶ 2805

The rate of tax charged to motor carriers is declared by statute to be the equivalent of the taxes imposed by the motor fuel tax. Accordingly, the rate is 7½¢ per gallon.

● *Payments and reports*

Payment of the motor fuel tax is required from distributors on or before the 20th day of each month, with respect to all gasoline, fuel oils, compressed petroleum gas, special fuel, and aviation gasoline sold or used in Georgia during the preceding month. The payment must accompany a report for the preceding month's activities on forms prescribed by the Commissioner. If payment is made on or before the 20th day of the month, the distributor will be entitled to deduct an allowance of 1% of the first 5½¢ per gallon paid in state tax to cover losses and expenses of reporting the tax to the state.

The road tax is paid by each motor carrier to the Commissioner quarterly, on or before the last day of the month following the calendar quarter for which payment is being made. It is calculated on the amount of motor fuel used by the motor carrier in its operations within the state. The amount of motor fuel used in the operations of any motor carrier within the state is in proportion to the total amount of motor fuel used in its operations within and without the state as the total number of miles traveled within the state bears to the total number of miles traveled within and without the state.

Any person or business owing more than $10,000 of tax must pay by electronic funds transfer.

Prepayment of taxes: A prepaid state tax must be collected on sales of motor fuel. The Commissioner of Revenue will issue the rate of prepaid state tax on a semiannual basis.

Collection allowance: An allowance of 1% of the tax is provided for distributors to cover losses and expenses incurred in reporting the motor fuel tax. The allowance is not deductible, however, unless payment of the tax is made on or before the 20th day of the month as required.

Transporters: Persons transporting motor fuel either in interstate or in intrastate commerce to points within Georgia must make reports of all deliveries of motor fuel. Each report made by a transporter of motor fuel must be filed by the 20th day of each calendar month to cover the preceding month's activities.

Motor carriers subject to the road tax are required to make quarterly reports to the Commissioner, on or before the last day of April, July, October, and January.

Two or more carriers regularly engaged in the transportation of passengers on through buses and on through tickets in pool service, at their option and with the consent of the Commissioner, may make joint reports of their entire operations within the state. Under this arrangement, the road taxes are calculated on the basis of the joint report as though the motor carriers were a single motor carrier. Liability for the tax, however, is joint and several.

¶ 2805

Part IX—Miscellaneous Taxes

¶ 2806 Motor Vehicles

Law: Secs. 40-2-20, 40-2-30, 40-2-37, 40-2-87, 40-2-88, 40-2-111, 40-2-112, 40-3-38, 48-5-471—48-5-474, 48-10-2, 48-10-2.1, 48-10-3, 48-10-7, 48-10-8, 48-10-10, 48-10-12, Code (CCH Georgia Tax Reports ¶ 50-005—50-090).

Every owner of a motor vehicle, including a tractor or a motorcycle, and every owner of a trailer, must register the vehicle and pay the required license fee for each year, unless specifically exempted.

Applications for motor vehicle registrations and transfers of motor vehicle registrations may be filed separately from applications for certificates of title.

Georgia, under statutory authority, has entered into the International Registration Plan (IRP), an agreement with other states and jurisdictions regarding the registration of motor carriers, and other fleets of vehicles. The IRP, administered by the American Association of Motor Vehicle Administrators, is designed to promote the fullest possible use of the highway system by authorizing proportional registration of fleets of vehicles and by recognizing vehicles proportionally registered in other jurisdictions. The IRP implements the concept of one registration plate per vehicle and grants exemptions from payments of certain fees when reciprocated by member jurisdictions.

IRP registration: Applications for registration or renewal of registration under the IRP must be submitted during the registration period applicable in counties that have a 12-month staggered registration period. Registration fees must be paid not later than 30 days from the date of the invoice, and license plates must be displayed on vehicles registered under the IRP not later than 30 days from the date of the invoice.

The following vehicles are exempt from registration requirements:

—motorized carts, including golf carts;

—heavy earth-moving machinery, fertilizer application equipment, and crop protection chemical application equipment, not including trucks, used primarily off the highway;

—mopeds;

—skidders, tractors and loaders (pieces of lumbering equipment) used only in the woods;

—tractors used only for agricultural purposes;

—trailers used exclusively to haul agricultural products from one place on the farm to another;

—trailers without springs used to haul unprocessed farm products to their market destination;

—trailers without springs that are pulled from a tongue and used primarily to transport fertilizer to a farm; and

—three-wheeled motorcycles used only for agricultural purposes.

● *Rates*

The following paragraphs outline the principal fees payable to the State Revenue Commissioner before May 1 of each year. A $1 additional fee is imposed for purchasing a license plate or revalidation decal by mail. Motor vehicles are also subject to property taxes.

The fee for each passenger motor vehicle not operated as a common or contract carrier for hire is $20.

License fees for trucks and other non-passenger-carrying motor vehicles, including leased trucks, that are operated as common or contract carriers for hire are based on owner-declared gross vehicle weight as follows:

Less than 14,000 pounds	$ 20
14,000 to 18,000 pounds	$ 25
18,001 to 26,000 pounds	$ 38
26,001 to 30,000 pounds	$ 85
30,001 to 36,000 pounds	$130
36,001 to 44,000 pounds	$215
44,001 to 54,999 pounds	$365
55,000 to 63,280 pounds	$575
63,281 to maximum permitted	$725

The fee for a straight truck that is not a truck-tractor or a leased truck will not be higher than $50. The fee for trailers used as common or contract carriers is $12.

License fees for most private trucks are based on the owner-declared gross vehicle weight as follows:

Less than 14,000 pounds	$ 20
14,000 to 18,000 pounds	$ 25
18,001 to 26,000 pounds	$ 38
26,001 to 30,000 pounds	$ 45
30,001 to 36,000 pounds	$ 70
36,001 to 44,000 pounds	$115
44,001 to 54,999 pounds	$190
55,000 to 63,280 pounds	$300
63,281 to maximum permitted	$400

Special fees apply to certain private trucks. The fee for a straight truck that is not a truck tractor may not be higher than $75, while the fee for a straight truck hauling fertilizer and agricultural products may not be higher than $31. The fee for a truck-tractor hauling fertilizer or milk may not be higher than $220.

Motor buses or van type vehicles that are used as common or contract carriers for hire in public transportation transporting passengers are subject to license fees according to their factory weight. The fee per 100 pounds of factory weight, or fractional part thereof, is as follows:

10,000 or less pounds	$1.90
10,001 to 15,000 pounds	$2.70
15,001 to 20,000 pounds	$3.45
More than 20,000 pounds	$3.75

A license fee of $20 is charged for farm trucks, and a $5 fee is charged for farm trailers that are not hauling agricultural products on the farm.

¶ 2806

Part IX—Miscellaneous Taxes 323

A fee of $38 is required for straight trucks and truck trailers pulling single pole trailers hauling logs from the woods to the sawmill. The fee for other truck-tractors used in transporting forest products is $220.

A fee of $31 is charged for each agricultural use vehicle.

Except as otherwise provided, the annual fee for all apportionable vehicles not operated as a common or contract carrier for hire based on owner declared gross vehicle weight or combined vehicle gross weight is as follows:

26,001 to 30,000 pounds .... $ 45
30,001 to 36,000 pounds .... $ 70
36,001 to 44,000 pounds $115
44,001 to 54,999 pounds $190
55,000 to 63,280 pounds $300
63,281 pounds to maximum permitted pounds $400

Except as otherwise provided, the annual fee for all apportionable vehicles operated as a common or contract carrier for hire in accordance with owner declared gross vehicle weight or combined vehicle gross weight is as follows:

26,001 to 30,000 pounds .... $ 85
30,001 to 36,000 pounds $130
36,001 to 44,000 pounds $215
44,001 to 54,999 pounds $365
55,000 to 63,280 pounds $575
63,281 pounds to maximum permitted $725

For each apportionable motor bus or van-type vehicle, the fee is $3.75 per 100 pounds of factory weight, or fractional part thereof. The maximum license fee for buses is $875. If a bus is operated over a route of 50 miles or less, the fee is reduced by one-half.

For buses that are part of an interstate fleet or combined interstate and intrastate fleet of two buses or more, the fee is a fraction of the full motor bus fee that is equal to the proportion that the fleets travel in Georgia during the preceding year bears to the total number of miles it traveled during the year.

The license fee for school and church buses is $5.

Apportionment of registration fees is restricted to private trucks, motor buses used as common or contract carriers for hire and trucks used as common or contract carriers, except private trucks and common or contract carrier trucks with owner declared gross vehicle weights of 14,000 pounds or less. Apportionment is as follows:

Registration between March 1 and May 31 . 3/4 of the annual license fee

Between June 1 and August 31 .... 1/2 of the annual license fee

Between September 1 and November 30 . 1/4 of the annual license fee

Vehicles other than passenger vehicles, trucks and buses are subject to the following license fees:

¶ 2806

Manufacturers and dealers:

Application fee for distinguished dealer's number	$62
Annual registration fee	$25
Motorcycles	$20
House, auto or boat trailers not for hire	$12
Motor driven hearses or ambulances	$20
Government-owned vehicles	$1
U.S. Department of Defense vehicles	$20
Certificate of title	$18
Replacement certificate of title	$8

The fee for a highway use permit for vehicles with gross weight of 18,000 lbs. or more used for transportation of merchandise or freight is not more than $200. A fee of not over $25 is charged per round trip into Georgia on trucks from states that impose a road tax on Georgia trucks, in addition to motor fuel taxes and registration fees.

The Georgia Supreme Court ruled, on September 7, 1988, in *Private Truck Council of America, Inc.,* that the permit and round trip fees imposed on trucks not registered in Georgia are unconstitutional. The Georgia Department of Revenue has suspended collection of the highway use tax.

● *Payments and reports*

Every motor vehicle owned by a natural person in the state of Georgia is subject to ad valorem taxation. The owner of the vehicle is required to make a return and pay the tax at the same time he or she is due to apply and pay for the vehicle's registration and license plate; the application for registration and purchase of the license plate may, in many instances, serve as the return.

A motor vehicle owned by a nonresident member of the armed forces of the United States temporarily stationed in Georgia as a result of military orders is not subject to tax. Not more than one motor vehicle jointly owned by the armed forces member and the member's nonresident spouse, if the nonresident spouse temporarily resides in Georgia at the temporary domicile of the armed forces member, is exempt from Georgia tax. The exemption does not apply to motor vehicles that are used in the conduct of a business.

In the case of an antique, hobby, or special interest motor vehicle, the due date for ad valorem taxes is the registration date.

A return and the payment of taxes is not required during the vehicle's initial registration period, or when the vehicle is transferred, unless the date of purchase or the application date of the initial registration is the same as the original owner's registration period.

Motor vehicles owned by dealers and held in inventory for sale or resale are a separate subclass of motor vehicles and are not subject to the ad valorem tax return, imposition, and collection requirements. Upon their transfer, however, inventory vehicles must be returned and the taxes due must be paid in full.

¶ 2806

Part IX—Miscellaneous Taxes

¶ 2807 Rental Vehicles

Law: Secs. 48-13-90—48-13-94, 48-13-97, Code (CCH GEORGIA TAX REPORTS ¶ 33-510, 33-520, 33-530).

Counties and municipalities may levy and collect an excise tax on rental motor vehicles. Counties are limited to levying and collecting the tax within the territorial limits of special districts. Each special district includes all of the territory within the county, except the territory located within the boundaries of any municipality that imposes the tax.

The excise tax is levied upon the rental charge collected by a rental motor vehicle concern when the charge is taxable for purposes of the sales and use tax. A "rental motor vehicle" is defined as a motor vehicle designed to carry 10 or fewer passengers and is rented or leased without a driver. "Rental charge" means the total value received by a rental motor vehicle concern for the rental or lease for 31 or fewer consecutive days of a motor vehicle, including, but not limited to, charges based on time or mileage and charges for insurance coverage or collision damage waiver. However, all charges for motor fuel taxes or sales taxes are excluded.

The tax may be imposed only at the time and place that a customer pays sales tax with respect to the rental charge. Any excise tax on rental motor vehicles must terminate no later than December 31, 2038.

Each person collecting the tax is allowed to deduct 3% of the tax due if payment is timely.

The local excise tax on certain rental motor vehicles may not be imposed if

—the customer picks up the rental motor vehicle outside the state and returns it in Georgia, or

—the customer picks up the rental motor vehicle in Georgia and returns it outside the state.

● *Rate*

The excise tax on rental motor vehicles is imposed at a rate of 3% of the rental charges.

¶ 2808 Motor Carriers

Law: Secs. 46-1-1, 46-7-9, 46-7-15, 46-7-16, 48-9-31, Code (CCH GEORGIA TAX REPORTS ¶ 50-110, 50-120, 50-130).

The term "motor common carrier" means every person owning, controlling, operating, or managing any motor propelled vehicle and the lessees, receivers, or trustees of such person, used in the transporting for hire of persons or property, or both, otherwise than over permanent rail tracks, on the public highways of Georgia as a common carrier.

This term (as well as the term "motor contract carrier") does not include the following:

—school vehicles transporting children and teachers to and from public and private schools;

—taxis, drays, trucks, buses and other vehicles operating within the corporate or police limits of cities and towns that regulate such vehicles;

—hotel passenger or baggage motor vehicles;

—nonprofit motor vehicles transporting no more than 15 elderly and handicapped passengers or employees under a corporate sponsored van pool program;

—granite trucks where transporting from quarry to finishing plant does not cross more than two counties;

—RFD carriers and star-route carriers carrying no more than nine passengers and U.S. mail, if no other motor carrier has a certificate to carry passengers along that route;

—trucks of railway companies operated within a 10-mile radius of a railroad freight or passenger depot;

—motor vehicles owned and operated by any subdivision of government;

—single source leasing from a leasing company to a private carrier;

—tow trucks or wreckers; and

—certain motor vehicles used in intercorporate hauling and the transportation of agricultural and dairy products and other commodities exempted by the Commission.

● *Rates*

Motor contract carriers and motor common carriers must obtain certificates of public convenience and necessity from the Public Service Commission and pay an application fee of

$75 if the applicant owns or operates less than six motor vehicles,

$150 if the applicant owns or operates six to 15 motor vehicles, and

$200 if the applicant owns or operates over 15 motor vehicles.

The fee for a transfer of certificate is $75 and the fee for intrastate emergency temporary authority is $50.

Any common or contract carrier engaged in interstate commerce or any common or contract carrier engaged in exempt commodity intrastate commerce must obtain a registration permit from the Commission upon payment of a $25 fee. The permit is valid as long as there are no changes in the carrier's operating authority. Every common or contract carrier operating pursuant to a certificate or permit must obtain an annual registration and identification stamp between October 1 and December 31. A fee of $5 is payable for the registration of each vehicle and the issuance of the stamp that is valid for a period beginning October 1 and continuing for 16 months. A fee of $8 is charged for each motor carrier operating as an emergency, temporary or trip-lease vehicle.

A road tax for the privilege of using the streets and highways of Georgia is imposed upon every motor carrier. The tax is equivalent to the motor fuel tax, and is calculated on the amount of motor fuel used by the motor carrier in its operations within Georgia. For details, see ¶ 2805, "Motor Fuel Taxes."

¶ 2808

Part IX—Miscellaneous Taxes

Reports: Reports must be filed with the Commission on or before the 10th day of each month.

¶ 2809 Environmental Taxes

Law: Sec. 12-8-40.1, Code (CCH GEORGIA TAX REPORTS ¶ 33-155, 33-160).

The tire tax is imposed by Sec. 12-8-40.1(h) of the Georgia Code.

● *Rate*

A fee of $1 per tire sold is imposed on the retail sale of all new replacement tires between July 1, 1992, and June 30, 2005. The fee is to be collected by retail dealers at the time each new replacement tire is sold to the ultimate consumer, and must be remitted quarterly to the Environmental Division of the Department of Natural Resources.

Georgia tire distributors who sell tires to retail dealers must collect the fees from dealers who do not possess valid scrap tire generator identification numbers. Also, the Environmental Protection Division of the Department of Natural Resources is authorized to contract with the Department of Revenue for collection of the fees.

● *Payments and reports*

Payments and reports: Distributors or retailers who collect, report, and pay the fees are allowed a deduction of 3% of the first $3,000, and ½ of 1% of the portion exceeding $3,000, of the total amount of all fees reported due, provided the amount due is not delinquent.

¶ 2810 Realty Transfer and Recording Taxes

Law: Secs. 48-6-1—10, 48-6-60—77, Code; Reg. Secs. 560-11-8-.01—.16 (CCH GEORGIA TAX REPORTS ¶ 25-125, 25-425, 33-310, 33-320, 33-330, 33-340, 33-360).

A real property transfer tax is imposed on deeds, instruments, and other writings by which lands, tenements, or other types of realty sold are granted, assigned, transferred, or otherwise conveyed or vested. A separate recording tax, discussed below, applies to long-term notes secured by real estate.

The real property transfer tax applies if the consideration or value of the property conveyed is more than $100, excluding the value of any lien or encumbrance that existed before the sale and was not removed by the sale.

Practitioner Comment: Transfers Among Affiliated Entities

Section 48-6-1 of the Georgia Code excludes from the calculation of taxable consideration the value of any lien or encumbrance existing prior to the sale and not removed by the sale of the real property. In order to reduce the amount of consideration upon which the tax is calculated, the transferor can grant a mortgage to an affiliated entity prior to the transfer, with the real property subsequently being transferred subject to the mortgage.

¶ 2810

The principal amount of the mortgage should be payable in less than three years in order to avoid the intangible recording tax imposed on long-term notes of greater than three years. The short-term mortgage between the affiliated entities must be negotiated at arms' length with a market interest rate, and interest must actually be paid by the mortgagor-entity to the mortgagee-entity.

Alston & Bird LLP

● *Exemptions*

The tax does not apply to the following:

—an instrument given to secure a debt;

—a deed of gift;

—any deed, instrument, or other writing to which the United States, the State of Georgia, any agency, board, commission, department, or political subdivision of the United States or Georgia, or any public authority or nonprofit public corporation is a party;

—a lease of realty or any estate, interest, or usufruct in realty;

—a transfer between husband and wife in a divorce case;

—an order for year's support awarding an interest in real property, made for a widow, minor or unborn child;

—a deed issued in lieu of foreclosure if it is made for a purchase money deed to secure debt that has been in existence, properly executed and recorded, for 12 months prior to the recording of the deed in lieu of foreclosure;

—a deed from the debtor to the first transferee at a foreclosure sale;

—the acquisition of property by donation, exchange, or prescription by the state;

—deeds of assent or distribution by an executor, administrator, guardian, trustee, or custodian;

—deeds or other instruments carrying out the exercise of a power of appointment;

—any instrument transferring real estate to or from a fiduciary; and

—any deed, instrument, or other writing that effects a division of real property among joint tenants or tenants in common if the transaction does not involve any consideration other than the division of the property.

Practitioner Comment: Transfer to Individuals

Georgia now provides an exemption for transfers to individuals (Sec. 48-6-2, Code). This has been interpreted to mean "natural persons" and therefore does not apply to any business entity.

Mary T. Benton, Esq., Alston & Bird

¶ 2810

Part IX—Miscellaneous Taxes   **329**

Practitioner Comment: Guaranty Agreements

Reg. Sec. 560-11-8-.14(4) exempts from the tax instruments that do not secure notes. The regulation specifically mentions guaranty agreements as an example of such an exempt instrument under Georgia law.

Alice M. Nolen, Esq., Alston & Bird

● *Rate*

The rate of tax is $1 for a value of $1,000 or less, plus 10¢ for every $100 (or fractional part of $100) over $1,000.

● *Payments and reports*

The tax is payable by the person who executes the deed or other instrument, or the person for whose use or benefit it is executed.

Payment is made to the clerk of the superior court in the county where the instrument is recorded (if recordation in more than one county is required, the tax is due only in connection with the first recording). The instrument offered for recording must be accompanied by a prescribed form showing the consideration or value of the realty interest. When the tax is paid, the clerk of the court will enter or attach a certification of payment. If payment is not made, no instrument subject to the tax will be recorded in any official state or county record.

The real estate transfer tax forms may be obtained from the Property Tax Unit, Real Estate Transfer Tax Section, Department of Revenue. The form currently in use is: Form PT-61 (Real Estate Transfer Tax Declaration).

● *Recording tax on long-term notes*

Every holder of a long-term note secured by real estate is required to record the note within 90 days in the county in which the secured real estate is located and pay a tax based on the face amount of the note. A note that matures within three years of the date of execution is considered to be short-term, and is not subject to this tax.

Rate of tax: The tax is imposed at the time of recording of the security instrument at the rate of $1.50 for each $500, or fraction thereof, of the amount of debt secured by the instrument. The maximum tax is $25,000 on a single note.

Practitioner Comment: Application of $25,000 Cap to Nonresident Lenders

Section 48-6-01 of the Georgia Code provides that the maximum amount of recording tax payable "with respect to any single note" shall be $25,000. Section 48-6-69(b) of the Code provides that if the subject real property is located both inside and outside of Georgia, the tax is "...that proportion of the tax which would otherwise by

¶ 2810

required under this article that the value of the real property within this state bears to the total value of all the real property within and outside this state ...." Nonresident lenders should be aware that Georgia regulation Sec. 560-11-8-.07(2)(b), arguably in conflict with the plain language of the statute, interprets Sec. 48-6-69(b) to require application of the $25,000 cap after the apportionment calculation. This will result in a much greater tax liability than if the maximum tax of $25,000 imposed under Article 3 of Chapter 6 were apportioned to the state.

Alston & Bird LLP

Refinancing: Intangible recording tax is not required to be paid on any part of the face amount of a new instrument securing a long-term note that represents a refinancing by the original lender and original borrower of unpaid principal of an existing instrument securing a long-term note secured by real estate still owned by the original lender, if the intangible recording tax was paid on the original instrument or the original instrument was exempt from the tax. Tax is due on any additional amount financed. The new instrument must contain a statement of what part of the face amount represents a refinancing of unpaid principal on the previous instrument. Likewise, two or more notes may be consolidated by the original borrower and lender into a single instrument securing a long-term note with a single deed to secure the debt. Tax would be due only on any additional amount financed.

Practitioner Comment: Aggregation of Multiple Notes

Notwithstanding the fact that Sec. 48-6-61 of the Georgia Code imposes the recording tax on an instrument securing a "long-term note," the statute has been interpreted to require application of the tax to instruments securing any series of obligations constituting a single debt. Therefore, an attempt to reduce the tax burden by breaking up a single debt into multiple notes, some of which will be due in less than three years, will likely not be successful as the value of the short-term notes will be aggregated with the long-term notes for purposes of calculating the total value of the single debt transaction. See 1960-61 Op. Attorney Gen. p. 519.

Alston & Bird LLP

¶ 2811 Utilities

Law: Secs. 46-2-10, 46-3-14, 46-3-170, 46-5-61, 46-5-101, 46-8-382, Code (CCH GEORGIA TAX REPORTS ¶ 80-005, 80-011, 80-012, 80-015, 80-052, 80-056, 80-100).

Most public utilities are subject to regulation by the Georgia Public Service Commission and are assessed a special fee to cover its operating costs. Utilities may be taxed when they engage in special occupations that are licensed. Some of the utilities must also submit miscellaneous reports and fees.

¶ 2811

Part IX—Miscellaneous Taxes

Utilities may be subject to county and/or municipal taxes or fees. "Special franchises" and utilities are subject to property taxes just as any other property located in the state. For details, see Chapter 26, "Property Taxes."

Municipalities may impose a franchise fee upon utilities in exchange for permission to use public ways with respect to maintenance of electric wires, poles, and other facilities. Further, a gross receipts tax may be imposed on utilities that would otherwise have been subject to a franchise fee of the same amount, but for the utility's lack of agreement to the terms of the franchise.

The Tennessee Valley Authority Act (16 U.S.C. § 831) does not contain any provision that would prevent the imposition of state and local taxes on any electric membership corporation granted a franchise by the State of Georgia, which purchases surplus power from the TVA (*North Georgia Electric Membership Corporation v. City of Calhoun* (Ga SCt 1994) 264 Ga 205; CCH Georgia TAX REPORTS ¶ 200-262).

● *Rate*

All public utilities regulated by the Public Service Commission are subject to a special annual fee, fixed by the State Revenue Commissioner upon each utility so that altogether a revenue of $1,050,000 per year is produced. The amount assessed against each utility is determined according to the value of its property as ascertained by the most recent state tax assessment.

The State Revenue Commissioner must notify each public service corporation or utility of the amount due by no later than April 1 annually, and the fee must be paid into the general fund by July 1 of each year.

A cooperative, nonprofit corporation organized to furnish telephone service in rural areas to the widest practicable number of users must pay an annual fee of $10, due by July 1, to the Secretary of State. A rural telephone cooperative is exempt from all other excise and income taxes.

If any utility defaults in paying the fee, the State Revenue Commissioner will proceed to collect in the same manner as franchise taxes are collected.

● *Payments and reports*

Every domestic and foreign corporation authorized to transact business in Georgia must file an annual report.

¶ 2812 Lodgings Taxes

Law: Secs. 48-13-51, 48-13-53, 48-13-53.1, 48-13-53.2, 48-13-53.6, 48-13-53.7, 48-13-58, Code (CCH GEORGIA TAX REPORTS ¶ 33-410 *et seq.*).

Counties and municipalities may levy and collect an excise tax upon rooms and accommodations furnished for value by a person or legal entity licensed or required to pay business or occupation taxes to that county or municipality for operating a hotel, motel, inn, lodge, campground, tourist camp, tourist cabin, or any other place where rooms, lodgings, or accommodations are furnished. The tax is the legal obligation or debt of the person or entity providing the accommodations, which is responsible for collecting the tax from the guest and remitting it to the government. The amount of the tax remitted is credited against the tax obligation of the innkeeper. The guest is liable for the tax to the person or entity providing the accommodations.

At no time may a county or municipality levy more than one local excise tax. Any action by a locality to impose or change the rate of the local excise tax authorized will become effective on the first day of the second month following its adoption.

● *Exemptions*

The local excise tax on rooms and lodgings is not levied upon the fees or charges for any rooms, lodgings, or accommodations furnished

—for those who certify that they are being accommodated as a result of the destruction of their home or residence by fire or other casualty,

—for continuous occupancy after the first 10 days of continuous occupancy,

—for use as meeting rooms and other such facilities, rooms, lodgings, and accommodations provided without charge, or

—for a period of one or more days for use by Georgia state or local government officials or employees when traveling on official business.

● *Rates of tax*

In general, the excise tax on rooms, lodgings, and accommodations may be imposed at a rate not to exceed 3%. However, local governing bodies may elect to impose the tax at higher rates up to 8% if revenues are allocated for certain purposes, such as funding a trade and convention center.

● *Returns and payments*

Lodgings tax returns and payments for a calendar month are generally due by the 20th day of the next following month and any tax not paid by that date is delinquent after that date. Assessments of lodgings tax by local taxing authorities must comply with the general statute of limitations for other Georgia taxes.

If an innkeeper's estimated lodgings tax liability for any taxable period exceeds $2,500 and the innkeeper's tax liability exceeded $2,500 per month for three consecutive months or more during the previous fiscal year, the innkeeper must pay estimated tax. The estimated tax due is equal to 50% of the "estimated tax liability," defined as an innkeeper's lodgings tax liability that is adjusted to account for any subsequent change in the tax rate or any substantial change in circumstances due to damage of the premises and is based on the innkeeper's average monthly payments for the last fiscal year. Estimated tax must be paid on the 20th day of the taxable period.

Innkeepers liable for lodgings tax, interest, or penalties must make a final return and payment within 15 days after the date of selling or quitting their business. Furthermore, an innkeeper's successors or assigns are required to withhold a sufficient amount of the purchase money to cover the innkeeper's liability until the innkeeper produces evidence from the local taxing authority that the tax, interest, or penalties are paid or not due. If the purchaser of a business fails to withhold an amount sufficient to cover the seller's tax

¶ 2812

Part IX—Miscellaneous Taxes

liability, the purchaser will be personally liable for paying the tax, interest, and penalty due.

Interest and penalties: Generally, the penalty for failure to file a lodgings tax return or pay the tax is 5% of the tax due or $5, whichever is greater, for the first 30 days and an additional 5% or $5, whichever is greater, for each additional 30 days. The penalty may not exceed 25% of the tax due or $25, whichever is greater.

¶ 2812

PART X

ADMINISTRATION AND PROCEDURE

CHAPTER 29

GEORGIA ADMINISTRATION AND PROCEDURE

¶ 2901	Authority of Department of Revenue
¶ 2902	Returns and Payments
¶ 2903	Recordkeeping Requirements; Confidentiality

¶ 2901 Authority of Department of Revenue

Law: Sec. 48-2-1, 48-2-12, Code (CCH GEORGIA TAX REPORTS ¶ 89-056, 89-060).

The Department of Revenue, headed by the Revenue Commissioner, administers all statewide taxes, except for corporate organization fees and insurance taxes. The Revenue Commissioner has sole rulemaking powers.

The Department administers and collects taxes on alcoholic beverages, bank gross receipts, corporate income, corporate net worth, estates, gasoline and other motor fuels, general property tax, individual income, motor vehicle registration fees, realty transfers, sales and use, and tobacco products.

Organization of DOR: For ease of administration and enforcement of the various tax types assigned to the Department, the Department is organized into the following divisions: Administrative, Alcohol and Tobacco, Compliance, Income Tax, Information Systems, Internal Administrative, Motor Vehicle, Property Tax, Sales and Use Tax, and Taxpayer Accounting.

The headquarters address is:

Georgia Department of Revenue
1800 Century Center Blvd. NE
Atlanta, GA 30345-3205

See Chapter 32 for additional contact information.

● *Administration of other taxes*

In addition to the Department of Revenue, the following administrative bodies administer and collect taxes in Georgia:

Secretary of State: The Secretary of State administers and collects corporate organization and qualification fees and charter renewal fees.

Insurance Commissioner: The Insurance Commissioner administers and collects the insurance companies premiums tax and insurance company license fees.

¶ 2901

Local officials: Local taxing officers administer and collect local property taxes. The Department of Revenue also has collection authority for state taxes.

¶ 2902 Returns and Payments

Law: Sec. 48-2-32, 48-2-39, Code; Reg. Sec. 560-3-2-.26, 560-12-1-.22, 560-12-1-.26 (CCH GEORGIA TAX REPORTS ¶ 89-102, 89-106, 89-108, 89-110, 89-112).

Georgia tax reporting and payment requirements vary according to the tax type. The governing body for overseeing tax collection and payment is the Department of Revenue.

● *Returns, payments, and due dates*

Specific information about forms, filing, and payment requirements is discussed under each tax.

● *Payment methods*

Taxes may be paid by check or money order. If a check is not honored, the taxpayer will be penalized 2% of the amount of the check, or the lesser of $15 or the face amount of the check if the check was less than $750.

Electronic filing: Personal income taxpayers who file their return electronically or by telephone (telefiling) must complete the payment voucher (Form 525-TV) and mail the voucher, together with a check or money order for any tax due, to the Department of Revenue. Electronic filing of personal income tax returns is discussed at ¶ 601.

● *Electronic funds transfer*

Taxpayers or employers with corporate estimated income tax, individual estimated income tax, withholding tax, sales and use tax, or motor fuel distributor tax liabilities in excess of $10,000 for the year must remit taxes using electronic funds transfer. The requirement for payment by EFT also applies to every employer whose Georgia personal income tax withheld or required to be withheld exceeds $50,000 for the 12-month period that ended the preceding June 30.

Taxpayers required to make payment by EFT may use either the automated clearing house (ACH) debit method or (with approval of the Department of Revenue) the ACH credit method. Taxpayers wishing to pay voluntarily by EFT may, upon approval, use the ACH debit method. In emergency situations, wire transfer through the Federal Reserve System may be permitted on a limited basis, as may certain transfers to a State of Georgia bank account, or a certified or cashier's check delivered to the Commissioner of Revenue.

● *Rounding to whole dollar amounts*

Georgia statutes and regulations are silent on whole-dollar reporting. However, because Georgia requires individual taxpayers to enter the adjusted gross income amount shown on federal Form 1040, federal Form 1040A, or federal Form 1040EZ, the whole dollar reporting amount for federal tax

Part X—Administration and Procedure

purposes is adopted by implication in Georgia for personal income tax purposes (Instructions to Individual Income Tax Form 500).

Whole dollar reporting is expressly adopted for corporate income tax on Form 600 (Instructions to Corporate Income Tax Form 600).

Under whole dollar reporting, cents may be rounded off to the nearest whole dollar by eliminating any amount less than 50¢ and increasing any amount from 50¢ through 99¢ to the next dollar.

● *Mailing rules and legal holidays*

Payments and returns are timely if they are postmarked by the due date, or received for delivery by FedEx, UPS, or another delivery service (*Letter from the Operations Manager, Income Tax Division,* April 16, 2001).

If a filing due date or a payment due date falls on a Saturday, Sunday, or legal holiday, the filing of the return, or other document, or the payment of the tax is deemed timely if postmarked by the next business day.

¶ 2903 Recordkeeping Requirements; Confidentiality

Law: Sec. 48-2-15, 48-3-29, 48-7-60, 48-7-111, 48-8-52, 48-9-8, 48-15-10, Code; Reg. Sec. 560-1-1-.19, 560-12-1-.23 (CCH GEORGIA TAX REPORTS ¶ 89-136, 89-142).

Georgia has provisions on record maintenance, as follows:

● *Corporate income tax*

Corporations must keep income tax records for three years and have those records readily available for inspection by the Revenue Commissioner. The types of records that must be kept, either in hard copy or electronically, include, but are not limited to accurate copies of all income records (*i.e.,* invoices, bills of lading, purchase orders, and exemptions).

● *Personal income tax*

Employers must keep records of all taxes withheld, as well as the compensation, including noncash forms of compensation, paid to their employees for a period of four years.

CCH Tip: Individual Recordkeeping

There are no formal recordkeeping requirements for individuals with regard to their personal income tax. However, the Department of Revenue may audit a taxpayer's personal income tax return for three years after it is filed. Accordingly, individuals keep all pertinent records related to their tax returns for at least three years.

¶ 2903

- *Sales and use taxes*

Dealers must keep adequate records for three years and make them available for examination by the Commissioner. A dealer may be required to appear before the Commissioner and produce the books, records, and papers of the business. The types of records that must be kept, either in hard copy or electronically, include, but are not limited to:

—suitable records of sales and purchases, and other books of account necessary to determine the amount of tax due;

—merchandise purchased (*i.e.*, bills of lading, invoices, and purchase orders);

—daily records of all cash and credit sales;

—records of all tangible property used in the conduct of the business;

—inventory of stock on hand;

—a record of all deductions and exemptions claimed in filing sales or use tax returns, including exemption and resale certificates; and

—a record of all tangible personal property used or consumed in the conduct of the business.

Additional information on recordkeeping requirements for sales and use tax is at ¶ 2306.

- *Motor fuels*

Every person selling motor fuel at retail must maintain records of the gallons received and sold for a period of three years. Licensed motor fuel distributors and aviation gasoline dealers must keep records of all motor fuel received, sold, delivered, or used within Georgia and all motor fuel exported from Georgia for a period of three years. Any other person who receives motor fuel for sale or distribution in Georgia is also required to keep records of motor fuel received, including all invoices, bills of lading, and any other records setting forth the amount of fuel received or sold for a period of three years.

- *Electronic recordkeeping and retention*

Taxpayers required to keep electronic records must maintain their records according to regulatory standards. These standards differ, depending upon whether the taxpayer maintains its electronic records in machine-sensible format or by using electronic data interchange.

- *Confidentiality*

Information obtained by the Commissioner or any of his or her agents is confidential and privileged. Information related to the amount of income earned in a tax year disclosed in any report or return may not be released by the Department unless a court order so directs. However, effective May 13, 2004, confidential taxpayer information or records may be disclosed to, or discussed, with another party if the taxpayer has granted express written authorization to the Georgia Commissioner of Revenue or an officer or employee of the Department of Revenue (Act 501 (H.B. 1461), Laws 2004).

¶ 2903

Part X—Administration and Procedure

An exception to the confidentiality statutes exists for the use of tax information in proceedings in which the particular taxpayer's liability is at issue. See ¶ 3001 with regard to the Commissioner's authority to share audit information.

The Commissioner of Revenue may publish in the media or on the Internet any or all information related to executions issued for the collection of any tax, fee, license, penalty, interest, or collection costs due Georgia if the amounts posted are recorded on the public records of any county.

See ¶ 3101 for information on the taxpayers' rights.

Practitioner Comment: Information Sharing

Act 501 (H.B. 1461), Laws 2004, added a provision in O.C.G.A. § 48-2-15.1 that allows the Department of Revenue to disclose confidential taxpayer information to another party if the taxpayer consents to such disclosure. The Department has, for example, included in settlement agreements a provision that allows the Department to disclose the terms of the settlement to other taxpayers.

Timothy J. Peaden, Esq., Alston & Bird

ADMINISTRATION AND PROCEDURE

CHAPTER 30

AUDITS, ASSESSMENT, AND COLLECTION OF TAX

¶ 3001 Audits and Assessments
¶ 3002 Collection of Tax
¶ 3003 Penalties and Interest

¶ 3001 Audits and Assessments

Law: Secs. 48-2-16, 48-2-35(b), 48-2-46, 48-2-49, 48-7-2, 48-7-82, 48-8-52, 48-8-104, 48-8-109, 48-9-12, 48-9-19, 50-13-14, Code; Reg. Sec. 560-7-2-.07, 560-7-2-.08, 560-12-1-.01 (CCH Georgia Tax Reports ¶ 89-132—89-148, 89-230).

The Commissioner may examine the books, records, inventories, or business of any taxpayer for the purpose of determining liability for taxes collected directly by the Commissioner. The Compliance Division of the Department of Revenue is responsible for performing tax audits.

> *Practitioner Comment: Department's Power to Collect Information*
>
> Although the Department has broad investigative powers, they are not unlimited. Any information requested by the Department must be relevant to any potential tax liability. In addition, tax advice generally should be privileged, either under the common-law "attorney-client" privilege or the statutory "accountant-client" privilege.
>
> *Timothy J. Peaden, Esq., Alston & Bird LLP*

Information sharing: Agents of the Department of Revenue may share information contained in tax returns, reports, and related schedules and documents filed in Georgia, or contained in the report of an audit or investigation made with respect to a Georgia tax return or report, with any other state, the District of Columbia, the United States, or any U.S. territory that grants reciprocal information sharing privileges to Georgia. The information contained in income tax returns, reports, related schedules, and documents is confidential and remains confidential if the Commissioner shares information contained in the return with another jurisdiction pursuant to a reciprocal information sharing agreement.

Georgia is an associate member of the Multistate Tax Compact. However, Georgia does not participate with respect to the article on interstate audits (*Telephone conversation with Department of Revenue,* February 7, 2001).

● *Tax-specific audit provisions*

Income tax: The Office Audit section under the Chief of Office Operations (part of the Compliance Division) performs an office audit on all individual, fiduciary, and partnership tax returns, and will write assessments for additional taxes on any returns containing errors that do not require a field audit. The accounting section processes the returns audited by the office audit section.

The Field Operations office is comprised of two sections: the individual field audit section; and the corporations section. The individual field audit section receives returns from the office audit section containing errors that require a field audit. The section visits taxpayers to examine taxpayer auditing books, records, or any other evidence required to determine the correct tax liability, and prepares a proposed assessment showing any changes with explanations.

The corporations section consists of three subsections: domestic; foreign; and *Fieri Facias* (fi fa) collection. The domestic section reviews all Georgia corporate income tax returns and assigns returns requiring a field audit to an auditor who can inspect the corporation's books and records on site. The foreign section performs the same functions for out-of-state corporations with Georgia corporate income tax liability as the domestic section performs for Georgia corporations. The fi fa collection subsection receives and records all past-due income tax accounts, and contacts delinquent taxpayers and those owing past-due taxes. The fi fa collection subsection can issue and record Writs of *Fieri Facias* and use levies and garnishments to enforce collection.

Sales and use taxes: The Director of the Sales and Use Tax Unit is immediately responsible to the Revenue Commissioner for the administration of the sales and use taxes. Dealers must keep adequate records of taxable transactions for a period of three years, and the Director or any designated officer or employee may examine the taxpayer's books and records and conduct investigations to determine the correct tax liability.

The Commissioner administers and collects local sales and use taxes in the same manner and subject to the same provisions, procedures, and penalties as provided for state sales and use taxes. Local governments are not authorized to conduct sales and use tax audits.

CCH Tip: Audit Methodology

Although there is no statutory provision for the use of block sampling in sales and use tax audits, the Department of Revenue will use block sampling with the taxpayer's permission. The number of sample months used will vary based on the size and type of business of the taxpayer. In addition, the Department has a small staff of computer audit specialists who, at the election of the taxpayer, can conduct a stratified random sample audit using ACL software. *Telephone conversation with Clark Ramirez, Audit Pro-*

Part X—Administration and Procedure

gram Manager, Department of Revenue, Compliance Division, January, 2001.

Taxpayers disputing an assessment resulting from an audit may request a conference with the Regional Office Manager. Any decision made by the Regional Office Manager is subject to review by the Director.

Motor fuels tax: The Commissioner may enter into cooperative agreements with other states for either a cooperative audit of interstate motor fuel users' records or the exchange of information contained in those records. Under those agreements, officers and employees of other states are authorized agents of Georgia when auditing returns and reports, and those audits or parts of audits have the same effect as similar audits made by Georgia. The Commissioner may utilize the audit findings received from another state as the basis upon which to propose assessments of gasoline or other motor fuel taxes against a motor carrier as though the audit was actually conducted by the Commissioner.

● *Managed audits; voluntary disclosure*

Georgia does not have any provisions for managed audits. A managed audit is a variation of the traditional field audit in which the Department of Revenue provides the audit planning, direction, and scope, and the taxpayer provides the records retrieval and internal accounting expertise.

Voluntary disclosure program: Georgia has a voluntary disclosure program administered through the Compliance Division. Taxpayers who were contacted by the Department prior to initiating the disclosure process are not eligible. For all other taxpayers, the Department will determine taxpayer eligibility on a case-by-case basis.

The following taxpayer benefits apply to participants in the voluntary disclosure program:

—if sufficient nexus exists for sales and use tax or corporate and net worth tax, the Department will generally agree to limit prior period exposure to the lesser of three years or the date that nexus was established;

—if the taxpayer collected sales tax from customers and did not remit the tax to the Department, the prior period exposure will be extended to include all liabilities of this type;

—the Department will waive all penalties of taxpayers eligible and participating in the voluntary disclosure program, provided the tax and interest due is paid; and

—if the existence of nexus or tax liability is questionable, the Department may agree to prospective filing or to a shorter prior period exposure.

● *Limitations period for assessments*

The Department of Revenue may not assess a tax deficiency for any tax type unless it mails notice to the taxpayer within three years from the date that the taxpayer filed its return. An assessment may be made at any time in

¶ 3001

the case of a false or fraudulent return, where there is intent to evade the tax, or in the case of the failure to file a return.

Practitioner Comment: Limitations Period When Failure to File a Return

Despite the statutory language that indicates an unlimited period for assessment if a taxpayer fails to file a return, the Georgia Supreme Court has indicated that there is nonetheless a seven-year period for the Department to assess taxes. See, e.g., *Suttles v. Dickey*, 192 Ga. 382, 15 S.E.2d 445 (1941). In making this determination, the Court relied upon the seven-year limitation period for enforcing a tax execution in Sec. 48-3-21, Code.

Timothy J. Peaden, Esq., Alston & Bird LLP

Income tax: A special longer assessment limitation period applies to corporate and personal income tax if the taxpayer omits an amount in excess of 25% of gross income less expenses, or if the taxpayer wrongfully omits an amount distributed in liquidation of a corporation. In such cases, the tax may be assessed or a court proceeding may commence without assessment at any time within six years of the date that the return was filed.

- **Conferences**

Taxpayers and/or their legal representatives may request a conference with a tax conferee to determine if additional information or facts are necessary to reach a legal and equitable disposition of the case.

- **Appeal**

There are no specific provisions to contest audit findings. A taxpayer may contest any proposed assessment by filing with the Commissioner a written protest within 30 days from the date of the notice of assessment. If a different time limit is specified by the notice, the protest must be filed within that time limit. The filing of a written protest, a petition for redetermination of a deficiency, or a written request by the taxpayer for additional time for filing such a petition tolls the period of limitations for making an assessment until the petition is denied by the Commissioner or the request is withdrawn in writing by the taxpayer.

The taxpayer has the right to demand a hearing on any matter involving tax liability. The hearing is subject to the Administrative Procedure Act.

After review of all the information presented by the taxpayer at the hearing, the Commissioner must make a final assessment of the tax and notify the taxpayer of the Commissioner's decision. A taxpayer may appeal that decision to the superior court.

For information on judicial appeals, see ¶ 3101.

¶ 3001

Part X—Administration and Procedure

Practitioner Comment: Department Review of a Protest

If a taxpayer files a written "protest" of a proposed assessment, the matter is referred to the division within the Department responsible for that particular tax (e.g., Income Tax, Sales and Use Tax). Within each division, there are one or more individuals who have the title of "Conferee" and are responsible for considering the protest and determining whether to sustain or reject the proposed assessment.

Timothy J. Peaden, Esq., Alston & Bird LLP

¶ 3002 Collection of Tax

Law: Secs. 18-3-1, 48-2-9, 48-2-18.1, 48-2-49, 48-2-45, 48-2-48, 48-2-51, 48-2-54.1, 48-2-55, 48-2-60, 48-2-80, 48-3-1, 48-3-3, 48-3-3.1, 48-3-19, 48-3-29, 48-5-513, 48-7-162—48-7-164, 48-8-57, Code (CCH GEORGIA TAX REPORTS ¶ 89-162—89-186).

In seeking to collect any tax due, the Department of Revenue must first assess the tax against the taxpayer and provide the taxpayer with notice (¶ 3001). If the tax is not timely paid, it becomes delinquent. The taxpayer may petition for a redetermination after a notice of deficiency is received.

● *Methods of collection*

The Department of Revenue has the following methods of collection available:

Jeopardy assessment: If the Revenue Commissioner ascertains that the return of any taxpayer contains mistaken, false, or fraudulent statements, or that it contains statements or omissions of data otherwise incorrect or misleading, thereby causing the improper or inadequate assessment of taxes, the Commissioner may determine and fix the amount of the taxes due by the taxpayer.

The Commissioner may declare the taxable period of a taxpayer terminated, and demand immediate payment of the tax due, under the following circumstances:

—the taxpayer gives evidence of the taxpayer's intention to leave the state or to remove the taxpayer's property from the state;

—the taxpayer conceals himself or herself, or his or her property;

—the taxpayer discontinues its business; or

—the taxpayer does any other act tending to prejudice or render wholly or partly ineffective any proceedings to compute, assess, or collect any state tax.

Executions for the collection of tax: The Revenue Commissioner may issue a writ of execution for the collection of any tax due the State. A writ of execution (*fieri facias*) is a formal process issued by a court that evidences the debt of the taxpayer and commands the sheriff to take the taxpayer's property in satisfaction of the tax liability. The execution must be directed to all Georgia sheriffs, commanding them to levy upon the goods, chattels, lands, and tenements of the taxpayer. See also ¶ 3001.

The county tax collector or the Commissioner may issue an execution for nonpayment of tax at any time after 30 days have elapsed since the tax official has notified, in writing, the taxpayer of the fact that the taxes have not been paid and, unless paid, an execution will be issued. Notices are not required for taxes due on personal property, and executions may be issued on the day after taxes are due.

Sale of an execution: Third parties may pay deficient taxes after an execution is issued. The execution will be transferred to the third party who now stands in the position of the tax collector and has the right to seek reimbursement from the delinquent taxpayer, and holds a lien on the taxpayer's property. The transferred execution must be recorded within 30 days on the general execution docket of the county in which the execution was issued, and in the county in which the delinquent taxpayer resides. If the third-party payer to whom the execution was transferred fails to record the transfer, the third party loses its lien upon the property.

Levy and sale of property: When a taxpayer refuses or neglects to pay any taxes, fees, licenses, penalties, interest, or collection costs due the state, the Revenue Commissioner may levy upon all property and rights to property belonging to the taxpayer, other than exempt property. The levy covers the amount due, interest on that amount, any penalty for nonpayment, and all other fees, costs, and levy expenses.

The Commissioner may conduct judicial sales in the manner provided by law for sales by sheriffs and constables.

Offsets: The collection of debts owed the state may be accomplished by setting off the debts against any tax refunds. If the Department determines that a taxpayer is owed a refund of at least $25, and the taxpayer owes a debt to the state, the Department must apply the refund against the debt owed. If the amount of the taxpayer's refund is greater than the taxpayer's debt, the Department will refund the excess within a reasonable period of time.

Prior to transferring a refund to satisfy a taxpayer's debt, the Department must notify the taxpayer that the refund is being applied as an offset against another debt owed the state. The taxpayer has a right to a hearing to contest the offset. To request a hearing, the taxpayer must apply in writing for a hearing with the claimant agency named in the notice within 30 days of the date that the notice of offset was mailed.

Attachment: The Commissioner may attach the property of a delinquent taxpayer when he or she:

—resides outside the state;

—moves or is about to move his or her domicile outside the state;

—absconds;

—conceals himself or herself;

—resists legal arrest;

—moves his or her property beyond the limits of the state; or

Part X—Administration and Procedure   347

—liquidates his or her property in an effort to avoid payment of the tax.

Garnishment: When a tax collector or tax commissioner can find no property of the delinquent taxpayer upon which to levy a tax execution, the revenue official must first make an entry to that effect on the execution. Then, the collector or commissioner can issue a garnishment summons against any person the revenue official believes to be indebted to the delinquent taxpayer or who has property, money, or effects belonging to the taxpayer.

Revocation of corporate charter: The Commissioner may revoke a Georgia corporation's charter, or a foreign corporation's permission to transact business within Georgia, if the corporation fails to file a return by the due date or pay any tax owed.

The Commissioner of Revenue may publish, in the media or on the Internet, any or all information related to executions issued for the collection of any tax, fee, license, penalty, interest, or collection costs due Georgia if the amounts posted are recorded on the public records of any county (Sec. 48-3-29, Code, CCH GEORGIA TAX REPORTS ¶ 93-885a). The Commissioner of Revenue may also charge to the taxpayer's account any costs or fees that are charged to the Commissioner by the United States Treasury Financial Management System for offsetting federal refund claims against any Georgia tax liability that the Commissioner is responsible for collecting (Sec. 48-2-54.1, Code, CCH GEORGIA TAX REPORTS ¶ 93-762a).

● *Requirement to post bond or security*

The Revenue Commissioner can require a taxpayer to file a bond or post security if the taxpayer shows an intention to do any of the following:

—leave the state;

—remove property from the state;

—conceal property;

—discontinue business; or

—perform any other action limiting the state's ability to collect taxes.

If the Commissioner finds, after fair notice and a hearing, that a dealer is chronically delinquent or in default of remitting sales and use taxes, the dealer may be required to file a bond with a Georgia-licensed surety or to post securities in an amount between $1,000 and $10,000, as determined by the Commissioner. After serving notice by mail or in person, the Commissioner may sell any security to recover delinquent taxes plus interest and penalties.

● *Civil action*

If a taxpayer is delinquent in the payment of tax, the Revenue Commissioner may file a suit for collection. The Georgia Attorney General can assist the Commissioner in any judicial proceeding for the collection of tax.

¶ 3002

● *Reciprocal enforcement*

Georgia courts recognize and enforce tax liabilities lawfully imposed by other states that extend like comity to Georgia.

● *Agreements in compromise of tax*

The Revenue Commissioner, or a designee, can settle and compromise proposed tax assessments, final tax assessments, and tax *fieri facias* (writs of execution), as well as develop procedures for the acceptance or rejection of offers in compromise of tax due. Such a settlement, compromise, or other offer must contain a verified statement that the offer is, in the opinion of the Attorney General, in the best interest of the state.

● *Intergovernmental tax collection agreements*

There are a number of agreements among governmental agencies to provide for assistance in tax collection, both between the Internal Revenue Service and the states and among the states themselves.

Agreement with IRS Abusive Tax Avoidance Transactions (ATAT) Memorandum of Understanding: The Small Business/Self-Employed Division of the Internal Revenue Service signed ATAT Memorandums of Understanding with 40 states, including Georgia, and the District of Columbia on September 16, 2003, which provide for information-sharing on abusive tax avoidance transactions (*Memorandum of Understanding,* Internal Revenue Service). The Memorandum authorizes the IRS and Georgia to:

—exchange tax returns and return information,

—share audit results from ATAT participant cases,

—exchange information on identified types of ATAT schemes, and

—share audit technique guides.

The IRS will provide states with a list of participants in a particular ATAT scheme on a semi-annual basis on July 31 and January 31. The IRS generally refers to an abusive tax shelter arrangement as the promise of tax benefits with no meaningful change in the taxpayer's control over or benefit from the taxpayer's income or assets.

¶ 3003 Penalties and Interest

Law: Secs. 33-5-33, 48-2-35, 48-2-38, 48-2-40, 48-2-60, 48-5-148, 48-5-150, 48-5-242, 48-5-493, 48-5-7.5, 48-7-2—48-7-5, 48-7-57, 48-7-57.1, 48-7-61, 48-7-81, 48-7-86, 48-7-112, 48-7-120, 48-7-121, 48-8-7, 48-8-9, 48-8-10, 48-8-37, 48-8-54, 48-8-66, 48-9-16, 48-9-45(c), Code (CCH GEORGIA TAX REPORTS ¶ 89-202—89-210).

Georgia has separate provisions on interest and penalties for various tax types, instead of general administrative provisions for all taxes. However, individuals who default on any federal, state, or local tax, including Georgia personal income tax and property tax, are ineligible to hold public office (Constitutional Amendment 1; H.R. 126, Laws 2002). To be ineligible for office, the officeholder or candidate will have to be finally adjudicated to owe the tax. The impediment to office is removed when the tax is paid, or a payment plan begun.

¶ 3003

Part X—Administration and Procedure   349

● *Civil penalties—income taxes*

Late returns or payment: A penalty is assessed for the failure to file a timely corporate or personal income tax return if the failure is not due to a reasonable cause. The penalty is 5% of the tax required to be shown on the return for each month or fractional part of the month during which the violation continues. The penalty in the aggregate may not exceed 25% of the tax. For purposes of fixing the penalty, the tax required to be shown is reduced by any part of the tax that was paid on or before the due date, and by any credits against tax claimed on the return.

If a copy of an approved federal income tax extension of time is filed with the state income tax return, and the state return is filed within the period specified in the federal extension of time, no penalty due to lateness is incurred, and no state application for extension need be filed.

Filing frivolous return: In addition to any other penalties that may be imposed, a $1000 penalty is assessed against any person or entity filing what purports to be a return, but which either does not contain information on which the substantial correctness of the amount of tax shown to be due may be judged, or contains information that on its face indicates that the amount of tax shown to be due is substantially incorrect. This additional penalty applies only if:

   (1) the conditions discussed had been due to the taxpayer's taking a frivolous position, or

   (2) the return contains information demonstrating a desire to delay or impede the administration of the income tax laws.

Failure to pay tax shown on return: A penalty is assessed if the amount shown as tax on a return is not paid by the due date. The penalty is an additional 0.5% for each month that the taxpayer fails to pay the tax liability. The amount of tax shown on the return is reduced, for the purpose of computing the addition for any month, by the amount of any part of the tax that is paid on or before the beginning of the month and by the amount of any credit against the tax that is claimed on the return.

Underpayment of tax: Underpayment of tax due to a negligent or intentional disregard of rules and regulations, but without intent to defraud, is subject to a penalty of 5% of the underpayment.

Dishonored check: A 2% penalty is imposed on a taxpayer whose check or money order to the Commissioner for $1,250 or more is not honored when presented to the issuer for payment. If a check or money order is less than $1,250, the penalty is $25.

Fraud: If any part of an underpayment of tax required to be shown on a return is due to fraud, an amount equal to 50% of the underpayment is added to the tax. This amount is in lieu of the 5% penalty normally assessed for an underpayment. If the 50% penalty is assessed for an underpayment of tax that must be shown on a return, neither the penalty for failure to file a return, nor the penalty for failure to pay the tax shown on the return is assessed, with respect to the same underpayment.

False independent contractor claim: Effective July 1, 2004, it is unlawful for any person to knowingly coerce, induce, or threaten an individual to falsely

¶ 3003

declare himself or herself an independent contractor, or to falsely claim that an individual employed by that person is an independent contractor, in order to avoid or evade the withholding or payment of any Georgia tax. In addition to any other authorized penalties, for a first offense, a person who violates this provision in connection with a contract with the state or any political subdivision or authority of the state is subject to a fine equal to the total amount of the tax owed. For a second offense, the person is subject to a fine equal to double the amount of tax owed. For third and subsequent offenses, the applicable fine is equal to four times the amount of tax owed. A violation in connection with a contract constitutes one offense, regardless of the number of individuals improperly coerced or falsely claimed to be independent contractors. These provisions are repealed July 1, 2014. (Act 525 (S.B. 491), Laws 2004.)

Underpayment of estimated tax: A penalty is assessed for the underpayment of estimated tax in an amount equal to 9% of the underpayment, for the period of the underpayment. The period of the underpayment runs from the date that the installment was required to be paid to the earlier of (1) the 15th day of the fourth month following the close of the taxable year or (2) with respect to any portion of the underpayment, the date on which the portion is paid. A payment of estimated tax on the 15th day of the first month of the succeeding taxable year is considered a payment of any previous underpayment only to the extent that the payment exceeds the amount of the installment then due.

Effective for taxable years commencing on January 1, 2003, the 9% annual penalty on underpaid Georgia estimated income tax is applied to the lesser of the excess of: (1) the amount of the installment required to be paid if the estimated tax were equal to 70%, or 66 2/3% for certain farmers and fishermen, of the tax shown on the return for the taxable year, or the tax for the year if no return was filed; or (2) the amount of the installment required to be paid if the estimated tax were equal to 100% of the tax shown on the return for the preceding taxable year, as long as the preceding taxable year was 12 months and a tax return was filed; over (3) any amount of the installment paid on or before the last date prescribed for payment.

● *Civil penalties—property tax*

Penalty provisions for the failure to return or pay property tax are discussed at ¶ 2608.

● *Civil penalties—Motor fuel tax*

Distributors who fail to pay the motor fuel tax, or any part due, are subject to a penalty of 10% of the amount of unpaid taxes due. A penalty of $50 is imposed on any person who fails to file a required motor fuel tax report for each occurrence.

● *Civil penalties—sales and use taxes*

Filing a false or fraudulent return: A penalty of 50% of the tax due is assessed for filing a false or fraudulent return.

¶ 3003

Part X—Administration and Procedure **351**

Failure to file a return: A penalty of 5% of the tax due or $5, whichever is greater, is imposed on each 30-day period that a dealer fails to file a return, up to a maximum penalty of 25% or $25, whichever is greater.

● *Criminal penalties—income taxes*

The following criminal penalty provisions apply to corporate and personal income taxes:

—failing to furnish information, file a return, keep or exhibit records, or pay tax, is a misdemeanor;

—assisting in filing false income tax returns is a misdemeanor, subject to a fine up to $1,000, six months imprisonment, or both;

—advising disregard of income tax regulations is a misdemeanor, subject to a fine between $100 and $500, six months imprisonment, or both;

—divulging confidential income tax information is a misdemeanor, subject to the immediate removal from office and prohibition from holding public office for five years, if the offender is a Georgia officer or employee; and

—attempting to evade or defeat tax in excess of $3,000 is a felony, subject to a $100,000 fine for individuals and a $500,000 fine for corporations, imprisonment for one to five years, or both.

● *Criminal penalties—property tax*

A person who transports or moves a mobile home without a decal, which evidences possession of a mobile home location permit, is guilty of a misdemeanor subject to a fine between $200 and $1,000, 12 months imprisonment, or both.

● *Criminal penalties—sales and use taxes*

A dealer's failure to collect sales and use taxes is a misdemeanor punishable by a fine of not more than $100, up to three months imprisonment, or both.

The filing of a false or fraudulent dealer's return with the intent to evade tax is a misdemeanor punishable by a fine between $100 and $300, imprisonment between 30 days and three months, or both.

A dealer's failure to file a required return is a misdemeanor.

A dealer, wholesale dealer, or jobber who fails to keep records or open his or her records for inspection is guilty of a misdemeanor.

Any person advertising or representing to the public that sales tax will be absorbed or that the purchaser is relieved from payment of the tax is guilty of a misdemeanor punishable by a fine between $25 and $250, up to three months' imprisonment, or both.

● *Interest*

Interest on unpaid corporate and personal income taxes, property tax, estate tax, motor carriers' road tax, and sales and use taxes is imposed at a rate of 1% per month, beginning with the due date of the tax.

¶ 3003

For unpaid property tax, as a general rule, interest is assessed from December 20 until the time of payment. However, certain counties can charge interest from an earlier date.

Interest on unpaid tax imposed on insurance companies for independently procured coverage is compounded annually at the rate of 1%.

The rate of interest on refunds of any erroneously or illegally assessed and collected Georgia taxes or fees is 1% per month from the date of payment of the tax or fee to the Revenue Commissioner.

Overpayments: The 1% per month rate of interest also applies to:

—amounts refunded as overpayments when an employee's credit for personal income tax withheld, together with other credits allowed by law, is in excess of the employee's personal income tax liability for the year, and

—amounts refunded as overpayments when a taxpayer's credit for estimated personal income tax paid, together with other credits allowed by law, is in excess of the taxpayer's tax liability for the year.

However, the amounts refunded as overpayments bear interest only after 90 days from the later of the filing date of the final return showing the overpayment or the due date of the final return.

● *Abatement or cancellation of penalties or interest*

The Revenue Commissioner can refund a penalty, and any interest paid on the penalty, if it was collected without suit, and the Commissioner determines that the circumstances giving rise to the penalty were reasonably beyond the control of the taxpayer. The Commissioner may waive the penalty only within three years after the date of payment. Waiver of penalties and interest is a feature of the voluntary disclosure program, discussed at ¶ 2903.

Property taxes: A local tax collector or tax commissioner may waive a property tax penalty or any applicable interest with the written approval of the county governing authority if the delay in the payment of taxes was due to reasonable cause and not due to gross or willful neglect or disregard of the law.

ADMINISTRATION AND PROCEDURE

CHAPTER 31

TAXPAYER REMEDIES

| ¶ 3101 | Taxpayer Rights and Remedies |

¶ 3101 Taxpayer Rights and Remedies

Law: Secs. 48-1-9, 48-2-35, 48-2-59, 48-2-60, 48-7-84, 50-13-12, 50-13-40—50-13-44, Code (CCH GEORGIA TAX REPORTS ¶ 89-222—89-240).

The Revenue Commissioner must provide a taxpayer with a statement of taxpayer rights:

—upon a taxpayer's request;

—when the Commissioner deems it appropriate;

—when a proposed assessment is made against a taxpayer; or

—when the Department of Revenue requests an examination of a taxpayer's records.

These rights, which are applicable to all taxes administered by the Department, unless specifically stated otherwise, include the rights to:

—fair and courteous treatment in all dealings with the Department;

—prompt and accurate responses to all questions and requests for tax assistance; and

—a fair and timely hearing on a dispute of any tax liability as provided by law.

The statement of taxpayer rights must also set forth:

—the rights of taxpayers and the obligations of the Commissioner during any tax audit or examination;

—any procedures for the appeal of unfavorable Commissioner opinions;

—any procedures for processing refund claims and taxpayer complaints; and

—any procedures for enforcing Georgia's revenue laws (including the filing and enforcement of liens).

Property taxes: The following additional rights are applicable to property taxes:

—the prevention of any indirect tax increases resulting from an increase to existing county property values due to inflation; and

—the enhancement of an individual property owner's rights when objecting to, and appealing, a county board of tax assessors' increase to the value of the owner's property.

● *Refunds*

Taxpayers who overpay their state taxes may file a claim for a refund of any overpayment within three years after the later of the date of the payment of the tax or, in the case of income tax, within three years after the due date for filling the applicable income tax return, including any extensions of time to file the return.

A written claim for refund must include information reasonably required by the Georgia Revenue Commissioner and a summary statement of the grounds for the refund claim. The DOR has no special form for filing a refund claim. DOR Form IT-550, which is provided to claim a refund of erroneously or illegally collected income tax, should be used only for estimated tax payments or extension payments made in error. Income tax refund claims should be included on an amended income tax return, DOR Form 600 in the case of corporate filers and DOR Form 500 or 500X in the case of individual filers.

Class actions prohibited: A refund claim for a tax that was erroneously collected or illegally assessed may not be submitted by a taxpayer on behalf of a class consisting of other similarly situated taxpayers.

Extension for military service: Any individual who is prevented from filing a claim within the usual three-year limitations period as a result of service in the armed forces may begin the period of limitation from the date of his or her discharge from the service. If the taxpayer wants a conference or hearing before the Commissioner concerning a claim for refund, the taxpayer must request that meeting in its written claim.

Suit for refund: The Department of Revenue has one year to rule on a taxpayer's claim. If no ruling is made within one year of filing the claim, or if the refund claim is denied, the taxpayer may sue for a refund in the superior court of the taxpayer's county of residence (or in Fulton County Superior Court for nonresidents).

Property tax: Information on property tax refunds is found at ¶ 2609.

Contribution option: Taxpayers have the opportunity on their Georgia personal income tax forms either to donate all or part of any refunds owed them, or else make voluntary contributions, to the Georgia Greenspace Trust Fund.

Practitioner Comment: Limitations on Interest for Certain Sales Tax Refunds

While there is no general provision in the Georgia sales tax statute that requires a taxpayer to seek approval of an exemption prior to claiming a refund, a new provision added by the 2004 Legislature (Act 563 (H.B. 1239), Laws 2004) will have that effect. O.C.G.A. § 48-2-35.1 provides that a refund of sales and use taxes will be made without interest unless that taxpayer has obtained a ruling

¶ 3101

from the Department prior to the transaction that the purchaser is entitled to purchase the tangible personal property or taxable services free of tax.

Timothy J. Peaden, Esq., Alston & Bird

● *Appeals*

Taxpayers may appeal any final order, ruling, or finding of the Revenue Commissioner. Appeals may go either to the Office of State Administrative Hearings (OSAH) under Georgia's Administrative Procedure Act (APA) or to superior court, at the election of the taxpayer. In either case, appeals are filed with the Revenue Commissioner within 30 days of the final assessment. The appeals are then transmitted by the Commissioner to OSAH for hearing or certified to the superior court, as appropriate.

Small claims hearings: Georgia has no provision for small claims hearings.

Taxpayers' rights: Taxpayers have the following rights in connection with an administrative hearing:

—to present evidence on any relevant issue;

—to be represented by counsel at the taxpayer's expense;

—to subpoena witnesses and documentary evidence; and

—any other rights conferred by law or OSAH's rules.

Generally, a decision is issued within 30 days of the date that the hearing ended (*Facts and Questions,* Office of State Administrative Hearings).

Practitioner Comment: OSAH Hearings

Upon the completion of the OSAH hearing, the administrative judge issues an "initial decision." Either the taxpayer or the department can request the Commissioner to reject the "initial decision." The Commissioner typically requests briefs on the issues in the case. The Commissioner then will issue a "final decision," which either party can appeal to superior court. On questions of fact, the superior court will only reverse the Commissioner's "final decision" if there is no evidence that would support such a decision.

Timothy J. Peaden, Esq., Alston & Bird LLP

● *Appeal to superior court*

Ordinarily, an appeal may be taken to the superior court of the county where the taxpayer resides. However, if the taxpayer is a public utility or nonresident, the appeal of either party must be to the superior court of the county in which is located the taxpayer's principal place of doing business or in which the taxpayer's chief or highest corporate officer residing in Georgia maintains his or her office.

¶3101

If the taxpayer is a nonresident individual or a foreign corporation having no place of doing business and no officer or employee residing and maintaining an office in Georgia, the taxpayer may appeal to the Superior Court of Fulton County or to the superior court of the county in which the current Commissioner resides.

Payment of taxes as condition of appeal: As a matter of the court's jurisdiction, a taxpayer who is appealing must first enter with the court a written statement of agreement to pay on the due dates all taxes that the taxpayer admits are due. With respect to any disputed taxes, the taxpayer has 30 days from the date of the Commissioner's decision to file a bond with the court clerk, if required. In a case where the value of the appellant's title or interest in real property owned in Georgia is in excess of the tax amount in dispute, a surety bond is not required. The appeal can be dismissed if the taxpayer fails to pay all taxes admittedly owed upon the due date or dates.

Payment upon final judgment: Unpaid tax for which the taxpayer is adjudged liable is payable on the due date. If the tax has already become due at the time of final judgment, the taxpayer must pay the tax immediately with interest. Irrespective of whether the tax has or has not become due at the time of final judgment, the taxpayer is liable for court costs if the final judgment is adverse to the taxpayer.

Compromise settlements: Suits, actions, or other judicial proceedings may only be settled by agreement, compromise, or judgment in open court. A compromise or an agreed judgment must contain a verified statement that the proposed judgment is, in the opinion of the Attorney General, in the best interest of the state.

Prohibition against injunctions: No suit for the purpose of restraining the assessment or collection of any income tax may be maintained in any court.

Practitioner Comment: Direct Appeals

If the taxpayer chooses to appeal an assessment directly to superior court pursuant to Sec. 48-2-59, instead of an appeal pursuant to the Administrative Procedures Act, the superior court provides a de novo review. For cases involving factual questions, this is a distinct advantage compared with the APA proceeding. As noted above, the review by the superior court of an APA factual determination is an appellate-level review.

Timothy J. Peaden, Esq., Alston & Bird LLP

Practitioner Comment: Appellate Review

Neither a taxpayer nor the Department has a right to appellate review of a superior court decision involving state-administered taxes. (By contrast, there is a right of appeal for ad valorem property tax cases administered by the local jurisdictions.) Either party must file a petition with the appropriate appellate court under the discretionary appeal procedure (generally the Court of Appeals), seeking the court's permission to file a notice of appeal. If

¶3101

granted, then the party will file a notice of appeal pursuant to the normal appellate procedure.

Timothy J. Peaden, Esq., Alston & Bird LLP

● *Federal court actions*

An assessment may be appealed to a federal court if there is a question involving the U.S. Constitution or a federal statute. However, the right to bring a federal suit is limited by the Tax Injunction Act and the fundamental principle of comity. The Tax Injunction Act prohibits an injunction in a federal district court against the assessment, levy, or collection of any state tax when there is a "plain, speedy, and efficient remedy" in state court (28 U.S.C. § 1341). Because this federal provision has been the subject of considerable litigation, the case law interpreting this provision should be researched if a federal action is contemplated.

In addition, any appeal of a state tax case to a federal court is subject to established principles of federal jurisdiction and abstention.

ADMINISTRATION AND PROCEDURE

CHAPTER 32

GEORGIA RESOURCES

Department of Revenue—*Headquarters*
1800 Century Center Blvd., N.E.
Atlanta GA 30345-3205
    Taxpayer Information Programs and Services (TIPS) .... (404) 417-4177 or (877) 602-8477
    Internet: www2.state.ga.us

Department of Revenue—*Income Tax Division*
Individual returns .... (404) 417-2300
Withholding, Suite 7100........................... (404) 417-2311
Refund inquiries, Suite 10300 .... (404) 417-4470
    Email: inctax@gw.rev.state.ga.us

Department of Revenue—*Sales and Use Tax Division*
Information...................................... (404) 417-3209
Registration .... (404) 417-4490
    Email: salesuse@gw.rev.state.ga.us

Department of Revenue—*Motor Fuel Tax Unit*
Information...................................... (404) 417-6712
IFTA information................................. (404) 417-3212
    Email: fueltax@gw.rev.state.ga.us

Department of Revenue—*Property Tax Division*
4245 International Parkway, Suite A
Hapeville, GA 30354-3918 .... (404) 968-0707
    Email: protax@gatax.org

Department of Revenue—*Estate Tax Section*
P.O. Box 49432
Atlanta, GA 30359 .... (404) 968-0707

Department of Revenue—*Alcohol and Tobacco Tax Division*
Alcohol and tobacco taxes .... (404) 417-4870
    Email: attax@gw.rev.state.ga.us

Department of Community Affairs
60 Exec Park South
Atlanta GA 30329 404-679-4940
   Internet: www.dca.state.ga.us

Department of Administrative Services—*Governor's Small Business Center*
200 Piedmont Ave., Ste 1304, West Tower
Atlanta GA 30334 404-656-6315
   Email: gsbc@doas.ga.gov

Secretary of State—*Corporations Division*
315 West Tower, #2 Martin Luther King, Jr. Drive
Atlanta, GA 30334-1530 .... (404) 656-2817
   Fax: (404) 657-2248
   Internet: www.sos.state.ga.us/corporations
   Online filing: https://www.ganet.org/sosonline

Insurance Commissioner
704 West Tower, #2 Martin Luther King, Jr. Drive
Atlanta, GA 30334 .... (404) 656-2070
   Fax: (404) 657-8542
   Internet: www.gainsurance.org
   Email: inscomm@mail.oci.state.ga.us

PART XI

DOING BUSINESS IN GEORGIA

CHAPTER 33

FEES AND TAXES

| ¶ 3301 | Domestic Corporation Costs |
| ¶ 3302 | Foreign Corporation Costs |

¶ 3301 Domestic Corporation Costs

Law: Secs. 14-2-122, 14-2-129, 14-2-201.1, 14-2-1006.1, 14-2-1105.1, 14-2-1403.1, 14-4-1, 14-4-183, 14-11-1101, 15-6-77, Code (CCH GEORGIA TAX REPORTS ¶ 1-110, 1-205, 1-210, 1-410, 1-420, 1-430, 1-505, 1-510, 1-630, 1-701, 1-805).

The following paragraphs provide the fees and costs required to be paid by domestic corporations. See ¶ 3302 for the requirements for foreign corporations.

● *Initial fees and taxes*

The information reported in this section concerns the fees imposed in connection with the incorporation of domestic corporations. Fees required in connection with the filing of corporate documents are payable to the Secretary of State at the time the papers are delivered.

Registration of name (good for 30-days) $25

Articles of incorporation fees: The following fees are required:

$100 as the Secretary of State's fee for filing the articles and issuing a certificate of incorporation;

$40 to pay for two insertions of the incorporation notice in a newspaper (paid directly to the newspaper).

Corporations chartered by Secretary of State; fee: Banking, trust, insurance, railroad, canal, navigation, express, and telegraph corporations are chartered by the Secretary of State. The Secretary of State's fee for filing a petition for charter is $100.

Fee for amended or restated articles: A $40 fee is required for publication of notice of change of name in a newspaper (paid directly to the newspaper).

Mergers and share exchange fees: The following fees are required:

$20 for the clerk of the superior court of the county in which the registered office of the surviving or new corporation will be located; and

¶ 3301

$40 to pay for the publication of notice of the merger or share exchange in a newspaper (paid directly to the newspaper).

Dissolution fees: The following fees are imposed in connection with dissolution:

$40 for two insertions in a newspaper of statement of intent to dissolve (paid directly to the newspaper); and

$20 for filing a notice of intent to dissolve and $20 for filing the Articles of Dissolution.

Miscellaneous fees: In addition to the fees noted above, the Secretary of State collects fees for miscellaneous services as listed below:

Domestic Business Corporations Generally	**Fee**
Application for certificate of authority	$225
Annual registration	$30
Certificate of existence	$10
Civil penalty for each year or part thereof during which a foreign corporation transacts business in Georgia without a certificate of authority	$500
Statement of change of address of registered agent—$5 per corporation but not less than	$20
Application for reinstatement	$100
Other documents required or permitted to be filed	$20

Fees imposed on limited liability companies: The fees imposed on limited liability companies are specified by statute.

Annual report fee: A $30 fee is payable to the Secretary of State for filing the report. Annual registration may be accomplished online at the Secretary of State's secure website. Go to https://www.ganet.org/sosonline

Penalty for signing false document: A person who signs a document he knows is false in any material respect with intent that the document be delivered to the Secretary of State for filing is guilty of a misdemeanor and, upon conviction, is subject to a fine not to exceed $500.

CCH Tip: *Expedited Filing*

For expedited processing and filing of any document, a separate check for $100, payable to the Secretary of State, should be included. For expedited processing of a certificate request, the additional fee is $50.

¶ 3302 Foreign Corporation Costs

Law: Secs. 14-2-122, 14-2-1502, 14-8-57, Code (CCH Georgia Tax Reports ¶ 2-110, 2-205, 2-630, 2-701, 2-710, 2-805).

The following paragraphs provide the fees and costs required to be paid by foreign corporations. See ¶ 3301 for the requirements for domestic corporations.

● *Initial fees and taxes*

Transacting business by a corporation in a state other than the state of incorporation is a privilege upon which conditions may be imposed and for which fees may be charged. The information reported in this section concerns the fees imposed by Georgia upon a foreign corporation seeking the privilege of doing business within the state. Fees required in connection with the filing of corporate documents are payable to the Secretary of State at the time the papers are delivered.

Certificate of authority fee: The Secretary of State charges a fee of $225 for filing an application for a certificate of authority to transact business in Georgia and issuing the certificate. For a nonprofit corporation, the fee is $70.

An application for certificate of authority must be accompanied by a certificate of existence in good standing issued by the corporation's home state no more than 90 days before filing the application.

Annual report fee: A $30 fee is payable to the Secretary of State for filing the report. Annual registration may be accomplished online at the Secretary of State's secure website. Go to https://www.ganet.org/sosonline

Fees imposed on foreign limited liability partnerships: The following fees are imposed upon foreign limited liability partnerships:

—application for certificate of authority to transact business, $200;

—statement of change of registered office or agent, $5 per company, but not less than $20;

—annual registration, $30; and

—other required documents, $20.

Transacting business without authority: A foreign corporation that transacts business in Georgia without authority and has not obtained a certificate of authority is subject to a penalty of $500 for each year or part of a year during which it transacts business. Foreign corporations that have not obtained a certificate of authority within 30 days after the first day on which business was transacted in Georgia are also liable for civil penalties.

LAW AND REGULATION LOCATOR

This finding list shows where sections of Georgia statutory law and administrative regulations referred to in the *Guidebook* are discussed.

Law Sec.	Discussion at ¶
LAW	
3-2-6	2802
3-4-2	2802
3-4-60	2802
3-5-60	2802
3-5-61	2802
3-5-90	2802
3-6-3	2802
3-6-50	2802
3-6-70	2802
3-6-71	2802
12-8-40.1	2809
14-2-122	3301, 3302
14-2-129	3301
14-2-201.1	3301
14-2-1006.1	3301
14-11-1104	101, 703
14-2-1105.1	3301
14-2-1403.1	3301
14-2-1502	3302
14-4-1	3301
14-4-183	3301
14-8-57	3302
14-11-1101	3301
14-11-1104	902
15-6-77	3301
18-3-1	3002
20-3-630	207, 310
33-5-31	2804
33-5-33	2804, 3003
33-5-35	2804
33-7-4	2804
33-7-9	2804
33-8-4	2804
33-8-5	2804
33-8-6	2804
33-8-7	2804
33-8-8.1	2804
33-8-8.2	2804
33-8-8.3	2804
33-15-28	2804
33-21-2	2804
33-40-5	2804
33-41-22	2804

Law Sec.	Discussion at ¶
36-62-5.1	913
36-88-1—36-88-10	2604
36-89-3	2604
36-89-4	2604
40-2-20	2806
40-2-30	2806
40-2-37	2806
40-2-87	2806
40-2-88	2806
40-2-111	2806
40-2-112	2806
40-3-38	2806
46-1-1	2808
46-2-10	2811
46-3-14	2811
46-3-170	2811
46-5-61	2811
46-5-101	2811
46-7-9	2808
46-7-15	2808
46-7-16	2808
46-8-382	2811
47-7-61	2804
48-1-2	101, 701, 807, 902, 1002
48-1-3	606
48-1-9	2609, 3101
48-1-10	2004
48-2-1	801, 1501, 2901
48-2-9	3002
48-2-12	801, 1501, 2901
48-2-15	2903
48-2-16	3001
48-2-18.1	3002
48-2-30	1406, 2302
48-2-31	2302
48-2-32	604, 610, 1406, 2302, 2902
48-2-33	605, 2302
48-2-35	801, 1501, 1502, 2302, 3001, 3003, 3101
48-2-36	603, 1401, 1404, 1406, 2302
48-2-37	2401
48-2-38	3003
48-2-39	601, 1401, 1406, 2302, 2902
48-2-40	2608, 3003

365

Law Sec.	Discussion at ¶	Law Sec.	Discussion at ¶
48-2-44	2608	48-5-41	2604
48-2-45	1502, 2302, 3002	48-5-42	2604
48-2-46	802, 2302, 3001	48-5-43	2604
48-2-47	802	48-5-44	2604
48-2-48	802, 2401, 3002	48-5-45	2604
48-2-49	802, 2302, 3001, 3002	48-5-47	2604
48-2-50	2302	48-5-47.1	2604
48-2-51	1502, 2302, 3002	48-5-48.1	2604
48-2-52	2406	48-5-48.2	2604
48-2-54	1502	48-5-52	2604
48-2-54.1	3002	48-5-71—48-5-74	2604
48-2-55	3002	48-5-84	2608
48-2-56	1502	48-5-127	2606
48-2-58	1502, 2302	48-5-148	2606, 2608, 3003
48-2-59	2513, 3101	48-5-150	2606, 2608, 3003
48-2-60	3002—3101	48-5-220	2602
48-2-80	3002	48-5-242	2908
48-2-100	304	48-5-260—48-5-261	2605
48-2-110	304	48-5-269	2605
48-3-1	2607, 3002	48-5-299	2602, 2607, 2608
48-3-3	2607, 3002	48-5-311	2609
48-3-3.1	3002	48-5-342	2605
48-3-8	2607	48-5-350	2602
48-3-9	2606, 2607	48-5-351	2602
48-3-12	3002	48-5-356	2604
48-3-19	2607, 3002	48-5-380	2609
48-3-21	2607	48-5-420	2605
48-3-29	2903, 3002	48-5-423	2605
48-4-1	2607	48-5-440	2604
48-4-2	2606, 2607	48-5-441.1	2605
48-4-6	2607	48-5-442	2605
48-4-20—48-4-22	2607	48-5-443	2605
48-4-40—48-4-48	2607	48-5-444	2606
48-4-61	2607	48-5-451	2608
48-4-64	2607	48-5-470.1	2604
48-4-65	2607	48-5-471	2604, 2806
48-4-76—48-4-81	2607	48-5-472	2604, 2806
48-5-1	2605	48-5-473	2606, 2806
48-5-2	2605	48-5-474	2806
48-5-4	2604	48-5-478.2	2604
48-5-5	2604	48-5-491	2605
48-5-7	2605	48-5-493	2608, 3003
48-5-7.1—48-5-7.4	2603, 2605, 2608	48-5-494	2606
48-5-7.5	2608, 3003	48-5-507	2608
48-5-9—48-5-18	2606	48-5-511	2605, 2608
48-5-10	2603, 2605, 2606	48-5-513	2608, 3002
48-5-11	2603, 2606	48-5-519	2605, 2608
48-5-12	2603, 2606	48-5-520	2605
48-5-16	2603, 2606	48-5-540	2605
48-5-23	2606, 2608	48-5-541	2605, 2608
48-5-24	2606	48-5-542	2605
48-5-28	2607	48-5-543	2605
48-5-32.1	2602	48-6-1—48-6-10	2810
48-5-40	2604	48-6-60—48-6-77	2810

Law and Regulation Locator **367**

Law Sec.	Discussion at ¶
48-6-90	1901
48-6-90.1	1901
48-6-91	1901
48-6-93	919, 1901—1905
48-6-95	919, 1901—1906
48-7-1	102, 504, 902, 907
48-7-2	3001
48-7-2—48-7-5	3003
48-7-20	101, 103, 105, 121, 501, 701
48-7-21	901, 902, 904, 905, 1001—1004, 1006—1008, 1101—1104, 1201—1205, 1403
48-7-22	101, 701, 807
48-7-23	101, 702
48-7-24	702
48-7-25	901, 903, 1005
48-7-26	104, 301
48-7-27	103, 104, 108, 201—203, 205—207, 301—306, 308—310, 401—404, 608
48-7-28	120
48-7-28.1	119
48-7-28.2	307, 1206
48-7-29	118
48-7-29.1	128
48-7-29.2	111
48-7-29.3	115, 914
48-7-29.4	122, 919, 1002, 1906
48-7-29.5	123
48-7-29.6	124, 922
48-7-30	501, 502, 503
48-7-31	901, 902, 905, 1301—1303, 1305, 1306, 1308, 1310
48-7-32	1307
48-7-33	106, 107, 907
48-7-34	505, 1301, 1309
48-7-35	1301, 1304
48-7-36	108, 603
48-7-38	305, 1205
48-7-39	204, 1007
48-7-40	913, 916
48-7-40.1	913
48-7-40.2	913, 916
48-7-40.3	913, 916
48-7-40.4	913, 916
48-7-40.5	112, 909
48-7-40.6	114, 911, 1104
48-7-40.7	916
48-7-40.8	916
48-7-40.9	916
48-7-40.10	918
48-7-40.11	907, 918
48-7-40.12	906, 917
48-7-40.13	912
48-7-40.15	924
48-7-40.16	116, 915

Law Sec.	Discussion at ¶
48-7-40.17	920
48-7-40.18	920
48-7-40.19	116, 915
48-7-40.20	921
48-7-40.21	125, 913
48-7-40.22	126, 913, 923
48-7-40.24	925
48-7-40.25	926
48-7-41	113, 910
48-7-42	906
48-7-50	602
48-7-51	1402, 1403, 1507
48-7-52	1402
48-7-53	602, 702
48-7-56	108, 601, 603, 1401, 1404
48-7-57	3003
48-7-57.1	3003
48-7-58	1301, 1310, 1401, 1502
48-7-59	1502
48-7-60	2903
48-7-61	3003
48-7-80	605, 1406
48-7-81	3003
48-7-82	601, 1401, 1502, 3001
48-7-83	1508
48-7-84	3101
48-7-85	504
48-7-86	109, 3003
48-7-100	607
48-7-101	607, 608, 609
48-7-102	608
48-7-103	610
48-7-105	608
48-7-106	609, 610
48-7-107	610
48-7-108	607
48-7-109	607
48-7-111	2903
48-7-112	3003
48-7-114	604
48-7-115	604
48-7-116	604
48-7-117	1405
48-7-119	1406
48-7-120	604, 1502, 3003
48-7-121	3003
48-7-126	607
48-7-128	609, 610, 808, 901
48-7-128	1508
48-7-129	609, 610
48-7-162—48-7-164	3002
48-7A-1	117
48-7A-2	117
48-7A-3	117

Law Sec.	Discussion at ¶
48-8-1	2002, 2202
48-8-2	2002—2006, 2101, 2301, 2405
48-8-3	2002, 2004—2006, 2101, 2201, 2202
48-8-4	2201
48-8-5	2201
48-8-6	2103
48-8-7	3003
48-8-9	3003
48-8-10	3003
48-8-30	2002—2006, 2101, 2102, 2202, 2301, 2306, 2404, 2405
48-8-31	2105
48-8-32	2003
48-8-33	2003, 2301, 2405, 2805
48-8-34	2003, 2006, 2202, 2301, 2405
48-8-35	2003, 2301, 2405
48-8-36	2301
48-8-37	3003
48-8-38	2002, 2004, 2201
48-8-39	2002, 2101, 2201
48-8-39.1	2004
48-8-40	2004
48-8-42	2203
48-8-44	2101
48-8-45	2101
48-8-46	2407
48-8-48	2407, 3002
48-8-51	2401, 2403
48-8-52	2306, 2401, 2903, 3001
48-8-53	2306
48-8-54	3003
48-8-55	2303, 2401
48-8-57	3002
48-8-58	2101
48-8-59	2304
48-8-60	2304, 2406
48-8-61	2304
48-8-62	2304
48-8-63	2004, 2201
48-8-65	2002
48-8-66	3003
48-8-81—48-8-83	2103
48-8-85	2103
48-8-86	2103
48-8-92	2103
48-8-102	2103
48-8-103	2103
48-8-104	3001
48-8-109	3001
48-8-110—48-8-112	2103
48-8-141	2103, 2105
48-9-2	2805
48-9-3	2805
48-9-8	2805, 2903

Law Sec.	Discussion at ¶
48-9-9	2805
48-9-12	3001
48-9-14	2805
48-9-16	3003
48-9-19	2805, 3001
48-9-30—48-9-34	2805
48-9-31	2805, 2808
48-9-37	2805
48-9-45	3003
48-10-2	2806
48-10-2.1	2806
48-10-3	2806
48-10-7	2806
48-10-8	2806
48-10-10	2806
48-10-12	2806
48-11-2	2803
48-11-3	2803
48-11-5	2803
48-11-8	2803
48-11-10	2803
48-11-11	2803
48-11-13	2803
48-11-14	2803
48-13-51	2812
48-13-53	2812
48-13-53.1	2812
48-13-53.2	2812
48-13-53.6	2812
48-13-53.7	2812
48-13-58	2812
48-13-70	1602
48-13-71	1603
48-13-72	1601, 1602
48-13-73	1604, 1605, 1701, 1803
48-13-74	1701, 1804, 1902
48-13-75	1604, 1701, 1702, 1902
48-13-76	1801, 1803
48-13-77	1801
48-13-78	1601, 1801, 1802
48-13-79	1801, 1903
48-13-90—48-13-94	2807
48-13-97	2807
48-15-10	2903
50-13-12	3101
50-13-14	3001
50-13-20	3101
50-13-40—50-13-44	3101

Reg. Sec.	Discussion at ¶
REGULATIONS	
391-3-25-.01	116, 915
560-1-1-.19	2902
560-1-1-.23	2902

Law and Regulation Locator

Reg. Sec.	Discussion at ¶	Reg. Sec.	Discussion at ¶
560-3-2-.26	2902	560-12-1-.26	3202
560-7-2-.07	3001	560-12-1-.27	2101
560-7-2-.08	3001	560-12-1-.28	2102
560-7-3-.06	1101, 1201	560-12-1-.30	2405
560-7-3-.08	702	560-12-1-.31	2304, 2407
560-7-4-.01	208	560-12-1-.32	2203
560-7-4-.02	304	560-12-1-.33	2302
560-7-7-.03	902, 1301, 1305, 1306, 1310	560-12-1-.34	2101
		560-12-1-.35	2101
560-7-8-.01	602	560-12-2-.01	2004
560-7-8-.20	118	560-12-2-.02	2004, 2005
560-7-8-.33	608, 610	560-12-2-.03	2201
560-7-8-.34	609, 610	560-12-2-.04	2201
560-7-8-.35	609, 1508	560-12-2-.06	2004
560-7-8-.36	913	560-12-2-.07	2004
560-7-8-.37	916	560-12-2-.08	2004
560-7-8-.39	609	560-12-2-.09	2004, 2101
560-7-8-.40	916	560-12-2-.10	2004
560-7-8-.42	917	560-12-2-.12—560-12-2-.15	2004
560-7-8-.43	111	560-12-2-.17	2004, 2201
560-7-8-.44	111, 128	560-12-2-.18	2004
560-8-7.14	920	560-12-2-.19	2004, 2201
560-9-2.02	2805	560-12-2-.21	2004, 2201
560-9-2.04	2805	560-12-2-.23	2004, 2201
560-9-2.06	2805	560-12-2-.24	2004
560-9-2.07	2805	560-12-2-.25	2201
560-9-2.08	2805	560-12-2-.26	2004, 2302, 2303, 2304
560-9-2.10	2805	560-12-2-.28	2004, 2201
560-9-2.11	2805	560-12-2-.30	2004, 2201
560-9-2.12	2805	560-12-2-.31	2201
560-11-2-.20	2603	560-12-2-.32	2004, 2201
560-11-2-.22	2605	560-12-2-.33	2004, 2201
560-11-2-.54	2604	560-12-2-.34	2004, 2201
560-11-4-.03	2605	560-12-2-.35	2201
560-11-6-.03	2605	560-12-2-.36	2004
560-11-8-.01—.16	2810	560-12-2-.37	2201
560-11-9-.03	2606	560-12-2-.38	2004
560-12-1-.01	3001	560-12-2-.39	2304
560-12-1-.02	2101	560-12-2-.40	2004, 2201
560-12-1-.05	2102, 2301	560-12-2-.41	2004, 2201
560-12-1-.06	2101, 2302	560-12-2-.42	2005
560-12-1-.07	2201	560-12-2-.43	2004
560-12-1-.08	2201	560-12-2-.44	2302
560-12-1-.09	2304	560-12-2-.45	2101
560-12-1-.10	2304	560-12-2-.46	2004
560-12-1-.11	2003, 2301, 2405	560-12-2-.47	2005
560-12-1-.13	2302	560-12-2-.48	2201
560-12-1-.14	2101	560-12-2-.49	2004
560-12-1-.15	2306	560-12-2-.50	2201
560-12-1-.16	2305	560-12-2-.51	2004, 2201
560-12-1-.17	2101	560-12-2-.52	2004, 2201
560-12-1-.19	2101, 2302	560-12-2-.53	2005
560-12-1-.22	2302, 2902	560-12-2-.54	2201, 2202
560-12-1-.23	2306	560-12-2-.55	2004, 2005
560-12-1-.25	2101		

Reg. Sec.	Discussion at ¶	Reg. Sec.	Discussion at ¶
560-12-2-.56	2201	560-12-2-.91	2201
560-12-2-.57	2004	560-12-2-.96	2004
560-12-2-.58	2004	560-12-2-.97	2005
560-12-2-.60	2004	560-12-2-.98	2004
560-12-2-.61—560-12-2-.64	2201	560-12-2-.100	2004
560-12-2-.65—560-12-2-.67	2004	560-12-2-.102	2004
560-12-2-.68	2005	560-12-2-.106	2201
560-12-2-.70	2304	560-12-2-.107	2201
560-12-2-.71	2201	560-12-2-.109	2201
560-12-2-.72—560-12-2-.77	2004	560-12-3-.02	2304
560-12-2-.78	2201	560-12-3-.03	2304
560-12-2-.79	2004, 2201	560-12-3-.04	2302
560-12-2-.80	2201	560-12-3-.09	2302
560-12-2-.81	2201	560-12-3-.13	2201
560-12-2-.82	2004	560-12-3-.20	2401
560-12-2-.84	2004	560-12-3-.21	2401
560-12-2-.85	2004	560-12-4-.02	2105
560-12-2-.86	2304	560-12-5-.02	2105
560-12-2-.87—560-12-2-.89	2201	560-12-6-.02	2105
560-12-2-.90	2004		

TOPICAL INDEX

References are to paragraph numbers.

A

Abatement
- corporate income tax 3101
- personal income tax 3101

Absorption of tax
- sales and use taxes 2301
- . penalties 3003

Accounting periods and methods—see also Separate accounting
- corporate income tax 907
- . federal/state key feature comparison 45
- personal income tax 106
- . decedent's return 107
- sales and use taxes 2302

Acquisitions—see Corporate reorganizations; Mergers, consolidations, and acquisitions

Addition modifications
- corporate income tax 1101
- . child care property depreciation deduction 1104
- . federal obligations 1009
- . income taxes deducted on federal return 1103
- . state or local obligations income 1009; 1102
- personal income tax
- . child care property depreciation deduction 404
- . income taxes deducted on federal return 403
- . lump-sum distributions 402
- . state or local obligations income . 401

Administration and procedure
- authority of Department of Revenue 2901
- deficiency assessments 3001
- interest 3003
- jeopardy assessments 3001
- payment of tax 2903
- penalties 3003
- returns 3003
- statute of limitations ... 2903; 3001; 3101
- taxpayer remedies 3101

Admissions, entertainment, and dues
- sales and use taxes 2004
- . exemptions, school functions ... 2201

Advertising
- sales and use taxes 2004

Advertising display service
- sales and use taxes
- . exemption 2004

Affiliated corporations
- corporate income tax
- . assignment of credits 906
- . net income 1308
- . subtraction modification 1203

Aged—see Elderly

Agricultural fuel, products, and supplies
- property taxes
- . exemptions 70; 2604
- sales and use taxes
- . exemption 65; 2004; 2201

Agricultural property
- property taxes
- . assessment 2605
- . classification 2603
- . exemptions 70; 2604
- . penalties 2608

Aircraft
- sales and use taxes
- . exemptions 2201

Airline companies
- property taxes 2605
- . penalties 2608

Alcoholic beverages taxes 2802

Allocation and apportionment—see also Formula apportionment
- bank and financial institutions tax .....
- . allocation of local business license taxes 1904
- corporate income tax 1301
- . allocation, investment income .. 1303
- . allocation, special cases 1304
- . apportionment, three factor formula 1305
- . doing business 1302; 3301; 3302
- . net business income, intangible property 1303
- . net income, subsidiaries and affiliates 1308
- . no throwback rule 1302
- . property owned 1302
- . railroad and public service corporations 1307
- . returns based on books of account 1309
- . Revenue Commissioner's power to determine income attributable to state 1310
- . special definitions and rules 1306
- corporate net worth (franchise) tax
- . apportionment of net worth, foreign corporations 1702
- personal income tax
- . computation of tax, nonresidents 501
- . deduction of expenses, nonresidents 503
- . formula apportionment, nonresidents 502
- . nonresident income 501
- . part year residents 504
- . returns based on books of account, nonresidents 505
- . separate accounting, nonresidents 501
- . withholding 609

American Jobs Creation Act (AJCA) of 2004
- corporate income tax 1002
- personal income tax 201

AME

372 Guidebook to Georgia Taxes

References are to paragraph numbers.

Amortization
- corporate income tax
  - bond premium 1009
  - federal/state key feature comparison 45
  - intangibles 1009
  - pollution control facilities 1009
  - reforestation 1009
- personal income tax
  - start-up expenditures 209

Annual returns
- sales and use taxes............. 2302

Annuities
- personal income tax
  - withholding 609

Appeals
- administration and procedure.... 3001
- corporate income tax........... 3101
- corporate net worth (franchise) tax ... 3101
- property taxes 2609

Apportionment—see Allocation and apportionment; Formula apportionment

Appraisal
- property taxes 2605

Arbitration
- property taxes 2609

Armed forces personnel—see Military personnel

Art and artifacts
- sales and use taxes
  - exemption 2201

Assessment date
- property taxes 2605

Assessments
- administration and procedure.... 3001
- corporate income tax
  - jeopardy assessments...... 1502; 3001
  - statute of limitations .. 2903; 3001; 3101
- corporate net worth (franchise) tax
  - assessment or revision by Commissioner 1804
- personal income tax
  - deficiencies 802; 3003
  - jeopardy assessments 3001
  - statute of limitations .. 2903; 3001; 3101
- property taxes 2605
- sales and use taxes
  - deficiency assessments 2401
  - jeopardy assessments......... 2403

Asset expense election
- corporate income tax
  - federal/state key feature comparison 45
- personal income tax
  - federal/state key feature comparison 40

Atlanta Urban Enterprise Zone Act .. 2604

Auctions
- sales and use taxes............. 2004

Audits
- generally 3001
- sales and use taxes............. 2402

B

Bad checks
- sales and use taxes............. 3003

Bad debts
- corporate income tax
  - federal/state key feature comparison 45
- personal income tax
  - federal/state key feature comparison 40
- sales and use taxes............. 2101

Bankruptcy and receivership
- corporate income tax........... 1507
- personal income tax............. 807

Banks—see Financial institutions

Basis of tax
- banks and financial institutions tax 1902
- corporate income tax............. 904
- corporate net worth (franchise) tax ... 1604
- personal income tax............. 103
- sales and use taxes............. 2101

Bazaars and school carnivals
- sales and use taxes............. 2004

Benefits
- unemployment compensation.... 2705

Beverages
- sales and use taxes............. 2004

Bibles
- sales and use taxes
  - exemption 2004

Blind persons
- personal income tax
  - deduction 302

Blood banks
- sales and use taxes
  - exemption 2004

Bonds
- amortization
  - corporate federal/state key feature comparison.................. 45
- personal income tax
  - interest................. 40, 303, 401
- premiums, amortization
  - corporate federal/state key feature comparison.................. 45

Books of account
- corporate income tax........... 1301
  - returns 1309
- personal income tax
  - nonresident returns............ 505

Bracket schedule
- sales and use taxes............. 2105

Broadcasting
- sales and use taxes............. 2004

Business deductions
- personal income tax
  - federal/state key feature comparison 40

AMO

Topical Index

References are to paragraph numbers.

Business expansion
. personal income tax 1301
.. credit 125
Business incentives .... 50—75
. corporate income tax
.. credits 60
.. enterprise zones, incentives 2604
. insurance gross premiums tax 75
. personal income tax 55
. property taxes 70
. sales and use taxes 65
Business income
. corporate income tax
.. exempt organizations, unrelated
   business income 1005
.. net income from intangible property .
   1303
.. net income, subsidiaries and affiliates
   1308
Business successor liability
. sales and use taxes 2407

C

Cable television services
. sales and use taxes 2004
Calendar year
. corporate income tax
.. accounting periods and methods . 907
.. payment of tax, due date 1406
.. returns, due date 1401
. personal income tax
.. accounting periods and methods . 106
.. payment of tax, due date 605
.. returns, due date 601
Camps
. sales and use taxes 2004
Capital gains and capital losses
. personal income tax 202; 209
.. federal/state key feature comparison
   40
Carrybacks
. corporate income tax
.. net operating loss 3003
. personal income tax
.. net operating loss 208; 3003
Carryovers
. corporate income tax
.. credits .... 909—915
Casual sales
. sales and use taxes
.. exemptions 2201
Catalogs
. sales and use taxes
.. exemption 2004
Cellular telephones
. sales and use taxes 2004
Cemeteries
. property taxes
.. exemption 2604
Certificate of registration
. sales and use taxes 2304

Charitable contributions
. corporate income tax 1009
.. federal/state key feature comparison
   45
. personal income tax 209
. federal/state key feature comparison
   40
Charitable organizations
. corporate income tax
.. exemptions 901; 903
. corporate net worth (franchise) tax ...
   1603
. property taxes
.. exemption 2604
Child care
. corporate income tax
.. credit, employer-provided child care .
   .... 60; 911
.. depreciation deduction, child care
   property 1104
. personal income tax
.. credit, employer-provided child care .
   .... 55; 114
.. depreciation deduction, child care
   property 104
.. federal/state key feature comparison
   40
. sales and use taxes
.. exemption, nonprofit child care
   organizations 2201
Cigarette and tobacco taxes 2803
Cigarette exports
. corporate income tax
.. credit 60; 921
Civil penalties—see Penalties
Claim for refund of taxes
. administration and procedure 2903
. corporate income tax 2903
.. statute of limitations .. 2903; 3001; 3101
. personal income tax
.. statute of limitations .. 2903; 3001; 3101
Classification of property
. property taxes 2603
Clean-fuel vehicles
. corporate income tax
.. federal/state key feature comparison
   45
Clean-room equipment
. sales and use taxes
.. exemption 2201
Cleaning and laundry services
. sales and use taxes 2004
Coin-operated amusement devices
. sales and use taxes
.. exemption 2004
Coins, currency, and bullion
. sales and use taxes
.. exemption 2201
Collection of tax
. administration and procedure
.. authority of Department of Revenue .
   2901
.. levy 3002
. corporate net worth (franchise) tax ...
   .... 1004, 2901
. lodging taxes 2812

COL

Collection of tax—continued
. motor fuel taxes 2805
. property taxes 2607
. sales and use taxes 3002
.. discounts 2302

College meals
. sales and use taxes
.. exemption 2201

Colleges and universities
. property taxes
.. exemptions 2604

Combat zone
. personal income tax
.. military personnel 108; 603

Comity—see also Reciprocity
. administration and procedure
.. statute of limitations .. 2903; 3001; 3101

Commercial fishing
. sales and use taxes
.. crab bait exemption 2201
.. dyed diesel fuel exemption 2201

Commercial property
. property taxes
.. classification 2603

Commingled goods
. sales and use taxes 2004

Common carriers
. sales and use taxes 2004

Common ownership
. sales and use taxes 2004; 2006

Compromise of tax
. administration and procedure
.. authority of State Revenue
    Commissioner 2901
. corporate income tax 3101
. personal income tax 3101

Computation of income
. corporate income tax 1001; 1002
.. adjustments—special rules 1004
.. basis of tax 904
.. corporate reorganizations—mergers
    and acquisitions 1008
.. depreciation, business property . 1007
.. exempt organizations—unrelated
    business income 1005
.. federal elections 1003
.. federal/state comparison of key
    features 45
.. federal taxable income as starting
    point 1002
.. net operating losses, NOL carryovers
    .... 1002; 1008
.. subchapter S elections 1006

Computation of tax
. personal income tax
.. federal/state comparison of key
    features 40
.. nonresidents 501
.. withholding 609

Computers and computer services
. sales and use taxes 65; 2004
.. equipment exemption 65; 2201

Conditional sales—see Installment, lay-away, and conditional sales

Confidentiality
. administration and procedure 2903

Conservation use property
. property taxes
.. assessment 2605
.. classification 2603
.. penalties 2608

Consolidated returns
. corporate income tax
.. computation of income 1403
.. federal/state key feature comparison
    45
. corporate net worth (franchise) tax ...
    1801
. sales and use taxes 2302

Consolidations—see Corporate reorganizations; Mergers, consolidations, and acquisitions

Construction contractors
. sales and use taxes 2004; 2304

Consumer liability
. sales and use taxes 2404

Contact lenses—see Eyeglasses and contact lenses

Containers—see Returnable containers; Storage

Corporate dissolution
. corporate income tax 1508

Corporate distributions and adjustments
. corporate income tax
.. federal/state key feature comparison
    45

Corporate income tax
. abatement 3101
. accounting periods and methods .. 907; 1009
.. federal/state key feature comparison
    45
. addition modifications 1101
.. child care property depreciation
    deduction 1104
.. federal obligations 1009
.. income taxes deducted on federal
    return 1009; 1103
.. state or local obligations income ....
    .... 1009; 1102
. administration 1501
. allocation and apportionment 1301
.. allocation, investment income .. 1303
.. allocation, special cases 1304
.. apportionment, three factor formula .
    1305
.. by agreement 1310
.. doing business 1302
.. net business income, intangible
    property 1303
.. net income, subsidiaries and affiliates
    1308
.. property owned 1302
.. railroad and public service
    corporations 1307
.. returns based on books of account ..
    1309
.. Revenue Commissioner's power to
    determine income attributable to
    state 1310
.. special definitions and rules 1306

COL

Topical Index

References are to paragraph numbers.

Corporate income tax—continued
. alternative minimum tax
. . federal/state key feature comparison 45
. amortization
. . bond premium 1009
. . intangibles 1009
. . pollution control facilities 1009
. . reforestation 1009
. appeals 3101
. assessments 1502; 3001
. . statute of limitations 3001
. asset expense deduction
. . federal/state key feature comparison 45
. bad debt deduction
. . federal/state key feature comparison 45
. banking institutions 919; 1009
. . federal/state key feature comparison 45
. bankruptcy and receivership 1507
. basis of tax 904
. carryovers................. 909—915
. charitable contributions
. . federal/state key feature comparison 45
. capital gains and losses
. . federal/state key feature comparison 45
. clean-fuel vehicles
. . federal/state key feature comparison 45
. compensation, deferred plans 1009
. compromise of tax 3101
. computation of income 1001; 1002
. . adjustments—special rules 1004
. . basis of tax 904
. . corporate reorganizations—mergers and acquisitions 1008
. . depreciation, business property . 1007
. . exempt organizations—unrelated business income 1005
. . federal elections 1003
. . federal taxable income as starting point 1002
. . net operating losses, NOL carryovers 1002; 1008
. . subchapter S elections 1006
. consolidated returns 1403
. . federal/state key feature comparison 45
. corporate dissolution 1508
. corporate distribution and adjustments 1009
. . federal/state key feature comparison 45
. corporate partners.............. 1301
. corporations required to file 1402
. court action 3101
. credits against tax 908
. . alcohol fuel................... 1009
. . approved retraining programs . 60; 909
. . assignment of credits to affiliated entities 906
. . bad debts 1009
. . basic education 60
. . basic skills education programs .. 60; 910
. . business expansion 60; 913
. . business growth 60; 912
. . child care 60; 911

Corporate income tax—continued
. credits against tax—continued
. . cigarette exports 60; 921
. . clean fueled vehicles and equipment 60; 915; 1009
. . consistent net taxable income growth 912
. . diesel particulate emission reduction technology equipment 915
. . disabled access 1009
. . employer-provided child care .. 60; 911
. . employer-provided transportation 60; 923
. . employer social security ... 1009; 1206
. . employment increases (job tax credits) 913
. . enhanced oil recovery 1009
. . enterprise zone job 2604
. . enterprise zone property tax exemption.................. 2604
. . environmental remediation 1009
. . establishing headquarters in Georgia 920
. . expenditures 1009
. . federal qualified transportation fringe benefits 60; 914
. . foreign tax 1009
. . fuel from nonconventional source 1009
. . Georgia headquarters 60
. . historic property rehabilitation 60; 925
. . income reduction for payments to minority subcontractors ... 55; 1205
. . incremental research expenditures 1009
. . Indian employment 1009
. . investment (former law) 920; 1009
. . investment tax 60; 916
. . job tax 60; 913
. . low-income housing...... 60; 922; 1009
. . manufacturing and telecommunications facility investments 916
. . new manufacturing facilities .. 926, 927
. . new markets 1009
. . orphan drug.................. 1009
. . port traffic increases 60; 913; 924
. . qualified research 60; 913; 917
. . qualified electric vehicles 1009
. . renewable electricity production 1009
. . safe harbor leasing (pre-1984 leases) 1009
. . water conservation 60; 918
. . water conservation equipment... 918
. . water conservation facilities 918
. . work opportunity 1009
. deductions 1009
. . asset expense election 1009
. . barriers removal 1009
. . dividends received 1009; 1203
. . fertilizer 1009
. . tertiary injectants 1009
. . deemed dividends 1009
. deferred compensation plans
. . federal/state key feature comparison 45
. deficiencies—procedure 1502
. interest....................... 3003

Corporate income tax—continued
- depletion
  - federal/state key feature comparison 45
- depreciation 1009
  - bonus depreciation 1007; 1009
  - federal/state key feature comparison 45
  - pre-1984 property 1007; 1009
- disabled access expenditures
  - federal/state key feature comparison 45
- dividends
  - federal/state key feature comparison 45
- due dates
  - payment of tax 1406
  - returns 1401
- electronic funds transfer
  - estimated taxes 1406
- environmental remediation costs
  - federal/state key feature comparison 45
- estimated taxes
  - declarations 1405
  - installment payments 1406
  - overpayment 2903
  - underpayment 1502; 3003
- examination of returns 1502
- exempt organizations 903; 1009
  - federal/state key feature comparison 45
- extension of time 1401; 1404; 1406
- extraterritorial income
  - federal/state key feature comparison 45
- federal changes 1401; 2903; 3001
- federal/state comparison of key features 45
- filing extensions 1401; 1404; 1406
- foreign source income
  - federal/state key feature comparison 45
- forms 1407
- gains
  - federal/state key feature comparison 45
- imposition of tax 901; 902
- installment payments
  - estimated taxes 1406
- insurance companies
  - federal/state key feature comparison 45
- intangibles, amortization
  - federal/state key feature comparison 45
- interest
  - deficiencies 3003
  - federal obligations 1009
  - federal/state key feature comparison 45
  - indebtedness 1009; 1202
  - overpayments and refunds 2903
- jeopardy assessments 1502; 3001
- liability
  - transferee.................. 1508
- liability.................... 1004; 1009
- mergers and acquisitions 1008
- losses
  - federal/state key feature comparison 40

Corporate income tax—continued
- net operating loss 3003
  - federal/state key feature comparison 45
- nonresidents
  - property transfers 1508
- overpayments.................. 2903
- overview 901
- payment of tax 1406
- penalties 3003
- pollution control facilities, amortization
  - federal/state key feature comparison 45
- rate of tax 5; 905
- refunds 2903
- research expenses
  - federal/state key feature comparison 45
- returns 1401
- S corporations
  - federal/state key feature comparison 45
- setoffs 1502; 2903
- settlements................... 3101
- start-up expenditures, amortization
  - federal/state key feature comparison 45
- statute of limitations
  - assessments 3001
  - refund claims 2903
- subtraction modifications 1201
  - deductions eliminated by federal jobs tax credit.................. 1204
  - depository financial institutions ..919; 1905
  - dividends, foreign source or affiliated corporation................. 1203
  - federal employer social security credit..................... 1206
  - federal obligations income 1202
  - interest on indebtedness....... 1202
  - minority subcontractors, payments 55; 1205
- tax paid deduction
  - federal/state key feature comparison 40
- tax evasion
  - federal/state key feature comparison 40
- taxpayer remedies
  - abatement 3101
  - appeals..................... 3101
  - compromise of tax 3101
  - court action 3101
  - interest on overpayments and refunds 2903
  - refunds..................... 2903
  - setoffs 1502; 2903
  - settlements 3101
  - statute of limitations, refund claims.. 2903
- transferee liability.............. 1508
- underpayment, estimated tax 1502; 3003
- withholding 1508

Corporate net worth—see Corporate net worth (franchise) tax

Corporate net worth (franchise) tax
- administration 1804; 2901
- appeals 3101

Topical Index

> References are to paragraph numbers.

Corporate net worth (franchise) tax—continued
- apportionment of net worth, foreign corporations 1702
- assessment or revision by Commissioner 1804
- basis of tax 1604
- collection of tax 1901
- consolidated returns 1801
- corporate net worth 1701
- due dates
  - . payment of tax................ 1802
  - . returns 1801
- exempt corporations 1603
- filing extensions 1801
- gross receipts 1702
- imposition of tax............ 1601; 1602
- initial tax period .... 1801—1803
- interest 3003
- overview 1601
- payment of tax 1802
  - . period covered................ 1803
- penalties 3003
- rate of tax 10; 1605
- returns 1801
- taxpayer remedies 3101

Corporate officer's personal liability
- sales and use taxes............. 2406

Corporate partners
- corporate incomme taxes 1301

Corporate reorganizations—see also Mergers, consolidations, and acquisitions
- corporate income tax
  - . mergers and acquisitions 1008

Corporations subject to tax—see Imposition of tax

Cost price
- sales and use taxes
  - . defined 2101

County taxes
- administration and procedure
  - . refund claims 2903

Coupons, premiums, and cash discounts
- sales and use taxes.............. 2101

Court action
- administration and procedure
  - . suit for refund of taxes 2903
- corporate income tax............ 3101
- estate tax
  - . jurisdiction 2507
- personal income tax............. 3101
- property taxes
  - . taxpayer remedies............. 2609

Crab bait
- sales and use taxes
  - . exemption 2201

Credit card data processing
- corporate income tax
  - . apportionment, special rules ... 1306

Credits
- administration and procedure
  - . interest on credits 3003
- against corporate income tax
  - . banks and financial institutions tax 1905

Credits—continued
- corporate income tax............ 908
  - . alcohol fuel................... 1009
  - . approved retraining programs . 60; 909
  - . assignment of credits to affiliated entities 906
  - . basic education 60; 910
  - . business expansion 60; 913
  - . child care 60; 911
  - . cigarette exports 60; 921
  - . clean fueled vehicles 60; 915
  - . consistent net taxable income growth 60; 912
  - . diesel particulate emission reduction technology equipment 915
  - . disabled access 1009
  - . employer-provided child care .. 60; 911
  - . employer-provided transportation 60; 923
  - . employer social security 1009
  - . employment increases (job tax credits) 60; 913
  - . enhanced oil recovery 1009
  - . enterprise zone job 2604
  - . enterprise zone property tax exemption 2604
  - . establishing headquarters in Georgia. 60; 920
  - . federal qualified transportation fringe benefits 60; 914
  - . federal/state key feature comparison 45
  - . foreign tax 1009
  - . fuel from nonconventional source 1009
  - . Georgia headquarters 60; 920
  - . historic property rehabilitation . 60; 1009
  - . income reduction for payments to minority subcontractors ... 60; 1205
  - . incremental research expenditures 1009
  - . Indian employment 1009
  - . investment tax............... 60; 916
  - . job tax 60; 913
  - . low-income housing........... 922
  - . manufacturing and telecommunications facility investments 60; 916
  - . new manufacturing facilities .. 926, 927
  - . new markets 1009
  - . orphan drug 1009
  - . port traffic increases 60; 924
  - . qualified research 60; 917
  - . qualified electric vehicles 1009
  - . renewable electricity production 1009
  - . water conservation 60; 918
  - . water conservation equipment... 918
  - . water conservation facilities..... 918
  - . work opportunity 1009
- federal/state key feature comparison
  - . corporate income tax 45
  - . personal income tax 40
- estate tax 2502
- insurance tax 2804
- personal income tax............. 110
  - . accessible residence 128
  - . adoption expenses 209
  - . aged and disabled caregiving expenses 111
  - . approved retraining programs . 55; 112

CRE

378 Guidebook to Georgia Taxes

References are to paragraph numbers.

Credits—continued
. personal income tax—continued
. . basic skills education programs . . 55; 113
. . business expansion 125
. . clean fueled vehicles 55; 116
. . disaster assistance recipients. . . . 122
. . driver's education expenses 123
. . earned income 209
. . education assistance 209
. . employer-provided child care . . 55; 114
. . employer-provided transportation 55; 126
. . federal qualified transportation fringe benefits 55; 115
. . federal/state key feature comparison 40
. . historic property rehabilitation 55; 127
. . income reduction for payments to minority subcontractors . . . 55; 1205
. . low-income housing 124
. . low-income residents and working poor persons 55; 117
. . rural physicians 55; 118
. . taxes paid another state 120
. . taxes paid—returned income amounts 119
. . taxes withheld and estimated tax. 121
. sales and use taxes 2203

Criminal penalties—see Penalties

D

Day care—see Child care

Dealer
. sales and use taxes 2004
. . defined 2002
. . delinquent dealer 3002
. . import dealers 2304
. . returns 2302

Debit telephone cards—see Prepaid (debit) telephone cards

Decedents
. personal income tax
. . accounting method on return 107

Deductions
. corporate income tax
. . addition modification 1103
. . subtraction modification 1204
. . federal/state comparison of key features 45
. personal income tax 203
. . addition modification 403
. . alimony 209
. . asset expense election 209
. . bad debts 209
. . charitable contributions 209
. . contributions to qualified pension, profit-sharing, or stock bonus employee plans 209
. . deduction of taxes 209
. . estates and trusts 104; 301
. . expenses, nonresident 503
. . federal/state comparison of key features. 40
. . health insurance, itemized 403
. . medical savings account 209

Deductions—continued
. personal income tax—continued
. . mine development and exploration 209
. sales and use taxes 2302

Deferred compensation plans
. corporate income tax
. . federal/state key feature comparison 45

Deficiency assessments
. administration and procedure 3001
. corporate income tax 1502
. . interest 3003
. personal income tax 802
. . interest 3003
. . statute of limitations 3001
. sales and use taxes 2401

Definitions
. cigarette and tobacco taxes
. . retail dealers 2803
. . wholesale dealer or jobber 2803
. corporate income tax
. . corporation 902
. . estimated tax 1405
. . gross receipts 1305
. . manufacture 1306
. . original cost 1305
. . qualified investment property. . . . 916
. . sale 1306
. motor fuel taxes
. . liquefied gas 2805
. motor vehicle registration
. . fleet 2806
. personal income tax
. . fiduciary 701
. . partnership 702
. . resident 102
. . taxable nonresident 102
. property taxes
. . fair market value 2605
. sales and use taxes
. . cost price 2101
. . dealer 2002
. . gross sales 2301
. . lease or rental 2002
. . qualified municipality 2103
. . retail sale 2002
. . retailer 2002
. . sale 2002
. . sale at retail 2002
. . sales price 2101
. . storage 2006
. . tangible personal property 2002
. . use 2006
. unemployment compensation
. . wages 2702

Delinquent taxes
. administration and procedure 3002
. property taxes
. . installment payments 2608
. sales and use taxes
. . dealers 3002

Delivery charges
. sales and use taxes 2101

Dental supplies
. sales and use taxes 2004
. . exemption 2201

CRI

Topical Index — 379

References are to paragraph numbers.

Department of Revenue—see Georgia Department of Revenue

Dependent exemptions
. personal income tax 1; 104; 301

Depreciation
. corporate income tax
.. business property 1007
.. federal/state key feature comparison
.... 45
. personal income tax 204; 209
.. federal/state key feature comparison
.... 40
. property taxes 2605

Diesel fuel
. motor fuel taxes 2805

Direct payment permits
. sales and use taxes............. 2305

Disabled persons
. corporate income tax
.. federal/state key feature comparison
.... 45
. personal income tax
.. credit, caregiving expenses...... 111
. property taxes
.. exemptions 2604

Disabled veterans—see Veterans

Disaster assistance recipients
. personal income tax
.. credit 122

Disclosure
. administration and procedure
.. authority of State Revenue Commissioner 2901

Discount cards—see Coupons, premiums, and cash discounts

Distributions
. personal income tax
.. nonresidents 609

Dividends
. corporate income tax
.. federal/state key feature comparison
.... 45
.. filing requirements, corporations paying dividends............ 1402
.. received 1009; 1203
.. subtraction modification....... 1203

Doctors—see Physicians

Domestic international sales corporations (DISCs)
. corporate income tax............ 902

Doing business
. corporate income tax
.. apportionment................ 1302
. domestic corporations.......... 3301
. foreign corporations 3302

Domestic corporations
. corporate income tax..... 901; 902; 3301
. corporate net worth (franchise) tax
.... 1601; 1602
.. basis of tax 1604
.. corporate net worth 1701
.. rate of tax.................... 1605
.. doing business 3301; 3302
.. fees and taxes 3301; 3302

Domestic service employees
. unemployment compensation.... 2702

Driver's education expenses
. personal income tax
.. credit 123

Drop shipments
. sales and use taxes
.. exemptions 2202

Drugs—see Prescription drugs

Due dates
. alcoholic beverages taxes 2802
. cigarette and tobacco taxes 2803
. corporate income tax
.. payment of tax............... 1406
.. returns 1401
. corporate net worth (franchise) tax
.. payment of tax............... 1802
.. returns 1801
. estate tax 2508
. insurance taxes................. 2804
. lodging taxes................... 2812
. motor fuel taxes 2805
. motor vehicle registration 2806
. personal income tax
.. estimated taxes 604
.. payment of tax................ 605
.. returns 601
.. special rules 3001
.. statement to employees 608
.. withholding 608; 610
. property taxes 2606
. sales and use taxes............. 2302
. unemployment compensation.... 2704

Dues—see Admissions, entertainment, and dues

Durable medical equipment
. sales and use taxes
.. exemption 2201

E

Economic Growth and Tax Relief Reconciliation Act (EGTRRA)
. personal income tax............. 101

Educational assistance benefits
. personal income tax
.. federal/state key feature comparison
.... 40

Educational institutions and organizations
. corporate income tax
.. exemption 901; 903
. corporate net worth (franchise) tax
.. exemption 1603
. property taxes
.. exemption 2604

Educational local option tax 2103

Elderly
. personal income tax
.. credit, caregiving expenses...... 111
.. deduction 202
. property taxes
.. exemptions 2604

Electricity
. sales and use taxes
.. exemption, manufacturing 2201

ELE

Electronic commerce 2004
Electronic filing
. personal income tax 601
Electronic funds transfer (EFT)
. administration and procedure 2902
. corporate income tax
. . estimated taxes 1406
. personal income tax
. . estimated taxes 604
. . returns 601
. . withholding 610
. sales and use taxes 2302
Employee meals
. sales and use taxes 2004
Employee organizations
. sales and use taxes 2004
Employers and employees
. corporate income tax
. . credits .... 909—924
. personal income tax
. . credits .... 112—115; 121; 126
. . deduction 307
. . withholding .... 607—610
Employment
. corporate income tax
. . credit, employment increases (job tax credits) 129; 913
. unemployment compensation 2702
Empowerment zones
. corporate income tax
. . federal/state key feature comparison 45
Energy systems or facilities
. property taxes 2604
Enterprise Zone Employment Act ... 2604
Enterprise zones
. corporate income tax
. . job credit 913
. property taxes
. . exemptions 2604
. occupational tax, regulatory fee, and business inspection fee abatement or reduction 2604
Entertainment—see Admissions, entertainment, and dues
Entities subject to tax
. banks and financial institutions tax 1901
Environmental remediation costs
. corporate income tax
. . federal/state key feature comparison 45
Environmental taxes 2809
Environmentally sensitive property
. property taxes
. . classification 2603
Equalization
. property taxes 2605
Estate tax
. additional 2503
. court jurisdiction 2507
. credits 2502
. due dates 2508
. final determination 2507

Estate tax—continued
. interest 2508
. nonresidents 2504
. overpayments 2508
. overview 2501
. payment of tax 2508
. property subject to tax 2506
. rates of tax 20; 2502
. refunds 2508
. returns 2509
Estates and trusts
. estate tax 2502
. personal income tax
. . deductions 104; 301
. . fiduciaries 701
Estimated taxes
. corporate income tax
. . declarations 1405
. . installment payments 1406
. . overpayment 2903
. . underpayment 1502; 3003
. lodging taxes 2812
. personal income tax 604
. . credit 121
. sales and use taxes 2302
Examination of returns
. administration and procedure
. . authority of State Revenue Commissioner 2901
. corporate income tax 1502
Excise taxes
. sales and use taxes 2101
Exclusions
. personal income tax
. . withholding 609
. . gain on sale of residence 209
Exempt corporations—see Exemptions
Exempt organizations
. corporate income tax
. . federal/state key feature comparison 45
. . unrelated business income 1005
Exemption certificates
. personal income tax 608
Exemptions
. alcoholic beverages taxes 2802
. banks and financial insititution tax 1901
. corporate income tax
. . enterprise zone property tax exemption 2604
. . exempt corporations 901; 903
. corporate net worth (franchise) tax
. . exempt corporations 1603
. lodging taxes 2812
. military zone compensation 209
. motor vehicle registration 2806
. personal income tax 104; 301
. property taxes 2604
. . agricultural real property 70
. . freeport 70
. . other agricultural property 70
. . pollution control property 70
. . realty transfer taxes 2810
. . state historic preservation tax incentives 70

Topical Index

Exemptions—continued
- sales and use taxes 2004; 2201
- . agriculture 2201; 2604
- . broadcasting and film production   65; 2201
- . computer equipment........ 65; 2201
- . computer software 65; 2201
- . delivery/installation charges ... 2201
- . homesteads 2604
- . interstate transactions 2202
- . manufacturing 2201
- . packaging..................... 2201
- . pollution reduction equipment .. 2201
- . research and development 55; 60
- . telecommunications, broadcasting and film products 2201
- unemployment compensation.... 2702

Exports—see Imports and exports

Express services
- corporate income tax
- . apportionment provisions...... 1307

Extension of time
- corporate income tax
- . filing returns 1401; 1404; 1406
- corporate net worth (franchise) tax
- . filing returns 1801
- personal income tax............. 603
- sales and use taxes............. 2302

Extraterritorial income exclusion
- corporate income tax
- . federal/state key feature comparison 45
- personal income tax
- . federal/state key feature comparison 40

Eyeglasses and contact lenses
- sales and use taxes
- . exemption 2201

F

Fair market value
- property taxes
- . defined 2605

Farm equipment and machinery
- sales and use taxes
- . exemption 2201

Farm products
- sales and use taxes
- . exemption 2201

Farmers and fishermen
- personal income tax
- . estimated taxes 604
- sales and use taxes
- . farmers and market masters ... 2304

Federal adjusted gross income (AGI)—see Federal taxable income

Federal areas
- sales and use taxes............. 2201

Federal changes
- corporate income tax
- . assessments 3001
- . overpayment 2903
- . returns 1401
- personal income tax
- . returns 601

Federal government transactions
- sales and use taxes
- . exemption 2201

Federal obligations
- corporate income tax
- . subtraction modification....... 1202
- personal income tax
- . interest 209; 303
- . subtraction modification........ 303

Federal returns
- corporate income tax
- . addition modification 1103
- . examination 1502
- personal income tax
- . addition modification 403

Federal/state key feature comparisons
- corporate income tax............. 45
- personal income tax............. 40

Federal taxable income
- corporate income tax
- . starting point 1001; 1002
- personal income tax
- . federal AGI starting point 103; 201
- . subtraction modification........ 300

Fees and taxes
- domestic corporations.......... 3301
- foreign corporations 3302

Fertilizers
- property taxes
- . exemptions 2604
- sales and use taxes
- . exemption 2201

Fiduciaries
- personal income tax............. 701
- . defined 701
- . estimated taxes 604

Filing dates—see Due dates

Filing extensions—see Extension of time

Filing requirements
- corporate income tax........... 1402
- corporate net worth (franchise) tax 1801
- personal income tax............. 602
- . time and place of filing 601

Filing status
- personal income tax............. 209

Final returns
- sales and use taxes............. 2302

Finance charges
- sales and use taxes............. 2101

Financial asset securitization investment trusts (FASITs)
- corporate income tax
- . federal/state key feature comparison 45

Financial institutions
- banks and financial institutions tax
- . allocation of local business license taxes 1904
- . basis of tax.................. 1904
- . credit against corporate income tax 1905
- . entities subject to tax 1901
- . rate of tax................... 1903
- . returns and payments......... 1906

FIN

Financial institutions—continued
- corporate income tax
  - credit card data processing 1306
  - depository financial institutions .. 919; 1906

Fiscal year
- corporate income tax
  - accounting periods and methods . 907
  - payment of tax, due date 1406
  - returns, due date 1401
- personal income tax
  - accounting periods and methods . 106
  - payment of tax, due date 605
  - returns, due date 601

Fishermen—see Farmers and fishermen

Food
- sales and use taxes 2004
  - exemptions 2201

Food stamps
- sales and use taxes
  - exemption 2201

Foreign contractors
- sales and use taxes 2004

Foreign corporations
- corporate income tax 901; 902
- corporate net worth (franchise) tax 1601; 1602
  - apportionment of net worth 1702
  - basis of tax 1604
  - corporate net worth 1701
  - rate of tax 1605
- doing business 3301; 3302
- fees and taxes 3301; 3302

Foreign educational and cultural institutes
- sales and use taxes
  - exemption 2004

Foreign sales corporations (FSCs)
- corporate income tax 902

Foreign source income
- corporate income tax
  - federal/state key feature comparison 45

Foreign tax credit
- corporate income tax
  - federal/state key feature comparison 45

Foreign vendors
- sales and use taxes 2302

Forms
- corporate income tax 1407
- lodging taxes 2812
- personal income tax 606
- sales and use taxes
  - certificates of registration 2304
  - exemptions 2201
  - notice of assessment.......... 2401
  - resale certificates 2004
  - returns, extensions 2302
  - unemployment compensation.... 2704

Formula apportionment—see also Allocation and apportionment
- personal income tax
  - nonresidents 502

Franchise tax—see Corporate net worth (franchise) tax

Fraternities
- sales and use taxes
  - exemption, meals 2201

Freeport exemption
- property taxes 2604

Funerals
- sales and use taxes 2004

Fungicides
- sales and use taxes
  - exemption 2201

Furniture and storage warehousemen
- sales and use taxes 2005

G

Gains
- corporate income tax
  - federal/state key feature comparison 45

Gambling—see Lottery and gambling

Gasoline
- motor fuel taxes 2805

Georgia Department of Revenue
- corporate income tax
  - administration 1501
- corporate net worth (franchise) tax
  - administration 1804; 2901
- generally
  - administration and procedure . 2901—3101
- personal income tax
  - administration 801

Georgia taxable income
- personal income tax
  - differences between federal, Georgia taxable income 201

Gifts and promotional merchandise
- sales and use taxes 2004

Girl Scout cookies
- sales and use taxes
  - exemption 2201

Golf and country clubs
- sales and use taxes 2004

Government contractors
- sales and use taxes
  - exemption 2201

Government employees
- sales and use taxes 2201

Government and public property
- property taxes
  - exemption 2604

Government transactions
- sales and use taxes 2004
  - exemptions 2201

Grocery items
- sales and use taxes
  - exemption 2201

Gross premiums tax—see Insurance taxes

FIS

Topical Index

References are to paragraph numbers.

Gross receipts
. corporate net worth (franchise) tax ...
.... 1702

Gross receipts factor
. corporate income tax
.. apportionment formula 1305
.. special rules 1306

Gross receipts tax—see Utilities

Gross sales
. sales and use taxes
.. defined 2301

H

Handicapped persons—see Disabled persons

Harvesting equipment
. sales and use taxes
.. exemption 2201

Head of household
. personal income tax
.. returns 105; 602

Headquarters, establishing in Georgia
. corporate income tax
.. credits 920

Health insurance
. personal income tax
.. subtraction modification 309
.. self-employed taxpayers 209

Health maintenance organizations (HMOs)
. insurance taxes
.. payment and reports 2804

Hearing aids
. sales and use taxes
.. exemption 2201

Herbicides
. sales and use taxes
.. exemption 2201

Higher education savings
. personal income taxes
.. contributions 310
.. withdrawals 207

Historic property
. property taxes
.. assessment 2605
.. classification 2603
.. state preservation tax incentives .. 70
.. rehabilitation credit
.. corporate income tax 60; 925
.. personal income tax 55; 127

Homestead option sales and use tax . 2103

Homesteads
. property taxes
.. exemption 2604

Hospitals
. property taxes 2604
. sales and use taxes 2004; 2201

Household goods
. property taxes
.. exemption 2604

Housing authorities
. sales and use taxes 2201

Husband and wife
. personal income tax
.. estimated taxes 604
.. innocent spouse relief 109
.. rate of tax 105
.. returns 602
.. withholding 608

I

Ice
. sales and use taxes
.. exemptions 2004; 2201

Imports and exports
. sales and use taxes
.. exemptions 2202
.. import dealers 2304

Imposition of tax
. alcoholic beverages taxes 2802
. cigarette and tobacco taxes 2803
. corporate income tax 901; 902
. corporate net worth (franchise) tax ...
.... 1601; 1602
. insurance taxes 2804
. lodging taxes 2812
. motor fuel taxes 2805
. personal income tax 101
. property taxes 2602
. sales and use taxes 2002; 2004

In-transit property
. property taxes
.. exemption 2604

Incidence of tax
. sales and use taxes 2002; 2101

Industrial materials
. sales and use taxes
.. exemption 2201

Industrial property—see also Manufacturing and industrial property
. property taxes
.. classification 2603

Inheritance or estate taxes—see Estate tax

Initial tax period
. corporate net worth (franchise) tax ...
.... 1801—1803

Innocent spouse relief
. personal income tax 109

Insecticides
. sales and use taxes
.. exemption 2201

Installation services—see Repair, installation, and warranties

Installment, lay-away, and conditional sales
. sales and use taxes 2101

Installment payments
. administration and procedure 3003
. corporate income tax
.. estimated taxes 1406
. insurance taxes 2804
. personal income tax
.. estimated taxes 604
. property taxes 2606
.. penalty, late payments 2608

INS

Insulin
. sales and use taxes
.. exemption 2201
Insurance agents
. unemployment compensation
.. exemption 2702
Insurance companies
. corporate income tax
.. exemption 901; 903
.. federal/state key feature comparison
.... 45
. corporate net worth (franchise) tax
.. exemption 1603
Insurance premiums, self-employed
. personal income tax
.. federal/state key feature comparison
.... 40
Insurance taxes 75; 2804
. credits
.. low-income housing 75; 2804
.. small business investment ... 75; 2804
Intangible property
. corporate income tax
.. net business income 1303
. property taxes 2601
Intangible property holding companies
. corporate income tax 902
Intangibles, amortization
. corporate income tax
.. federal/state key feature comparison
.... 45
Interest
. administration and procedure 3003
. corporate income tax
.. deficiencies 3003
.. federal obligations . 45; 1009; 1102; 1202
.. state obligations 1009
. corporate net worth (franchise) tax
.. penalties.................... 3003
. lodging taxes 2812
. personal income tax
.. deficiencies 3003
.. overpayments and refunds 2903
.. withholding 607; 609
. property taxes 2608
. sales and use taxes 3003
. unemployment compensation 2703
Intergovernmental tax collection agreements
. IRS abusive tax avoidance transactions memorandum 3002
Internal Revenue Service
. intergovernmental tax collection agreements 3002
Internet services
. sales and use taxes............. 2004
Interstate transactions
. sales and use taxes
.. exemptions 2202
Inventory
. property taxes
.. exemption 2604
Investment income
. corporate income tax
.. allocation 1303

Investment income—continued
. corporate income tax—continued
.. investment tax credit 60

J

Jeopardy assessments
. administration and procedure.... 3001
. corporate income tax....... 1502; 3001
. personal income tax............ 3001
. sales and use taxes............. 2403
Job Creation and Worker Assistance Act
. corporate income tax.... 901; 1002; 1007
. personal income tax... 101; 204; 208; 209
Job tax credits
. corporate income tax.......... 60; 913
.. enterprise zone 2604
.. new manufacturing facilities .. 926, 927
.. subtraction modification....... 1204
. personal income tax............. 129
Jobbers—see Wholesalers and jobbers
Joint county and municipal sales and use tax......................... 2103
Joint returns
. personal income tax
.. husband and wife, rate of tax 105
.. innocent spouse relief 109
.. penalties.................... 3003
Joint ventures
. corporate income tax
.. apportionment, special rules ... 1305; 1306
Judicial review—see Court action
Judicial tax foreclosure
. property taxes 2607

K

Kennels
. sales and use taxes............. 2005

L

Labels and tags—see also Packaging
. sales and use taxes
.. exemption 2201
Land bank authority
. property taxes 2607
Laundry services—see Cleaning and laundry services
Lay-away sales—see Installment, lay-away, and conditional sales
Leased departments
. sales and use taxes............. 2302
Leases
. sales and use taxes............. 2004
Levy
. administration and procedure
.. collection of tax 3002
. sales and use taxes............. 3002

Topical Index

Liability for tax
. corporate income tax
. . transferee 1508
. personal income tax
. . employer, withheld taxes 607
. . transferee liability 808
. sales and use taxes
. . business successor 2407
. . consumer 2404
. . corporate officer's personal liability . .
.... 2406
. . seller 2405

Libraries—see Public libraries

Liens
. corporate income tax 1502
. property taxes 2607
. sales and use taxes 3002

Life insurance

Limited liability companies (LLCs)
. corporate income tax 902
. personal income tax 703
. . distributions, withholding 609

Linen supplies—see Cleaning and laundry services

Livestock and livestock feed
. property taxes
. . exemption 2604
. sales and use taxes
. . exemption 2201

Local tax chart
. sales and use taxes 2104

Local taxes
. property tax 2601
. sales and use taxes 2103

Lodging
. miscellaneous taxes 2812
. sales and use taxes 2004

Losses
. corporate income tax
. . federal/state key feature comparison
.... 45
. personal income tax
. . federal/state key feature comparison
.... 40
. . not otherwise compensated 209

Lottery and gambling
. personal income tax
. . withholding, lottery proceeds 609
. sales and use taxes
. . exemption 2201

Low-income housing
. corporate income tax
. . credit 922
. insurance tax 75; 2804
. personal income tax
. . credit 124

Low-income residents
. personal income tax
. . credit 117

Lump-sum distributions
. personal income tax 209; 402

M

Machinery and equipment
. sales and use taxes
. . exemptions 2004; 2201

Magazines
. sales and use taxes 2004

Manufacturing and industrial property
. corporate income tax
. . apportionment, special rules ... 1306
. . new manufacturing facilities credits . .
.... 926, 927
. sales and use taxes
. . exemptions 65; 2004; 2201

Married persons—see Husband and wife

Maternity homes
. exemption, sales and use taxes ... 2201

Meals
. sales and use taxes 2004
. . exemptions 2004; 2201

Medical supplies
. sales and use taxes 2004
. . exemption 2201

Mergers, consolidations, and acquisitions—see also Corporate reorganizations
. property taxes 2605
. sales and use taxes
. . exemption 2201

Metropolitan Atlanta Rapid Transit Authority (MARTA) tax 2103

Military equipment
. sales and use taxes
. . exemption 2201

Military personnel—see also Nonresidents
. personal income tax 108
. . extension of time to file 603
. property tax
. . exemption, vehicles owned by armed forces members 2604
. sales and use taxes 2004

Millage rates 2602

Miscellaneous taxes
. alcoholic beverages taxes 2802
. cigarette and tobacco taxes 2803
. environmental taxes 2809
. insurance taxes 2804
. lodging taxes 2812
. motor carrier taxes 2808
. motor fuel taxes 2805
. motor vehicle registration 2806
. overview 2801
. realty transfer taxes 2810
. rental vehicle taxes 2807
. utilities taxes 2811

Mobile Telecommunications Sourcing Act
. sales and use taxes 2802

Modifications—see Addition modifications; Subtraction modifications

MOD

Mortgage interest
. personal income tax
. . subtraction modification 308
Motion pictures
. sales and use taxes 2004
Motor carriers 2808
Motor fuels
. motor fuel taxes 2805
. sales and use taxes
. . exemptions 2201
Motor fuel taxes 2805
Motor vehicle registration 2806
Motor vehicles
. corporate income tax
. . credit, clean fueled vehicles .. 60; 915; 1009
. miscellaneous taxes 2806
. . carriers 2808
. . rental vehicles 2807
. personal income tax
. . credit, clean fueled vehicles ... 55; 116
. property taxes
. . assessment 2605
. . exemptions 2604
. . penalties 2608
. sales and use taxes 2004

N

Natural gas
. motor fuel taxes 2805
. sales and use taxes 2201
Net business income—see Business income
Net operating loss
. corporate income tax 1002
. . carryback 1009; 3003
. . federal/state key feature comparison
.... 45
. personal income tax 208; 209
. . carryback 208
. . federal/state key feature comparison
.... 40
Net taxable income—see Taxable net income
Net worth
. corporate net worth (franchise) tax ...
.... 1701
. . apportionment of net worth, foreign corporations 1702
Newspapers
. sales and use taxes 2004
Nexus
. sales and use taxes 2003
No-par-value stock
. corporate net worth (franchise) tax ...
.... 1701
Nonbusiness deductions
. personal income tax 302
Nonprofit organizations
. corporate income tax
. . exemption 901; 903
. corporate net worth (franchise) tax
. . exemption 1603

Nonprofit organizations—continued
. property taxes
. . exemption 2604
. sales and use taxes 2004
. . exemptions 2004; 2201
. unemployment compensation
. . nonprofit employers 2702
Nonresidents—see also Military personnel
. corporate income tax
. . property transfers 1508
. estate tax
. . property subject to tax 2506
. . taxable transfers 2504
. personal income tax
. . allocation and apportionment of income .... 501—505
. . definition, taxable 102
. . income 501
. . military personnel 108
. . partners and partnerships 702
. . property transfers 609
. . shareholders 206
. . withholding, distributions 609
. property taxes
. . exemption, armed forces members..
.... 2604
. . returns 2606
. sales and use taxes 2004
. . exemption 2202
Notices
. administration and procedure 3002
Nursing homes
. sales and use taxes 2004

O

Obligations—see Federal obligations; State or local obligations
Occasional sales
. sales and use taxes
. . exemptions 2201
Optical services and supplies
. sales and use taxes 2004
. . exemption 2201
Organ donation expenses
. personal income tax subtraction ... 311
Orphans' homes
. sales and use taxes
. . exemption 2004
Out-of-state dealers
. sales and use taxes 2003
. . leases and rentals 2004
Out-of-state transactions
. sales and use taxes 2006
Overpayment of tax
. corporate income tax 2903
. . interest 2903; 3003
. personal income tax 2903
. . interest 2903; 3003
. property taxes
. . interest 2609
Overwithholding
. personal income tax 610

Topical Index

References are to paragraph numbers.

Oxygen
. sales and use taxes
.. exemption 2201

P

Packaging—see also Labels and tags
. sales and use taxes
.. exemptions 65; 2201

Painters and paperhangers
. sales and use taxes............. 2005

Parent-teacher organizations
. sales and use taxes
.. exemptions 2201

Part-year residents
. personal income tax............. 504

Partners and partnerships
. corporate income tax
.. apportionment, special rules ... 1305; 1306
. personal income tax............. 702
.. defined 702
.. distributions, withholding 609
.. returns 602

Passenger vehicles
. motor vehicle registration 2806

Payment of tax
. administration and procedure.... 2903
. alcoholic beverages taxes 2802
. cigarette and tobacco taxes 2803
. corporate income tax........... 1406
. corporate net worth (franchise) tax ...
.... 1802
.. period covered............... 1803
. estate tax 2508
. insurance taxes................ 2804
. lodging taxes.................. 2812
. motor fuel taxes 2805
. personal income tax.......... 604; 605
.. withholding 607; 610
. property taxes 2606
. realty transfer taxes 2810
. sales and use taxes............. 2302
.. prepayment 2303

Payroll factor
. corporate income tax
.. apportionment formula........ 1305
.. special rules................. 1306

Pecan harvesting
. sales and use taxes
.. exemption 2201

Peddlers and street vendors
. sales and use taxes............. 2304

Penalties
. administration and procedure.... 3003
. corporate income tax........... 3003
. corporate net worth (franchise) tax ...
.... 1903
. lodging taxes.................. 2812
. personal income tax............ 3003
.. withholding 607; 609; 3003
. property taxes 2608
. sales and use taxes............. 3003
. unemployment compensation.... 2703

Pensions
. personal income tax
.. withholding 609

Personal exemptions
. personal income tax.......... 104; 301

Personal income tax
. abatement 3101
. accounting periods and methods .. 106
.. decedent's return 107
.. separate accounting, nonresidents ..
.... 501
. addition modifications
.. child care property depreciation deduction 404
.. income taxes deducted on federal return 403
.. lump-sum distributions 209; 402
.. state or local obligations income . 401
. administration 801
. allocation and apportionment, nonresident income
.. computation of tax 501
.. deduction of expenses 503
.. formula apportionment......... 502
.. nonresident income 501
.. part year residents 504
.. returns based on books of account ..
.... 505
.. separate accounting 501
. alternative minimum tax 209
. amortization 209
. annuities
.. withholding 609
. apportionment of withholding 609
. assessments
.. deficiencies 802
.. interest...................... 3003
.. statute of limitations 3001
. asset expense election
.. federal/state key feature comparison
.... 40
. bad debt deduction
.. federal/state key feature comparison
.... 40
. bankruptcy and receivership 807
. basis of tax 103
. books of account, nonresident returns .
.... 505
. business deductions
.. federal/state key feature comparison
.... 40
. calendar year
.. accounting periods and methods . 106
.. due dates 601; 605
. capital gains and capital losses
.. federal/state key feature comparison
.... 40
. charitable contributions
.. federal/state key feature comparison
.... 40
. capital gains election 202
. carryback 208; 209
. compromise of tax 3101
. computation of tax
.. nonresidents 501
.. withholding 609
. contributions
.. qualified pension, profit-sharing, or stock bonus employee plans ... 209
.. Teachers Retirement System of Georgia 207
. court action 3101

PER

Personal income tax—continued
- credits 55
  - adoption expenses 209
  - aged and disabled caregiving expenses 111
  - approved retraining programs . 55; 112
  - basic skills education programs . . 55; 113
  - business expansion 125
  - child tax 209
  - disaster assistance recipients 122
  - driver's education expenses 123
  - earned income 209
  - employer-provided child care . . 55; 114
  - employer-provided transportation 55; 126
  - federal qualified transportation fringe benefits 55; 115
  - historic property rehabilitation 55; 127
  - low-emission vehicles 55; 116
  - low-income housing 55; 124
  - low-income residents and working poor persons 117
  - residence, accessible 128
  - rural physicians 55; 118
  - taxes paid another state 120
  - taxes paid—returned income amounts 119
  - taxes withheld and estimated tax . 121
  - work opportunity 209
- deductions
  - alimony 209
  - asset expense election 209
  - bad debts 209
  - business deductions 209
  - charitable contributions 209
  - employer social security 307
  - estates and trusts 104; 301
  - health insurance 209
  - itemized 209
  - medical savings account 209
  - mine development and exploration 209
  - nonresident expenses 503
  - payments to minority subcontractors 55; 305
  - prior year income 203
  - withholding, standard deduction allowance 608
- deficiency assessments 802; 3001
  - interest 3003
- depreciation 209
  - bonus depreciation 204
  - federal/state key feature comparison 40
  - pre-1987 property 204
- distributions
  - lump-sum 402
  - withholding 609
- due dates
  - estimated taxes 604
  - payment of tax 605
  - returns 601
  - special rules 3001
  - statement to employees 608
  - withholding 608; 610
- Economic Growth and Tax Relief Reconciliation Act (EGTRRA) 101
- educational assistance benefits
  - federal/state key feature comparison 40

Personal income tax—continued
- electronic funds transfer (EFT)
  - estimated taxes 604
  - withholding 610
- employee
  - exemption certificate 608
  - payment of tax 607
- employer
  - liability for tax withheld 607
  - sale of business 609; 610
- estates and trusts
  - deductions 104; 301
  - estimated taxes 604
  - credit 121
  - exclusions, withholding 609
  - gain on sale of residence 209
- exemption certificate, employee . . . 608
- exemptions 104; 209; 301
- extraterritorial income
  - federal/state key feature comparison 40
- extensions of time 603
- farmers and fishermen
  - estimated taxes 604
- federal changes 601
- federal/state comparison of key features 40
- fiduciaries 701
- filing requirements 602
  - time and place of filing 601
- filing status 209
- fiscal year
  - accounting periods and methods . 106
  - due dates 601; 605
- forms 606
- formula apportionment, nonresidents 502
- head of household 105; 602
- higher education savings withdrawals 207
- historic property
  - rehabilitation, credit for 55; 127
- husband and wife
  - estimated taxes 604
  - innocent spouse relief 109
  - rate of tax 105
  - returns 602
  - withholding 608
- imposition of tax 101; 201
- installment payments, estimated taxes 604
- insurance premiums, self-employed
  - federal/state key feature comparison 40
- interest
  - deficiencies 3003
  - federal obligations 209; 303
  - federal/state key feature comparison 40
  - indebtedness 209
  - refunds 2903
  - withholding 607; 609
- jeopardy assessments 3001
- Job Creation and Worker Assistance Act 101; 204; 208; 209
- joint returns 105; 109
- kiddie tax 209
- liability for tax
  - employer, withheld taxes 607
  - transferee liability 808
- limited liability companies 703
  - distributions, withholding 609

PER

Topical Index

References are to paragraph numbers.

Personal income tax—continued
- losses
  - federal/state key feature comparison 40
  - not otherwise compensated 209
  - prior year income 203
- lottery proceeds
  - withholding 609
- lump-sum distributions 209; 402
- military personnel 108
  - extension of time to file 603
- military zone compensation exemptions 209
- net operating losses 208
  - federal/state key feature comparison 40
- nonresidents
  - allocation and apportionment .. 501—505
  - computation of tax 501
  - deduction, expenses 503
  - definition, taxable 102
  - income 501
  - military personnel 108
  - partners and partnerships 702
  - property transfers 609
  - separate accounting 501
  - shareholders 206
  - withholding, distributions 609
- nonwage income
  - withholding 609
- overpayments 2903
- overview 101
- overwithholding 610
- part year residents 504
- partners and partnerships 702
  - distributions, withholding 609
  - returns 602
- payment of tax 604; 605
  - withholding 607; 610
- penalties 3003
  - withholding 607; 609
- pensions
  - withholding 609
- periodic payments
  - withholding 609
- prior year income 203
- property
  - depreciation 205
  - sale or exchange 204
  - transferee liability 808
  - withholding, transfers by nonresidents 609
- protest procedures
  - assessments 802; 3001
- railroad employees
  - retirement benefits 304
- rate of tax 1; 105
- refunds 2903
  - claims, statute of limitations ... 2903
  - interest 2903
- residency 102
- retirement benefits 209
- retirement plans
  - federal/state key feature comparison 40
- returns
  - due dates 601
  - electronic filing 601
  - estimated taxes 604
  - extensions of time 603
  - federal changes 601

Personal income tax—continued
- returns—continued
  - filing requirements 602
  - forms 606
  - head of household 105; 602
  - husband and wife 105; 109; 602; 604
  - joint returns 105; 109; 3003
  - nonresidents, books of account .. 505
  - partnerships 602
  - payment of tax 604; 605
  - time and place of filing 601
  - withholding 610
- S corporations 206
  - distributions, withholding 609
- self-employed health insurance
  - federal/state key feature comparison 40
- separate accounting
  - nonresidents 501
- setoffs 2903
- settlements 3101
- statute of limitations
  - assessments 3001
  - refund claims 2903
- subtraction modifications
  - contributions to higher education savings 310
  - dependent exemptions 301
  - employer social security deduction 307
  - federal obligations income 303
  - itemized nonbusiness deductions 302
  - minority subcontractors, payments 305
  - mortgage interest 308
  - moving expenses 209
  - organ donation expenses 311
  - personal exemptions 301
  - retirement income 304
  - salary, wage expenses eliminated for federal jobs tax credit purposes 306
  - self-employed, health insurance costs 309
  - standard deductions 302
- taxable net income 202; 209
- taxpayer remedies
  - abatement 3101
  - compromise of tax 3101
  - court action 3101
  - interest on overpayments and refunds 2903; 3003
  - protest procedures on assessments 802; 3001
  - refunds 2903
  - setoffs 2903
  - settlements 3101
  - statute of limitations on refund claims 2903
- tax rates
  - capital gains and capital losses ... 209
- taxes paid deduction
  - federal/state key feature comparison 40
- Teachers Retirement System of Georgia
  - contributions 207
- transferee liability 808
- underpayments
  - estimated taxes 604
- underwithholding 610

PER

Guidebook to Georgia Taxes
⟫⟶ *References are to paragraph numbers.*

Personal income tax—continued
. wages 607
. withholding 607
.. amounts subject to withholding .. 608
.. annuities..................... 609
.. apportionment................ 609
.. computation of tax 609
.. credit 121
.. distributions, nonresidents 609
.. due dates 608; 610
.. electronic funds transfer........ 610
.. employee exemption certificate .. 608
.. employee payment of tax 607
.. employer liability 607
.. employer sale of business 609; 610
.. exclusions 609
.. exemption allowance........... 608
.. husband and wife.............. 608
.. interest.................... 607; 609
.. limited liability companies....... 609
.. lottery proceeds 609
.. nonresidents 609
.. nonwage income 609
.. overwithholding............... 610
.. partnerships.................. 609
.. payment................... 607; 610
.. penalties................... 607; 609
.. pensions 609
.. periodic payments............. 609
.. property transfers, nonresidents . 609
.. returns 610
.. S corporations 609
.. standard deduction allowance ... 608
.. underwithholding............... 610
.. wages 607

Personal property—see Tangible personal property

Personal services
. sales and use taxes 2004; 2005; 2201

Persons subject to tax—see Imposition of tax

Pesticides
. sales and use taxes
.. exemption 2201

Pet shops
. sales and use taxes............ 2005

Photography
. sales and use taxes............ 2004

Physicians
. personal income tax
.. credit, rural physicians 118

Pilot training schools
. sales and use taxes............ 2005

Pipelines
. corporate income tax
.. apportionment, special rules ... 1306

Pollution and cleanup equipment
. sales and use taxes
.. exemption 2201

Pollution control facilities
. corporate income tax
.. federal/state key feature comparison
   45
. property taxes
.. exemption 70; 2604

Pollution reduction equipment....... 65

Postmark
. administration and procedure
.. due dates 3002

Poultry feed
. sales and use taxes
.. exemption 2201

Preferential property
. property taxes
.. classification 2603

Prepaid (debit) telephone cards
. sales and use taxes............ 2004

Prepayment of tax
. sales and use taxes............ 2303

Prescription drugs and devices
. sales and use taxes
.. exemption 2201

Presumption of taxability
. sales and use taxes............ 2002

Printing
. sales and use taxes
.. exemption, supplies........... 2004

Private colleges and universities
. sales and use taxes
.. exemptions 2004

Private schools
. sales and use taxes
.. exemptions 2004; 2201

Professional services
. sales and use taxes 2004; 2005; 2201

Property
. corporate income tax
.. apportionment............... 1302
. personal income tax
.. depreciation.................. 205
.. sale or exchange 204
.. transferee liability 808
.. withholding, transfers by
   nonresidents................ 609

Property factor
. corporate income tax
.. apportionment formula........ 1305
.. special rules 1306

Property subject to tax—see also Imposition of tax
. estate tax 2601
. property taxes 2903

Property taxes
. appraisal 2605
. assessment................... 2605
. classification of property 2603
. collection of tax 2607
. due dates 2606
. equalization................... 2605
. exemptions 70; 2604; 2605
. imposition of tax............... 2602
. interest 2608
. liens......................... 2607
. overview 2601
. payment of tax 2606
. penalties 2608
. property subject to tax 2603
. rate of tax 2602
. redevelopment 2605
. refunds 2609
. returns 2606

PER

Topical Index

Property taxes—continued
. statute of limitations
. . tax executions 2607
. taxpayer remedies 2609
. valuation 2605

Prosthetic devices
. sales and use taxes
. . exemption 2201

Protest procedures
. personal income tax
. . assessments 802; 3001

Public libraries
. property taxes
. . exemptions 2604
. sales and use taxes
. . fund raising exemptions 2004

Public property—see Government and public property

Public schools
. sales and use taxes............. 2004
. . exemptions 2004; 2201

Public service corporations
. corporate income tax
. . apportionment provisions...... 1307

Public transit
. sales and use taxes
. . exemptions 2004; 2201

Public utilities—see Utilities

Publishing
. sales and use taxes............. 2004

Purple Heart recipients
. property tax
. . motor vehicle exemption 2604

Q

Qualified investment property
. corporate income tax
. . defined 916

Qualified municipality
. sales and use taxes
. . defined 2103

Qualified research credit 60; 917

Quarterly returns
. sales and use taxes............. 2302

R

Railroad employees
. personal income tax
. . retirement benefits 304
. unemployment compensation
. . exemption 2702

Railroad Unemployment Insurance Act 2702

Railroads and rolling stock
. corporate income tax
. . apportionment provisions...... 1307
. property taxes
. . valuation and assessment...... 2605
. . penalties................... 2608

Rate of tax
. alcoholic beverages taxes 2802
. banks and financial institutions tax 1903
. cigarette and tobacco taxes 2803
. corporate income tax.......... 5; 905
. corporate net worth (franchise) tax 10; 1605
. estate tax 2502
. insurance taxes................ 2804
. lodging taxes.................. 2812
. millage rate 2602
. motor fuel taxes 2805
. motor vehicle registration 2806
. personal income tax........... 1; 105
. property taxes 2602
. realty transfer taxes............ 2810
. sales and use taxes........... 15; 2102
. sales tax holidays 2102
. unemployment compensation.... 2703

Real estate agents
. unemployment compensation
. . exemption 2702

Real estate investment trusts (REITS)
. corporate income tax
. . federal/state key feature comparison 45

Real estate mortgage investment companies (REMICs)
. corporate income tax
. . federal/state key feature comparison 45

Real property
. administration and procedure
. . levy of property 3002
. property taxes
. . classification 2603

Realty transfer taxes 2810

Receipts factor—see Gross receipts factor

Reciprocity—see also Comity
. sales and use taxes
. . reciprocal tax enforcement 3002

Recordkeeping requirements
. generally 2903
. sales and use taxes............. 2306

Redemption of property
. administration and procedure.... 3002
. property taxes 2607

Refunds
. administration and procedure.... 2903
. . interest on refunds 2903
. corporate income tax........... 2903
. . claims, statute of limitations ... 2903
. . interest 2903
. estate tax 2508
. personal income tax............ 2903
. . interest 2903
. property taxes 2609
. sales and use taxes............. 2903

Regulated investment companies (RICs)
. corporate income tax
. . federal/state key feature comparison 45

Regulations—see Rules

Religious institutions and organizations
. corporate income tax
. . exemption 901; 903
. corporate net worth (franchise) tax
. . exemption 1603
. property taxes
. . exemption 2604
. sales and use taxes
. . exemptions 2004

Remedies—see Taxpayer remedies

Remittance of tax
. sales and use taxes 2301

Rental vehicles 2807

Rentals
. sales and use taxes 2004

Repair, installation, and warranties
. sales and use taxes
. . exemption 2201

Reports—see Returns

Repossessions
. sales and use taxes 2101

Resale certificates
. sales and use taxes 2004

Resales
. sales and use taxes 2004

Research and development
. corporate income tax
. . credit, research expenses 55, 917
. . federal/state key feature comparison
     45

Resident
. estate tax
. . computation of tax 2502
. personal income tax
. . credit, low-income residents ... 117
. . defined 102
. . estimated taxes 604
. . returns 602

Residential property
. property taxes
. . classification 2603

Residential transitional property
. property taxes
. . assessment 2605
. . classification 2603

Restaurants
. sales and use taxes 2004

Retail dealers
. cigarette and tobacco taxes
. . defined 2803

Retail sale
. sales and use taxes
. . defined 2002

Retirement income
. personal income tax
. . computation 304
. . subtraction modification 304

Retirement plans
. personal income tax
. . federal/state key feature comparison
     40

Returnable containers—see also Storage
. sales and use taxes 2201

Returns
. administration and procedure 3003
. alcoholic beverages taxes 2802
. banks and financial institutions tax ....
     1905
. cigarette and tobacco taxes 2803
. corporate income tax 1401
. corporate net worth (franchise) tax ...
     1801
. estate tax 2507
. insurance taxes 2804
. lodging taxes 2812
. motor fuel taxes 2805
. personal income tax
. . due dates 601
. . estimated taxes 604
. . extensions of time 603
. . federal changes 601
. . filing requirements 602
. . forms 606
. . head of household 105; 602
. . husband and wife 105; 109; 602; 604
. . joint returns 105; 109; 3003
. . nonresidents, books of account .. 505
. . partnerships 602
. . payment of tax 604; 605
. . time and place of filing 601
. . withholding 610
. property taxes 2606
. realty transfer taxes 2810
. sales and use taxes 2302
. unemployment compensation 2704

Revenue Commissioner—see State Revenue Commissioner

Rock Eagle 4-H Center
. sales and use taxes
. . exemption 2004

Rules
. administration and procedure
. . authority of State Revenue
     Commissioner 2901
. no throwback 1302

S

S corporations
. corporate income tax 902; 1009
. . federal/state key feature comparison
     45
. personal income tax 206
. . distributions, withholding 609

Safe harbor leases
. corporate income tax
. . federal/state key feature comparison
     45

Sales and use taxes
. absorption of tax 2301
. application 2002
. audit procedures 2402
. bad debts 2101
. basis of tax 2101
. bracket schedule 2105
. collection of tax 3002
. . discounts 2302
. credits against tax 2203
. deficiency assessments 2401
. direct payment permits 2305
. due dates 2302
. electronic funds transfer (EFT) ... 2302

Topical Index

References are to paragraph numbers.

Sales and use taxes—continued
- estimated tax payments 2302
- exemptions 65; 2004; 2201
- .. interstate transactions 2202
- extension of time 2302
- forms
- .. certificates of registration 2304
- .. exemptions 2201
- .. notice of assessment.......... 2401
- .. resale certificates 2004
- .. returns, extensions 2302
- imposition of tax........... 2002; 2004
- incidence of tax 2002; 2101
- interest 3003
- jeopardy assessments 2403
- levy 3002
- liability for tax
- .. business successor 2407
- .. consumer 2404
- .. corporate officer's personal liability.. 2406
- .. seller...................... 2405
- liens 3002
- local power to tax 2001
- local taxes.................... 2103
- .. local tax chart 2104
- Mobile Telecommunications Sourcing Act 2002
- nexus 2003
- nonresidents moving to Georgia .. 2202
- overview 2001
- payment of tax 2302
- .. prepayment of tax............ 2303
- penalties 3003
- persons, transactions subject to tax... 2004
- presumption of taxability 2002
- rate of tax 15; 2102
- reciprocal tax enforcement 3002
- recordkeeping requirements 2306
- refunds 2411
- remittance of tax 2301
- resales...................... 2004
- returns 2302
- sales tax holidays 2102
- samples..................... 2101
- self-produced goods............ 2002
- statute of limitations 3001
- streamline sales tax project...... 2003
- taxable services 2005
- Uniform Sales and Use Tax Administration Act 2003
- use tax...................... 2006
- vendor registration............. 2304
- voluntary disclosure 2003
- warrants 3002
- withholding, by contractors 2303

Sales factor—see Gross receipts factor

Sales price
- sales and use taxes
- .. defined 2101

School carnivals—see Bazaars and school carnivals

School districts
- property taxes 2601

School lunches
- sales and use taxes
- .. exemption 2201

School property and services
- sales and use taxes
- .. exemption 2004

Schools—see also Private schools; Public schools
- sales and use taxes............. 2004
- .. exemptions 2004; 2201

Scientific organizations
- corporate income tax
- .. exemption 901; 903
- corporate net worth (franchise) tax
- .. exemption 1603

Seeds and seedlings
- sales and use taxes
- .. exemption 2201

Self-employed
- personal income tax
- .. subtraction modification........ 309

Self-employed health insurance
- personal income tax
- .. federal/state key feature comparison 40

Self-produced goods
- sales and use taxes......... 2002; 2101

Seller liability
- sales and use taxes............. 2405

Senior citizens—see Elderly

Separate accounting—see also Accounting periods and methods
- personal income tax
- .. nonresidents 501; 502

Service contracts—see Warranties and service contracts

Service providers—see Personal services; Professional services

Setoffs
- corporate income tax....... 1502; 2903
- personal income tax............ 2903

Settlements
- corporate income tax........... 3101
- personal income tax............ 3101

Short-period returns
- corporate net worth (franchise) tax 1801

Situs
- property taxes 2603

Social and fraternal organizations
- sales and use taxes............. 2004

Software
- sales and use taxes
- .. exemption, custom software ... 2004

Sororities
- sales and use taxes
- .. exemption, meals 2201

Special county sales and use tax 2103

Special franchises
- property taxes 2605

Special period returns
- sales and use taxes............. 2302

Stables
- sales and use taxes............. 2005

STA

Start-up expenditures, amortization
. corporate income tax
. . federal/state key feature comparison
. . . . 45

State and local transactions
. sales and use taxes
. . exemption 2201

State contractors
. sales and use taxes
. . registration requirement 2304

State or local obligations
. corporate income tax
. . addition modification 1102
. personal income tax
. . addition modification 401

State Revenue Commissioner
. corporate income tax
. . abatement—protest 3101
. . administration 1501
. . authority to waive penalty and
       interest 3003
. . power to determine income
       attributable to state 1310
. corporate net worth (franchise) tax
. . assessment or revision 1804
. estate tax
. . final determination 2507
. personal income tax
. . abatement—protest 3101
. . accounting periods and methods . 106;
       107
. . administration 801
. property taxes
. . supervision of taxes 2601
. sales and use taxes
. . remittance of tax 2301

Statute of limitations
. administration and procedure 2903;
     3001; 3101
. corporate income tax
. . assessments 3001
. . refund claims 2903
. personal income tax
. . assessments 3001
. . refund claims 2903
. property taxes
. . tax executions 2607
. sales and use taxes 3001

Stock—see No-par-value stock; Treasury stock

Storage—see also Returnable containers
. sales and use taxes
. . defined 2006
. . exemption 2201

Street vendors—see Peddlers and street vendors

Subcontractors
. corporate income tax
. . subtraction modification 1205
. personal income tax
. . subtraction modification 305
. sales and use taxes 2004

Subsidiaries
. corporate income tax
. . net income 1308

Subtraction modifications
. corporate income tax 1201
. . deductions eliminated by federal jobs
       tax credit 1204
. . depository financial institutions . . 919;
       1905
. . dividends, foreign source or affiliated
       corporation 1203
. . dividends received 1009
. . federal employer social security
       credit 1206
. . federal obligations income 1202
. . minority subcontractors, payments
       . . . . 60; 1205
. personal income tax
. . contributions to higher education
       savings 310
. . dependent exemptions 301
. . employer social security deduction . .
       307
. . federal obligations income 303
. . itemized nonbusiness deductions . . .
       302
. . minority subcontractors, payments
       . . . . 55; 305
. . mortgage interest 308
. . moving expenses 209
. . personal exemptions 301
. . retirement income 304
. . salary, wage expenses eliminated for
       federal jobs tax credit purposes . . .
       306
. . self-employed, health insurance costs
       309
. . standard deductions 302

Successors in business
. sales and use taxes 2304

Suit for refund
. administration and procedure 2903
. corporate income tax 2903

T

Tangible personal property
. property taxes 2602
. . classification 2603
. sales and use taxes
. . defined 2002

Tax evasion
. criminal penalty 3003
. . federal/state key feature comparison
       45

Tax executions
. corporate income tax 1502
. property taxes 2607

Tax liens—see Liens

Tax rate—see Rate of tax

Tax sales
. property taxes 2607

Taxable net income
. corporate income tax 1002
. . basis of tax 904
. . credit, consistent growth 912
. . personal income tax 202; 209
. . fiduciary 701

Taxable services
. sales and use taxes 2005

Topical Index

Taxable transfers
. estate tax 2504

Taxes paid deduction
. corporate income tax
.. federal/state key feature comparison
.... 45
. personal income tax
.. federal/state key feature comparison
.... 40

Taxicabs
. sales and use taxes............ 2004

Taxpayer Bill of Rights 2609

Taxpayer protest—see Protest procedures

Taxpayer remedies
. administration and procedure.... 3101
. corporate income tax
.. abatement 3101
.. appeals 3101
.. compromise of tax 3101
.. court action 3101
.. interest on overpayments and refunds 2903
.. refunds 2903
.. setoffs 1502; 2903
.. settlements 3101
.. statute of limitations on refund claims 2903
.. refunds 1904
. personal income tax
.. abatement 3101
.. compromise of tax 3101
.. court action 3101
.. interest on overpayments and refunds 3003
.. protest procedures on assessments .
.... 802; 3001
.. refunds 3101
.. setoffs 2903
.. settlements 3101
.. statute of limitations on refund claims 2903
. property taxes 2609

Taxpayers subject to tax—see Imposition of tax

Teachers Retirement System of Georgia
. personal income tax
.. contributions 207

Telecommunications
. sales and use taxes............ 2004
.. exemption 2201
.. manufacturing equipment 65

Telegraph companies
. corporate income tax
.. apportionment provisions...... 1307

Telephone companies
. corporate income tax
.. apportionment provisions...... 1307

Timber
. property taxes 2604
.. assessment 2605
.. penalties................... 2606

Tobacco taxes—see Cigarette and tobacco taxes

Trade-ins
. sales and use taxes............ 2101

Trading stamps
. sales and use taxes............ 2004

Trailer parks
. sales and use taxes............ 2004

Trailers
. motor vehicle registration 2806

Transferee liability
. corporate income tax........... 1508
. personal income tax............ 808

Transportation
. corporate income tax
.. apportionment, special rules ... 1306
.. credit, employer provided transportation 60; 923
.. credit, federal qualified transportation fringe benefits .. 914
. personal income tax
.. credit, employer provided transportation 55; 126
.. credit, federal qualified transportation fringe benefits .. 115
. sales and use taxes............ 2004

Transportation equipment
. sales and use taxes
.. exemptions 2201; 2202

Treasury stock
. corporate net worth (franchise) tax ...
.... 1701

Trusts—see Estates and trusts

U

Underpayment of taxes
. administration and procedure.... 2903
. corporate income tax........... 3003
.. estimated taxes 1502; 3003
. personal income tax
.. estimated taxes 604

Underwithholding
. personal income tax............ 610

Unemployment compensation
. benefits 2705
. coverage 2702
. due dates 2704
. exemptions 2702
. forms 2704
. history 2701
. interest 2704
. overview 2701
. penalties 2704
. rate of tax 2703
. returns 2704
. tax base................... 2703
. wages
.. defined 2702

Universal Sales and Use Tax Administration Act
. sales and use taxes............ 2003

Universities—see Colleges and universities

Urban transit
. sales and use taxes
.. exemption 2004

URB

Use
. sales and use taxes
.. defined 2006
Use tax
. consumer liability 2404
. overview 2006
. seller liability 2405
Utilities
. miscellaneous taxes 2811
. property taxes
.. penalties, public utilities 2608
.. valuation and assessment, public utilities 2605
. sales and use taxes 2004; 2201
Utility property
. property taxes
.. classification 2603

V

Valuation
. property taxes 2605
.. underpayments; overpayments . 2609
Vehicles—see Motor vehicles
Vending machines
. sales and use taxes 2004
Vendor registration
. sales and use taxes 2304
.. foreign vendors 2302
Veterans
. property taxes
.. exemption, disabled veterans... 2604
. sales and use taxes
.. exemption, disabled veterans... 2004
Videotapes
. sales and use taxes 2004
Vocational training schools
. sales and use taxes 2004

W

Wages
. personal income tax
.. withholding 607
. unemployment compensation
.. defined 2702
Waivers
. administration and procedure
.. waiver of collection and enforcement 3002; 3101
.. waiver of penalty 3003
. corporate income tax
.. waiver of penalty and interest .. 3003
. sales and use taxes
.. waiver of penalty or interest 3003
Warranties and service contracts
. sales and use taxes
.. exemption 2201

Warrants
. administration and procedure.... 3002; 3101
. sales and use taxes 3002
Water
. corporate income tax
.. credit, conservation 918
. sales and use taxes
.. exemption 2004
Wheelchairs—see Durable medical equipment
Wholesalers and jobbers
. alcoholic beverages taxes 2802
. cigarette and tobacco taxes 2803
. sales and use taxes
.. recordkeeping requirements ... 2306
Withholding
. corporate income tax 1508
. personal income tax 607
.. amounts subject to withholding .. 608
.. annuities 609
.. apportionment 609
.. computation of tax 609
.. credit 121
.. distributions, nonresidents 609
.. due dates 608; 610
.. electronic funds transfer 610
.. employee exemption certificate.. 608
.. employee payment of tax 607
.. employer liability 607
.. employer sale of business 609; 610
.. exclusions 609
.. exemption allowance 608
.. husband and wife 608
.. interest 607; 609
.. limited liability companies 609
.. lottery proceeds 609
.. nonresidents 609
.. nonwage income 609
.. overwithholding 610
.. partnerships 609
.. payment 607; 610
.. penalties 607; 609
.. pensions 609
.. periodic payments 609
.. property transfers, nonresidents . 609
.. returns 610
.. S corporations 609
.. standard deduction allowance ... 608
.. underwithholding 610
.. wages 607
. sales and use taxes
.. contractors 2303
Working Families Tax Relief Act (WFTRA) of 2004
. corporate income tax 1002
. personal income tax 201
Working poor persons—see Low-income residents

USE